PREHISTORIC MESOAMERICA

Maria A. Liston
Gilcrease Museum
Tulsa, Ok
27 April 1997
with Margaret + Julie G.

PREHISTORIC MESOAMERICA

REVISED EDITION

by Richard E.W. Adams

University of Oklahoma Press : Norman and London

By Richard E.W. Adams
Prehistoric Mesoamerica (Boston 1977)
(ed.) *The Origins of Maya Civilization* (Albuquerque, 1977)
Prehistoric Mesoamerica, rev. ed. (Norman, 1991)

Unless noted otherwise, photographs are by the author and drawings are the property of the author.

Library of Congress Cataloging-in-Publication Data

Adams, Richard E.W., 1931–
    Prehistoric Mesoamerica / by Richard E.W. Adams.—Rev. ed.
        p.   cm.
    Includes bibliographical references and index.
    ISBN 0-8061-2304-4 (cloth)
    ISBN 0-8061-2834-8 (paper)
        1. Indians of Mexico—Antiquities. 2. Indians of Central America—
    Antiquities. 3. Mexico—Antiquities. 4. Central America—
    Antiquities. I. Title.
    F1219.A22   1991
    972'.01—dc20   90-50679
                                                                              CIP

The paper in this book meets the guidelines for permanence and durability of the Committee on Production Guidelines for Book Longevity of the Council on Library Resources, Inc. ∞

3   4   5   6   7   8   9   10   11   12

FOR JOEY, 1966–1975

CONTENTS

ILLUSTRATIONS

Figures

Maps

Tables

PREFACE TO THE REVISED EDITION

In each age humanity attempts to understand its past. In our own, if we accept the universality of human cultural experience, we must also attempt to understand the past of cultures other than our own. This book is a synthesis of archaeological findings from Mexico and Guatemala and an interpretation of them. It is built on the work of predecessors who worked in the prehistoric past, sixteenth-century chroniclers, and several generations of more contemporary scholars. It was written to fill the void created by the unfortunate loss of native records, but it also deals with matters that presumably were never thought of by native historians and philosophers of Mesoamerica. The goal is simple: to present an up-to-date, interpretative synthesis of Mesoamerican prehistory—to aid the reader in understanding those alien and destroyed cultures which form a part of the New World's heritage. It is intended for the student as well as for the curious person who has somehow become intrigued with the past native civilizations of Mexico, Guatemala, Belize, Honduras, and El Salvador.

The first immigrants to the New World about twenty thousand years ago came from what is now northeastern Siberia. They moved through a world still locked in the grip of the last ice advance, into increasingly warmer zones to the south of the glaciers. Many generations and thousands of miles later, their descendants laid the economic basis for civilization by beginning that tinkering with plants that led to the ultimate control of crops by humans. From that point on, the story continues to run from earliest to latest until we consider the Aztec and their contemporaries in the final chapter.

In the previous edition, I presented the Aztec first and then reverted to a sequential review. This approach was based on some twenty-five years of teaching Mesoamerican archaeology at the college level and was more successful for me than the standard approach. It had the advantage of dealing first with a Mesoamerican civilization that was seen in full tide by the first Europeans in Mexico, and it also served to introduce in this more familiar context some of the archaeological and anthropological concepts on which presentation of the later material depends. This approach is still possible if the instructor wishes to assign the Aztec chapter first and then return to chapter 2 to continue. The presentation is aimed not just at dusting off the ancient pots and pans, but at reconstructing ways of life and making functional interpretations based on archaeology. The reader should thus have an impression of the earlier cultures which will be akin to that given for the Aztec even if it is lacking in the wealth of historical events and personalities.

This book, then, is an interpretation of the technical archaeological data. It does not aim at encyclopedic completeness of coverage. It is an interpretation which can be documented, however; it is not made out of whole cloth. When there are theoretical alternatives, these will usually be indicated and discussed and the evidence given.

Appendix A deals with technical matters of chronology, spatial divisions within Mesoamerica, and definitions of sociopolitical organization. These subjects have been placed in a separate section in order not to disturb the flow of the book, but the student and professional will probably want to know, for example, the bases on which I have categorized the Early Classic Maya and Formative Olmec as "pristine states."

Several themes run through the book. (1) The native civilizations of Mesoamerica are worth knowing about not just because they are exotic examples of human behavior, but also because their historical and cultural experiences are worth considering. They faced universal problems of human existence and either solved them or failed. We can learn from their successes and failures, if we will. (2) Mesoamerica was a sphere of cultural interaction. Part of what made civilization possible was the interaction among the diverse cultures that flourished there. The varieties of culture and their interrelationships through time and space are fascinating and involve not only economics and militarism but also religion and ideology; interaction took place along all of these lines. Occasionally personality and character break through the flow of historical process, especially where we can read some of the texts left us in the form of native writing systems. (3) Civilization, in the sense of complexity and sophistication of development, was in the main a phenomenon of the elite class. (4) There are continuities between the deep past and the Indian cultures of the colonial and modern worlds. Much that we see in Mexico and Guatemala today is related to the historic past, although the ties are usually unrecognized.

The richness and diversity of the native cultures of Mesoamerica are attractive to us of the West if only because they document the endless variety of forms in which human behavior, society, and artifacts occur. I hope that the reader can gain an understanding of some of the Native American cultural experience and thereby also better understand that of our own tradition.

It is up to the readers to judge how well I have succeeded in bringing together the finds of the past and interpreting these findings. My colleagues and predecessors have my gratitude, but I accept responsibility for any shortcomings of this book.

Thanks are due to Donald Brockington, Ronald Spores, David Grove, K. V. Flannery, Wigberto Jimenez-Moreno, Jacinto Quirarte, and all my colleagues not otherwise mentioned in the seminars sponsored by the School of American Research on the origins, collapse, and settlement patterns of Maya civilization. I am deeply grateful to Douglas Schwartz, Director of the School of American Research, for the exciting opportunities afforded to examine these questions. Special intellectual debts are owed to G. R. Willey, Demitri Shimkin, and W. T. Sanders.

Franklin Graham, then of Little, Brown and Company, encouraged me with the production of the first edition. Critical appraisals were made then and later by George Cowgill, Barbara Price, Margaret Bond, and George Stuart and have been very useful and stimulating. David Grove was especially kind in writing long and thoughtful letters answering my questions about the new perspectives on the Olmec and their contemporaries. Professor Ross Hassig read a draft of the second edition and commented on it to my great benefit. Professor William Fowler performed the same service from a different perspective and with great care and perspicacity. Professor Frederic Hicks advised me on a number of queries regarding the Aztec *calpulli* and social organization. Edward Calnek and Henry Nicholson also aided me in these problems. All of these have gone beyond the call of duty in pointing out systemic and factual errors as well as new information that should be added. If at times I have not taken their advice, the decision has not been lightly made.

John A. Graham provided me with many new illustrations for the Olmec section and from his work at Abaj Takalik. He also brought to my attention the important new work at La Venta and that of his student James Porter. For these and many other kindnesses I thank him. Rebecca Gonzalez Lauck very kindly furnished me with an original copy of the new map of La Venta. I am much indebted to her and to the Instituto Nacional de Antropología e Historia de México for permission to publish a version of it here. My colleague and good friend Miguel Orrego of Guatemala kindly provided new data from his project at Abaj Takalik. The Guatemalan Institute of Anthropology and History has given me unrivaled opportunities for field research. Many of the results are incorporated into this book. I especially thank Licda. Edna Nuñez de Rodas, Lic. Rafael Morales, and Lic. Miguel Valencia for their many kindnesses and enormous aid.

John Paddock carefully read the material on Oaxaca for the first edition and wrote a detailed commentary on it. David Kelley helped me greatly with matters of hieroglyphic writing, calendrics, and other arcane matters. I thank them both.

The late Robert Heizer furnished badly needed photographs. Joseph

Campbell kindly aided with the pronunciation guide, Clemency Coggins with a problem in hieroglyphs, and Frank Saul with one in physical anthropology. Special thanks go to Nancy Reidand Olivia Rodriguez, who prepared the finely drawn art.

Austin Long and Rene Kra of the University of Arizona AMS Laboratory very kindly allowed me to cite the startling new dates on primitive corn. Evelyn Rattray was most generous with her new data from the Merchants Barrio of Teotihuacan and gave me a copy of the superb report that she had prepared.

The hieroglyphic and linguistic section of this edition was discussed and critiqued by Robert Spencer to my great advantage. Frank and Susan Ambuhl copy-read about two-thirds of the manuscript and turned up an embarrassing number of errors. Jane Adams also keyboarded sections of this edition and copy-read endless reams of material. I am in debt to all of these friends and colleagues.

As with any such book, this is the expression of an intellectual adventure. For me, the adventure has spanned forty years. The late Eduardo Noguera introduced me to fieldwork in Mesoamerican archaeology, and I remember him fondly. To E. M. Shook, the late Linton Satterthwaite, and W. R. Coe, who gave me my first Maya field experience, I am deeply obliged. E. A. Hoebel, R. S. Spencer, and Elden Johnson at the University of Minnesota encouraged me in the beginning stage of this project. J. W. Wagener of the University of Texas at San Antonio performed the same service for the revised edition. I hope that the result does not disappoint them.

Finally, my wife, Jane Jackson Adams, and our children sustained me in this endeavor, as in much else.

RICHARD E. W. ADAMS

San Antonio, Texas

PREHISTORIC MESOAMERICA

CHAPTER 1

INTRODUCTION

*There were writers from each branch of knowledge. Some composed
the historical annals, setting in order the events that took place
every year, stating the day, month, and hour. Others recorded the
genealogies and descendants of the kings, lords, and personages of
high lineage; they would make note of those who were born and cancel
the dead. Others painted the limits, boundaries and border stones of
the cities, provinces and villages, and of the fields and plantations,
indicating their owners. Yet others made records of the laws, and the
rites and ceremonies performed in pagan times. The priests made
records regarding the temples of the idols, and of their idolatrous
doctrines and the feasts of their false gods and their calendars. And
finally, there were philosophers and wise men among them who recorded in picture writing the sciences they were versed in.*
—Ixtlilxochitl in Bernal, 1964:xxv.

*These writings would have enlightened us considerably had not igno-
rant zeal destroyed them. Ignorant men ordered them burned, be-
lieving them idols, while actually they were history books worthy of
being preserved instead of being buried in oblivion as was to occur.*
—Durán, 1971:396.

THE HISTORY OF Mesoamerican studies can be formally divided into five
periods. The first period is that of the Spanish Conquest and immediate
aftermath of approximately fifty years, 1519–70. Hernán Cortés himself
wrote five famous and lengthy letters to Charles V reporting on the
progress of the exploration and conquest of Mexico (Cortés, 1963), and
many others did the same over the next forty years or so. Francisco de
Montejo, conqueror of Yucatan, wrote official reports and documents,
for example (in Chamberlin, 1948). Several conquerors wrote memoirs,
the most famous being Bernal Díaz del Castillo's account (1968). Cortés
evidently dictated his autobiography and story of the Conquest to his
chaplain in Spain, Francisco López de Gómara (1964). Even the "Anonymous Conqueror" left us his tale (1917). All of these personal and

eyewitness stories have substantial quantities of information on native life and civilization in them, although they are often frustratingly vague and are also frustratingly spotty in distribution.

Formal compilations of information were begun shortly after the Conquest by Father Andrés Olmos, who set the standards for later chroniclers. Olmos developed the system of collecting all the native books available to him, having them translated, and supplementing them by systematic interviews of persons of high and low estate who had lived before the Conquest. Unfortunately, Olmos's account is lost, but Father Bernardino de Sahagún followed the same research methods, as did many other illustrious writers, including Landa, Durán, Burgoa, Ixtlilxochitl, Tezozomoc, and, much later, Boturini. In a sense, all of these men were doing ethnology and ethnohistory, using participant observation when possible and documents where they existed. Diego Durán grew up in Texcoco across the lake from Aztec Tenochtitlan, and in the days of his youth there were many Aztec buildings still in use or at least visible. All of these priests wrote to provide guides to aid in the conversion and further instruction of Indians and to guard against unrecognized heresy. The Spanish bureaucracy provided much information on the working of native society, especially that of the Aztec, since they found these data to be of practical administrative use. The first viceroy of New Spain (Mexico), Antonio de Mendoza, had the Codex Mendoza compiled as a guide to the amounts of tribute that the Aztec had received from their conquered vassals and what the Spaniards therefore might reasonably expect.

Documents that fall into this and later periods are those written by natives or mestizos, who, having taken an interest in their own origins and illustrious pasts, gathered as much information as they could. Many of these documents are written in native languages. Some of them are frankly attempts to save knowledge and information that the Spanish would not have approved of, being ritually important and definitely non-Christian. The *Popol Vuh* (1971) and *Rabinal Achi* (Carmack, 1973) and the books of *Chilam Balam* are all examples of this category. Many are also self-serving in the sense that they are attempts at bolstering the social and economic statuses of survivors of the native elites. Withal, and despite the chaotic nature of the material and the attendant difficulties, these documents make up an immense treasure house of information which grows in value each year as it is confirmed, elucidated, or amplified by further historical and archaeological work.

A second period is that from 1570 to 1790. The documentary data from this period include not only some materials from the above categories, but also more formal administrative questionnaires, known generally as the *Relaciones geográficas* (reviewed in *HMAI* 12). There are two main sets, the best being the earliest, dating from 1578 to 1580. The second set dates from the dying days of the Spanish Empire, 1742–92, and is much less complete. Supplemented with accounts of ecclesiastical visits by bishops to native towns (for example, that of Father Cortés y Larraz of Guatemala), native lawsuit records (for example, the "Mapa de Teozacoalco" from Oaxaca), and miscellaneous papers, a remarkable amount of information was produced by the last two hundred years of Spanish colonial rule, in spite of its being further removed in time from the native cultures with which it dealt.

Toward the end of the Spanish colonial era, the third period of Mesoamerican studies began—that of exploration, broad scholarly participation from several fields and individuals, and awakened national interest within the various former colonies. Antonio del Río and Guillelmo Dupaix were Spanish army officers commissioned to investigate the reports of ruins in Mexico. Del Río went to the newly discovered ruins of Palenque in 1787, and his report was published in 1822, stimulating further exploration. Dupaix, a retired Royal Dragoons officer, made a good first survey of some of the major archaeological sites in Mexico. By roundabout circumstances, his report was published in the Kingsborough volumes, which appeared from 1830 to 1848 (Brunhouse, 1973).

As the Spanish Empire crumbled and the former colonies achieved independent national status, they came more and more into contact with the outside world. After centuries of purposeful isolation from non-Spanish Europe, suddenly the remarkable features of the Americas became known. The first activity stimulated by these curiosities created collections of documents. An Englishman, Lord Kingsborough, beggared himself in collecting and publishing many of these materials in a hand-colored edition of sumptuous size and cost.

Scarcely a generation after the achievement of independence came the fourth period of scholarship, led by a remarkable group of historians (Cline, 1973). They revived the tradition of document collection and comparative studies that had lapsed after the sixteenth century. José Ramírez, Joaquín Icazbalceta, Alfredo Chavero, and Franciso Paso y Troncoso all made collections of immense historical value during the nineteenth century. Manuel Orozco y Berra, however, was the principal person to attempt to apply the newly developed sophistication in historiography to these collections, and his *Historia Antigua* is a noteworthy achievement. He attempted a first synthesis of what was known about the pre-Columbian cultures as part of this magnum opus. These collections, explorations, and the resultant studies of the natural and cultural wonders of the Americas stimulated a series of more systematic explorations which led directly to the development of present-day Mesoamerican archaeology.

The first great explorers were John Lloyd Stephens, a New York lawyer, and his colleague, Frederick Catherwood, an English architect. These men explored the Maya Lowlands and, with Catherwood's superb drawings, presented an extraordinarily accurate picture of a largely unrecorded ancient civilization. They published their travels in four volumes which were best-sellers in their day—1841 and 1843 (Stephens, 1949, 1963).

Teobert Maler worked in Guatemala and Yucatan for the Peabody Museum of Harvard University in the late nineteenth century, recording ruins and texts by photography and producing a series of excellently illustrated volumes (Wauchope, 1965). A P. Maudslay's monumental archaeological supplement to a giant English work on the biology of Central America concentrated again on the Maya area. Brasseur de Bourbourg discovered many native language texts, including the *Popol Vuh* (Mace, 1973). W. W. Holmes, an American anthropologist, traveled through most of Mexico and northern Yucatan in the 1890s making accurate drawings and descriptions of the ruins. Leopoldo Batres, an official in charge of antiquities under Porfirio Díaz, did the first excavation at Teotihuacan in preparation for the celebration of the Mexican centennial of independence from Spain; however, the quality of his work is best left uncommented on, especially when compared with the work of others of the period. Desire Charnay traveled extensively and dug occasionally in places such as Tula and Teotihuacan in the 1870s and 1880s and also produced a well-illustrated book.

None of the above explorers were trained archaeologists; indeed, there was hardly such a profession as archaeology yet in existence. Certainly none of them had available the kinds of historical and ethnohistorical information which are routinely consulted today. Most of that data lay undiscovered and untranslated in archives, in private collections scattered throughout Europe, in obscure Latin American parish churches, and in other places equally difficult of access. The Mexican historians had started to publish some of the documents, and Kingsborough earlier had put a great deal (somewhat inaccurately, alas) into print. It remained for the great Eduard Seler to begin the systematic comparative studies of chronicles, native documents, and archaeological remains. Stephens had made a start in this direction, but Seler, with his intense and profound scholarship, was able to produce a magnificent series of commentaries on the religious picture manuscripts of the Borgia group of codices from central Mexico. He explained the divinatory purposes of the native calendars and other complexities of native civilizations (Nicholson, 1973).

At about the same time (late nineteenth and early twentieth centuries), Ernst Förstemann, J. T. Goodman, and Charles Bowditch were independently working out the basic features of the Maya arithmetical and calendrical system (Thompson, 1950). Indeed, much exploration done during the early twentieth century was directly stimulated by the need to record more texts and sculptures in aid of this decipherment work. David Kelley (1976) has written a critical history of these developments.

Archaeology, developed as part of the physical and natural sciences in

Europe and as part of anthropology in the United States, became a field study in its own right. At the point during the early twentieth century when all of these traditions began to combine into a coherent focus on native cultures, both prehistoric and ethnographic, Mesoamerican studies came into being. If one has to pick a date at which archaeology began to assume its modern form as a part of this intellectual development, 1910 is a likely selection. Seler, together with Alfred Tozzer of Harvard and Franz Boas of Columbia University, founded the School of American Studies in Mexico City in 1908, with Seler as its first director. Boas, the founder of modern anthropology in America, became director in 1910 and recruited Manuel Gamio as his associate.

Gamio had already done extensive excavation in the sites around the Valley of Mexico, but, in the style of the time, his work had been more in the nature of digging for things than for information. In 1910, probably because of Boas's influence, he suddenly began to dig by metric stratigraphy, thus introducing a fundamental field method into New World archaeology and also setting up a ceramic sequence for the Valley of Mexico. Gamio already had intellectual ties with the Mexican historical tradition through his chief, Nicolás León, director of the National Museum, who had been a member of the group of nineteenth-century Mexican historians mentioned above. Gamio continued to prepare himself through graduate studies at Columbia and then returned to Mexico to put into practice one of the most far-reaching plans for integrated anthropological research ever conceived. He proposed to study every aspect of several major regions of Mexico.

The Teotihuacan Valley was the first region to be selected, and a government project began there in 1917 with Gamio as director. The project's breadth of conception, amazing for its time, comprehended ethnographic studies of the modern populations, historical studies of the colonial period, and archaeological studies of the prehistoric past. These were supplemented with geological and geographical projects. Gamio's work was interrupted by personal political troubles, during which he had to leave the country, and after he returned to Mexico in 1929, his interest became concentrated on problems of integrating modern Indian populations into the national fabric and remained so until the end of his life. He had shown the way, however, in prehistoric studies.

In the Maya area from about 1908 until 1914, S. G. Morley was working under various auspices, recording Maya glyphs. In 1914, Morley persuaded the Carnegie Institution of Washington to undertake a long-term program of intensive research that would deal with selected sites from all known periods. From 1914 until 1958, when the program was abruptly abolished, the Carnegie group, led by A. V. Kidder, Sr., worked at many Maya lowland and highland sites in Guatemala, Mexico, and Honduras establishing the basic outlines of Maya prehistory and provid-

ing the critical mass of data needed to begin to attack the most sophisticated questions (Adams, 1969). The Carnegie group produced a monumental series of publications packed with data and with excellent
illustrations. Their standards of scholarship and field techniques were
very high.

Kidder was by then perhaps the preeminent person in American archaeology and an innovator in field excavation techniques developed in his
work at Pecos in the U.S. Southwest. He carried these methods into the
Maya area and developed them further. His ability to synthesize and to
carefully, if conservatively, theorize on the meanings of the data was a
great part of his scholarly strength (Willey, 1967). However, he has been
stringently criticized for not having been explicit enough in his theoretical
constructions (Taylor, 1948).

Alfonso Caso began his remarkable professional life in 1927 and continued his active scholarship until his death in 1970. His amazing luck,
combined with a powerful intellect and a gift for lucid analysis and
writing, made him outstanding in his field. Caso focused early on the
Valley of Oaxaca and began work at Monte Alban near the city of Oaxaca
early in the 1930s. His concurrent studies in calendrical matters carried
on the momentum built up by Seler in the decipherment of writing
systems. To round off his career, he produced a remarkable series of
commentaries on the historical-genealogical books of the Mixtec.

Caso and Gamio were the founders of modern anthropology in Mexico,
and their intellectual descendants carry on today. Likewise, the Carnegie
group in the Maya area formed a tradition which has influenced workers
coming afterward in that field.

The work of George Vaillant in the Maya Lowlands and later in the
Valley of Mexico was of great importance in establishing basic chronologies. Indeed, during the 1930s and 1940s the major issues of Mesoamerican archaeology were largely tied up with time-space relationships. Vaillant, however, was somewhat ahead of his time; he was willing to wring
the data for more implications than were most of this contemporaries.
His gift for large-scale synthesis and his almost poetic feeling for the
ancient cultures of Mexico are nowhere better shown than in his book
Aztecs of Mexico (1962). Vaillant, with Matthew W. Stirling, Alfonso
Caso, and Miguel Covarrubias, was one of the first to recognize the
importance of the series of finds on the Gulf Coast and in the central
highlands which ultimately were shown to be traces of the earliest civilization in Mesoamerica, that of the Olmec. His tragic death in 1945 cut
short what would undoubtedly have been further major contributions.

In the fifth and most recent period of Mesoamerican studies, integration
of the various fields seems finally to be taking form. Since about 1960 it
has become evident that the new generations of field workers are not
satisfied with simply sorting things out in terms of time and space but

also demand that data be collected and interpreted to deal with whole societies. Culture process—the study of cultural change—has become the major objective of research in this area. More sophisticated theory derived from cultural ecology, general systems theory, comparative history, and general anthropology has stimulated interpretations which are testable in the scientific sense. A certain daring and willingness to hypothesize from data are more evident in this younger group.

Present-day Mesoamericanists are a much more heterogeneous group than those that came before. From a field largely dominated by Mexican and U.S. scholars from few institutions, the effort has become one enlisting many researchers from U.S. state universities as well as from Ivy League schools. Further, the Mexican national effort has deepened in numbers of people involved and the sophistication of their training. French, German, and English research groups have appeared and are making significant contributions. Guatemala and Honduras now have small but active research groups that are growing in professional skills. Theoretical systems such as cultural ecology and field techniques such as settlement-pattern studies have taken hold of the whole field. The Selerian tradition continues, as does the Mexican ethnohistorical school of studies, but these are now much integrated into other branches of scholarship.

As will be seen, we have not yet, and likely never will, achieve a completely satisfactory understanding of Mesoamerican prehistory. (Indeed, our colleagues in European history seem dissatisfied with their control over their long-established field.) The work of our illustrious predecessors who pioneered in the field has made it possible for us to set up and test complex models of social, historical, and ecological dynamics by amassing the vast amounts of requisite information. The field continues to develop new data in an exponential manner. Partly by necessity, as much work has been done in the past forty years as was done in the preceding hundred. Archaeological data are unique and limited and are being rapidly destroyed by "ignorant zeal," not of religious enthusiasts this time, but of zealots of development and aesthetic admirers. The archaeologist today engages in a desperate race with bulldozer, dambuilder, and antiquity hunter to retrieve and record the ever-shrinking data which will aid in understanding the unique civilizations that developed in Mesoamerica.

Geography

One of the most formidable barriers to understanding the Mesoamerican past is the place-names, which at first glance may seem to non-Mesoamericans bizarre and unintelligible, let alone forgettable. Many centers or regions had similar or identical names. Some of this confusion comes from the fact that many names are descriptive. For example, a very important late Mixtec center in coastal Oaxaca was named Tututepec, but

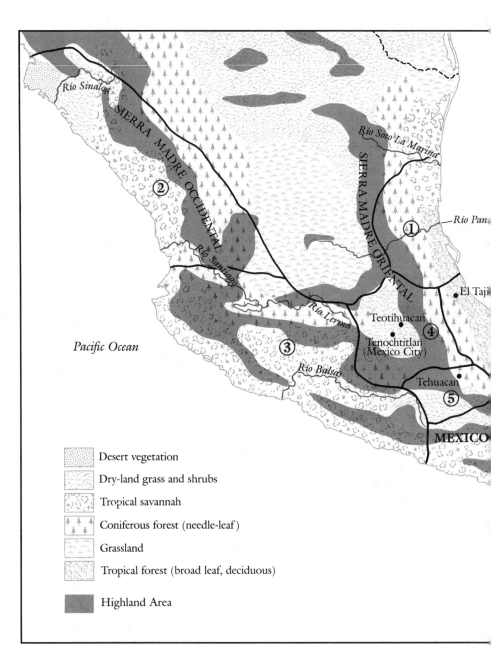

Map 1–1. Physiographic and culture areas of Prehistoric Mesoamerica.

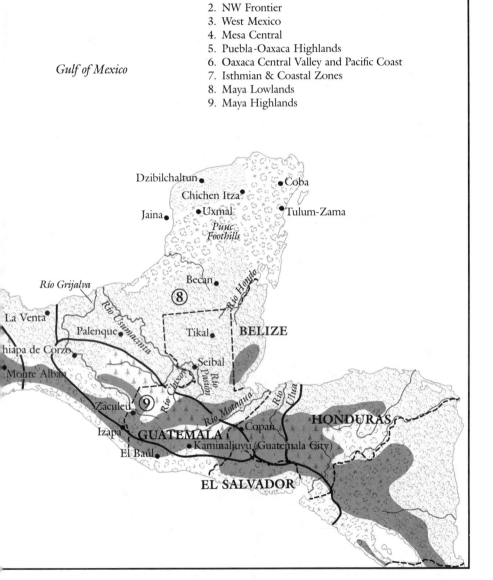

1. NE Frontier
2. NW Frontier
3. West Mexico
4. Mesa Central
5. Puebla-Oaxaca Highlands
6. Oaxaca Central Valley and Pacific Coast
7. Isthmian & Coastal Zones
8. Maya Lowlands
9. Maya Highlands

Gulf of Mexico

Dzibilchaltun
Coba
Chichen Itza
Jaina
Uxmal
Tulum-Zama
Puuc Foothills

Río Grijalva
Becan
Río Hondo
⑧
La Venta
Río Usumacinta
Palenque
Tikal
BELIZE
hiapa de Corzo
Seibal
Río Pasión
Monte Albán
Río Chixoy
Zaculeu
⑨
Río Motagua
Río Ulúa
Izapa
HONDURAS
GUATEMALA
Copan
El Baúl
Kaminaljuyu (Guatemala City)
EL SALVADOR

there was also the Huastec center of Tutotepec far to the north in Hidalgo; both names mean "Hill of the Bird." To further complicate matters, during the sixteenth century many non-Aztec place-names were translated into Nahuatl, creating a more apparent uniformity than was really the case. Tututepec's Mixtec name was originally Yucu Dzaa, which means the same thing: "Hill of the Bird." Historical charisma was another reason for duplication of names. The great Toltec center of Tula was commemorated by having its name applied to a number of smaller and usually less important places. The matter is more than a technicality. The cultural differences among places of the same name were often as great as those which exist between Paris, France, and Paris, Texas.

Frequent reference to the maps in this book or elsewhere can help prevent some of the confusion. In addition, the geographical features of each major cultural area will be discussed as we explore each one in the text. However, there are some general features that are important aids in understanding the ecological stage on which the Mesoamerican drama was played out. The modern nation-states of Mexico, Guatemala, Honduras, and El Salvador and the commonwealth country of Belize occupy the space once controlled by various native high cultures (Map 1-1). Mesoamerica is thus a culturally defined area. The northern border of this

Fig. 1–1. Highland Mesoamerica. A portion of the Valley of Oaxaca, in the Tlacolula branch, looking northeast from Yagul.

Fig. 1–2. Highland Mesoamerica. The broken terrain around Mixco Viejo in the central highlands of Guatemala.

Fig. 1–3. Highland Mesoamerica. Haystack hills and a gorge in the northern Maya Highlands of Guatemala.

culture area is roughly at the Sinaloa River in the northwest and the Soto la Marina River in the northeast. A dip in the middle excludes the central desert of Chihuahua, Nuevo León, and Coahuila. This desert zone was known to ancient Mesoamericans as the Gran Chichimeca, and civilized life existed only fitfully and fragilely in it. The southern frontier runs from the mouth of the Ulua River in Honduras, angling south in Salvador to end at the Gulf of Fonseca on the Pacific Coast. These borders frame an area of about 1,015,300 square kilometers (392,000 square miles). The borders fluctuated through time, and the frontiers given here represent the maximum extensions of Mesoamerican culture.

Extraordinary diversity compressed into a relatively small space characterizes Mesoamerica. The surface configuration is broken up by great

Fig. 1–4. Highland Mesoamerica. Native housing of thatch and pole construction on the road near Tactic, Guatemala.

mountain ranges which are part of the circum-Pacific volcanic ranges. The resulting compartmentalization of ecology has caused complex patterns of climate, vegetation, and animal life. Robert West (1964) notes that rainfall and altitude are the most crucial factors in determining the climate of any given region. All of this diversity, both ecological and cultural, can generally be organized into two polarities—highland and lowland. However, as Sanders and Price (1968) have pointed out, zones from both these categories were often economically combined into what can be called symbiotic regions. The compressed ecological diversity of Mesoamerica allowed cultural evolution to take place, but similar and widespread cultural forms were needed to organize Mesoamerica in order to realize the maximum potential that it eventually achieved. Interaction among cultures adapted to very different ecological areas is a constant and recurring phenomenon in Mesoamerican prehistory.

The following are the major cultural areas of Mesoamerica; they are both major physiographic zones and the centers of development of major cultural patterns:

1. The northeast: the Huasteca.
2. The northwest frontier.

Fig. 1–5. *Highland Mesoamerica. Eruption of Volcán Fuego near Antigua Guatemala in 1962.*

Fig. 1–6. Highland Mesoamerica. Native housing of thatch and pole construction in the Cotzal Valley, Guatemala.

Fig. 1–7. Lowland Mesoamerica. Jungle scene at Tikal, Guatemala. (Courtesy Alexandre Nikouline)

Fig. 1–8. Lowland Mesoamerica. Jungle waterhole covered with water plants, near Kohunlich, Campeche, Mexico.

Fig. 1–9. Lowland Mesoamerica. Lake Peten Itza, Guatemala.

3. West Mexico.
4. The Mesa Central: the Basin of Mexico and the surrounding valleys of Morelos, Puebla, and Toluca.
5. The Puebla-Oaxaca Highlands.
6. Oaxaca: Central Valley and Pacific Coast.
7. The Isthmian Zone: Gulf Coast Veracruz, the Isthmus of Tehuantepec, and the Guatemalan Pacific Plain.
8. The Maya Lowlands.
9. The Maya Highlands: Chiapas and Guatemala.

Mesoamerica as a Cultural Concept

Walter Lehmann in the 1920s and Paul Kirchoff in 1943 developed the concept of Mesoamerica as a large area of interaction with a basic cultural unity, a co-tradition area. These scholars depended heavily on historical and ethnographic traits in their definitions. Later, Gordon R. Willey, Rene Millon, and Gordon Ekholm reworked the concept to make it operational for archaeology (1964). In turn I have made adjustments in definition to take account of the latest research.

Basic agricultural technologies tended to be extensive in the tropical lowlands and intensive in the highlands. This distinction blurred in periods of high populations, when intensive agriculture was practiced in both sorts of zones. Regional crop lists always included varieties of corn (maize), squash, and beans, but varied greatly in regional plants such as cacao, avocados, tropical fruits, and many sorts of vegetables. Settlement patterns tended to conform to these differing subsistence systems; they were dispersed in the lowlands and nucleated in the highlands. However, again, this distinction was a matter of degree, as will be seen in the discussion of varieties of urbanism in the final chapter.

Stone Age technologies were common to all Mesoamerican cultures. New World cultures lacked the wheel, possessed few useful domesticated animals, and did not use the true arch. Metal was not ordinarily used for utilitarian purposes. Movement of goods and people was largely by canoe or by foot.

Organization of society and economy centered on the agricultural village. Aristocratic leadership controlled all affairs of import through civil servants. Merchants, warriors, and artisans formed special social classes ranking above the main class of farmer-laborers. Temple centers in both highlands and lowlands functioned as headquarters for the elite and bureaucratic classes, both initially and later when the centers had been transformed into varieties of urban communities. Market systems were integrated with the various population centers and furnished the sinews that bound together the symbiotic regions. The dispersed and nucleated towns, cities, and metropolises all were built of stone, plaster, and mortar. A variety of architectonic forms were expressed in these materials, and they were decorated with art styles which were intimately connected with the elite classes. Other manifestations of hieratic art appeared in elaborate pottery, murals, sculpture, and jewelry. After the establishment of state-level organizations, the city-state was the basic and stable unit; combinations of city-states made up the larger political structures of kingdom and empire.

Intellectually, there were certain cross-cutting philosophical and religious principles. One set was bound up with the fatalistic cosmologies of the Mesoamericans. Humans lived in a hostile world with capricious gods. Mathematics, hieroglyphic writing systems, astronomy, and calendrical systems were all tied to these philosophical tenets. Two ritual games were widely played: the ball game and the *volador* ceremony. Both still survive in isolated regions.

These and other characteristics which bound Mesoamerica together varied from region to region. But Willey has characterized Mesoamerica as a vast diffusion sphere; that is to say, whatever happened of importance in one area sooner or later had some effect on most of the other areas.

Prehistoric Development

Let us now quickly survey the main features of Mesoamerican prehistory by stages of development. These stages will be used in organizing the material in each of the following chapters. Again, I refer to Willey, Millon, and Ekholm's synthesis (1964), but I have made several modifications to that evolutionary terminology. First, I have lengthened the Lithic stage

Fig. 1–10.   Field archaeology. A palm-thatched archaeological field laboratory at Altar de Sacrificios, Guatemala.

Fig. 1–11. Field archaeology. Excavation of two associated burials and an interior terraced platform at Altar de Sacrificios. Burial 96 was located in the upper terrace, and Burial 128 in the lower terrace.

considerably to include what now seems to be good evidence for much earlier human occupation than formerly appeared likely. Second, I have adopted the now commonly used term *Archaic*. Third, I have employed the term *Formative*, which has come to be used interchangeably with *Preclassic*. This newer label has nearly as many problematic implications as the older and more commonly used term, but it seems to have become more common usage and therefore I have chosen to adopt it. Finally, it might also be noted that I have chosen to avoid the "value-free" chronological system espoused by a group of archaeologists who work mainly in the Valley of Mexico (Wolf, 1976). This scheme, which conceptually derives from one developed for the Andean area, uses terminology such

Fig. 1–12. Field archaeology. Excavation of the mosaic serpentine mask at La Venta, Veracruz, Mexico, by the late Robert Heizer and associates. (Courtesy Robert Heizer and John A. Graham)

as First Intermediate phase, Second Horizon, and the like. I do not use this system in dealing with Mesoamerica as a whole because of its technical nature and complexity and because it is so evolutionarily tied to the Valley of Mexico.

Lithic (25,000–7000 B.C.). Humans filtered into the New World as immigrants in an Upper Palaeolithic state of culture and gradually developed a radically distinctive set of New World variations. The earliest certain settlers in Mesoamerica now seem to date from about 25,000 B.C., but possibly there were people there as early as forty thousand years ago.

Archaic (7000–1500 B.C.). Transitions from hunting and gathering cultures took place during this stage, and agricultural village societies were established all over Mesoamerica by 1500 B.C. The major events were the beginning of sedentary life based on intensive hunting and gathering patterns, with a shift to agriculture and all of the consequences of that change.

Fig. 1–13. Field archaeology. Unusually good stratigraphy in which a plaster floor sealed the pottery vessels below and supported the later temple platform above. The small Formative temple was, in turn, buried by a defensive parapet around the site of Becan, Campeche, Mexico.

Formative (1500 B.C.–A.D. 150). Development of most of the early civilizations is based on cultural elaboration that took place during these 1,650 years. The Olmec seem to have been the earliest floresence and appeared near the beginning of the period, although there are now seen to have been possible predecessors to them on the Pacific Coast. A number of other Formative cultures in the central highlands were in existence and interacted with the Olmec. By A.D. 150 most of the features defining Mesoamerica and distinguishing it from North American and Central American cultural areas were in existence. In certain selected regions of Mesoamerica precocious developments led to what have been called Protoclassic cultures. However, it is clear that this second floresence is really a part of the Classic period. Because a textbook is no place to be innovative in basic chronology, I have shortened the Formative period, and in effect, the earliest Classic cultures overlap between Formative and Classic periods.

Classic (A.D. 150/300 to A.D. 650/900). A rise in populations and the appearance of elaborate cultural institutions led to the highly developed cultures of the Classic stage. The ending date is strictly dependent on the area with which one deals. Tendencies started in Formative cultures came to fruition in exotic variety during the Classic stage.

Early Postclassic (A.D. 650/900 to 1250). The reformulation of regional cultures after the collapse of most Classic cultures in Mesoamerica was the major feature of this period. New and hybrid cultures appeared at the beginning. Paradoxically, these new cultures led to more standardized and secularized forms of states.

Late Postclassic (A.D. 1250–1519). Essentially, this stage is the culmination of the reformulated cultures put together in the preceding period. We also have historical and native documents as well as eyewitness accounts for this time.

The above schemata frame the subject matter in terms of time, space, and content. We shall now turn to the earliest evidence for the presence of humans in Mesoamerica and the data which show the slow development of the economic basis for Mesoamerican civilization.

CHAPTER 2

FIRST IMMIGRANTS AND THE ESTABLISHMENT OF SETTLED LIFE

O protector of all, O giver of life, O Titlacauan (Tezcatlipoca), pity me, give me what it is necessary for my life and for my strength—of thy gentleness and sweet essence. For now there is want; there is fatigue in gaining one's needs. . . . Take pity upon me.
—*Sahagún, 1963, Book 3: 11.*

If one looks closely he will find that everything (these Indians) did and talked about had to do with maize; in truth they fell little short of making a god of it. And so much is the delight and gratification they got and still get out of the corn fields, that because of them they forget wife and children and every other pleasure, as if their corn fields were their final goal and ultimate happiness.
—*"Crónica de la Santa Provincia de Santíssimo Nombre de Jesús de Guattemala," in Morley, 1946:2.*

IT IS NEARLY an article of faith among archaeologists that the earliest inhabitants of the New World came from northeast Asia, crossing at the Bering Strait. The probabilities are that the first migrations were about thirty thousand years ago and not more than forty thousand at the outside. Recent finds in northern Chile date to about 15,000 B.C. (Dillehay, 1986). MacNeish's earliest complex in the central Andes dates to about 22,000 B.C., but there is skepticism about the validity of its artifacts. In North America the best documented and most convincing data from this early time are perhaps from Meadowcroft rock shelter in western Pennsylvania, dating about 15,000 B.C. (Adovasio *et al.*, 1978). Meso-america is geographically bracketed by these finds, and the best possibilities for this magnitude of age are the sites around Valsequillo in Puebla and that of Tlapacoya in the Valley of Mexico. First, however, we need to set the context by discussing as a whole New World materials of older date than 14,000 B.C.

No evidence for morphologically primitive humans has yet been found in the Americas. All skeletal material falls well within the range of variation of native groups as they are known from the five hundred years of

European contact. A few uncertainly dated skeletal remains discovered in
Minnesota and Texas can possibly be dated earlier than 13,000 B.C., and
may be more "primitive," but they are incompletely published, discredited
by incorrect orientation of skulls in publication, or not in the literature
at all.

There is a body of material, nearly all uncertainly dated and scattered
among dozens of sites throughout all of the Americas, which consistently
lacks the developed projectile point form in the inventory of stone tools.
These sites also fairly consistently show an emphasis on the cruder means
of manufacturing tools, that is, by percussion or direct blows of one stone
on another. Thus, most of the forms produced are flakes and choppers
or generalized scraping, digging, and gouging tools. It is claimed that
this material represents the real beginning of man's habitation of the New
World and that it may go back in time to around one hundred thousand
years ago. This claim seems exaggerated to many.

This is not the place to discuss in detail the various arguments about
early man in America except as they apply to Middle America. However,
note that the earliest stone tool, or lithic, complex in MacNeish's highland
Peruvian sequence, the Paccaicasa, tentatively dated at 22,000 B.C., dis-
plays the general characteristics noted above for the pre–projectile point
sites. Considering the distances involved between the Bering Strait and
Peru, and the necessarily halting and random nature of the earliest migrant
movements, MacNeish (1971) thinks that one hundred thousand years
is not an unreasonable estimate for the entry into the Americas of men
and tools ancestral to Paccaicasa. However, as Cowgill points out, this
estimate would assume that early humans were extraordinarily infertile
and that there were only tiny groups in the New World for eighty-five
thousand years, after which a population explosion occurred. The other
alternative is that men did not get here until thirty thousand to thirty-
five thousand years ago.

Taken together, the above indications suggest that man was a relatively
late arrival from Asia, perhaps as late as thirty thousand years ago, and
that later arrivals may have brought with them a set of ideas about stone
tools which included the punched blade technique and the lanceolate
point. It also may be the case that the lancelike point was a New World
invention. Nearly all of the material from North America dating to after
14,000 B.C. includes some sort of lancelike projectile point designed to
be attached to a shaft to form a dart or spear.

Pre–projectile point material in Middle America is best represented by
Cynthia Irwin-Williams and Juan Armenta's sites in Puebla. Valsequillo
is a well-known locality, with at least five sites that show human habitation. Most of the stone tool assemblages there lack obvious projectile
points, but one is associated with some interesting pictures of Ice Age
mammoths incised on elephant bone. The depictions were found with

the tools in gravels which seem to be of Wisconsin glaciation age. (The Wisconsin is the last of the four major glacial stages in North America and ended about 7000 B.C.) There has been some difficulty in dating the Puebla materials, because dates before 200,000 B.P., clearly outrageous and unbelievable, have been produced by uranium series techniques on bone. An initial estimate of six hundred thousand years of age on the Valsequillo gravels on a geological basis also strongly conflicts with the archaeological evidence. In addition, many of the associated artifacts are a rather nondescript group of flakes, chips, choppers, and other generalized stone items. Other dating estimates have indicated that the Valsequillo material may be between forty thousand and twenty thousand years old. This seems to be now accepted by many archaeologists (Stark, 1981).

Although the possible projectile points are not of the later lanceolate form, there are three of them in Deposit I of Hueyatlaco site, and they are associated with Ice Age fauna, including elephants. The Tlapacoya site in the southern Basin of Mexico has produced good evidence of human remains from this period. Period I at the site is dated about 25,000 to 20,000 B.C. based on radiocarbon assays of carbon from one of three fire hearths. These hearths are associated with jumbles of bones of bear, deer, and a sort of stag, all Ice-Age fauna again. Most convincingly, some twenty-five hundred stone flakes, blades, and cores were found in this level (Niederberger, 1976).

Another possibly very ancient find is that of a carved sacrum of a Pleistocene camelid, related to such present-day animals as the llama and vicuña. The carving seems to be that of a dog's, wolf's, or coyote's face. The find was made in 1870 at Tequixquiac in the Basin of Mexico. Later reevaluation of the site has indicated that the find was made at the bottom of the Pleistocene lake deposits known as the Becerra formation. Simple stone scrapers and splinters of mammoth bone have been found at the same site, perhaps evidence of early man's animal killing and processing activities. The splinters would represent butchering and perhaps marrow extraction, and the scrapers could have been used as general cutting tools and also to scrape pieces of hide. Dating is insecure, but the bottom of the Becerra deposits are thought to have been laid down beginning about forty thousand years ago.

If MacNeish's and Dillehay's finds in South America are dated correctly, then there should be finds of the age suggested by Valsequillo, Tequix-quiac, and Tlapacoya in Middle America. Based on recent work, indeed there seems to be such material. Stark (1981) has named this period Paleoindian I.

Elephant Hunters or Daring Plant Collectors?

Solid evidence for early human presence in Mesoamerica after 14,000 B.C. (Stark's Paleoindian II) still rests mainly on the finds made by Luis

Aveleyra Arroyo de Anda (1964) at two kill sites near the small town of Santa Izabel Ixtapan in the northern Basin of Mexico. The sites have similar stratigraphy and represent similar situations. A couple of layers of recently deposited soil overlay a level candidly called the "green muck," which is part of the upper Becerra. The mammoth skeletons are mired in the green muck and are the remains of animals chased into the marshy edges of the Pleistocene lake, stabbed and irritated with javelins and spears, and literally "worried to death." Six stone tools were found with one mammoth, and three other artifacts with the second.

There are some difficulties with the dating of these items, because some of them resemble stone points from elsewhere in North America (Scottsbluff, for example) which are pretty securely dated as being in use from 7000 to 5000 B.C. However, the carbon 14 dates on the mammoth remains and upper Becerra fall between 9000 and 14,000 B.C. The difficulty has been resolved by the fact that the typological resemblances are not exact and that therefore the dating of the Mexican points need not be exactly the same as that of the somewhat similar points from the Great Plains area. This being so, it seems best to accept the median date on the upper Becerra and the mammoth bones, which is about 11,000 B.C. and which nicely overlaps the earliest securely dated material in western North America: Clovis points and their associated tool types.

West Mexico has produced some finds of early projectile points, for example, at Zacoalco, Jalisco. Clovislike points have been found elsewhere, notably at the Ladyville site in the Maya Lowlands near Belize City (Hester, Kelly, and Ligabue, 1981). The site of Tapiales in Guatemala, dated at probably about 8000 or 9000 B.C., has produced a Clovislike point and a large number of woodworking tools. A very large number of probably lithic stage sites also have been found in the same zone of Guatemala by Kenneth L. Brown (1980).

Cave sites in the Tehuacan Valley to the southeast of the Basin of Mexico and in Tamaulipas, far to the north, have produced approximately contemporary remains in the form of somewhat nondescript collections of scrapers, flakes, and chips. Inasmuch as the rest of the Tehuacan and Tamaulipas sequences show definite and increasing reliance on small animals and plant gathering, MacNeish suggested that big-game hunting as a way of life never existed in the form that it did on the North American Great Plains. Indeed, MacNeish has made the statement that in central Mexico if a man killed a mammoth, he probably never stopped talking about it. The view of Mesoamerican Lithic-stage people as engaging in plant gathering and small animal hunting and only occasionally and opportunistically hunting big game accords with the geographical and faunal evidence. As ecologically favorable as it was for many purposes, Mesoamerica did not have the vast and grassy plains to support large numbers of Pleistocene megafauna. Mammoths and other large game animals did occur, of course, but their numbers were small, and the kinds of specializations in meat eating and hunting which parallel the European Ice Age cultures were simply not possible.

An argument over the role of man in the extinction of large Ice Age game has become quite heated. Some authorities think that the changing climatic conditions after the retreat of the glaciers are the prime factor in the extinction of large herd animals such as the mammoth. Paul S. Martin has argued, persuasively, that man, in combination with natural factors, played an important role (Martin and Mehringer, 1965). However this argument may eventually be resolved in regard to the North American plains, in the restricted environmental zones of Mesoamerica, where the populations of large animals were relatively thin, this certainly seems to be a reasonable explanation of their extinction.

The physical remains of early human life in Mesoamerica were ingeniously found by Helmut de Terra in 1948 in the Basin of Mexico near the small town of Tepexpan. Unfortunately, the circumstances of discovery and excavation techniques left much to be desired, and for some time there was grave doubt whether Tepexpan "man" was actually a Pleistocene individual. The skeleton was found by means of a mine detector, which also detected a number of water pockets in the former lake bed. Finally, after many false alarms, the bones came to light, apparently in association with the upper Becerra formation. However, the association was not certain, and proof had to wait for the later discoveries of the mammoths at nearby Santa Izabel Ixtapan. The fluorine content of the mammoth bones is the same as that of the human bones, indicating that the human is indeed about the same age as the elephants. The individual was female and between twenty-five and thirty years old. It is interesting that the skeleton is morphologically modern and well within the normal range of various present-day Indian populations of central Mexico. Tepexpan woman, if resurrected and dressed correctly, could lose herself in present-day Mexico City crowds without comment. These characteristics fit with most other data from North America and again are possible indications of a relatively late human migration to the New World.

The Archaic: Plant Collectors and Incipient Cultivation, 7000–1500 B.C.

The record is not continuous between the first glimpse of the earliest cultures at the Iztapan and Tepexpan sites and the earliest remains in the dry cave sites of Tehuacan and Tamaulipas. As noted, there are hints that plant collecting and small animal hunting and trapping were always very important for the diet of early humans. Indeed, the pattern of life developed during these periods never entirely died out. Even as late as Aztec times there were people called Chichimeca living near the Valley of Mexico. Durán says of these people:

They lived among the peaks and in the harshest places of the mountain where they lived a bestial existence. They had no human organization, but hunted food like beasts of the same mountain, and went stark naked without any covering on their private parts. They hunted all day for rabbits, deer, hares, weasels, moles, wildcats, birds, snakes, lizards, mice, and they also collected locusts, worms, herbs, and roots. *Their whole life was reduced to a quest for food*. . . . These people slept in the hills inside caves, or under bushes, without any heed for sowing, cultivating, or gathering. They did not worry about the morrow, but ate what they had hunted each day. [Durán, 1964:12]

These statements are a fair match for the archaeological reconstruction of life during the long buildup toward village communities based on cultivation. However, it should be noted that Durán is speaking of the survivors of this way of life in the sixteenth century who had been relegated to the least desirable zones. From 7000 to 1500 B.C. most people lived on wild foods and had access to the best and most fruitful zones. The views of Durán are also tempered by the prejudices of civilized people toward "more primitive" peoples. On the other hand, it is clear that most of human existence in these early times revolved around getting the next meal, even if the task was easier than in the sixteenth century.

Social and Ecological Factors

Social organization during the late Ice Age and early Postpleistocene epoch is reconstructed as having been family centered with, at most, organization in "bands." Apparently, at certain favorable times of the year these blood-related groups came together temporarily to form larger social groups. This type of fluctuating society was necessary when population was thin and the way of life nomadic. Following Julian Steward's lead in archaeology and ethnology (Steward, 1938), MacNeish (1964) has characterized the smaller family groups as "microbands" and the larger, multifamily groups as "macrobands." The yearly economic rounds involved a continual breaking up and regrouping of these two types of groups. This same kind of society is the one that developed Mesoamerican agriculture and that formed the basis for the later village farming societies.

With the advantage of knowing the principal food plants that were important among later peoples, we can trace some of the ancestry of these plants through the archaeological sequences. Wild corn pollen detected from a core taken from beneath the Palace of Fine Arts in downtown Mexico City has been dated at about 80,000 B.P. This and distributional evidence indicate that the central highlands of Mexico were one of the zones where wild corn *(Zea maize)* grew. The Oaxacan and Maya highlands also seem to have been areas which contained many of the wild ancestors of maize and others of the eventually cultivated plants.

The inventory of wild plants for any single region of Mesoamerica, even if all of the plants were developed to the point of being productive when cultivated, would not have been sufficient to support village life. The plants would have been neither diverse nor productive enough. About fifty food plants of New World origin are for sale at present in Tehuacan's market, and most of them certainly did not originate or occur as wild plants in the valley at 7000 B.C., when plant domestication began there. However, the compressed ecological diversity within Mesoamerica, noted earlier, along with easy communication among the diverse zones, meant that a necessary condition was present: the possibility of trading both wild and "improved" (semidomesticated or domesticated) plants from zone to zone. That this necessary condition was taken advantage of in central Mexico is self-evident; we do have the rise there of village life based on agriculture. However, we apparently do not have the sufficient conditions, whatever those may have been in the Maya Highlands, to have led to the innovative establishment of village farming life in that area. This is to say that just because the ecological conditions existed for something to happen, there was no inherent necessity for that event— the move to agriculture in this case—to have occurred. Ecological or environmental determinism does not explain all, then. Historical and other factors must be brought into the explanation. We will consider some of these factors after a review of the archaeological evidence. In the meantime, the environmental stage is set with the existence of the vast diversity of topography and associated diverse plant and animal communities crammed into a relatively small geographic area.

The Archaeological Evidence

The two major sequences which reflect the development of highland agriculture have been traced by R. S. MacNeish, who in an extraordinary and sustained effort, beginning in 1948 and continuing until 1975, recovered the major features of this botanical and social evolution from a series of dry, dusty caves in the mountains of northeastern and central Mexico.

The Tehuacan Sequence. To the southeast of Mexico City, the modern provincial resort town of Tehuacan is located in a semiarid highland valley about 1,676 meters (5,500 feet) above sea level. The valley rises toward the south and is delimited by mountainous terrain on the east and west. Better-watered zones occur on the margins and in the canyons of the area, and it was in these favored environments that the wild ancestors of corn grew. Porous rock formations in these mountains allowed the development of shelters and caves, favored sites of habitation by early human populations. Families and groups of families visited the caves frequently, carrying their gathered plants and the animals they trapped and hunted with them for processing and eating. Wild plant seeds were

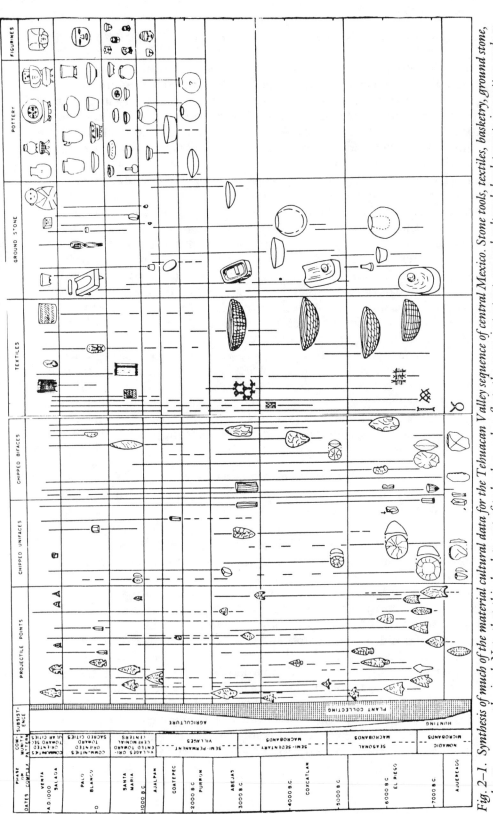

Fig. 2–1. Synthesis of much of the material cultural data for the Tehuacan Valley sequence of central Mexico. Stone tools, textiles, basketry, ground stone, and pottery are emphasized. Note that this development of technology only reflects the more important general cultural developments in matters such as social organization, agricultural techniques (for example, irrigation), political structure, and so on. (Courtesy Richard MacNeish)

ground on convenient stones, and the animals were skinned (or some-times not) and cooked and eaten. Seeds, fragments of animal bones, the grinding stones, pieces of gourd rind, fireplaces, human feces, bits of basketry and netting, chipped stone tools, and other debris littered these caves when they were in use. These discarded and lost items gradually built up in layers, preserving the record of man's activities and his increasingly successful manipulation and use of plants.

Archaeologists divide long periods of settlement in a region into conve-nient segments or phases, each of which is defined by a certain group of stone tools, plants used, and, later, pottery. A chronology chart of the phases in the Tehuacan Valley stretches from about 7000 B.C. to A.D. 1500, one of the longest, most continuous, and most informative of sequences in Mesoamerica (Fig. 2-1). About ten thousand pieces of plant remains, more than eleven thousand zoological specimens, and over one hundred pieces of human feces were recovered from Tehuacan sites. The last are very important for dietary information, representing as they do complete meals and direct evidence of human consumption. A scientist named Callen has ingeniously devised a way in which to restore these feces to their prestine condition. Although this procedure has its disadvan-tagés, it also results in such information as the proportion of meat in a diet. Hair and bone fragments even allow identification of animal species consumed.

The earliest Tehuacan phase, Ajuereado, is clearly one of a society adapted to hunting small animals and collecting wild plants at about 7200 B.C., although antelope and Ice-Age horses were present as well. Over 40 percent of the diet was derived from wild plants and some 54 percent from meat. These trends continued into the better known El Riego phase, which begins about 7000 B.C. At least nineteen kinds of wild plants were used in that phase, but three plants already show evidence that they were domesticated; the most important of them is a type of squash *(Cucurbita mixta)*. Chile peppers and avocados were also probably early domesti-cates, but all three contributed less than 5 percent to the diet. Many uncultivated cactuses, grass seeds (especially *Setaria*), and mesquite beans were eaten. Amaranth, important among the later Aztec as a cereal, was also important during El Riego as a gathered plant. Callen's basic data tell us that meat was eaten, but he could not identify the species. Population of the valley is estimated to have been three family groups, or twelve to twenty-four people.

During the Coxcatlan phase (5500–4500 B.C.) human population was still thin. However, the amounts of food from gardening activities rose to 14 percent and included primitive corn, chiles, squash, and amaranth. For both El Riego and Coxcatlan times the principal subsistence activities were rabbit drives, stalking game with darts, and collecting fruits, pods, and seeds, all of which were more important than gardening. These mainly wild foods were eaten after they were boiled (vegetables and fruits), milled (grass seeds), and steamed or boiled (meat). Marrow was extracted from the bones. Meat and plant products were also eaten raw. Life was still somewhat nomadic, although gardening and gathering allowed groups to stay in one spot from spring to fall. Nearly all of the stone technology was devoted to exploitation of natural resources. Chipped flint points tipped the darts used for hunting, game was skinned with flint flakes, and hides were prepared by scraping with special stone tools. Hide preparation was aided by bone awls for punching holes. Large choppers represent general digging tools which could be used for digging into rodent burrows and for grubbing up roots. In both El Riego and Coxcatlan phases stone bowls are found that probably were mortars. A certain amount of ritual in the lives of these people revolved around the burial of the dead. Some offering accompanied the bodies—probably blankets, baskets, and perhaps food. No permanent housing or special buildings of any sort are known.

The next two phases of the sequence, Abejas and Purron, are the last Tehuacan phases that we shall consider, although the sequence continues into the sixteenth century. Abejas and Purron represent a block of time from about 3500 to 1500 B.C. During these phases, agricultural output provided first 21 percent and later 35 percent of the diet. In fact, after these phases agriculture continued to increase in productivity until, about A.D. 600, agricultural products reached a peak of 75 percent of all food-stuffs. On the other hand, the proportion of meat in the diet diminished steadily throughout the sequence, falling from nearly 55 percent in Ajuereado (7200 B.C.) to 17 percent about A.D. 600. Major factors in these changes were plant improvement through various genetic modifications and continual addition of plants that were not native to the Tehuacan Valley, such as various races of beans.

The major event in the domestication of plants took place at about 3000 B.C.—the introduction of corn into the inventory of plants. This is a redating based on the use of the newest radiocarbon techniques (Long et al., 1989).

The history of corn is an excellent example of genetic change and one that has been reconstructed by Paul Mangelsdorf of Harvard University (Mangelsdorf, 1974, esp. pp. 45–52 and 180–85). Wild corn was a primitive and unpromising plant, and one wonders why it was selected for development at all. It was both a pod and popcorn, with the individual tiny kernels wrapped each in its own glume. The cobs were less than 20 mm long (the width of a one-cent piece). Quids from the 7000 B.C. material show that ancient people ate corn by simply chewing it up for the juices and then spitting out the remainder. Early corn might have had a dispersal problem because of the kernel wrapping, but in compensation the ear was placed high on the plant. Fertilization might have been a problem for the same reason—the kernel wrapping—but that was not the case, since each ear had its own tassel carrying pollen. Mangelsdorf and his associates, through a series of genetic experiments, tried to reproduce the primitive ancestor of corn (Mangelsdorf, MacNeish, and Galinat, 1967). They did not precisely succeed, but, as Mangelsdorf says, they did achieve the world's most unproductive corn.

To reach the productivity and characteristics of modern corn, one of the world's great cereal crops, an extraordinarily complex series of genetic changes and crosses had to take place. Mangelsdorf and his colleagues have worked these out through experimentation and theoretical genetics, and their reconstructions have been partially confirmed by archaeology and recent discoveries in field botany (Mangelsdorf, 1983). Corn was domesticated not only in Mesoamerica but also in the South American west coast of Peru and Ecuador, where races of wild maize occurred. The primitive domesticate from Mesoamerica almost certainly crossed with the equally primitive domesticate in South America. This crossing dropped certain genetic barriers, and another crossing took place between the improved corn and *Tripsacum*, a grass that grows in Bolivia and other parts of the Andean area. The second crossing resulted in explosive evolution, with changes in ear and kernel sizes and in other characteristics. For example, the tassel moved to the top of the plant, and ears lost their individual tassels. The improved corn was traded back to Mesoamerica, and there it crossed with another native grass, teosinte. Teosinte has its own complicated history and seems to have been an offspring of primitive corn and *Tripsacum*. The third crossing—improved South American corn with teosinte—led to a second explosive evolution and resulted in the modern races of maize. This result still was not the extraordinary series of races of modern hybridized corn with which we are familiar but more resembled North American dent corn.

The long-quiescent controversy about the origins of corn and the place of teosinte in its evolution has proven to be only dormant and not dead. George Beadle, former provost of the University of Chicago, retired to his teosinte patch and built a case for teosinte as the direct ancestor of corn (Beadle, 1972).

Beadle's arguments revolve around the fact that teosinte is the closest relative of corn, with a genetic difference on the order of only four or five genes. In Beadle's view that renders acceptable the hypothesis that teosinte might be ancestral to corn, especially since Mangelsdorf now suggests that wild corn is possibly the ancestor of both maize and teosinte. If one accepts the latter, Beadle argues, then why not consider the reverse: that is, that teosinte is the ancestor of both corn and modern teosinte? Teosinte is the more successful wild plant and therefore a more likely candidate for a common ancestor. Further, teosinte can be rendered into a good food by either popping or grinding it. Beadle argues that the earliest archaeological corn, as found in the Tehuacan sequence, represents a transitional form between teosinte and maize and not an ancestral wild maize. He is forced to speculate, however, that domestication began much earlier than the evidence indicates.

Mangelsdorf has replied in his magnum opus, entitled *Corn* (1974), and has added new data and arguments since the publication of his monograph (1983). He accepts the fact that teosinte is the closest relative of maize and that it can be eaten if popped or ground. His main refutation rests on the argument that Beadle's possibilities are not probabilities and, indeed, go against all the factual evidence now in hand. No evidence has ever been found for the extensive use of teosinte as food in either ancient or modern times. Ground teosinte is over half kernel shell, which, if it had been eaten, would have shown up in prehistoric human feces. None of the Tehuacan coprolites had teosinte kernel fragments in them. Further, although Beadle himself once consumed 150 grams (5.25 ounces) of ground teosinte a day, Mangelsdorf points out that this amount would yield only one-sixth of an adult's average daily caloric needs. A meal does not make a diet. Mangelsdorf also says that teosinte's characteristics are much more specialized than those of maize and that the transition from teosinte to maize would therefore have been more difficult than the reverse process. The largest part of the rebuttal rests on the massive archaeological evidence, which is compatible with Mangelsdorf's theory and incompatible with the teosinte theory.

The Tamaulipas Sequence. The other major sequence showing a series of phases of domestication is that from Tamaulipas. The northeastern corner of modern Mexico is mountainous, and much of it today is semiarid mesquite country and thus drier than the Tehuacan zone. An indication of the hotter climate might be noted in R. S. MacNeish's (1958) phase names for the sequence, one of which is Infiernillo (Inferno). Again, this sequence shows a long developmental buildup through phases beginning about 7200 B.C. and culminating with the establishment of full-time agricultural communities and villages about 1500 B.C. The sequence and the timing of the appearance of plants is different from that of Tehuacan. In Tamaulipas, as in Tehuacan, squash was also the first domesticate, but it was of a different species *(Cucurbita pepo)* and presumably represents the domesticated version of the local wild plant. The same intensification of gathering and gardening activities took place together with the same social changes from nomadic bands to seminomadic groups and, finally, to semipermanent villages. Early Tehuacan squash *(Cucurbita mixta)* does not occur at the Tamaulipas sites until well after A.D. 1.

Corn first appears at Tamaulipas sites about 3000 B.C., nearly contemporary with its appearance in the Tehuacan Valley. It is also an improved variety in its first appearance, albeit not greatly so. The implications are that from one end of Mesoamerica to the other, corn was being experimented with and improved, and that there is no heartland of domestication for this plant. There are contrasts in the appearance of crucial food plants: varieties of beans, for example. However, enough has been said to make the point that domestication and development of food plants was a process in which all of Mesoamerica was involved, and at times even areas outside Mesoamerica made their contributions. By 1500 B.C. nearly every major region of the cotradition area had achieved a village farming level.

It is noteworthy that there were no domesticated animals of great food importance. Dogs show up as domesticates about 3000 B.C. and certainly were eaten as well as being used in hunting, but dogs are no substitute for cattle, sheep, goats, or pigs, all of which were important in the Old World Neolithic but lacking in the New World.

Possible and Early Lowland Villages

There is no direct evidence from the tropical lowlands for domestication of food plants, but important plants certainly are of lowland origin: vanilla, cacao, various squashlike vegetables such as *huisquil,* and many fruits. MacNeish has considered these data and has recently completed a project in the Maya Lowlands (MacNeish, Wilkerson, and Nelken-Terner, 1980) that suggests a comprehensive explanation for the establishment of village life in both major altitude zones, and one which also explains certain later events (MacNeish, 1966). Although the latter was written before his lowland work, the basic theoretical structure still is sound.

Large shell mound sites exist on both the Gulf and Pacific coasts of Mesoamerica, but few have been even cursorily examined. Exceptions are the Sanja and Puerto Márquez sites, which are located on lagoons on the Pacific Coast of Guerrero. A date on material from their shell middens has been read as about 2900 B.C.; it is preceramic and seems to be associated with a clay (house?) floor. Another date, 2400 B.C., is associated with some of the earliest, if not the earliest, pottery in Mesoamerica. The mounds are large enough to suggest semipermanent village life.

Voorhies found a clay floor with two possible post holes at the not too distant Pacific Coast site of Tlacuachero (ca. 3100–2000 B.C.). Other hints of early communities come from some shell heaps on the Veracruz coast, where James Ford and Alfonso Medellín-Zenil found masses of chipped stone and fire-cracked rocks in large sites located on top of fossil sand dunes. No pottery was found on these sites, indicating a date possibly about 3000 B.C. at Palo Hueco (Wilkerson, 1975). The chipped stone tools from the Veracruz sites are roughly similar to those from the general period of 5000–3000 B.C. in the Tehuacan Valley. Not many grinding stones are present, indicating a reliance on food sources other than seeds. The locations of these sites suggest that shellfishing, fishing in the lagoons

and offshore, and hunting of small animals supported these semipermanent early lowland villages.

MacNeish (1966) suggests that this pattern of life and its subsistence
base developed between 7000 and 5000 B.C., when some highland groups
were taking their first halting steps toward cultivation and settled life.
Certainly, MacNeish thinks, permanent, sedentary villages were in existence on the coasts between 5000 and 3000 B.C., and thus a longer
tradition of sedentism belongs in the lowlands. These early villages were
in favored ecological situations, with the resources of the sea, lagoons,
estuaries, swamps, and several transitional types of microzones available
to them. This localization of several resource zones led to a stable pattern
of village life.

It is clear that after 3000 B.C. lowland societies began to acquire
domesticated plants and techniques both from their own experimentation
and by importation from the adjacent highlands. This development probably meant nearly instant food surpluses. The major centers of initial
lowland cultivation were probably along the river on the natural levees,
where, as Coe and Diehl (1980) point out, the most fertile land is located.
Lowe (1971) has suggested that population growth associated with the
possibilities of agriculture, and the anxieties that an agricultural way of
life brings, led to the establishment of more formal religious concepts.
The food surpluses, the longer tradition of sedentism in the lowlands,
and the motivation of religious assuagement of anxieties about crops and
hazards to them may well have combined to lead to the establishment of
formal ceremonial architecture dedicated to ritual. We shall return to this
argument when the origin of Olmec civilization is discussed.

Christine Niederberger has worked with materials from later levels at
Tlapacoya in the Valley of Mexico. Playa-phase material there seems to
be from hunter and gatherer groups who had made the transition to
sedentism by 5000 B.C. A natural disaster occurred in the form of a severe
volcanic eruption about 3000 B.C., and human life became impossible
over most of the basin for about five hundred years. About 2500 B.C.
there was a reoccupation of the zone, which was then on the edge of a
shallow lake or lagoon (Zohapilco phase). According to Niederberger
(1976), the data indicate that a permanent village in the vicinity had a
food subsistence base which combined both early domesticates, such as
corn, squash, and peppers, and wild species. Thus, the evidence from the
Basin of Mexico parallels in great degree that from the lowland coasts.
However, the zones where earliest and nonagricultural sedentary life was
possible in the highlands were definitely limited, whereas such zones were
extensive in the lowlands.

There are indications of early regional specifications in cultivated plants
in the lowlands as well as in the highlands. The Altamira site on the coast

of Chiapas, Lowe has suggested, is in a zone that is more suitable for the cultivation of the tropical root crop manioc than for maize. Although this site dates from about 1500 B.C., it may well reflect a continuation of a long-established tradition.

The archaic sequence of northern Belize in the Maya Lowlands presents new data and many problems. The sites there, developed by MacNeish, are open, their stone tools are similar to those of later Classic phases, and their stratigraphy is difficult. MacNeish and his colleagues (MacNeish, Wilkerson, and Nelken-Terner, 1980) have defined five phases running from 9000 to 2000 B.C. Assuming that the basic sequence is sound, the following seem to be the trends in the development of sedentary life in the Maya Lowlands: Early in the sequence, the evidence shows a reliance on hunting the remaining species of Ice-Age animals, including the giant sloth. Canoe construction is implied after 7500 B.C. by the presence of adzes, woodworking tools. After 5500 B.C. grinding tools appeared and increased in number and variety. Fishing and other exploitation of the sea and lagoons increased after 4200 B.C., with a goodly amount of plants also being processed and eaten. The final preceramic phase saw the appearance of sedentary villages, and the implications are that shellfishing and other lagoon exploitation gave way to a gradual increase in plant experimentation and improvement and, finally, to agriculture.

All of the above is somewhat unsatisfactory because of questionable facts and ambivalent evidence, but there is at least one thing in its favor. It fits the pattern of large-scale and intense interaction among the various parts of Mesoamerica which characterized the region in later periods of prehistory. The symbiotic patterns of Aztec times seem prefigured in the simpler, but no less significant, trading of early domesticates among the regions of the highlands. There is nothing to hinder the participation of the lowlands in this kind of interaction, and all of the hints in the archaeological record point toward that. It is clear that much more work is needed on this problem, and especially in the unglamorous but crucial excavation of shell middens.

At this time MacNeish's model seems the best explanation of the domestication of plants and the establishment of village life as the basis for later, more sophisticated communities. However, it does not explain certain processes that apparently were in operation to change hunters and gatherers into agricultural villagers. B. L. Stark (1981) has pointed out recently that a number of elements were probably involved in this transition. One was population growth. She notes that the Binfords (1968) and others have observed that mobile groups of humans apparently have a characteristically long birth spacing. This seems a result principally of the problems of caring for more than one small child at a time. If groups become less mobile or sedentary, then shorter birth spacing can be tolerated and population growth will probably occur. Further, there will also be a positive incentive for more children because they can help with the multitude of agricultural tasks.

Comparison with Old World Domestication

In going over the sequences of New World plant domestication one is struck by the inordinate length of time that it took to achieve a viable complex of food plants—over five thousand years. When we look at the record of this process in the Old World, we find that things moved much faster. In the Greater Middle East, the development of agriculture and animal domestication took place from about 8500 to 6000 B.C., about half the time of that of the New World. K. V. Flannery (1973, 1986) has suggested that this difference could be the result of three main factors. The first is the nature of the difference between the New World and Old World cereal crops; wheat is nearly as productive in the wild as it is under cultivation and needed little modification to be domesticated. Second, the larger numbers of animals available for domestication in the Old World apparently took up the slack during the chancy period when the first plant domesticates were being developed. Goats and sheep were domesticated first, and then cattle and pigs; all of them carry considerably more meat per animal than dogs and turkeys, the principal Mesoamerican domesticates. The third factor is the nature of the societies involved. Flannery suggests that because of the general lack of larger domesticable animals in the New World and the emphasis on gathering, there was not the specialization of labor by sex that one found in Old World hunting communities. Even a child can hit a lizard on the head, but it takes a man in full strength to attempt to domesticate and hunt wild cattle. In the Old World, men and women in Pleistocene societies had distinctive task roles which preadapted them for agricultural life, in which the women handled tasks around the village or base camp while the men were out cultivating. In New World hunting and gathering societies, apparently everyone did everything, and therefore it took time to develop social organization that would allow work specialization by sex, which, in turn, would confer the greater efficiency needed for agricultural life.

The Problem of the Origins of Mesoamerican Pottery

The earliest Mesoamerican pottery, found at Puerto Marquez on the Pacific coast of Mexico, was apparently fiber-tempered. Tempering (or grog) is material added to the clay to encourage more uniform expansion of the clay during firing. Otherwise, uneven expansion causes problems such as spalling and breakage, and other kinds of disappointments. The tempering material used in much early New World pottery was chopped grass or other organic material, which burns out or carbonizes during firing, leaving characteristically porous and lightweight ceramics called pox pottery. The earliest pottery in the Tehuacan sequence is similar to that found at Puerto Marquez, but dates to about 2000 B.C. It has been suggested that the stone bowls of the same form found in the sequence are prototypes from which the ceramic forms were developed. However, the dating of these bowls is not certain, and it may be the other way around; the stone bowls may be imitations of ceramic forms.

Fiber-tempered pottery from about 3000 B.C.—the earliest pottery of any kind to occur in the New World—is found at a site called Puerto Hormiga on the northern, Caribbean, coast of Colombia. Such pottery also shows up on the Atlantic coasts of Georgia and Florida from about 2500 B.C. The late James Ford (1969) argued that the first ideas about pottery were developed in South America, possibly from concepts introduced from Japan, and thence spread north and south over the North American continent. Whether or not we want to stamp all of this earliest pottery as "made in Japan," the similarity in form and tempering among all of the earliest ceramics and their dating sequence make it plausible to derive them from South America. At a site found by Eaton (1978) on the northern tip of Yucatan, a shell midden containing fiber-tempered pottery may well be a way-station in Ford's theoretical pottery diffusion from south to north.

In any case, clearly a horizon of large, round-sided, neckless jars and flat-bottomed, open pans, tempered with organic materials, is found in a wide distribution from about 2400 to about 2000 B.C. in Mesoamerica. From this basic horizon all the later regional, diverse, and very sophisticated ceramic traditions apparently stem.

There is no inherent quality in pottery, however, that means that any great cultural change is taking place. Pottery is simply an easily replaceable container material which has certain advantages over basketry; it can be used for cooking, for example, and water does not leak out of it so easily. It may reflect a greater sedentism in village life, with consequent accumulation of more storable material, although this is not necessarily so. It is certainly large in the consciousness of archaeologists, but this is mainly because of its utility as an analytical device for defining cultural regions and marking phase boundaries.

The Establishment of Regional Varieties of Village Life

Recent work by W. F. Rust and Rebecca Gonzalez Lauck has apparently confirmed much of MacNeish's theoretical formulation (Rust and Sharer, 1988). A now dry river channel, the Río Bari, lies north of the site of La Venta in lowland Veracruz. Natural levees built up along the once formidable river are the sites for Early and Middle Formative villages. The earliest site located, San Andrés, dates from between 1750 and 1150 B.C. and is buried at a depth of more than 5 meters (16 feet) below present ground level. "Small amounts of grit-tempered Early Preclassic

[Formative] pottery and marine mudflat-dwelling . . . mollusks" have been found there (Rust and Sharer, 1988). An associated deposit has shown possible evidence of cultivation of the zone. Although San Andrés, presumably a small village, is now 13 kilometers (8 miles) inland, evidence shows that it once was much closer to the Gulf and existed in an estuary environment.

The Barra phase is associated with mound building and manioc cultivation at the site of Altamira, located in the low, swampy coastal zone of Chiapas. The phase dates to about 1650 B.C. Nothing so far found ties it with the earliest Puerto Marquez pox pottery. Barra pottery is sophisticated in decorative techniques compared to either pox ceramics or the Purron-phase pottery of Tehuacan. At Altamira, the ceramics look like squashes or gourds, complete with the fluting and undulating surface which imitate the segmented surfaces of pumpkins or squashes. Lowe has also suggested that this early pottery developed when a preceramic group which had previously used gourds as containers adopted pottery from a South American source (Green and Lowe, 1967). They simply imitated the forms of their older containers. Obsidian chips found at Altamira are debris from the manufacture of other tools but certainly were not used for processing manioc, as Lowe has suggested (Lewenstein and Walker, 1984).

The Locona phase (ca. 1600 B.C.?), recently defined by John Clark and Michael Blake, appears to be the long-sought transition between Barra and Ocos phases. It is spread across the Isthmus of Tehuantepec and the coastal regions of Veracruz-Tabasco on the north side and the Chiapas-Guatemalan-Salvadorean Pacific Coast on the south. The Grijalva River trench seems to be included in this area. It is argued that this phase is characterized by ranked societies, which would have been associated with religious leadership. Finally, it should be noted that the Locona is now the first detectable period of large-scale cultural uniformity in Mesoamerica.

About 1500 B.C. another early ceramic complex, the Ocos, which is also possibly South American in origin, appeared on the Pacific coast of Guatemala. The Ocos-sphere complexes characterized by the use of very similar pottery and similar settlements, soon spread from the original Locona distribution zone over the isthmian area and are known from at least twenty-five sites. Most of these sites are in coastal, lagoon-estuary environmental settings, but some are on inland rivers at favored locations. Subsistence activities clearly were fishing the lagoons and farming the piedmont zones and the annually flooded river levees. The ceramics are again very sophisticated and distinctive, with large, globular jars (*tecomate* forms) and flat pans decorated typically with stamped designs of various sorts, including rocker stamping, zoned dentate stamping, and shell-back stamping as well as cord marking and fabric impression. This pottery was colored in iridescent stripes and in red bands of specular hematite around the mouths of the jars.

The Ocos-phase site of La Victoria is located on a former lagoon and even today is not far from the Pacific. Its excavator, M. D. Coe, has pointed out striking similarities between Ocos pottery and Chorrera-phase (about 1500 B.C.) ceramics in the Guayaquil coastal zone of Ecuador (Coe, 1960): the use of the open pan form, rocker stamping, and iridescent banding. The coast of western South America was noted in the sixteenth century for the development of seamanship and various sorts of watercraft, including sailing rafts of the sort made famous by the Kon-Tiki expedition. Coe has shown how currents and seasonal winds would aid and make possible voyages between the regions involved.

At this point, then, several things come together in a possible comprehensive explanation. As indicated several times already, South American contacts were possible in Mesoamerican prehistory. The earliest example is in the domestication of maize. Pottery-using communities may have intruded onto both the Mesoamerican coasts several times and at several places. It is possible that manioc was used in the Barra phase, and the emphasis on this plant was definitely more South American than Meso-american. The mechanism of contact would have been voyages across the Caribbean and Pacific, mainly coastal voyages or even inside the lagoons which stretch for miles and provide protected waters. However, there is every evidence that early sailors in the New World did not hesitate to leave the sight of land, at least for short distances. Recent work indicates that the West Indies were initially colonized by island-hopping sea travelers, again coming from South America at least by 5000 B.C.

Although ceramics were apparently introduced several times from outside Mesoamerica, directly from South America or from intermediate Central American regions, the Ocos horizon is the first which really took hold of and spread the idea of ceramics across a broad area. Almost certainly this concept was not carried by colonizing South American populations but was accepted by already sedentary Mesoamerican populations from visitors or a few settlers (Stark, 1981).

Coe and Gareth Lowe suggest that Ocos pottery is so sophisticated that some people must have spent almost all of their time producing it. If so, there must have been a new kind of society, one in which there were individuals that did not produce food and in which there were specialists of other sorts. If a group can support a potter at least part-time, it certainly can support a religious specialist, a shaman, equally well. Little information is available on religious concepts of the time, but female figurines that appear in this period and continue on into the Formative perhaps indicate the sort of fertility ideas with which they were associated in later Aztec times (Fig. 2–2). Lowe also suggests

Fig. 2–2. Formative-period clay figurines from Kaminaljuyu, Guatemala. The human figures date from about 300 B.C. and possibly were used by shamans in curing ceremonies.

that possession of the crucial agricultural and orchard crop resources by families might have led to high-status lineages and social stratification based on relative wealth.

Although the highlands of central and southern Mexico were clearly occupied by agricultural villagers during this period, and many of the lowland areas were being used by pioneer farmers using Ocos-horizon pottery, it seems equally clear that large areas of Mesoamerica were essentially vacant. Although a negative case is difficult to prove, it appears that some of the Maya Highlands and much of the tropical forest zone of the interior of the peninsula of Yucatan were empty zones exploited only for hunting and gathering. In much of the Guatemalan highlands there is only very weak evidence or no evidence at all of village agriculturalists, and in the Guatemalan lowlands the first colonists appear only about 1000 B.C. or perhaps 1200 B.C. at the earliest. However, human population was rapidly expanding elsewhere, and a significantly greater number of sites are known in other parts of Mesoamerica for the period 1350 to 1100 B.C. than for 1600 to 1350 B.C.

Ocos-horizon sites found in the wetlands of the Veracruz coast underlie at least two of the later greater ceremonial centers of Olmec civilization, San Lorenzo and probably La Venta. Ojochi, Bajio, and Chicharras phases at San Lorenzo are clearly developments from an Ocos base, and it is upon this base that the first and, in some respects, most spectacular civilization of Mesoamerica rests.

As will be seen, the relatively low Salvadoran mountain valleys, and even the Caribbean coastal lowlands of Honduras, were occupied by Ocos-horizon cultures. The Cuyamel Caves of Honduras have yielded bottle forms which are very similar to those found at San Lorenzo in the Bajio phase (1350–1250 B.C.; Coe and Diehl, 1980).

Note that MacNeish and Nelken-Terner (1983) have produced a synthesis of the preceramic period from a different point of view, but one not necessarily incompatible with that taken in this chapter.

CHAPTER 3

EARLY AND MIDDLE FORMATIVE CULTURES: VILLAGES, REGIONAL CENTERS, AND THE OLMEC

In 1862 I was in the region of San Andrés Tuxtla, a town in the state of Veracruz in Mexico. During my excursions, I learned that a Colossal Head had been unearthed a few years before in the following manner. Some one and a half leagues from a sugarcane hacienda, on the western slopes of the Sierra of San Martín, a laborer of this hacienda, while cutting the forest for his field, discovered on the surface of the ground what looked like the bottom of a great iron kettle turned upside down. He notified the owner of the hacienda, who ordered its excavation. And in place of the kettle was discovered the above-mentioned head. It was left in the excavation as one would not think to move it, being of granite and measuring two yards in height with corresponding proportions. . . . We went, and I was struck with surprise: as a work of art, it is without exaggeration a magnificent sculpture.
—*Melgar y Serrano, 1869, vol. 1:292.*

Emerald green Jade . . . its appearance is like a green quetzal feather. And its body is as transparent and as dense as obsidian. It is precious, esteemed, valuable. . . . It is one's lot, the lot of rulers, of the old ones.
—*Sahagún, 1963, Book 11:222.*

ARRIVING AT about 1500 B.C., we have reached the period when Meso-america began to take form and the time of development of the first known floresence, that of the Olmec. In the previous chapter we saw how, over a period of millennia, patterns of exploitation of wild foods changed and eventuated in food-producing communities. Based on the extraordinary richness of wild plants and on the resources of lakes, la-goons, estuaries, and the sea, some societies, it appears, achieved sedentary communities by 3000 B.C. or before. Pottery was either introduced or invented several times in this context of nonagricultural villages. These same communities, as well as those of the known plant experimenters of the highlands, became agriculturalists by about 1500 B.C. Based on the styles of ceramics, which seem partially to reflect ethnic and linguistic differences, several zones of Mesoamerica can be defined.

The Gulf Coast, Isthmus of Tehuantepec, and Pacific corridor of Guatemala form a geographical unit, the Isthmian Zone. Much later, this zone was one of the favorite ways to travel from the Mexican highlands to the Guatemalan highlands. By 1500 B.C. it was clearly a cultural zone tied together by the Barra-Locona-Ocos tradition of pottery; later, by the Cuadros-Jocotal tradition (Grove, 1981; Hatch, personal communication). Most of the societies and communities of this zone were reasonably simple villages, presumably concerned with the everyday and basic needs of life: food, shelter, child-rearing, security, and slow development of social and technological forms to aid in these concerns. Their ceramics were fairly sophisticated but, although partly painted and carefully decorated by other means, were mainly utilitarian. Art served the functions noted above. Similarly, religious life was probably basic and simple, and its explanations of the universe were available to all. The figurines that appear along with Barra and Ocos pottery and that multiplied in numbers and forms were probably household items for use in curing, worship, remembrance of ancestors, and the like. There is little evidence in most of these communities for much social differentiation until about 1400 B.C.

This characterization of the Isthmian Zone is also true for the highland areas that we know about—especially for the Valley of Mexico, but also for Morelos to the south. The styles of pottery and figurines there are different and set the central highlands apart from the lowlands, but the quality of life was comparable.

Within this broadly spread set of village cultures, which probably existed in regional forms in all of Mesoamerica, there were a few communities in which different matters were afoot. These communities and their supporting regions were not always the same through time, so we cannot speak of a "mother culture," yet they were characterized by two different activities—the creation of new and exotic forms of pottery and, even more impressive, the building of large platforms and mounds. Because these structures required the manpower of communities, not families, they have been termed "public architecture." The platforms presumably supported perishable buildings used by the whole community. Such public constructions may have occurred as early as the Ocos phase (1500–1300 B.C.) in Chiapas, which is part of the Isthmian zone defined above (Lowe, 1977), but the highlands were not far behind. By 1250 B.C., villages around the sacred peaks of Chalcatzingo had already built two public buildings. Although there are severe problems with the dating of these structures, it is possible that the inhabitants of the region built terraced, round adobe platforms at Cuicuilco as early as 1400 B.C. (Tlalpan phase). If one regards "public space" as a sign of increasing sophistica-

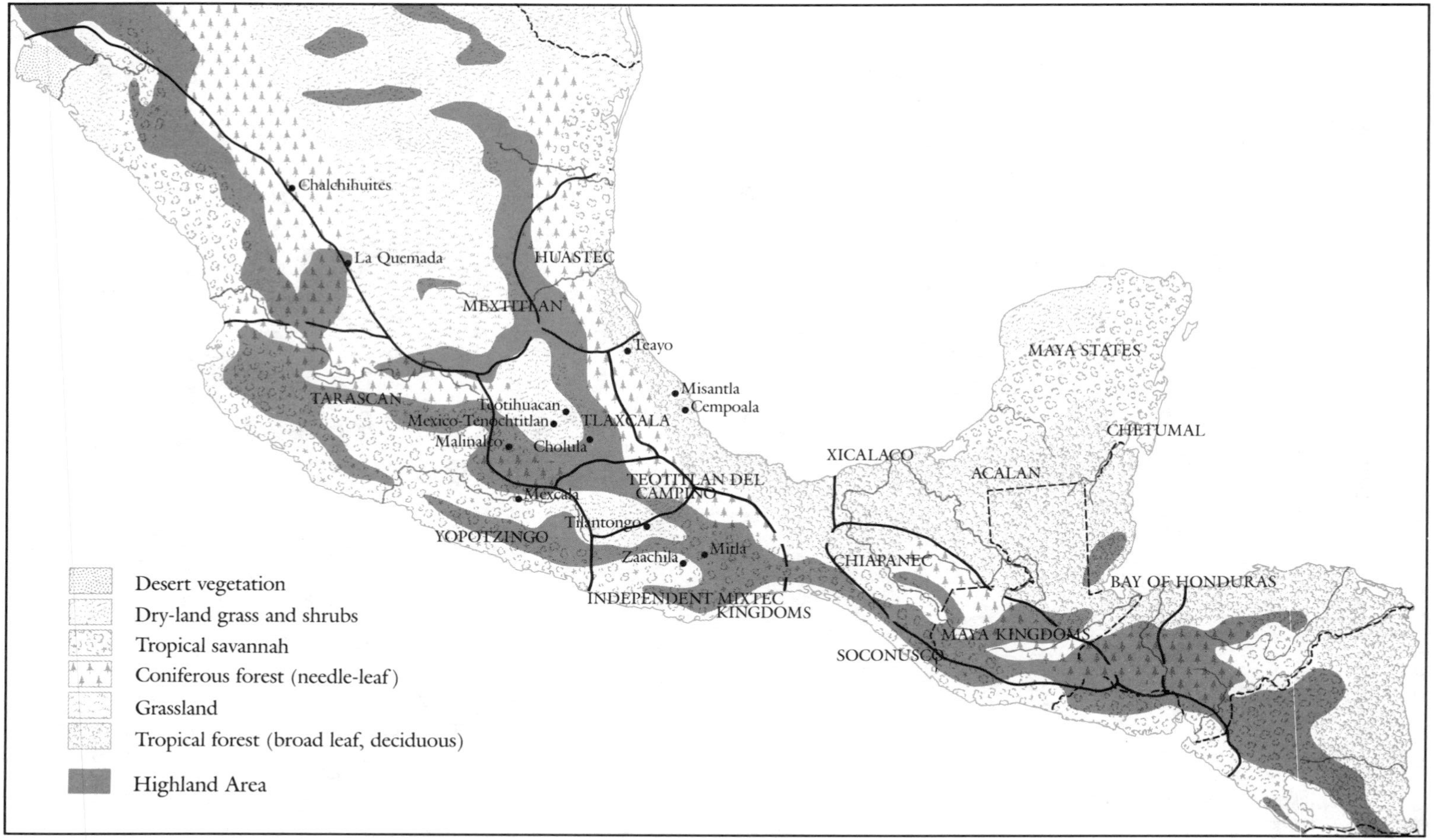

Map 3–1. Early and Late Formative Mesoamerican sites

Desert vegetation

Dry-land grass and shrubs

Tropical savannah

Coniferous forest (needle-leaf)

Grassland

Tropical forest (broad leaf, deciduous)

Highland Area

Chalchihuites

La Quemada

TARASCAN

HUASTEC

MEXTLAN

Teayo

Misantla

Cempoala

Teotihuacan

Mexico-Tenochtitlan

TLAXCALA

Malinalco

Cholula

Acna

Tilantongo

YOPOTZINGO

INDEPENDENT MIXTEC
KINGDOMS

TEOTITLAN DEL
CAMINO

Zaachila

Mitla

XICALACO

ACALAN

MAYA STATES

CHETUMAL

BAY OF HONDURAS

MAYA KINGDOMS

CHIAPANEC

SOCONUSCO

tion, it appears even earlier in the Oaxaca highlands at Gheo Shih, where a plaza was set apart by rows of boulders (Flannery, Marcus, and Kowalewski, 1981). However, one probably can also assume that this spatial definition was a common feature among most early Mesoamerican villages, one which will show up with more intensive research in other zones.

Returning to the lowlands, it is clear from the evidence at the Olmec site of San Lorenzo that massive public construction began by 1350 B.C. At this point then, we are confronted with the spectacular, but somewhat problematic, appearance of the Olmec. We must first define Olmec culture and its development. In this way we can clear away a great many mistaken interpretations that have plagued Mesoamerican archaeology. In the following section I have depended a great deal on the recently published work of M. D. Coe and Richard Diehl (1980) and of David Grove (1981 and 1987). Grove has elicited a great deal of order and sense from previous chaos and has corrected a number of fundamental errors in interpretation.

The Evolution of Olmec Culture

Olmec high culture eventually may be found to have first appeared in the Pacific coast of the Isthmian Zone. The early appearance of pottery and figurines, and the possible early appearance of public architecture, on this coastal shelf and in the adjacent Grijalva River trench hint at this. A current Guatemalan project at Abaj Takalik may confirm this possibility (Orrego and Hatch, personal communications, 1988).

Evidence of in-place evolution of complex culture in the heartland has come from the recent work of Rust and Gonzalez Lauck and from excavations at San Lorenzo as viewed in the new perspective (Grove, 1981). The already noted Bari material from near La Venta is the oldest known apparently agricultural village that has yet been found (1750–1400 B.C.; Rust and Sharer, 1988). Three villages from the later Bari phase (1400–1150 B.C.) possess thin *tecomate*-form pottery of the same sort that underlies the monumental site of La Venta. This pottery evidently represents the period of colonization of the La Venta salt dome area. Grinding stones of imported basalt and remains of charred palm nuts and mollusk shells give some hint of the diet of these early people.

At San Lorenzo three phases reflect this boot-strap development. The Ojochi phase (1500–1350 B.C.) is the local manifestation of the Ocos farming-village pattern and shows no major distinctions from other known sites, although presumably it has links to the Bari river-levee villages.

During the Bajio phase (1350–1250 B.C.) the process began which set the Olmec apart from their contemporaries. The hilltop location at San Lorenzo was modified into a large artificial plateau which may have required the piling up of over 2.13 million cubic meters (75 million cubic feet) of material. This work, clearly beyond the capacity for organization or labor of an ordinary village or even a group of villages, implies that social developments had already taken place which permitted such an enterprise. The later civic-religious function of this same zone also implies that this was the intended purpose of the construction from the beginning. One platform of sand and clay has also been located, and there is the likelihood of other buried structures from that time (M. D. Coe, 1981:124).

The Chicharras phase (1250–1150 B.C.) is probably Proto-Olmec, in the sense that most of the elements were then present which later characterized fully developed Olmec culture (Grove, 1981). Mound building presumably continued, and there are strong continuities in the ceramics, although new materials do appear. The pottery includes types made with kaolin, an exceedingly fine clay. Hollow, white-slipped figurines occur, and the first greenstone (jadelike) ornaments. Further, fragments of monumental stone carvings are found (see Coe, 1981:fig. 5–7). As Grove notes (1981), the differences between Chicharras and the following floresence of Olmec culture are quantitative rather than qualitative. The real point then, is that, notwithstanding Coe's interpretation that Chicharras represents "a host of new ideas and/or people" (1970:25), the more likely conclusion is that Olmec culture is a gradual and indigenous development.

Having considered the problems of origin of Olmec culture, we may now turn to its great period, that of Olmec II or, in terms of archaeological phases, San Lorenzo (1150–900 B.C.) and La Venta II (900–400 B.C.).

The Olmec Heartland: Natural Setting

Olmec civilization seemingly developed within a very limited geographical zone of 18,130 square kilometers (about 7,000 square miles) lying along the Gulf Coast and centering on the volcanic uplift called Los Tuxtlas Mountains. These mountains are primarily composed of extinct cinder cones and larger volcanoes, perhaps the largest caldera of which today contains Lake Catemaco. Two major drainage basins flank the mountains and make up the rest of what Bernal calls the "metropolitan Olmec area" (1969). The area is watery, swampy, and drowned by heavy rainfall and the annual flooding of the great rivers, which flow into marshes, estuaries, and lagoons on the edges of the sea. From 2 to 3 meters (80–125 inches) of rain per year fall in a period of six months (June to November). Rivers form the most important means of communication. Exuberant and flourishing vegetation covers the drier land between watercourses. As in most of the coastal tropical zones of Mesoamerica, there are rich plant and animal communities in the varied natural zones.

This area was probably occupied by what MacNeish described as early and primitive coastal villages living on wild resources, and certainly was occupied by about 1500 B.C. by the early pottery-using cultures of the Ocos horizon. These villagers were farmers, using slash-and-burn techniques to master the thick jungle, but they did not abandon the intensive hunting, gathering, and collecting techniques and schedules that had led to sedentary life in the first place. As described above, these farming villages laid the basis for the in-place development of Olmec culture.

It remains to suggest why this development occurred. Although we have mentioned the evolutionary evidence, we have not suggested any plausible reason why the earliest of complex cultures in Mesoamerica appeared here. The best that can be said at the moment is that, given the apparent priority of the coastal villages, the lowlands had a great deal more time in which population growth, with all the social consequences that comes with it, could occur. In addition, the ideological (political, religious, cosmological) basis for civilization could be developed during this considerable period. After all, sculpture and other art, as well as monumental architecture, are an expression of a set of philosophical, religious, political, and social ideas. These philosophical premises are the sine qua non for the material accomplishments of a society.

Chronology

Olmec culture lasted a long time, and in order to look more closely at the trends and events during this extended period, Ignacio Bernal (1969) has broken it up into three stages, which I have modified on the basis of more recent work. Based on rounded-off carbon 14 dating from the San Lorenzo project and earlier work at La Venta, and on stratigraphic and stylistic phasings, those three stages, including all the major events of Olmec culture history, are Olmec I, 1750–1150 B.C.; Olmec II, 1150–400 B.C.; and Olmec III, 400–100 B.C. In accepting this scheme, however, we should note that Olmec I may not be the earliest period of Olmec culture. R. Heizer (1968) and M. D. Coe (1968) have suggested that still earlier phases may lie hidden in the Tuxtlas Mountains. Olmec I is the local expression of Ocos-horizon culture, although Olmec features appear in this period. Olmec III may be a figment of carbon 14–fevered imagination, although there seems to be hard stratigraphic evidence for such a construction phase at the site of La Venta. Finally, we should note that Olmec II represents the floresence of high culture, and it is upon this period that we will focus here.

On the basis of work both in the highlands (Tolstoy and Paradis, 1970; Grove, 1987) and in the lowlands (Coe and Diehl, 1980), it is now possible to break down Olmec II into at least two tentative Mesoamerica-wide horizons based on the shifting importance of two of the four major lowland Olmec sites. The first is the San Lorenzo horizon (1150–900 B.C.), which is the period of apogee of San Lorenzo and possibly of the Laguna de los Cerros sites. Outside of the heartland, this horizon is marked by the appearance of hollow, white-slipped ceramic "babies" and bowls, dishes, and exotic bottles, some decorated with specific Olmec motifs such as the jaguar paw–wing motif. M. D. Coe (1977) thinks that the highland sites of Tlatilco and Tlapacoya in the Basin of Mexico, Las Bocas in Puebla, and the San José Mogote site in Oaxaca belong to this horizon. To this list should be added Chalcatzingo in Morelos in an early Formative phase. The second part of Olmec II is the La Venta horizon (900–400 B.C.), signaled in the heartland by the decline of San Lorenzo and the rise to power of La Venta. A different set of exported items marks this horizon in other parts of Mesoamerica. Hard white pottery decorated with double-line breaks and other decorative abstractions appears. In this horizon Coe notes the first appearance of jade among the Olmec and the export of finished carvings to places outside the heartland (1977). Chalcatzingo probably shows the presence of lowlanders (Grove, 1987), and the Oxtotitlan murals in Guerrero date from this horizon. Olmec culture was at its widest distribution in Mesoamerica, as indicated by its presence in Honduras far to the east as well as in Guerrero in western Mexico.

Overview of the Olmec

Before plunging into a mass of detail on the Olmec, it seems appropriate to give an overall view of the culture as we now know it. Briefly, the culture is made up of two components: a "civilized" elite and the older, simpler (and more persistent) "folk" component. The Olmec and some contemporaries in the highland valleys of Mexico were apparently the first in Mesoamerica to bring forth an elite component, and it was the elite who determined such matters as art style, complex political and economic affairs, and religious movements.

For the Olmec, the elite component centered on clusters of civic architecture in the Gulf Coast zone. These ceremonial centers were made up of large earthen pyramids and platforms, which probably supported perishable structures, in some of which lived an upper class. The leadership class and the centers were supported by the folk component, the mass of the population, who, because of their slash-and-burn style of agriculture, were unable to reside in true towns and cities but instead lived dispersed through the lowland area in hamlet- and village-sized communities.

Olmec leadership was handled by dynastic lineages of rulers who seem to have been identified with the basic deities of Olmec religion, especially with the jaguar-rain god. A magnificent art style expressed in sculpture and lapidary products depicted the Olmec gods and elite. The elite also developed a dynamic religious and social organization, which brought more people from throughout Mesoamerica into the Olmec orbit through trade, religious conversion, or military activity. Exotic goods, both sumptuary and religious, were either demanded by the elite class from various parts of Mesoamerica as tribute or gained through trade. The Olmec obtained obsidian, jade, cacao, iron ores, and other items through trade or, in some cases, through actual colonies. Trade relationships seem to have linked the Olmec with a series of highland Formative cultures which were themselves sufficiently sophisticated to appreciate Olmec religion, art, and status symbols. Grove has characterized the communities of the Basin of Mexico as the Tlatilco culture sphere, and one group of archaeologists argue that the influence was two-way; this controversy will be discussed later in this chapter.

Political and religious power seems to have shifted among the various centers of the Olmec heartland, but by 500 B.C. the Olmec became victims of their own precocity. Other more sophisticated and demographically more powerful centers were arising elsewhere in Mesoamerica at least partly due to the stimulus of the Olmec, and these later cultures finally overshadowed them.

Communities and Population

At least three food-producing systems were available in the Olmec zone. One was the early intensive gathering and hunting system which had led to settled life in the first place. There were also two major farming systems based on the kind of land used. The most favorable lands for cultivation were and are those of the river levees, which, like those of the Nile, are annually flooded and enriched by deposits of silt. This situation allows two or more crops per year to be planted using slash-and-burn techniques. Away from the rivers, and on the slopes of the Tuxtlas Mountains or the edges of the highlands, one crop per year is more usual. Coe (1968) suggests that the families who initially controlled the best lands along the rivers were those who eventually became the entrenched elite-class lineages. Indeed, this economic and social advantage can be seen in modern times: recent pioneer families who control the river lands are those who have the capital to go into retail trade in the small river towns and thus control the local economy (Coe and Diehl, 1980). Surpluses can be used for various purposes, and that which today is used for personal aggrandizement might have been used in ancient times to build up political and religious allegiances.

Bernal (1969:17) estimates that the 18,130 square kilometers (7,000 square miles) of heartland supported an average of some 19 persons per square kilometer (50 per square mile), or about 350,000 at its most densely populated. About 15 percent of the population were able-bodied men, so even if one objects to such a high density and accordingly cuts the figure in half, some 26,250 men would have been available for communal activities in addition to food production. This was a population based solely on slash-and-burn maize farming, and indeed, today corn makes up 90 percent of the diet in the region. However, data from the San Lorenzo center show that the Olmec also derived valuable protein from sources such as deer, wild pigs, and especially fish. Oxbow lakes and sloughs are especially favorable for seining, and robalo, tarpon, and gar were and are favored fish.

Given these subsistence and demographic resources, the Olmec elite developed the ceremonial centers. However, there were also certain restraints. Slash-and-burn agriculture, with its shifting fields and necessity for holding large amounts of land fallow, meant that population expanded physically as it expanded in numbers. In modern times, community size is generally limited, although large absolute populations can be sustained— theoretically up to 150 persons per arable square mile (58 per arable square kilometer). However, this population is dispersed over the cultivable land, and hence there may have been the ancient development of civic centers which were often virtually deserted during most of the year and where only a small elite class and its supporting population lived. Given the recent discoveries of vast zones of Classic-period intensive farming in the Veracruz and Maya lowlands (Siemens, personal communication; Adams, Brown, and Culbert, 1981), the possibility now exists that the Olmec may have depended, in part, on intensive farming. A discovery to this effect would mean that the Olmec would have had much greater economic resources and human populations. Such a pattern of intensive farming may be implied by the discovery by Rust of eight village sites contemporary with La Venta and of domestic remains inside La Venta proper (Rust and Sharer, 1988).

Olmec Centers

Bernal considers the Olmec centers to have been, functionally, dispersed cities. In this view, the centers operated as urban foci of complex social, political, religious, and economic behavior but did not have the permanent large concentrations of people that we would expect in a city. This interpretation, of course, ignores the possibilities of intensive farming.

Based on what remains to us, it appears that the Olmec built mainly in earth, the principal material at hand. Clay, either in bulk or in the form of adobe bricks, was heaped up and apparently plastered with adobe. Occasionally the facings of small structures were made of stone, but that material had to be imported to the zone with great effort and was mainly reserved for uses such as drains and sculpture. The amount of earth moved by Olmec builders is impressive. It is generally found in the form of very high or fairly low platforms. The Stirling group acropolis at La Venta, a large, flat platform, was made of at least 5 million cubic meters (177 million cubic feet) of material. In many sites, including La Venta, platforms are arranged in a linear fashion, about eight degrees west of true north. Barbara Stark's work has shown that this pattern was duplicated in several sites smaller than La Venta as well. Mounds were also arranged in groups around courtyards. There are up to ninety-five of the larger mounds at Laguna de los Cerros, occupying about 38 hectares (94 acres; Bove, 1978). Smaller platform mounds presumably supporting housing on the commoner level—wattle-and-daub huts with thatched roofs similar to those used today—are numerous. Some two hundred have been found in the vicinity of the center of San Lorenzo. All of these structures imply effort enough, but it is also possible that entirely artificial ridges of clay were piled up by the Olmec to serve as megaplatforms for formal architecture. The final form of the San Lorenzo plateau, comprising some 42 million cubic meters (1,483 million cubic feet) of material, is such an artificial feature (Coe and Diehl, 1980).

There are certainly three and probably four major Olmec sites known from the heartland area: La Venta, San Lorenzo, Tres Zapotes, and the more recently discovered sites of Laguna de los Cerros. Only the sites of La Venta and San Lorenzo have been somewhat satisfactorily sampled, and even these would yield a great deal more to excavation. A Mexican project sponsored by the National Institute of Anthropology and History (INAH) and led by Rebecca Gonzalez Lauck is at work on La Venta. Stark's surveys in the Papaloapan River basin (1977) also indicate that much more information will be yielded by further investigation.

San Lorenzo. San Lorenzo is located on a river, the Río Chiquito, but has a great deal more open country around it than La Venta, to the east. The Tuxtlas Mountains are in view from the site and within reasonably easy access. The main group of formal buildings, located over a salt dome which was artificially modified, consists of linear arrangements of mounds with closed courtyards. The ridge itself, Coe thinks, represents a bird flying east. Some twenty small lagunas, apparently water storage ponds, were found on the ridge. Large basalt conduits drain the plazas and some of the ponds on the ridge. The amount of stone used in these features is enormous; some thirty tons of basalt alone were used in a drain just 197 meters (650 feet) long, and this is only one of many such features. Much stone sculpture in the distinctive Olmec style represents not only artistic wealth but also a considerable effort invested in freighting the enormous tonnage of basalt from which it was carved.

Coe estimates the population of San Lorenzo at about one thousand persons, based on the more than two hundred house mounds found there. These people presumably were the immediate supporting retainers of the still smaller resident elite population. There were surely many more people under the control of the upper class, given the enormous amounts of building accomplished, even if the work was spread out over several centuries. Restricting available population to the immediate vicinity is as unrealistic as explaining the construction of European medieval cathedrals such as Chartres by the relatively small rural populations around them

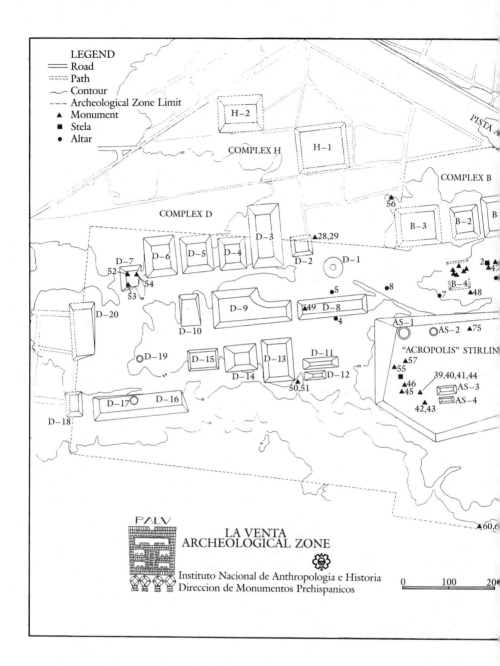

Map 3–2. Central section of the Olmec site of La Venta, Tabasco, Mexico. A great many very large earthen platforms have been recorded, although many others were undoubtedly destroyed by the Pemex oil refinery and town built on the island. (Courtesy INAH and Rebecca Gonzalez Lauck))

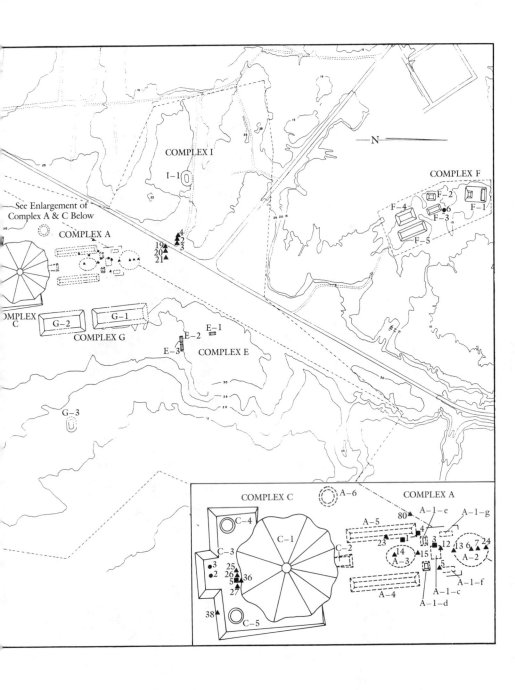

COMPLEX I

I-1

COMPLEX F

F-2

F-4

F-1

6

F-3

F-5

See Enlargement of
Complex A & C Below

COMPLEX A

19
20
21

4
2
3

N

COMPLEX
C

G-2

G-1

COMPLEX G

E-1

E-2

E-3

COMPLEX E

G-3

COMPLEX C

A-6

COMPLEX A

C-4

C-1

C-3

3
2

25
26

36

5

27

38

C-5

A-5

C-2

23

14

A-3

15

1

3

4

80

A-1-e

12

A-1-g

13 6

7

24

A-2

5

A-1-f

A-1-c

A-1-d

A-4

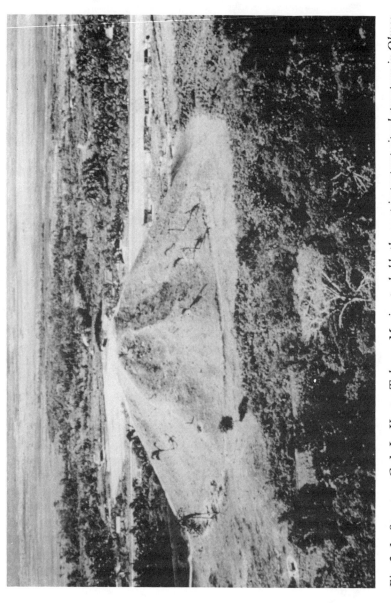

Fig. 3–1. Structure C–1, La Venta, Tabasco, Mexico, probably the most important ritual structure in Olmec La Venta. There is controversy over whether the fluted cone appearance is a result of deliberate construction or later erosion. It may be a man-made replica of nearby volcanic cinder cones. (Courtesy John A. Graham)

today. It seems more likely that we are dealing with an available population of tens of thousands.

San Lorenzo's great period is the earliest known among those of the four major sites. The end of the site's predominance—about 900 B.C.— is marked by the notable destruction of both architecture and sculpture. Deliberately mutilated sculpture was buried in lines. Some of the great stone heads were probably carried off to La Venta. Because these were likely the portraits of elite-class leaders, a political as well as religious turnover is indicated. Grove suggests that mutilation for sacred sculpture associated with sacred rulers was a means of releasing dangerous power inherent in such monuments. At any rate, when San Lorenzo lost its power and was deserted, Olmec culture continued to flourish and entered a still more dynamic phase at the large site of La Venta.

La Venta. La Venta is an island site in a swamp on the Tonala River and not obviously associated with any large zone of agricultural land. The island is formed by the upward bulge created by a salt dome. It was occupied from about 1400 to 600 B.C., its great period falling entirely within Olmec II times. Based on Gonzalez Lauck's remarkable and recently published map of the site, the center covered at least 200 hectares (500 acres; Map 3-2). The largest number of structures are large clay platforms which are aligned on the basic axis of the site: north-south. These platforms may have supported elaborate elite-class housing of wood and thatch. Test excavations in the G and E group zones have found not only domestic trash but also evidence of urn burials, large pottery openings, and a serpentine artifact workshop (Rust and Sharer, 1988).

La Venta is unusual in the symmetrical layout of one of its mound groups, Complexes A and C, which are really one functional unit. The large pyramid, C-1, may be an effigy volcano (Heizer, 1968). It is a fluted cone, the rills and ridges of which are argued to have astronomical significance (Fig. 3–1). This interpretation is disputed by those who believe the structure originally was rectangular but was modified by erosion. Be that as it may, there is a striking resemblance between this gigantic pile of earth and the cinder cones in the Tuxtlas Mountains from which came the basalt used in sculpture at La Venta.

Two low flanking mounds in front of the cone, in Complex A, lead to a kind of inner courtyard. In the late phase at La Venta the courtyard had a palisade of basalt columns erected around it, possibly for privacy. The famous group of sixteen jade figurines now on display in the National Museum of Anthropology in Mexico City has a similar palisade of six jade celts (Figs. 3–2, 3–3). The group probably depicts a ritual scene which originally took place within the basalt palisades in Complex A. The figurines represents a group of jostling onlookers, a file of participants, and a principal figure backed against the palisade.

Mounds like those of Complex A probably supported perishable build-

Fig. 3–2. *Group of Olmec jade figurines and celts anciently arranged into a ritual scene at La Venta. The celts form a fence similar to that found on La Venta's Southwest Platform, Group A. Note the figure standing against the fence, who observes four persons entering the enclosure. A crowd of people on the left completes this enigmatic scene.* (Courtesy John A. Graham)

Fig. 3–3. Beginning of excavations in the Southwest Platform, Group A, La Venta. Note the basalt-column fence around the platform, possibly represented by the jade celts in Fig. 3–2. (Courtesy John A. Graham)

ings, and the nearby Stirling Acropolis platform possibly supported sumptuous but perishable housing for the elite class. The various uses of log-
shaped basalt columns in both a tomb and the courtyard at La Venta
suggest that the perishable structures were partially made of upright logs.
The possibly elaborate nature of such wooden buildings is suggested by
the few examples of wooden Olmec sculpture and the ethnographic
analogy of the marvelously carved Maori wooden houses from New
Zealand. As at San Lorenzo, stone drains were built at La Venta to carry
rainwater away from the mounds and platforms (Fig. 3–4).

A great deal of monumental sculpture and many monumental offerings
are present at La Venta. The colossal stone heads are rulers' portraits in
the interpretation accepted here. James Porter (1989) has recently and
brilliantly analyzed the evidence for the recarving of the colossal heads
and convincingly demonstrated that many, if not all, were originally the
altar-thrones of Olmec rulers. Presumably, therefore, the rulers held forth
from their thrones during their lifetimes, and at their deaths the thrones
were converted to portrait-memorials. A recently found stela is interpreted by Gonzalez Lauck to represent a transfer of power from one ruler
to his successor.

The site of La Venta is still somewhat enigmatic, because it is so rich
in artifacts, precious objects, and fine sculpture. La Venta's location and
size are small enough to imply that not much of the supporting population
lived on the island, though the new Bari finds indicate that many villages
and subsidiary centers were located nearby. However, La Venta does
have the aspect of a religious pilgrimage center (Rust and Sharer's "temple
town") as well as that of an elite residential center. Victor Turner has
noted that major pilgrimage centers of modern Mexico are often outside
major population centers. This was also true in the later periods of pre-
Hispanic Mesoamerica. The island sanctuary of Cozumel off the east
coast of Yucatan drew people from throughout Mesoamerica and Central
America. La Venta as a pilgrimage center may fall within this pattern.

Tres Zapotes. The site of Tres Zapotes is located to the west of the
Tuxtlas Mountains and is poorly known except for its sculpture. There is
no adequate map of the site, although Stark's work may remedy this
problem. The ceramics of Tres Zapotes indicate that the center was
certainly contemporary with La Venta and San Lorenzo in Olmec II
(Stirling, 1943; Drucker, 1943b). Closed courts surrounded by earthen
or clay structures include monumental sculpture. This site was occupied
for a longer period than the other three known major centers, as indicated
by both ceramics and sculpture. A later and derivative sculptural style
called Izapan appears at Tres Zapotes as well.

All three sites have early Ocos horizons, or Olmec I remains. San
Lorenzo is the only site from which we have adequate information on
what happened to change the Olmec culture from a farming "folk" culture

Fig. 3–4. A covered drain at La Venta, probably designed to carry away the runoff from the torrential downpours which characterize the region. (Courtesy John A. Graham)

to the dynamic, innovative civilization that it became after 1300 B.C. M. D. Coe (1968) suggests that essentially Olmec culture derives from the lowland zone, although it may have taken its crucial steps toward civilization in the Tuxtlas Mountains. If this is so, then we still have to find the earliest developmental and evolutionary stages of Olmec culture history. Heizer points out that this may not be easy, because if these stages are to be found in the Tuxtlas, they may be hidden under deep deposits of volcanic ash from the recently active cinder cones of that vicinity. Several distinguished Mexican scholars have argued for the origin of Olmec culture in Guerrero, or the Mixteca of the highlands. Bernal, on the other hand, seems to feel that a local evolutionary origin in the lowlands is the best explanation. The latest research, limited as it is, supports Bernal's interpretation. We shall return to this question.

Olmec Art: Sculpture and Painting

Olmec sculpture is one of the most important defining qualities of the civilization. It tends to be massive and is found in life-sized and larger than life-sized pieces. It is both full round and bas-relief. The enormous human heads, of which twelve are known, are interpreted by M. D. Coe, (1965b) as being representations of elite-class rulers (Figs. 3–5, 3–6). The "football-helmet" headdress and the heavy quality of the facial features all fit Coe's characterization of these leaders as "tough warrior dynasts." Some of the sculpture is patently portraiture, as exemplified by the "wrestler" monument—a magnificent specimen of a man apparently flexing his muscles in a graceful exercise (Fig. 3–7).

Bas-relief on monuments, and on cliffs outside the heartland, tends to be much more complex. Several general themes can be detected. One is the presentation of a small jaguar-human, Coe's "were-jaguar," by an adult. In other scenes adults carry the were-jaguars. Coe identifies these beings as helpers of the jaguar rain deity. This principal deity is sometimes seen as a great head within whose mouth humans stand or sit. Thus, the were-jaguars would stand in the same relationship to the jaguar as the tlaloques did to the great rain god, Tlaloc, in Aztec times. However, the features of the were-jaguars remain to be explained. Characteristically, their faces combine human infantile features with everted lips, jaguar fangs, and often a cleft forehead. These features are especially clear in the many small jade statuettes depicting the were-jaguars. From two fragmentary sculptures M. D. Coe has derived a "basic Olmec myth" which not only explains these features but also allows him a coherent approach to Olmec art and religion.

At Laguna de los Cerros and Río Chiquito (near San Lorenzo) two badly damaged sculptures have been found which apparently show a jaguar copulating with a human female. These must have been some of the most eye-catching sculptures ever done when in their original condi-

Fig. 3–5. San Lorenzo Monument 1, a colossal head. There are twelve known colossal heads from San Lorenzo, La Venta, and Tres Zapotes. They appear to be portraits of rulers, and at least some were made from recarved thrones of the rulers, according to recent studies by James Porter. (Courtesy John A. Graham)

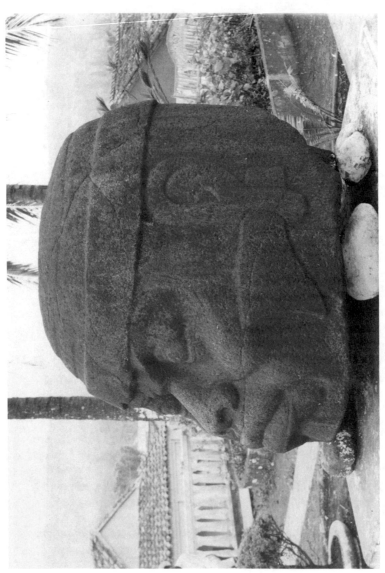

Fig. 3–6. Tres Zapotes Colossal Head No. 2. This smallest of the colossal heads weighs 8.5 tons. (Courtesy John A. Graham)

Fig. 3–7. The "Wrestler" statue, which appears to show an athlete engaged in warming-up exercises.

tion. At any rate, such a union would have produced the small part-jaguar assistants to the rain-god. However, this is not the complete explanation. Coe has also suggested that the cleft forehead and infantile features are explained by a familial genetic anomaly, spina bifida. Spina bifida infants are usually still-born and have cleft heads and characteristically snarling expressions. There are some etiological problems with this hypothesis, but it may be that the difficulties will be overcome. If this genetic anomaly did occur in Olmec populations, it might well have been interpreted by them as the result of the woman having mated with a jaguar. These intriguing explanations of the were-jaguars are not proven by any means, but they make more sense than any others yet advanced.

Another thematic group of sculpture is concerned with apparent military activity. In many bas-reliefs warriors bash other persons with clubs or simply hold clubs in threatening attitudes. Other depictions show warriors wearing "knuckle dusters," which may be what the name implies. Small floating figures above them represent several of the Olmec deities, including the were-jaguars. It is especially interesting that one of the most explicit scenes of violence is from the highland site of Chalcatzingo in Morelos (although the excavators of this site do not necessarily agree with this interpretation; Grove, 1987). This suggests that zones outside the heartland were controlled by not entirely peaceful means.

Petrographic and mineralogical studies leave no doubt that the basalt from which most of the major sculptures of the heartland sites are made was brought in from the Tuxtlas Mountains. This importation of tons of stone is impressive, but in fact, the jaguar-mask ceremonial deposits at La Venta are far greater in quantity (Figs. 3–8, 3–9). In these caches, roughly shaped and finished ashlars of serpentine—over a thousand tons of material—were laid down in layers in specially prepared pits. On top of the La Venta A-1-C deposit was found a large mosaic mask in Olmec style with the characteristic cleft head. It has been said to represent the jaguar deity of the Olmecs, but it must be something more complex, because the representation seems to have four eyes. In any case, the labor

Fig. 3–8. The mosaic serpentine mask found beneath Group Southwest Platform, La Venta. It is possible that the mask represents a jaguar with a typically notched Olmec head. (Courtesy John A. Graham)

Fig. 3–9. The immense stacks of serpentine blocks underlying the mosaic mask in Fig. 3–5. Imported material—several tons of it—was used to create a base for the mask and probably constituted something of an offering in itself. (Courtesy John A. Graham)

and amounts of material and skill expended on these deposits bespeak sophisticated social organization and arcane ritual. The serpentine is probably from upriver, the foothills zone. All of the material could only have arrived at La Venta by being rafted along the coastal waterway and in through the Tonala River or downriver from the edges of the highlands.

Ceremonial and ritual meaning is conveyed by the remainder of the scenes, with elite-class individuals apparently participating in worship and political protocol or acting out mythic and symbolic events. These symbolic events may have been of the sort that was used as a recurrent liturgy in the centers. At least one sculpture from La Venta, Altar 4, explicitly deals with dynastic continuity and legitimacy (Fig. 3–10). It is a table-top altar which, as Grove has discovered, was actually a throne. In the depiction on this monument the ruler sits in a rounded niche on the front, holding two twisted cords which appear to be attached to two individuals on either side of the throne. Examined carefully, these two people seem to be male and female and therefore the parents of the ruler, symbolically attached to him by umbilical cords.

A certain number of footprints, bird heads, and the like—possibly prototypes of hieroglyphic writing—are present on Olmec sculptures.

Fig. 3–10. La Venta Altar 4. An Olmec ruler sits within the niche, holding what are variously interpreted as ropes to captives or umbilical cords to his parents. Olmec altars have been conclusively demonstrated to be thrones. Moreover, at least some of these huge sculptures were later recarved into colossal heads as memorials to the rulers, according to the work of James Porter. (Courtesy John A. Graham)

Fig. 3–11. Oxtotitlan Mural, central section. The clearly Olmec figure is dressed in a bird costume and postures while seated on one of the "altar" thrones. The cave of Oxtotitlan is in the highlands of Guerrero, reflecting the far-reaching trade and political networks of the lowland Olmec. (After Grove 1970b)

The most convincing case yet made for the presence of at least pictographic symbols has been advanced by Grove in his study of the probable name glyphs of Olmec rulers. These occur on the great stone heads in the headgear of each one. However, no complex inscriptions with mathematical data and dates have been found. We shall discuss the invention of calendar systems and writing in Mesoamerica in the next chapter, but it is barely possible that these achievements were made during Olmec II times, at least in rudimentary form.

Fig. 3–12. *Chalcatzingo Monument 12 is a falling figure carved on a rock at the massive stone mountain of Chalcatzingo in highland Morelos. Angulo believes that the figure is that of a fast-moving ball game player. It is also possible that the figure represents an overthrown ruler, because of its posture common to captives in later sculpture.* (Courtesy David C. Grove)

Some remarkable murals discovered at the caves of Oxtotitlan, not too far from Taxco in Guerrero, and Juxtlahuaca show brightly colored scenes of pomp and elite-class ceremony, with a principal figure in each case seated on what appears to be a table-top altar throne (Fig. 3–11; Grove, 1969, 1970b). Another scene at Oxtotitlan with a dominant human figure in it has definite phallic overtones.

Olmec sculpture outside the heartland tends to be of a narrative style depicting both the military and ritual protocol themes (Fig. 3–12). Massive boulders and outcrops sculptured in place have been found by Navarrete at Pijijiapan, which is located at the entrance to the Guatemalan coastal plain. A rather imposing set of individuals, both conferring and aggressively advancing, are shown, along with one of the Olmec deities, who has a sprouting maize plant in his headdress. Further south on the coastal plain at Abaj Takalik, in Guatemala, the remains of a giant sculptured head together with other Olmec remains have been found. Given the political identification of this specific form, it seems likely that we have evidence here of physical Olmec presence and control, perhaps a colony. The farthest south that Olmec sculpture has been found is in the highlands of El Salvador at Las Victorias. Again we have a boulder carving which depicts Olmec personages in a dynamic scene in which they carry either clubs or plants in their arms. The Maya Lowland area thus far has but one site, that of Xoc, with a figure similar to those of Pijijiapan. More Olmec sculpture has been found in most of these zones, but enough has been said to make the point that there is a general distribution in two very specific zones of Mesoamerica. The artifact distribution is somewhat wider but includes the zones where sculpture occurs.

Small Works of Art and Other Artifacts

Portable expressions of Olmec style were made of exotic materials, jade being especially favored. Jade was probably obtained from the Balsas Valley in Guerrero (near the sacred caves of Oxtotitlan and Juxtlahuaca), from the Motagua River valley in Guatemala (Abaj Takalik and Monte Alto are on the way to this valley), and from other as yet unknown sources. American jade is variable, with the most highly prized being apple green in color. White streaks occasionally are found in pieces of it, and the color may run to a dark, turquoiselike blue. The small figurines of the were-jaguars were a favorite motif. Highly polished axe-celts with incised designs, including what appear to be rudimentary hieroglyphs akin to certain designs found on sculpture, are also fairly common. Other, rarer forms include canoelike pieces, were-jaguars with wings, and "letter-openers" probably used for blood-letting in religious ritual. Celts were especially favored in the heartland; in addition to the famous cache of figurines already described, cruciform deposits of celts were found at La

Venta. Most of the above-mentioned forms are also found in basalt, serpentine, and other stone.

Masks are especially well done. One in a private collection in Guatemala City is an extraordinary large piece of jade carved into a were-jaguar mask; it is said to come from La Venta. Another mask is of wood encrusted with jade, preserved by some miracle, and depicts a human face. Yet another mask, of marble, is a powerful evocation of the jaguar's face.

All of these items—celts, masks, figurines—are especially (and unfortunately) prized by modern collectors and were similarly regarded in ancient times. Apparently, many of the small, portable items were held as heirloom pieces, and one is to be found in the Vatican's collections covered with elaborate Italian gold work. It probably was sent back by a sixteenth-century Spaniard and might have come from an Aztec source, which would mean that it had been passed down through various hands for about twenty-eight hundred years. Religious symbolism made jades even more valuable to their ancient owners, although aesthetically motivated acquisition seems nearly to be a religion in the twentieth century.

Large hollow dolls of clay, made with baby-face features, appear consistently in graves in areas outside the Olmec heartland and as trash and discard within the San Lorenzo site. These dolls must have been exported to the Basin of Mexico and Morelos burial site of Las Bocas, where they occur.

Iron-ore mirrors, ground into concave reflecting surfaces, occur in the heartland sites, especially at La Venta and San Lorenzo. The source area of one variety of iron ore, magnetite, has been found in the Central Valley of Oaxaca, where Flannery and his associates have also located one of the villages and the houses of the specialists who made the mirrors at a site named San José Mogote. Within one of the houses of these highland craftsmen were found the characteristic hollow doll figures. These finds add the Valley of Oaxaca as an important resource zone for the Olmec.

Obsidian from about seven sources has been detected at San Lorenzo. Mineralogical analysis shows that obsidian came from near present-day Pachuca, north of Mexico City; from Orizaba Volcano, near Puebla; and from as far south as El Chayal, near Guatemala City. Obsidian was important as the prime cutting tool in ancient times.

In addition to the above items, mica, schist, flint, and bitumen were all imported into the Olmec heartland zone. Judging by the items found at the sites of La Venta and San Lorenzo, the Olmec should have suffered from a balance-of-payments problem, since they seem to have exported only the finished products. However, we must consider the nature of the Olmec-linked sites outside the heartland before we find an explanation for the matters outlined above.

Olmec Contemporaries: Colonies, Collaborators, or Competitors?

Four major zones appear to be in some manner contemporary with, in contact with, or even linked to the Olmec. From north to south, these are the Central Highlands (the Basin of Mexico and Valley of Morelos), the Balsas Valley and adjacent parts of Guerrero, the Central Valley of Oaxaca, and the Pacific Coastal plain of Guatemala and El Salvador. Some other occurrences of Olmec-linked culture occur in Honduras, not far from Tegucigalpa.

Basin of Mexico

Tlapacoya is located in the southeastern corner of the Basin of Mexico and was at least a large village in Olmec II times. Its location is at the entrance to the basin that one might use if approaching it from the Olmec heartland. Excavations by Tolstoy and Paradis (1970) indicate that Tlapacoya possesses the debris to be expected of an intensively occupied village, along with certain characteristic Olmec pottery forms, including the hollow dolls. This period is dated at about 1200 B.C. Across the basin and the lake was a contemporary village or villages now known as Tlatilco, and now under industrial Mexico City. The site is famous for its spectacular burials, of which some five hundred have been excavated. A great many more were dug up illegally and the contents of the graves sold to collectors.

Tolstoy and Paradis's research indicates that Tlatilco has about four periods represented in its burials, the earliest of which (Nevada phase) precedes the Tlapacoya material and dates to about 1500 B.C. Tlatilco seems to have been one or more villages with perishable housing, but it also possessed low one-or two-step clay platforms, which may have supported temple structures. Burials were apparently made under the floors of houses and among the trash pits which were present. At any rate, Tlatilco burials contain the characteristic Olmec hollow dolls from earliest times as well as other exotic and putatively Olmeclike pottery. Bowls in which excised jaguar-paw design are emphasized by red paint rubbed into them, with a surrounding black slip, are very similar to vessels found at San Lorenzo and La Venta. On the other hand, clusters of figurines with the burials are in non-Olmec style and show many life scenes: acrobats, diviners, and women carrying babies, for example. Much else in Tlatilco seems also to be in a native ceramic tradition. The famous "life-death" bowl, which shows a live face on one half with a skull on the other side, is such a piece. Greenstone and jade artifacts (the first is the substitute for the other) are quite rare but do occur.

Tlatilco burials also seem to reflect a ranked society because of the different offerings in each grave. Women and children received large amounts of offerings, and therefore ranking probably was ascribed, since children would not have had sufficient time before death to achieve status. It is interesting and perhaps significant that there is no earlier Formative material known for the basin than this period with an Olmec linkage. It should be noted that in the later phases (1250–900 B.C.), nearly every village in the region had Olmeclike material (7 percent) as well as an overwhelming amount of regional material (93 percent; Grove, 1981). The location of Tlatilco is also important, because it represents the exit point on the western side of the basin to Toluca and beyond. The commodities to be gained by that location are anybody's guess.

The Morelos Valley and Chalcatzingo

One of the most important of the highland Formative sites has recently been reported (Grove, 1987). Combined with previous work in the region (for example, Grove, 1970b) at other sites, the resultant sequence takes its place as one of the most reliable and interesting in the highlands.

Some of the earliest village material in Morelos occurs at sites on the Cuautla River, where the site of San Pablo Pantheon has yielded over two hundred burials. The ancient graves are in a stone-faced burial mound appropriately located next to a modern cemetery. Across the river is another zone with distinctive burials called La Juana. On the basis of stratigraphic and comparative material, Grove (1970a) says that La Juana is the older phase. Hollow ceramic "babies," spouted trays, roller stamps, blackware, and other San Lorenzo–horizon material indicate that he is right. On the other hand, the San Pablo Pantheon mound produced pottery which is characteristically in a variety of bottle forms: stirrup-spouted bottles, composite bottles, belted bottles, tubular-necked bottles, and so on. Less than 1 percent of the other Pantheon pottery has Olmec affinities, and therefore the picture is of an overwhelmingly regional development. The red-on-brown wares of both mounds also link them to western Mexico. Hollow D and K figurines of the type of the Valley of Mexico also occur. Grove dates the La Juana material 1100 to 900 B.C. and the Pantheon pottery 900 to 500 B.C.

Chalcatzingo's earliest villagers were few (about sixty-five), yet the site has two public buildings dating about 1500–1100 B.C. Clearly the site was a regional center drawing labor from many villages. The earliest pottery includes exotic bottle sherds. The location is an unusual one, and the two peaks that jut dramatically from the plain apparently were regarded as sacred features very early in the Formative. By 1000 B.C. the villagers were building a water control system and probably terracing. The terraces were residential and garden zones. By this period (Middle Formative) there was also a very large platform which later became an elite residence and burial place. A masonry replica of an Olmec altar-throne possibly was built at this time (before 700 B.C.) and later disassembled and reassembled (Terrace 25 Altar).

The most notable period of the site dates 700–500 B.C. and therefore is both Middle Formative and La Venta horizon. During this period Chalcatzingo became more than a small regional highland center and established definite links with the Olmec heartland. The center was not large in itself, but a big village, scarcely more than four hundred people at the most. The utilitarian pottery and figurines reflected its highland Formative Past. There are also Gulf Coast elements which consist of carved stone monuments that are both free-standing and in the form of cliff sculpture. The style is fully developed Olmec and of a form that Kann and Grove have defined as "Frontier Olmec." In this style, the symbolism is more overt and spelled out, as in the most famous of the cliff sculptures called "El Rey." In that scene, a human sits on a square stool in a cave formed by a jaguar's mouth. The cave is decorated with depictions of the local bromeliads which today grow in the crevices of the cliff. Clouds come from the cave, and rain falls from still more clouds, recalling the later Aztec belief that the Tlalocs lived in caves and that caves generated clouds and rain. There is still more rain and water symbolism in the sculptures at Chalcatzingo (Fig. 3–13). Clearly, the peaks were regarded as the residence of some form of rain deity.

Eight known public buildings, one of very large size (more than 26,000 cubic meters or 918,000 cubic feet), supported elite residences and were the location of elite burials. Jade and greenstone are relatively common in certain zones of the site. Jade figurines are attributed to the site as well. A form of figurine prosaically labeled C8 is argued by Gillespie to be a portrait form based on the great diversity of facial types as well. She suggests that it is associated with the "cult of the ruler," which contained an element of ancestor worship. Over twenty distinct individuals are depicted in the C8 series at Chalcatzingo. The altar throne was an integral part of the apparatus of Olmec rulers. Some pottery forms and their motifs are reminiscent of those found in the Gulf Coast sites.

Grove interprets the voluminous data to indicate the periodic presence of Gulf Coast people at Chalcatzingo. At least iron ores and kaolin would have made the region attractive. In addition, Chalcatzingo and the nearly totally looted site of Las Bocas would have controlled a suggested jade route which led west to Guerrero, where known deposits of jade occur along the Balsas River. One stela (carved erect stone) that may represent a woman from Guerrero is based on unique motifs which also occur at the newly discovered site of Teopantecuanitlan on one of four Olmec-style monuments (Fig. 3–14). Grove also suggests that local rulers may have gained legitimacy by adopting Olmec symbolism. The center was abandoned gradually after the heartland centers lost their uniqueness. It no longer had a function as a regional collection point for the Olmec heart-

Fig. 3–13. Monument 14. Chalcatzingo. A small lizard perches on a hill, and its exhalation forms a cloud which in turn brings rain, drops of which are seen falling on a squash vine, below. Grove notes that small lizards of this sort appear at Chalcatzingo about a month before the rains begin. (Courtesy David C. Grove)

Fig. 3–14. Chalcatzingo Monument 21 is a stela-type monument showing a woman who possibly was from Guerrero. The carving may commemorate a dynastic marriage between a local ruler and a distant but important community in Guerrero, the latter a source of Olmec jade. (Courtesy David C. Grove)

land rulers, and newer regional centers fulfilled new needs and fashions in the Late Formative.

The Central Valley of Oaxaca

Flannery and his colleagues (Flannery, Marcus, and Kowalewski, 1981) have considerably clarified the early phases of Oaxacan culture through a long-term project located in the Central Valley.

At least twenty villages date from the Tierras Largas phase, about 1400 to 1150 B.C. The first public structures were square, plastered buildings, with possible step altars in them, and are only found at the site of San José Mogote in the western arm of the valley. The ceramics of this phase are of a localized tradition similar in many respects to the earlier and not too distant Purron pottery. Figurines are well modeled and common. A few Ocos sherds occur. No perceptible contact with the Olmec is known during this period.

This Formative isolationism broke down in the San José phase (1150–850 B.C.). The village of San José Mogote grew considerably and became a regional center with an estimated population of a maximum of seven hundred persons. Households found within the village were occupied by part-time specialists who made concave, iron-ore mirrors of the type found at La Venta. Ornaments were also manufactured of shell and mica. There is little doubt about social ranking; burials reflect considerable difference in status, especially in the access to jade or greenstone. San José ceramics carry Olmeclike iconography. The fire-serpent and the were-jaguar motifs were used on different types of pottery. Careful and intensive excavations have revealed that there were east and west barrios in the village and that these used black and gray pottery with fire-serpent motifs. The north and south divisions of the village used white pottery with were-jaguar motifs. Flannery and his colleagues conclude that the motifs were symbols of descent groups, perhaps clans. This is a regionalized use of an imported symbolic system, probably for a function quite different from that intended in the origination area. However it is also the case that the symbols were of potent social and religious value, and this was probably the reason that they were adopted.

No Olmec presence is either suggested or plausible at San José unlike Chalcatzingo. Distribution patterns of iron used to manufacture the exported mirrors suggest definite wealth differences among the communities and among people within the communities of Middle Formative Oaxaca. Thus, it may be that status differences were created or exacerbated by Olmec contact, no matter how indirect.

The Guatemalan Pacific Ocean

The two sites of Monte Alto and Abaj Takalik are located on the Pacific coastal plain of Guatemala. Monte Alto has so far only produced information which implies that the place is a small-scale and not too impressive attempt to replicate the Olmec ceremonial centers of the heartland. A fairly intensive occupation is indicated by the heavy deposits of ceramics and other debris in association with large sculpture.

Excavation of the Abaj Takalik project is still in progress. Very substantial platforms, and a long series of sculpture in distinct styles, suggest to the excavators that the site is more than ordinarily important. The ceramic sequence opens in Early Formative Ocos and continues into the Late Classic period. The public architecture dates at least to the Middle Formative and possibly earlier (Miguel Orrego, personal communication, 1988). Several new sculptures have been found, and two are suggested as being "Proto-Olmec" in style by J. Graham. However, stratigraphic evidence is lacking to confirm this conjecture. One large sculpture seems to be the recarved remains of a colossal stone head (J. Graham, personal communication), and if so, it might imply rulership by an Olmec governor at Abaj Takalik. On the other hand it might also imply a common iconography of power among the regional centers of the Pacific and Gulf coasts.

Grove believes that the passage along the coast was probably a jade-cacao trade route. Ultimately it leads to the Motagua Valley and its jade boulders as well as to the enigmatic fortress of Los Naranjos near Tegucigalpa, Honduras, which is associated with pottery carrying the were-jaguar and fire-serpent symbols (Baudez and Becquelin, 1973).

The Southeastern Lowlands

The pleasant and fertile valley of Chalchuapa (El Salvador) is open to the Pacific coastal plain through the Ahuachapan Pass. A long sequence of cultural development there has been defined by Robert J. Sharer (1974), but only the Formative phases concern us at this point.

An early complex, Tok, dates from about 1200 to 900 B.C. It has close affinities with Cuadros-affiliated complexes, but no specific Olmec linkages. In other words, it is not linked to the San Lorenzo horizon of Olmec expansion. Sharer comments that Tok was a part of Lowe's expanding lowland, maize-cultivating tradition. These earliest inland populations apparently were colonists from the coastal plain.

The Colos ceramic complex (900–500 B.C.) is tied into the La Venta horizon by specific ceramic types: white-rimmed blackware, polished black pottery, streaky gray and white to buff pottery, as well as specific Olmec motifs. A large pyramidal structure at Trapiche was built to the imposing height of at least 20 meters (about 66 feet). Cacao, hematite, and Ixtepeque obsidian were desirables that attracted the Olmec. Twenty-five kilometers (15 miles) away at Ahuachapan, finds have been made of serpentine and jade Olmec figurines which indicate that there is probably an Olmec-linked regional center of the Chalcatzingo–Las Bocas variety there. Although the Olmec presence is impressive, and Sharer thinks that it stimulated cultural evolution, it is not massive. Grove's trading-station model seems to fit the Salvadoran situation well.

The Maya Lowlands

Only a few hints of Olmec linkage come from the Maya Lowlands as yet. One is the already noted cliff sculpture at Xoc (unfortunately destroyed by greedy looters). Another is the jade "letter-opener" (bloodletter) found in Xe (ca. 900 B.C.) at Seibal. The sculpture at Loltun Cave is no longer convincingly Olmec in style, now that we have better knowledge of both heartland and frontier varieties. No Olmec motifs show up in the Xe-sphere ceramics of the southern lowlands. However, the northern low-lands of Chiapas are poorly known except for the large sites, and it may be that some surprises await us. A general review of the Maya can be found in chapter 5.

Social and Political Implications

It is at this point that some of the most controversial problems about the Olmec arise. Economic and ritual motivations for the establishment of ties with all four areas noted above can be suggested. Obsidian and jade come from the zones around the Basin of Mexico and the Morelos Valley, and access was by passage through these highland areas. Iron ores made into mirrors came from the Valley of Oaxaca, and those from the Valley of Morelos were made into cosmetics. Kaolin for fine ceramics came from several areas, including the zone around Chalcatzingo. The Guatemalan-Chiapan Pacific plain produced the best and largest quantities of cacao of all Mesoamerica. This area, known as Soconusco in Aztec times, was conquered by the Aztec to assure control of that very valuable commodity. There is an emphasis on cacao in Late Formative art of this coastal shelf. In addition, this corridor led to sources for obsidian and jade from Guatemala.

In order to make some sense out of this material, it is necessary to deal with reconstruction of the social fabric of the Olmec heartland itself. It seems clear that Olmec society was stratified, with an elite or upper class which is depicted on the sculptured monuments. This elite engaged in religious ritual, warfare, and economic activities, judging by the depictions of them in action (Fig. 3–15). They commanded sufficient labor to accomplish the building of such large monuments as the C-1 effigy volcano at La Venta and the immense work of construction of the artificial plateau at San Lorenzo. They also defined and commanded the economically and ritually valuable commodities such as jade, magnetite, obsidian, probably cacao, and other perishable items. Socially significant, they commanded the services of craftsmen so skilled that they must have been full-time specialists by San Lorenzo times. We therefore get a picture of

Fig. 3–15. La Venta Stela 2. The central figure appears to be a ruler who is surrounded in the air by six supernatural or ancestral figures. All seem to be armed. (Courtesy John A. Graham)

Olmec society in the heartland as possessing an upper class, a group of artisan-craftsmen, and a mass of population of lower status. If this reconstruction is correct, then the Olmecs set a general pattern of stratified social organization which reappears among the Classic Maya, and thus it may have survived until about A.D. 900.

Olmec centers in the heartland probably acted as political capitals, nodes of economic exchange, and religious pilgrimage centers. This seems particularly true in the case of the largest centers. There is evidence that San Lorenzo achieved regional dominance first and was overlapped and then succeeded by La Venta. M. D. Coe (1970) thinks that the implications of these data are that the religious and political capitals were moved. However, Drucker (1981) makes a convincing case for the simultaneous existence of two to four Olmec autonomous, localized states at any given time. The positions of Tres Zapotes and Laguna de los Cerros in this political history are not yet clear because of lack of excavation at those sites.

The relationships of the Gulf Coast centers to the contemporary cultures of highland Mexico are clearer now that recent research has been published. Covarrubias saw the situation essentially as one in which the Olmec were derived from Guerrero, colonized the heartland zone, and then developed their pattern of civilization, which was adopted and adapted by all succeeding cultures in Mesoamerica (1946, 1957).

Bernal (1969) saw the various formative villages of the Mesa Central area (Tlatilco, Tlapacoya, Chalcatzingo, and Las Bocas) as being actual colonies of Olmecs contemporary with non-Olmec peoples living at small villages such as El Arbolillo in the Basin of Mexico. This view is now superseded by the latest evidence, which indicates contemporaneity and sophistication with the Olmec by these villages and regional centers, but not subordination. Chalcatzingo, indeed, seems to have been occupied periodically by Gulf Coast elites, but local and regional control was predominant.

Studies by linguists indicate that Mixe-Zoque is a likely candidate for the Olmec language (Campbell and Kaufman, 1976; Lowe, 1977). An older idea, mainly by nonlinguists, was that the Olmec possibly spoke Maya, but this is now discredited.

The Olmec and Their Role in Early Evolution of Complex Cultures

Olmec culture was precocious and advanced, and it undoubtedly influenced many later cultural developments. However, it existed, as we have seen, in the context of lively, vigorous general cultural developments over Mesoamerica as a whole. This process produced many known regional centers in the Early and Middle Formative and, no doubt, many that are yet to be found. Flannery (1968) and Grove (1987) have both argued strongly for a crucial role for these highland centers in an interactive relationship with the centers of the Gulf Coast. There is little doubt now that this interaction existed and that it was important to the Olmec as much as to their neighbors. That being said, however, it is not reasonable to go to the other extreme and argue that the Olmec were simply another player in a game which had several players of near cultural parity. The comparisons which have been made between the number of public works constructed in the Gulf Coast centers and those done at San José Mogote or Chalcatzingo make it clear that there was an order of magnitude difference and that it was heavily in favor of the Olmec. The immense amounts of earth moved, the numbers of platforms erected, the tons of stone moved and sculpted, and the treasures of valuable materials at the Gulf Coast centers have no parallel or match in the highlands. Analogously, sixteenth-century English towns such as Norfolk, while charming and lively, could not hope to match the resources drawn upon by London.

The preferred view of the Olmec taken here, then, is that they indeed did have cultural priority in Mesoamerica as a whole. They probably did invent and diffuse much of the cultural equipment used and reformulated in later cultures. On the other hand, like any other sophisticated culture, the Olmec had no inhibitions about adopting good ideas and new fashions from their neighbors. Therefore, interaction among the regional cultures of Mesoamerica on economic and cultural levels was as important in the Early and Middle Formative as in later times. The symbiotic relationships and interstimulation among these cultures were probably the most important factors in keeping up the evolutionary momentum of civilization in Mesoamerica.

It has already been seen that this interaction pattern was in existence in the preceding periods of the Archaic and was crucial in the development of agriculture. Willey (1962) has suggested that the Olmec's crucial role was in providing a vehicle for intensifying and accelerating that interaction and thus bringing many more areas of Mesoamerica into the process of evolution of civilization. He suggests that Olmec religion was a major motivation for this step-up in interaction patterns. This might be called the "Canterbury Tales" theory. Olmec religion seems to have been a powerful ideological force, and one which inspired a missionary fervor among its adherents. This proselytizing may have involved a kind of church militant that used force for conversions as well as to attain the resources necessary to maintain the prestige of the main centers of Olmec religion. The pattern of pilgrimages by culturally and ethnically diverse peoples to the lowland centers can be inferred from the archaeological record.

All the above fits a pattern that is somewhat like the historically recorded spread of Islam as a religious, cultural, and political movement. Persons traveling to religious centers exchanged ideas, goods, and even genes. This spiritual motivation to cultural evolution in Mesoamerica is particularly appealing because it was important in later times and because it has become apparent that cultural ecology does not give a full explanation. Irrigation farming leading to population growth and thence to urbanism and civilization is too mechanistic a scheme to explain all of the data, even as incomplete as it is now.

Thus, Mesoamerica was formed by the interaction of various early cultures, of which the Olmec became, for a time, an orienting and organizing force. The resulting patterns were regionalized and carried on. In the highlands there seem to have been still further qualitative developments in social organization. These were based in part on large numbers of people supported by irrigation farming. The Lowland Maya seem to have carried on Olmec-style cultural patterns until a new influence caused a somewhat radical change at the beginning of the Classic. From this point of view, Olmec culture did not die out but was absorbed and passed on in transformed variations. It is to the evidence from the Late Formative and the bridging cultures between Middle Formative cultures and their inheritors that we must turn.

CHAPTER 4

THE LATE FORMATIVE: DEVELOPMENT OF REGIONAL CULTURES AND CIVILIZATIONS

In the year and in the day
of obscurity and utter darkness,
before there were days and years,
the world being in deep obscurity,
when all was chaos and confusion,
the earth was covered with water,
there was only mud and slime
on the surface of the earth.
At that time . . .
there became visible
a god who had the name 1-Deer
and the surname Snake of the Tiger.
These gods are said to have been the beginning
of all the other gods.
      —Mixtec origin myth in León-Portilla,
                          1969:55.

Those who carried with them the black and red ink,
the manuscripts and painted book, the wisdom.
They brought everything with them, the annals,
the books and song and their flutes.
      —Sahagún, in León-Portilla, 1969:10.

Their dwelling place was as follows: . . . in the
middle of the town were their temples with beautiful
plazas, and all around the temples stood the houses of
the lords and the priests, and then [those of] the most
important people. Thus came the houses of the richest
and those who were held in the highest estimation
nearest to these, and at the outskirts of the town were
the houses of the lower class. And the wells, if there
were but few of them, were near the houses of the lords;
and they had their improved lands planted with wine

trees and they sowed cotton, pepper and maize, and
they lived thus close together for fear of their enemies.
                                            —*Landa, 1941:62*

THE RICH variation among Mesoamerican high cultures has its roots in
the Formative period. This variety of cultural texture and pattern reaches
back to the Early Formative but becomes more pronounced as one moves
forward through time to the cultures that succeeded the Olmec and their
contemporaries. At this point in our archaeological rediscovery of these
ancient predecessors of the Maya and Aztec, it is clear that there are
several clusters of Formative cultures. In their areal distribution they are
nearly templates for the major Classic civilizations. At least six of these
clusters can be defined at present: the Isthmian Zones, the Maya Highlands, the Maya Lowlands, Oaxaca, the Central Plateau, and West Mexico.
The isthmian cultures appear to be related to the Olmec patterns, albeit
obscurely in some cases. They have sometimes been called the epi-Olmec,
largely because they were all thought to share an art style that was derived
from the Olmec—the Izapan. Recent work has shown that at least two
distinct traditions were present in the Isthmian Zone, so the term *epi-*
Olmec has been discarded here in favor of regional labels. The early
Lowland Maya, like the Central Plateau and West Mexican cultures, seem
largely to have gone their own way without strong direct heritage from
the Olmec themselves. In other words, like the earlier Olmec, they
developed their own florescences largely on the basis of in-place evolution.
Before examining the individual clusters of cultures, we should observe
that not all of them achieved the status of civilizations during the Late
Formative or even during the Classic period. Culture in parts of the
Isthmian Zone retrogressed, and the West Mexican cultures waited for a
further circumstance before they evolved into more complex forms.

The Isthmian Culture Cluster

As during the great days of Olmec dominance, the Isthmus of Tehuantepec later formed an avenue of communication between the Gulf Coast
plain and the Pacific slope of Guatemala. The Late Formative cultures
in the zone are linked by art styles which seem to show commonalities in
symbolism, but distinctly regional aspects as well. This group of art styles
was formerly called by the name Izapan, from the site of Izapa, where
great numbers of monuments occur. Recent studies by the New World
Archaeological Foundation have shed a great deal of new light on this
site and period (Norman 1973, 1976; Lowe, Lee, and Martínez 1982).
It now appears that Izapan sculptural style is essentially confined to the
site from which it takes its name. Other sites with similar sculpture can
be regarded as either Olmec-derived (Cerro de las Mesas) or relatively

independent regional developments (Abaj Takalik, Kaminaljuyu, Chiapa de Corzo). The regionalism of these sculptural patterns is also reflected in other aspects of cultures. Thus we have a Late Formative continuation of the pattern established a thousand years before—that of regional cultural evolution. These processes and regions were linked by commonalities and occasionally and more intensively by a particularly vigorous and precocious culture, the Olmec formerly and the Izapan and Highland Maya latterly. Instead of the domination of one locality or area, we have a series of regional cultural traditions which interacted, played on one another, and yet maintained their own distinctiveness.

Olmec-derived Cultures: Cerro de las Mesas and Tres Zapotes

Cerro de las Mesas is located on the northern edge of the Tuxtlas Mountains, in the former Olmec heartland. Tres Zapotes is about 80 kilometers (50 miles) away. It is at both of these sites that we have the most direct continuation of the Olmec artistic tradition. Earthen platforms were built around plazas, stone monuments were erected, and about the final century B.C., a calendar system was devised.

Cerro de las Mesas may date to 600 B.C. or before. Unfortunately, the site was excavated with less than rigorous methods, and there is confusion about the sequence of pottery, burials, and other minutiae that archaeologists use to sort matters out. It may well overlap with Bernal's Olmec II period (1200–400 B.C.), but clearly the Cerro de las Mesas site represents a culture related to the Olmec—one which survived the closing of the older center and which bridges the evolutionary gap between the Olmec and the Classic civilizations. At the moment, however, the evidence is fragmentary, elusive, and tentative.

A ceremonial deposit (cache) of 782 jade and stone pieces was found at Cerro de las Mesas (Drucker, 1955). Of the cache Bernal considers only four pieces to be Olmec in style; they may well be heirloom items buried a long time after their manufacture. Most of the items are earspools, beads, and other personal jewelry. A burial in a small platform at the site produced a magnificently carved turtle shell which has as its principal motif the "long-lipped god." This same deity is found on the Izapan-related sculptures. Some of the sculptures at the site also reflect the later style of transformed Olmec heritage, with seated and standing figures of rulers associated with religiously powerful symbols which no doubt lent greater authority to those rulers.

At Tres Zapotes there is evidence of early writing, with Stela C probably representing the earliest found example of bar-and-dot numerals. Until recently the date of Stela C (32 B.C.) was somewhat in doubt, because the top of the notation was missing, but the missing part has been found and fully justifies the reading that Stirling, the discoverer, made in 1943. Taken together with the date of 99 B.C. on a small jade carving, the Tuxtla

Fig. 4–1. Izapa, Chiapas, Mexico. This Formative site is made up of many mound groups, of which this (F group) is one. Izapa Stela 67 (Fig. 4–2) is located here, out of sight to the right. (Courtesy Margaret N. Bond and Franklin C. Graham)

statuette, Stela C makes it certain that a complex calendar and notation system was in use in the former Olmec zone by 100 B.C.

Elsewhere, a recently discovered monument found at the bottom of the Acula River, La Mojarra Stela 1, has a very long and obscure text of 520 glyphs (Winfield Capitaine, 1988). Two dates on it read A.D. 143 and 156 in the Maya system. The human figure on the stela is in the Izapan style, and the headdress is very similar to that on Stela 11 of Kaminaljuyu, near Guatemala City. This monument was apparently associated with a set of as yet unexcavated mounds along the edge of the river. La Mojarra Stela 1 was probably in an area of the site now destroyed by the cutting of the river.

The oldest known monument in the Maya Lowlands at present is Stela 29 (A.D. 292) at the site of Tikal, although earlier indications of writing in the Maya Late Formative have been found in the past few years.

Izapa

Across the isthmus and down the Pacific Coast from Tres Zapotes and Cerro de las Mesas is the large center of Izapa, where there are more examples of Late Formative regional art than anywhere else in Mesoamerica (Fig. 4-1). Izapa, its beginnings in the Early Formative, was an Ocos village and then became a small regional center. Its great period was the Guillen phase (300–50 B.C.), during which it became a major regional center. Eventually it comprised eight courtyards of major architecture covering about 3.6 square kilometers (1.4 square miles), with a total of about 250,000 cubic meters (8.83 million cubic feet) of material. Boulder-faced clay platforms were arranged around each courtyard, each with its suite of stone monuments, which include stela/altar combinations, miscellaneous sculptures, and three thrones. There are 253 known stone monuments at Izapa, of which 119 were carved. The groups and the structures in them are oriented to solar solstices, equinoxes, lunar risings, and, above all, the impressive bulk of the huge Tacana volcano nearby.

Residential and ritual function are apparent in each group. The lower platforms apparently were intended to support elite residences built of timber, plaster, and thatch. Stone drains carried off the heavy rainfall of the region (in September 1988, over 25 centimeters [10 inches] of rain fell in nearby Tapachula in three days). Stone sculpture included basins and other water-related devices. A large group of monuments is located on a small peninsula by the Izapa River, and water also is a strong theme in the sculptures.

Linguistic studies indicate to Campbell and Kaufman (1976) that Izapa was Mixe-Zoque until the Postclassic, when Maya neighbors took over the region. It will be recalled that Mixe-Zoque was probably the language of the Olmec centers.

Over the period of 250 years comprising the Guillen phase, there was probably a shift in Izapan symbolism. However, the basic underlying concepts seem to have remained the same through this time. Lowe, Lee, and Martínez see an "orderly passion for commemorating cosmological or religious precepts with appropriate rituals" (1982:307). Periodically the courtyards were enlarged and the monuments reset. This ties in with the use of a ritual calendar in connection with agricultural and solar/lunar ceremonies. Lowe, Lee, and Martínez feel that the Izapan avoided the glorification of divine rulers that is so important among the later Classic Maya. Instead, they celebrated creation, fertility, the life cycles, and astronomical events.

The pictorial aspect of Izapan "narrative-style" art appeals readily to those unfamiliar with the iconography of more arcane Mesoamerican styles. Animals, gods, and humans are combined in scenes of action. Storm gods gather water and release it; jaguars are captive participants in human rituals; bird gods fly through the sky; gods in canoes ride over waves beneath which swim realistically depicted fishes (Fig. 4-2); other gods descend headfirst from heaven; seated humans tend incense burners; a warrior decapitates an enemy. These apparently straightforward depic-

Fig. 4–2. Stela 67, Izapa. A supernatural being or a human with a fish mask rides in a canoe upon sacred waters.

tions, however, had their deeper symbolism. Stela 5 depicts a ceremony engaging several persons and dominated by a huge tree. The tree has been named the "tree of life" and possibly represents the great ceiba tree, which in later Maya mythology was thought to hold up the heavens. Lowe, Lee, and Martínez interpret this monument as depicting creation.

Jacinto Quirarte (1973) has pointed out that among other elements appearing later in Classic Maya art is the double-headed monster figure (Stelae 5, 7, and 12). It is now problematical whether this form derived from a general iconography in eastern Mesoamerica or from Izapa's having had some ancestral role in the creation of later Maya art.

Izapa also lacks the dates and writing that are such a characteristic of the Cerros de las Mesas art or the contemporary and slightly later monuments at Kaminaljuyu. This would be consistent with the excavators' interpretation of Izapa as a residence for priest rulers and their acolytes and as a center for pilgrimages. Incense burning and the ritual deposition of large amounts of valued materials were parts of the liturgy. Large numbers of people built and sustained Izapa and probably a great number of other communities with formal architecture as well. Other, uninvestigated sites in the vicinity are of the same age and have several courtyards with buildings, but lack monuments. On the other hand, secular matters were not entirely ignored (aside from agriculture), because Izapa Group H has a very large plaza quite suitable as a marketplace. Later, and probably at that time as well, cacao was one of the most important crops, and traders came from long distances to acquire it. Such a location could have been the location for such commerce.

Abaj Takalik

Projects directed by John Graham and Miguel Orrego are providing new information on the large regional center of Abaj Takalik, which survived into the Late Formative (Fig. 4-3). As yet, not a great deal of detailed information about the site has been published, but stelae there are of undoubted Maya style, and at least one (Stela 5) dates to about A.D. 126 (Figs. 4-4, 4-5; J. Graham, 1978).

El Baúl

El Baúl, a nearby site in the piedmont zone of the Guatemalan south coast, has produced a stela that has been read by M. D. Coe as about A.D. 36, which is very early indeed.

Kaminaljuyu

Kaminaljuyu is an enormous site rapidly disappearing under the edges of modern Guatemala City. Fortunately it is now a national park which preserves much of interest. Also fortunately the Carnegie Institution of Washington during the 1930s and 1940s and the Penn State project of the 1960s and 1970s have preserved a rich haul of data which otherwise

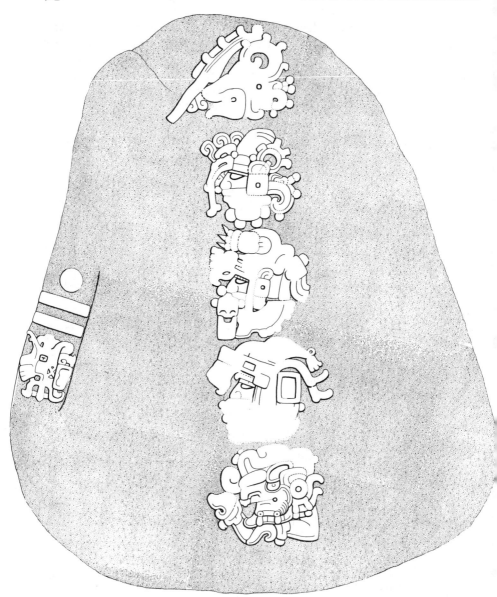

Fig. 4–3. Monument II at Abaj Takalik on the Pacific coastal plain of Guatemala. Possibly one of the earliest dated monuments in Mesoamerica, according to Graham. (Courtesy James Porter and John A. Graham)

would have been lost forever. Among the most crucial of the information gained from Kaminaljuyu is a long sequence of local sculptural expression. At this site it appears first in variable boulder pieces. The sculptures, which depict fat men, are perhaps as early as the late part of the Middle

Fig. 4–4. Abaj Takalik Stela 5, a very early dated monument in Maya style. (Courtesy James Porter)

Fig. 4–5. Abaj Takalik Stela 3. Note the similarity in the basal band and position of the feet to those same elements in Stela 5 (Fig. 4–4). (Courtesy John A. Graham)

Formative (ca. 500 B.C.; Fig. 4-6). These sculptures are regional in style, and their closest counterparts are mainly on the nearby south coast of Guatemala. Carved and uncarved angular pieces of basalt are from the Late Formative. Finally, the Kaminaljuyu tradition flowered into an exuberant and unique expression which includes depictions of "squashed frogs" (*ranas aplastadas*), silhouette sculptures of extraordinary complexity, and formal erect shafts which are clearly stelae, although most of them do not carry hieroglyphic texts. The extraordinary sculpture known as Kaminaljuyu Stela 11 shows a barefoot individual, otherwise richly attired, standing between two blazing incense burners. Incense burners of precisely the same type are to be seen on stelae at Izapa.

Stela 10, in the same excavation as Stela 11, is an equally interesting sculpture made of dense, black basalt (Fig. 4-7). In spite of the difficult stone, the skill of execution on Stela 10 is high, and the three human figures depicted on it in relief are among the best in Mesoamerican art. Great virtuosity is evidenced by the treatment of the feathers flowing from a backframe on the lefthand figure. Stela 10 also has a rather long hieroglyphic text which is incised to the side of a large relief-carved glyph.

Fig. 4–6. Miraflores-phase sculptures from Kaminaljuyu. These "Tweedle Dee and Tweedle Dum" pieces may represent surrogate worshiper figures designed to permanently accompany a major sculptured sacred image.

Fig. 4–7. Partial reconstruction of Kaminaljuyu Stela 10 (Miraflores phase), a very large sculpture which included at least two hieroglyphic texts. The left-hand human figure brandishes an elaborate ax set with a chipped flint blade. A possible ancestral figure hovers in the upper right corner. (Courtesy James Porter and John A. Graham)

Unfortunately, the stela was smashed in ancient times, and in any case the glyphs are indecipherable at present (Fig. 4-8). They resemble those on the newly found La Mojarra Stela 1 from the Gulf Coast. This regional style is apparently a result of a combination of indigenous development and interaction with Izapa and other centers, the same processes that

Fig. 4–8. Miraflores-phase sculpture from Kaminaljuyu. A fragment of Stela 10, a magnificently conceived and carved basalt slab. (Courtesy William R. Coe III)

operated so often, early and late, in Mesoamerican prehistory. Judging from the similar features of later Classic Maya Lowland stelae, it seems probable that these monuments partially memorialize temporal rulers and that the inscriptions may give some historical data about them. In later times, succeeding rulers often smashed the monuments of their predecessors.

As indicated above, Kaminaljuyu's beginnings are about 800 B.C., or Middle Formative, the time of development of so many other regional centers. All data suggest that the Valley of La Ermita (Guatemala City's present location) was occupied by a series of small villages, some of which might be classed by 500 B.C. as small regional centers. Thanks to the work of William Sanders and his associates, we now see that the settlement patterns and arrangements of ceremonial centers reflect what may be clan or lineage centers. Each of these dozen known groups possessed what appear to be temples of burial mounds around which were gathered small clusters of population (Michels, 1979a, 1979b; Sanders and Michels, 1969). The implication is that these were petty chiefs or leaders of kinship groups, with their ceremonial life focused on funerary and religious monuments. These platforms and buildings were supplemented by the carved and uncarved stones set in front of or on them.

By the Miraflores phase (100 B.C. to A.D. 200), five of these centers had grown to be major regional centers around which clustered the hamlets and houses of the kin-group members. Michels (1979a) believes that by 100 B.C. these groups represent Polynesian-style chiefdoms, each of which was divided along lines of duality (moieties), a classic and reasonably common traditional social structure. They also imply a rather loose political organization based on kinship and marriage ties among the local important families. Usulutan pottery, which has its apparent origins in what is now El Salvador, indicates outside contact. Total population for the valley is estimated at three thousand to six thousand persons. However, it is likely that many more persons were involved in the Kaminaljuyu societies. Sanders and his colleagues ignored some vital data in their calculations.

Guatemalan scholars Carlos Navarrete and Luis Lujan (1986) have studied the colonial aqueduct and concluded that the base of this formidable public work is pre-Hispanic and dates to the Miraflores period. The prehistoric earthwork was called "La Culebra" (the Serpent) in colonial documents, and indeed it probably is an effigy mound, as implied by the name. It is made of adobe bricks, runs sinuously for more than 4,100 meters (13,530 feet, or about 2.6 miles) and is probably incomplete. Judging from its location in the local topography, the earthwork may have been a boundary or military fortification guarding Kaminaljuyu from intrusions from the south. Navarrete and Lujan also consider the possibility that the structure was a pre-Hispanic aqueduct. In any case, the structure, in its incomplete condition, still has a volume of nearly 2 million cubic meters (70 million cubic feet). Michels calculates that other public architecture, some of which may date earlier, has a total volume of about 230,000 cubic meters (8 million cubic feet).

Another point to be added is that Kaminaljuyu is much diminished from its original state, many of the largest structures having been demolished with the establishment of the colonial capital in the vicinity about 1776 (Navarrete, personal communication). These putative structures, at least some of which would have dated from the Late Formative, would add to the total volume and, consequently, to the implied population.

Recent research by the Universidad del Valle, directed by Marian Hatch, has detected a major irrigation or drainage canal which dates at least to about 300 B.C. and perhaps earlier (Hatch, personal communication, 1988).

In addition, the elaborate Miraflores-phase burial in Str. E-III-3, implies complex social order (Shook and Kidder, 1952). It is an elaborate tomb, with a roof supported by massive timbers, containing the body of a man surrounded by hundreds of pottery vessels and other objects and by at least four people sacrificed to accompany him into the other world (Fig. 4-9).

With these additional data the Kaminaljuyu site becomes an order of magnitude greater than the contemporary centers of Izapa, Abaj Takalik, and even Cerro de las Mesas (as far as we know). The implied population and social organization to carry out the public works are matched only by the far earlier Gulf Coast centers such as San Lorenzo. It seems likely that Kaminaljuyu controlled tens of thousands of people instead of the suggested few thousand. It also becomes a possibility that the political organization of Late Formative Kaminaljuyu had evolved beyond the level of the chiefdom and entered the level that we must call a state. We will consider these matters further later in this chapter.

El Portón

The Valley of Salama is located in the north Maya Highlands (Alta Verapaz) of Guatemala. The small site of El Portón is an interesting example of a much smaller center which apparently was tracking Kaminaljuyu in its development. By the Late Formative, the now familiar platform-temple-courtyard complex had appeared there and carved stone monuments were erected (Sharer and Sedat, 1973). The best monument at the site is in the style of Kaminaljuyu Late Formative monuments. The political and social relationships of this center to the lowlands to the north or to Kaminaljuyu are not clear at the moment. It appears to have been a more or less independent, imitative, and provincial center which arose at that time. It was one of many.

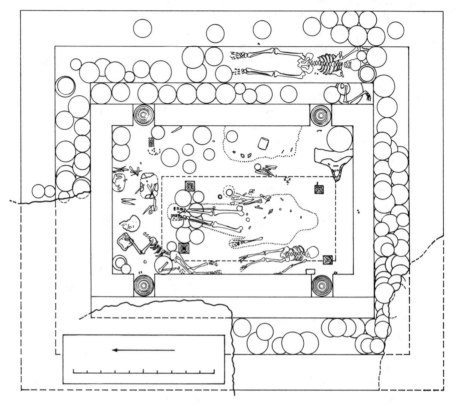

Fig. 4–9. Miraflores (Late Formative) Tomb II at Structure E-III–3, Kaminaljuyu. Note the supplementary skeletons and large numbers of pottery dishes set around the steps of the tomb. Posts formerly held up a timber roof.

Chalchuapa

The southeastern lowland cultures in the Chalchuapa area retained their precocity, and the later Formative remains there are represented by three ceramic complexes, Kal, Chul, and Caynac, which date from 400 B.C. to A.D. 200. During this period the Trapiche pyramid was rebuilt, and extensive new construction around Chalchuapa covered about half a square kilometer (one-fifth of a square mile). Numerous individual mound groups similar to those of contemporary Miraflores-phase Kaminaljuyu were the rule.

Monumental stone sculpture also appeared at the end of the phase. Monument 1 at Trapiche is especially important for its long and complex hieroglyphic text, which shows advanced features of the later Maya system. All things considered, Chalchuapa is a much smaller regional center than those of Kaminaljuyu or the next level down, Izapa.

Large quantities of ceramics and debris around Chalchuapa indicate a growth in population in the Late Formative period. Usulutan ware was adopted from its original zone in western El Salvador and intensively developed, and Chalchuapa may have been a manufacturing center for this important Late Formative trade ware in Eastern Mesoamerica (Demarest and Sharer, 1982). Tons of Usulutan ware are found throughout the valley.

The eruption of Ilopango Volcano apparently cut short this promising cultural development, and refugee populations may have found their ways into the adjacent highlands. Usulutan multiple-wavy-lined decorative techniques show up at this time in the lowlands in the very Late Formative complexes.

Chiapa de Corzo

Chiapa de Corzo is one of the most important sites in Mesoamerica because of its nearly continuous sequence, which runs from 1400 B.C. to the present, some 3,300 years. Pottery water bottles, jugs, and storage jars are the main evidence for earliest human occupation of this part of Chiapas. The site is in the lowland trench of the Grijalva River, a finger of tropical lowland environment that is the only part of the zone to produce early remains. The nearby highlands lack nearly any sign of early settlements, but small villages apparently lined the Grijalva River bottom, taking advantage of the same features that made the area around San Lorenzo so attractive to the Olmec peoples.

Continuity of culture and population is reflected in the sequence, with a slow series of changes producing the first pyramids and other civic buildings about 550 B.C.—about the same time that they show up in the Maya Lowlands. Public architecture became complex over time, and palaces of cut stone, plastered with heavy coats of polished stucco and roofed by beams and mortar, appeared by 150 B.C. These buildings are clearly suited for residences and are more elaborate than the more common thatched-roof, mud-walled houses that sheltered most of the population. Apparently some persons were important enough to rate superior housing built at cost to the community.

Social stratification is also reflected in the burials of the period, with Tomb 1 obviously representing a person of extraordinary importance. Tomb 1 is a formally built chamber of unfired brick. A long lance with an obsidian blade was in the grave, along with several unusual pottery vessels and jade jewelry—the latter always a symbol of high status. Also found were three elaborately carved human femurs that had been worked while the bones were fresh. Apparently the bones were originally set with feathers and used as aspergillums. Mythological subjects, such as a crocodile swimming through water, are portrayed on the bones in a style definitely related to Izapan and Cerro de las Mesas sculpture. Another bone shows a jaguar-masked person who is very similar to the depiction of a human on Kaminaljuyu Stela 11. To make the case tighter, fragments of Izapan-style sculpture have turned up at Chiapa de Corzo. Indeed, Chiapa Stela 2 may be one of the most anciently dated sculptured monuments known, with a reading of 36 B.C., according to M. D. Coe.

One of the most extraordinary finds in Mesoamerican archaeology was that of the palace structure of Chiapa de Corzo now called Mound 5 (Fig. 4-10). When archaeologists dug through the debris of the fallen roof, they found hundreds of smashed and burnt pottery vessels of outrageous variety in shape and decoration. Many of these vessels exhibited the hallmarks of the Late Formative in eastern Mesoamerica—mammiform feet; multiple, wavy-lined decoration; bridged spouts—characteristics that indicate contacts with the zones of Kaminaljuyu and with the Central Valley of Oaxaca. Some pottery from the latter region was actually traded into Chiapa de Corzo. Again, these finds strongly imply that political and economic ties linked these regional centers and provided stimulation one to another in various cultural fields. The palace and the pottery at Mound 5 were deliberately destroyed, indicating that the site of Chiapa de Corzo was abandoned by its former rulers. It was reoccupied shortly

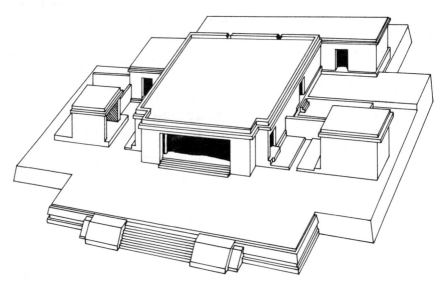

Fig. 4–10. Reconstruction drawing of Horcones-phase (Late Formative) palace at Chiapa de Corzo, Chiapas, Mexico. The structure was burned at the end of the phase, together with a great deal of ritual pottery of unusual shapes. (After Lowe 1962)

afterward, but the styles of pottery show that the new residents were new peoples.

About that time, the group of people known as the Zoque (already encountered as part of the Mixe-Zoque) pushed into the Grijalva Depression, according to linguistic evidence. This leaves us with the question of who built Chiapa de Corzo in its Late Formative (Horcones) phase and probably earlier phases. The answer is still speculative, but it seems possible that this is a case of Maya-speakers being shoved out of their original positions and displaced into their historical locations. The Zoque are non-Maya. On the other hand, it will be recalled that the highlands adjacent to the Grijalva Trench were very thinly or not at all occupied during most of the Formative. They are also the historical homeland of the Highland Maya. The intrusion of the Zoque or their ancestors and the movement of the Maya into the highlands would account for the sudden appearance of Early Classic remains in that region. The deliberate destruction of the Mound 5 palace at Chiapa de Corzo, in this scheme, would have been the last act of ritual abandonment by the Maya as they left their ancestral center for a new homeland. The Zoque, in turn, seem to have been displaced into remoter zones of the central depression of Chiapas starting about A.D. 500. The Chiapanec were the group occupying the zone of Chiapa de Corzo in the sixteenth century.

The appearance of Izapan-style sculpture at the highland sites of Tonina and Chinkultic may indicate the regions in which the Chiapa de Corzo elite took refuge (Norman, 1973). On the other hand, these sites may merely represent further contemporary regional centers like that of El Portón. It is important that we now have Maya Highland sites with Izapan-style sculpture which are geographically next to the Maya Lowlands. Such adjacency allows for the possible derivation of the first known Maya sculpture from the earlier sculptural traditions discussed here.

The Oaxacan Late Formative

The Central Valley of Oaxaca is a highland area of mountainous beauty. It covers some 3,375 square kilometers (1,303 square miles) and lies at about 1,550 meters (5,115 feet) above sea level. Seven hundred square kilometers (270 square miles) are located in the most desirable valley bottom.

The earliest phases of a long and continuous sequence have already been discussed in regard to the Early Formative. The earliest villages in the central valley are located within the valley bottom and in a zone where water is available within 3 meters (10 feet) of the surface. This is exactly the situation chosen by present-day farmers for a type of simple irrigation called pot irrigation. Modern Zapotec farmers of the zone lay out rectangular fields, plant their corn and other crops in hills, and dig wells to the shallow water table along the fields' edges. After lowering their pots into the wells, they water the nearest plants by pouring a potful on each hill. They then move to the next well and continue to water the adjacent plants. Flannery (1968) believes that the locations of the earliest villages were determined by the requirements of this irrigation technique. A well dating to about 600 B.C. which has been found in this zone seems to bear out the theory.

It is worth noting that this intensive technique does not depend on large-scale construction or on large masses of people and elaborate social organization. From about 1300 B.C. to 350 B.C. what we seem to have is a series of widely spaced independent villages with their dependent hamlets. San José Mogote by about 500 B.C. served an estimated thirteen hundred people. Larger communities of this kind possessed a formal leadership and more public architecture, probably associated with marketing and religious activities.

Ignacio Bernal did an extensive survey of the valley and found that from 300 to 100 B.C. a major population expansion took place (1965a). Thirty-nine sites were occupied during this time, including Monte Alban, which was later to become the political center for the entire valley. Many of these sites have civic architecture, and one has a residential area of 80 hectares (198 acres). Expansion into the agriculturally less desirable sloping piedmont zones also shows the effect of population growth. This change in quantity was followed by one in quality. For the period between 100 B.C. and A.D. 300, only twenty-three sites are known, but these are all larger than earlier sites and have massive ceremonial and civic architecture. Seven of the twenty-three were major centers, but Monte Alban, which is one of them, is not significantly different from the other six. This indicates that the valley was probably divided into at least seven petty states at this period. Flannery and his colleagues would see this politically fragmented but culturally convergent process as a confirmation of the Palerm-Wolf theory (Flannery, Kirkby, and Williams, 1967).

Briefly, the Palerm-Wolf theory states that civilization arose in zones where primitive agricultural techniques were easiest and then spread to more difficult zones as more advanced techniques were developed to meet special cultivation needs (Palerm and Wolf, 1960). A highland variant of slash-and-burn cultivation, *tlacolol,* is one of the oldest systems. Irrigation systems with long underground channels, dams, feeder ditches, and other features came much later. Primary centers were those which were able to accumulate techniques. That is, primary centers never discarded the older techniques; they kept them in the repertoires and used them to keep special zones in cultivation. Therefore, primary areas tended to be those, like the Valley of Oaxaca, which were ecologically diverse and which could maintain masses of population by continually developing new subsistence techniques and bringing into cultivation what had formerly been marginal lands. While it is too mechanistic an explanation of the origins of civilized life, this theory does explain certain later features of Mesoamerican prehistory. The spread of Oaxacan Formative communities from the valley bottoms to the piedmont zones, and still later into semiarid areas, can be explained by the theory. Massed population and economic power gave these areas of Mesoamerica, Oaxaca included, a decisive edge over the supposedly more uniform zones like that of the Gulf Coast (the Olmec region). The Valley of Mexico was another such zone of massed demographic and economic power.

The large amount of recent work in the Valley of Oaxaca has produced considerable additional data and theory on the Late and Terminal Formative origins of civilization in that zone. These ideas are better considered in connection with a survey of fully developed Zapotec civilization centered on Monte Alban.

The Central Mexican Formative

Again, in central Mexico we face the picture of a large basin with ecological diversity and, more to the point, cultural diversity very early in the sequence. The chronology chart (Fig. 2-1) outlines the sequences of phases. These phases are largely defined on the basis of pottery, but they have been correlated with the surveys of W. T. Sanders and his associates (Sanders, 1981; Sanders, Parsons, and Santley, 1979).

As noted before, the Basin of Mexico is most favorable for primitive agriculture in its southern sector. Frosts occur less frequently there, and rainfall is greater. The southern basin was the scene of most early events and changes. The first agriculture-based communities occurred in this zone, as did the previously noted first sedentary hamlets. There was a gradation of population density and social evolution from south to north through the Formative period. Sanders notes that there are no permanent village sites known from the northern basin much before 900 B.C. It is possible that the Tlalpan phase from Cuicuilco dates to about 1600 B.C. and that it represents a simple farming hamlet whose inhabitants did hunting and fishing on the side. Pottery made by these people closely resembles that of the early Barra phase in the isthmus. There is no hint of ceremonial architecture.

As noted in the previous chapter, the first securely dated material from permanent settlements appears from about 1300 B.C., is somehow related to the Olmec, and is found at Tlatilco in the middle valley and at Tlapacoya in the southern part. Garbage from Tlapacoya dating from about 1100 B.C. includes tiny maize cobs. Bones of deer, rabbits, gophers, domestic dogs, and people were all found in contexts that suggest that all were used for food. Mud turtles and water birds were eaten, although fish are mysteriously absent from the earliest phases. The Ayutla and Justo subphases have both these traits and Olmec features, which include white-rimmed black ware, large hollow doll figurines, and Olmeclike motifs—the already noted were-jaguar and fire-serpent symbols—on pottery.

The sophisticated traits of Olmec-linked culture drop out about 950 B.C., and the villages of the southern valley seem to suffer a cultural simplification. Even if this is really the case, population growth accelerated from 900 to 100 B.C. Sanders estimates that by 900 B.C. there were only about six thousand people in the valley but that by about 650 B.C. there were twenty thousand. Villages multiplied from about twenty-eight to seventy during the same time, and there are indications that by 600 B.C. the southern lake was solidly edged with communities. Native ceramic traditions slowly evolved, and attractive monochrome brick red, charcoal black, and chocolate brown pottery was made and traded throughout the zone. Red-and-white and red-and-yellow decorations relieved the single-color themes, as did experimentation with form. Low bowls and large water jars are the most common forms, but long-footed plates began to appear toward the end of the Formative period. Modeling in pottery continued. Jade was used in ear ornaments and other personal jewelry, although this material was uncommon, since quite probably the stone already had assumed its mystical and high-status properties and was restricted to persons of high social rank.

From the early phase of the Formative on into the Aztec and early colonial periods we have an uninterrupted series of figurine styles. Made by hundreds of people in dozens of communities over at least three thousand years, thousands of the small relics have been collected and sold to generations of tourists and are still to be found. Many Formative types have female characteristics and are thought to have been associated with the idea of fertility. Human fertility and that of the earth were intertwined; we know that the Aztec hung strings of these little figures over their fields. Another likely function was their use in curing ceremonies; the figurine represented the person and his or her particular ailment. In most contemporary societies that employ them, such figures are discarded or become children's playthings after their primary function has been completed. An extraordinary number of these figurine styles blend into and succeed one another in the Basin of Mexico. They reflect not only an artistic and aesthetic continuity, but also a philosophical-religious continuum.

Clay platforms and more formal architecture appeared certainly at Tlatilco by 1300 B.C. At Cuicuilco, the first round platforms made out of adobe were built about 400 B.C. but were soon replaced by a larger model made of stone, which was about 60,000 cubic meters (over 2 million cubic feet) in volume. These platforms and other public architecture were built in a large town by people using ditch irrigation for subsistence. By 200 B.C. Cuicuilco was large—at least 20 hectares (50 acres) in extent, with about twenty thousand people living in house compounds possibly arranged on a grid pattern. It was the primary community of its time. Tlapacoya built a sophisticated stone platform for ritual purposes about the same time. Obviously these communities were not the only important ones in the valley. There was considerable difference between these large towns with their politico-religious precincts and the rural hamlets which continued the lifeway of the past. Most of the sophisticated communities were clustered in the southern valley, presumably because of its more favorable environment.

In the northern reaches of the basin, the Teotihuacan Valley had a few scattered villages which were contemporary with Zacatenco in the south about 1300 B.C., and these were located on the valley floor near the springs and river. In one of these villages, known as Cuanalan, houses from this early period have been found in apparent clusters inside walls. Such household compounds are reported for Aztec times and are still in use within the Teotihuacan Valley to this day. Present-day compounds are composed of the houses of a man and his wife and their married children, together with a few shacks for cooking and storage. The compound consists of a dusty beaten earth floor, and most of the families' daily work is done under the shade of the trees within the wall. Formative hamlets in the northern valley consisted of groups of these family compounds. This extraordinary continuity of lifeway for some thirty-five hundred years demonstrates, at the least, why archaeologists are interested in traditional communities in the areas in which they work.

While Cuicuilco was building pyramids and performing other wonders, the Teotihuacan Valley finally started to build public architecture. This change, at about 400 B.C., was accompanied by a shift of most communities in the valley up to the tops of small but defensible hills and off the prime farmlands. Many small projectile points are found on these sites. Central to each community is a small pyramid, at least one of which was deliberately destroyed in ancient times. All of these features suggest to Sanders, the discoverer (1965), that during the Late Formative the Valley of Teotihuacan was divided among several warlike communities which headed six small competing states. The motivations of competition were population pressures and the consequent pressures on land. More efficient and competitive social organization may well have developed as a result of this situation of scarce resources and multiplying people.

Cuicuilco was destroyed by a volcanic eruption about 150 B.C., effectively eliminating one of the northern basin's strongest competitors. The lava flow on which the modern University City is built covers the former town. Only the round platforms remain. Unfortunately, a pioneer archaeologist used dynamite to excavate the circular stone structure, and for years it was not certain which came first, lava or pyramid. This was finally clarified by the excavations of Eduardo Noguera.

The Tlaxcala-Puebla Valleys

More than one hundred articles have been published on this area in recent years, based largely on the work of the West German Scientific Mission (Aufdermayer, 1970, 1973; Garcia Cook, 1981). A partial result of this intensive work is a long Formative sequence that begins with agricultural villages dating about 1600 B.C., after which a rapid population buildup evidently began. During the earliest part of this period, about 1200 B.C., nineteen villages are known, thinly scattered over a region of about 2,000 square kilometers (775 square miles). Each village had from ten to twenty-five residences arranged in lines. Houses were also placed on terraces. These small communities used similar pottery which also resembles that of adjacent regions. By 800 B.C. there were more than 150 settlements, and a few larger communities from that time show signs of public architecture in the form of small platforms and probable altars. A few residences were more elaborate, indicating the appearance of social stratification. Agricultural terracing was carried on from the preceding phase and became more elaborate and widespread. The only indication of any contact with Olmec ideas is the rather dubious association made through a limited number of figurines. All in all, the course of cultural evolution seems to have been quite indigenous, although it is clear that these people were in contact with the Valley of Mexico.

During the Middle Formative (ca. 800–400 B.C.) there were great advances in irrigation, with use of pond reservoirs, dams, canals, and large-scale terracing. The recent work of Melvin Fowler (1987) at Amalucan is a clear example of this development of ever more intensive farming techniques. At Amalucan the first moves were toward drainage of an area about 700 B.C. These canals were converted to a full-scale and independent irrigation system at the beginning of the Middle Formative and used until about 200 B.C. The irrigation system was provided with ponds at the upper and lower ends of the network of ditches (Fowler, 1987:fig. 8). This intensification of agriculture was probably spurred by further growth of population to a figure double that of the preceding period. The people lived in a diverse set of communities ranging from hamlets to large towns with populations of from one hundred to more than two thousand. Some of the towns display the features of enclosed plazas, streets, and drainage systems. Sculpture appeared at sites such as Tlalancaleca, and there are some indications of the use of the 260-day calendar and writing. About three hundred towns, villages, and hamlets were arranged in a hierarchy of importance presumably reflecting an administrative organization. Each political system seems to have been associated with a hydraulic system (Fowler, 1987:66). Fortified sites appear about 400 B.C. It seems clear that the Tlaxcala-Puebla zone was tracking the Basin of Mexico in its general evolutionary trends, although it seems to have had a much more rural flavor at this time.

The Late Formative (400 B.C.–A.D. 100) in the Tlaxcala-Puebla area produced a regional florescence as in other parts of Mesoamerica, but one less intense than that in the Basin of Mexico to the west. Population reached a maximum at this time, as did the number of settlements, with the appearance of a few true cities. The nature of the hierarchical settlement pattern leads Angel Garcia Cook (1981) to suggest that the standard political organization was the "city-state," of which there were perhaps twenty. Cholula built its first pyramid during this period. Impressive efforts increased the control over irrigation water for farming and included dikes in rivers as well as the appearance of raised fields (*chinampas*). Many of the better-known deities of Aztec times, including the gods of death and of the morning stars, appeared. An interesting development is that of the increasing ruralization of the region toward the end of the period. This loss of urban features seems to be correlated with the rise of Teotihuacan in the Basin of Mexico. While Garcia Cook feels that a migration of people from the Tlaxcala-Puebla region established the superior social organization of Teotihuacan, another explanation seems more economical. As will be seen in the later prehistory of the basin, Teotihuacan drew in great numbers of people from other towns and cities of the region, effectively depopulating those rival urban centers. It seems likely that the same may have happened to the adjacent Tlaxcala-Puebla region as well.

West Mexican Formative Cultures

Western Mexico is a convenient label for an area which was a vast reservoir of ecological, human, and cultural diversity. If any one statement characterizes the area, it is that there is no apparent unifying cultural or natural pattern to it. No area of Mesoamerica is like it; but then, no area of Mesoamerica is like any other. Modern political definition of the area includes the states of Michoacan, Jalisco, Guanajuato, Colima, Nayarit, and Aguascalientes (Map 4-1), encompassing about 209,151 square kilometers (80,732 square miles).

According to Robert West (1964) the area's geography is created by two major and related environmental factors: volcanic activity and a peculiar hydrography. Large internal drainage basins cover much of the surface between surrounding volcanic features. Large, composite volcanoes, swarms of cinder cones, and many scoria mounds dot the landscape. Some eight hundred cinder cones are to be found between Uruapan and Morelia. The basins are most important for human habitation. A few major rivers pierce the mountainous fence around the plateau and find their ways to the Pacific Ocean. The Río Balsas on the south

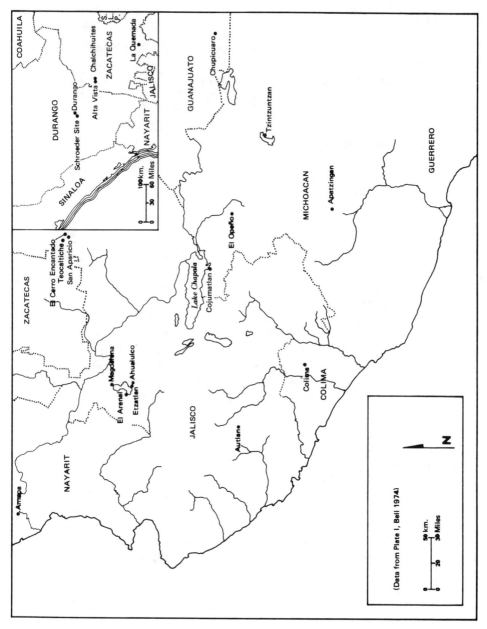

Map A-1. Western and Central Mexican Formative sites

and the Río San Pedro on the north frame the coastal zone, with at least eight other rivers between them. Culturally, the presence of so many waterways is important; they provided easy access from the coast to the interior plateau.

As noted, the first evidence for sedentary communities in the west is from the shell middens of Puerto Márquez, which have preceramic levels certainly earlier than 3000 B.C. This estuarine, seacoast, gathering way of life persisted late on the Pacific Coast, as evidenced by the San Blas phase in Nayarit (ca. 200 B.C.). The earliest sedentary interior material is from only about 1500 B.C. Clearly, in this area, which is as large as the Maya Lowlands, much more work needs to be done to fill in even the most fundamental data on time-space relationships of the ancient cultures.

Western Varieties of the Formative

Most of the archaeological remains of the West Mexican Formative cultures so far studied are of tombs and burials. Even so, it seems that this area of Mesoamerica emphasized death and death ritual more than other Formative cultures. Family crypts appear at about 1300 B.C. and continue until about A.D. 500. These crypts include varieties of chamber tombs. Development of an exuberant and regionally varied tradition of ceramic figures is linked to an emphasis on funeral activities. The sociopolitical level seems to have been that of linked or independent villages with kinship ties as the major integrating force. It is notable that West Mexico was apparently largely isolated and relatively free of interaction with outside cultures, especially the Olmec. This would reinforce the impression that sociopolitical organization was somewhat undeveloped in the west. Flannery's argument (1968) that the Olmec tended to deal with societies of equal sophistication might explain the lack of sustained contact. Only in Michoacan and Guanajuato do traces of contact with Tlatilco show up. In any case, the West Mexican area by 1300 B.C. established a distinctive cultural tradition which was only disturbed by outside events beginning about A.D. 350, when the Mesoamerican high cultures began to penetrate the area. It is uncertain whether there were continuities between the Formative tradition and the historic Tarascan who inhabited some of the same area. At the moment, it seems best to assume that such continuities were indirect at the most.

Earliest Known Cultural Complexes

Aside from the already discussed Puerto Márquez ceramic complex in Guerrero, there is a somewhat later preceramic phase called Matanchen (Meighan, 1972). Matanchen is a mollusk-gathering site in Nayarit, as indicated by the usual mound of shells. It should be pointed out that many people died during the Russian Revolution trying to live on mollusks (M. D. Coe, personal communication); there is a dietary imbalance in such a regimen. Therefore, it is entirely likely that Matanchen represents a periodically or seasonally occupied site at the most. A carbon 14 date of 2000 B.C. was obtained for it.

At approximately 1450 B.C. a ceramic complex known as Capacha appears on the Colima coast, with the pottery found mainly in simple extended burials. Stirrup jars, belted jars, (*bules*), *tecomates,* water jars, and composite forms make up the inventory of shapes, which are decorated by monochrome slipping, zoned punctation, zoned incision, zoned dichrome, and red-on-cream slipping. Similar pottery has been found in Jalisco, Michoacan, and Nayarit, indicating that the western ceramic tradition had begun by that early date, but no close relationships are known outside of the west. On the basis of the stirrup spout form, I. Kelly, the discoverer (1974), suggests that there must be a South American connection of origin to that form. As will be seen, stirrup-spouted jars elsewhere in Mesoamerica date from considerably later. In South America one example has been found in a seacoast culture of Ecuador (Machalilla) which is of about the same date. However, this similarity seems quite a weak one to rely upon. Machalilla culture itself is probably a seacoast variant of Chorrera culture, as we can see in the evidence presented by the excavators (Meggers and Evans, 1962); yet Machalilla is said to be earlier than Chorrera. At present no resolution to this confusion can be made. Therefore, it is specious to defer to a South American priority when basic time-space-content matters are not yet clear for Machalilla. However, this problem is eventually settled, Capacha is the earliest widespread ceramic complex in West Mexico.

In archaeological terms, El Opeño chamber burials of 1300 B.C. are only a little later in date. Work by Eduardo Noguera (1965) and José Arturo Oliveros (1974) has produced good data on the earliest formal tombs known from the west. Nine tombs were found to be dug into a hillside in two lines, all facing west toward the setting sun. All the crypts are similar in construction and are of the simple chamber type, entered by a flight of stairs cut into the volcanic ash subsoil (*talpetate*). Ovoid chambers are found at the base of the stairs. The tombs contained multiple burials, with as many as ten individuals in one chamber. In Tomb 3, nine skulls were found piled separately from the long bones which were sorted and stacked—an indication of disturbance and rearrangement. In several tombs there was evidence of repeated entrance and reuse, not only in the piling of bones but also in the layering of burials one above another.

The Opeño ceramic complex is actually a funerary subcomplex, lacking the almost certainly contemporary utility types of pottery. Nonetheless, the group is quite diagnostic and is related to Capacha as well as to some late Tlatilco pottery. Late San Pablo ceramics in Morelos are also similar.

Ceramic similarities are reinforced by similarities in obsidian point types to some found at Tlatilco. Many of the considerable number of solid figurines from El Opeño are like those from the Valley of Mexico. On the other hand, some figurines are regionalized in style and may relate to Chupicuaro types. An Olmec-style motif, the St. Andrew's cross, was incised on a greenstone pectoral, and Caribbean seashells confirm wide connections at El Opeño about 1300 B.C. All of this is a stronger indication of outside contact than that known for any other early western complex. Unfortunately, we do not have a clue to the nature of the community that used the Opeño area as a cemetery.

Later Varieties of Formative Cultures and Chambered Tombs

The lower Balsas River has produced a phase which is approximately Middle Formative, or dating to about 800–500 B.C. Infiernillo-phase burials, located on beaches, have yielded pottery which consists mainly of globular jars decorated by zoned incision, with pendant triangles and opposed triangles as a characteristic motif. One such burial also contained bracelets of shell, decorated with incised parrots. Small reddish bone carvings of "ducks" were found in the same grave.

By the beginning of the Late Formative stage (250 B.C.) a distinctive set of burial customs was operating in the west. The strongest expression of this funerary philosophy is in the shaft-tomb area, which is a geographic arc running from southern Nayarit south through Jalisco and curving west into Colima and to the Pacific Coast. Chamber tombs in this arc consist of deep vertical shafts 3 to 18 meters (10 to 60 feet) deep, with ovoid tombs either directly off the shafts at various levels or connected with the shafts by lateral tunnels (Fig. 4-11). Burial offerings from these tombs are distinctive and patterned. Large hollow-pottery figures, which are common, vary stylistically from zone to zone, but there are often mixtures of styles within a single chamber. Elaborate polychrome pottery accompanied the dead, as well as slate-backed pyrite-mosaic mirrors and conch-shell trumpets.

This complex of offerings is also found in zones where shaft-tomb burials do not occur. For example, in the Magdalena Lake district of Jalisco, the complex occurs in mound burials, "as it also does in regular burials in the Lake Chapala Basin" (M. Bond, personal communication, 1976). At Cerro Encantado to the northeast, the complex is found with both simple burials and some chamber tombs something like the earlier El Opeño models. Regardless of the wildly variant styles of tomb figures, there was a widespread similarity in funeral ritual in the west beginning about 500 B.C., and it lasted a thousand years (to A.D. 500).

Worse hit by pot hunters than most areas of Mesoamerica, all the west has suffered from looting, which has been fantastic in its proportions. Only at the Cerro Encantado and El Arenal sites have archaeologists

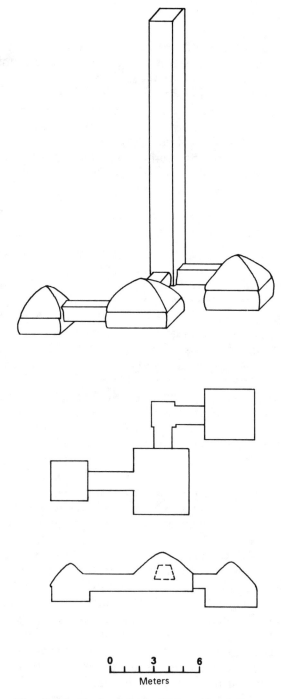

0　　3　　6
Meters

Fig. 4–11. Shaft tombs at El Opeño, Michoacan.

found undisturbed or semidisturbed burials which show stratigraphic and other associations among the artifacts. Philip Weigand (1974) estimates that the Etzatlan region alone has yielded eight to ten thousand tomb figures to the antiquity market. Even so, Peter Furst estimates that only 30 percent of the tombs have been found in one badly ravaged area.

Almost endless detailed variation in the styles of the figurines has led to a rough classification of the hollow types. The Chinesca type is a grouping of figurines with vaguely oriental features; apparently it comes from the Nayarit zone. Colima redware is from Colima, San Sebastian red and Arenal brown figures are localized in northern Jalisco, and Horned (Cornudo) figures come from northeastern Jalisco and southern Zacatecas. These categories are based on stylistic similarities and undoubtedly have some basis in reality. How much so we will be able to judge only when archaeologists find the figures in context and association.

Although less revealing than the Nayarit village scenes to be discussed below, the hollow figurines do give a good deal of information about social life and other affairs in the ancient past. Warriors in armor, men and women in everyday dress or undress, women with babies, people sitting, and other scenes give an impression of attempts at portraiture. The famous dog figures bark, snarl, sleep, and seem faithful enough. Perhaps the figures were meant to surround the dead persons in their tombs with a semblance of the actual life with which they had once been surrounded.

Until Weigand's recent work (1974) we have had practically no information on the settlement patterns and communities that supported these rich burials. Let us now turn to that research.

Etzatlan and El Arenal Tomb. Weigand and his colleagues have examined an area of several hundred square kilometers and classified some 348 sites. Some of these sites are only activity locations: kill spots, hunting stations, and workshops. All of the other sites are grouped into patterns of habitation mounds: semicircles or circles around a central burial mound. The simplest kind of group designated "type 4," is typically a single burial mound with a semicircle of house mounds around it. It is also the most common type of site and was probably the sort of small hamlet in which most of the ancient populations lived. Type 4 sites are eight to fourteen times as numerous as type 2 and type 3 sites. The simplest tombs, accompanied by one or two pottery figures, are found in these type 4 hamlet sites.

The larger sites (types 2 and 3) have correspondingly more elaborate tombs and burial goods. The famous shaft tomb of El Arenal is in a type 2 site, and in spite of its clandestine excavation in the 1930s, Eduardo Noguera (1965) recovered a great deal of valuable information about the skeletal and pottery arrangements in it. Another tomb was found nearby at San Sebastian, and Furst (1974) salvaged information about it. Some seventeen hollow figures were in a chamber along with forty polychrome vessels which probably had held food at the time of burial. The pottery figures were of several styles and were grouped around the skeletons of a dozen individuals. Boxes with covers, shell trumpets, and obsidian mirrors were also in the burial. A carbon 14 date of A.D. 250 was obtained. The figurines in the Etzatlan–zone tombs and burials are most often of ball players, warriors, and pregnant women. Weigand (1974) says that many of the tombs were originally painted with murals, although these had been poorly preserved.

Weigand thinks that the hierarchically arranged communities were linked through kinship ties, specifically through ranked lineages. Each tomb figure style may symbolically represent a lineage as well as a community craft specialty.

There is only one type 1 site in the valley, Ahualulco, which is a combination of types 2, 3, and 4. Ahualulco's mounds and ceramics cover about 1.3 square kilometers (0.5 square mile), with obsidian artifacts found over about 3.9 square kilometers (1.5 square miles). Weigand (1974) has set up a local sequence as follows:

Phases	Ahualulco Chronology
Etzatlan	A.D. 1200 to 1522
Huistla	A.D. 800 to 1200
Tenuchitlan	
(Late Classic)	A.D. 350/400 to 900
Ahualulco	
(Late Formative–	
Early Classic)	A.D. 150/200 to 350/400
El Arenal	1000 B.C.(?) to A.D. 150/200

At this point we are interested only in the two earliest phases, Arenal and Ahualulco. Weigand thinks that during Arenal times, all communities in the valley were more or less on a parity. After A.D. 150 or so, Ahualulco became larger than any other center and politically dominated the whole valley. An early contact with Teotihuacan may have something to do with the integration of the whole valley into Ahualulco's orbit. About A.D. 350, contact with Teotihuacan became much more direct, and the great central plateau city dominated this western valley. Ahualulco lost its importance, and shaft-tomb burial began to die out. The prestige of dominant local lineages may have been destroyed by Teotihuacan, and therefore the symbolic and status-reinforcing burial rituals dropped into disuse.

Cerro Encantado

Betty Bell (1974a) has excavated this important site in the arid region northeast of Jalisco. As noted before, the shaft-tomb artifactual complex is found at the site, even though the tombs themselves are absent. Bell found an undisturbed burial with a pair of Horned (Cornudo) figures in it. Actually, these figures are typically male-female pairs, with only the males having the mushroom-shaped horns on their heads. An associated carbon 14 date indicated A.D. 100–250 for this style. Pottery at Cerro Encantado shows relationships to the Chupicuaro culture group to the east and to the Canutillo and Alta Vista phases (A.D. 200 to 500) of Chalchihuites culture to the north.

Nayarit Villagers

The southern highlands of Nayarit was the homeland of an extraordinarily lively set of ceramic models which reflect everyday life in an amusing and detailed manner (Fig. 4-12). No southern Nayarit figurine or model has ever been found by an archaeologist in an undisturbed context. Gifford thought that these models belonged to a period dating from about A.D. 1 to 500 (early Ixtlan). This remarkable type of anecdotal sculpture has been categorized and analyzed by Hasso von Winning (1974; von Winning and Hammer, 1972). Most of its scenes fall into the following types: house models showing domestic life; ball games played in courts; and village scenes of infinite variety. War, tragedy, gaiety, life crises, and mundane, quiet domesticity are all shown. The village models show funeral processions in which catafalques are carried on pallbearers' shoulders through crowds of people. Adults mourn dead children; a small figure lies on the ground within a circle of seated persons who gaze at the child. Volador ceremonies take place on poles erected in the center of a group of houses; a man balances on his stomach on the top of a pole. Dignitaries are carried in elaborate litters by groups of men. Villagers dance and drink in riotous festivals. Family groups engage in quiet conversation outside their houses. Women prepare meals for their families. Women in childbirth are assisted by midwives. Groups of warriors on hills defend their villages against other groups. Figures strapped on beds are suggested by von Winning to be bodies ready for interment. Bloodletting ceremonies, involving piercing the cheeks with rods, are frequent. Sometimes the rod runs through several persons' cheeks as they stand in line. In short, we are provided with a rare look at daily life which is as close as the archaeologist gets to doing ethnography.

The pottery models from Nayarit undoubtedly have some regional distinctiveness, but they may generally reflect the quality of life and its major features throughout these Late Formative times.

Judging from the figures and the scenes, the villages were socially stratified and had specialized leadership, but that organization stopped short of urban complexities. Village models show elaborately decorated and complex houses, but they are no more so than are the houses of ethnographically known Chiapas villages and ceremonial centers. On the

Fig. 4–12. Ceramic model, probably from Nayarit, of a domestic scene in a village house.

other hand, there is little depicted of civic architecture. Small round platforms in the centers of villages, some ball courts probably with clay walls, and rather low platform foundations for houses are the extent of formal architecture. These features do not reflect access to manpower above the village level. Nor does housing show significant differences above the ranked levels found in most village societies. The models also indicate that most men engaged in warfare, but there is no sure evidence of specialist warriors (Fig. 4-13). Funerary activities were extremely important, and kinship ties undoubtedly were the main principle of social organization. The great men of the western villages probably were such partly because of their superior lineages. The inferences which can be drawn from these Nayarit scenes are remarkably congruent with the data from Etzatlan settlement patterns.

The Chupicuaro Culture Group

The Chupicuaro site is gone forever under a lake created by a modern dam. During the archaeological salvage project in the 1940s, however, some 390 burials, many richly furnished with brilliant pottery, were dug out. Some forty-six dog burials accompanied human graves. Muriel Porter Weaver (Porter, 1953), who made the most extensive report on the site, defined two periods, early and late, but Bennyhoff and McBride have suggested that the periods she defined should be reversed—that is, that early is really late and late is really early (Chadwick, 1971). Because Weaver (1981) accepts these revisionist arguments, which are based on the figurine sequence of the Valley of Mexico, we may do so as well. Such figurines are found in the Chupicuaro burials, and thus they can be ordered by a knowledge of the sequence of appearance of figurine types in the valley from whence they originated. The argument is over the correct seriation of figurines. However, rather than confuse things even more, and to avoid absolute bedlam should Bennyhoff and McBride prove to be mistaken, we will call early Chupicuaro the Chupicuaro Black Ware phase and late Chupicuaro the Chupicuaro Brown Ware phase.

The Chupicuaro Brown Ware phase, now considered probably earlier, dates from about 200 B.C. to A.D. 1, according to McBride. Common to both phases are red, red on buff, painted pattern, and black polychromes, but the Brown Ware phase is characterized by a heavy reliance on, of course, brown wares, including brown polychrome, as well as by specific Protoclassic forms in all types. Tetrapod bowls with swollen feet are especially diagnostic. Shoe-shaped pots are a favorite form, as are fruit stands, boxes, and linked cylinders. Many textilelike designs are found on the black polychromes.

Chupicuaro Black Ware phase, apparently the later phase, emphasizes black-slipped pottery. The pottery has been simplified, and red-rimmed, red, red on buff, and black polychromes are characteristic. In both periods are found large, hollow figures painted black and red on cream and figures strapped to a bed. The intimate connection of the hollow-figurine and the bed-figurine traditions with the figurines of the chamber tombs farther west perhaps indicates a commonality of burial ritual and belief.

In both periods, graves were furnished with a wealth of domestic tools and ornaments. Many items of bone possibly useful in textile manufacture were found, as well as a number of musical instruments. The latter

Fig. 4–13. Ceramic model of a Late Formative West Mexican warrior.

consisted of the usual complement of Mesoamerican ocarinas, rattles, rasps, and turtle-shell drums. Again, as at so many sites, we have at Chupicuaro a cemetery without information about its supporting communities, but there is no doubt that Chupicuaro represents an exuberant ceramic tradition in full flower. Chupicuarolike ceramics are distributed widely over Guanajuato state and into the Tula area (Tepeji del Río) and the Teotihuacan Valley (at Cuanalan). Clearly, Chupicuaro was an affluent variant of Late Formative Mesoamerica.

The Ortices complex in Colima is mainly known from its great variety of extraordinarily fine red-ware hollow figures: cleverly and deftly done animal, vegetable, and human effigies. These figures apparently come from the shaft tombs in the southern end of their distribution arc. The Chanchopa tomb is one example; it also yielded a thin orange pot from Teotihuacan II (Miccaotli), and it had a carbon 14 date of A.D. 10.

Deposition of the Morett midden site on the Colima coast probably began in the Late Formative period. Certain incised types of pottery at Morett resemble Tuxcacuesco ceramics, a type of pottery in Jalisco dominated by red wares. Solid figurines included in the complex have similarities to Ortices figurines.

A number of other regional complexes dot the west during this period but are less well defined, and in any case, pottery is not people. We can only say that the west seems to have been thoroughly settled by peoples with a fairly unified set of beliefs expressed in a variety of funeral customs. Ceramic linkages among the various regions indicate widespread trade and contact, but not on any basis more sophisticated than the village market level.

Maya Beginnings in the Lowlands

Like all of the major areas of Mesoamerica, the Maya Lowlands are ecologically diverse within themselves (Sanders, 1973, 1977). Annual rainfall there varies from a semiarid 50 centimeters (20 inches) on Yucatan's north coast to an overwhelming 635 centimeters (250 inches) in a small zone of the southwestern lowlands on the Chiapas escarpment. Vegetation varies accordingly, with lower scrub thorn jungle in the north giving way about 60 kilometers (37 miles) north of the present Guatemalan border to higher tropical forest, and finally, along the Pasión and Usumacinta rivers, to three- and five-canopy forest. Technically, the jungle is monsoon forest, adjusted to an annual cycle of distinct dry and rainy seasons. These seasons fall into a Mesoamerica-wide period of January to May for the dry months and June to December for the rainy months. Water is carried off by the great rivers of the southern lowlands and replenishes the lakes of the central Peten. The coastal zones of the Gulf and Caribbean consist of flood plains of substantial rivers, such as the Belize, up to a line running across the peninsula from Champoton to

Chetumal. North of a series of fault lines which run east-west through the central Peten, there is very little surface water either inland or on the coasts. Instead, the rain drains down through the massive unbedded limestone to a water table far out of reach of wells. Small water catchments (*aguadas*) supply a certain amount of water during the dry season, but many dry up as May approaches. In the far northern lowlands, the water table is only twenty feet or less below the surface, and in many cases the subsurface streams have worn away the bedrock, which has dropped through to form large natural wells locally called *cenotes*. Early populations clustered around these sources, and the later Maya developed reservoir techniques to stretch dry-season water supplies.

Communication from one part of the lowlands to another is usually not difficult, only tedious. In the south, the main rivers give access to the interior from the Gulf and the Caribbean coasts. North of the Central Peten lakes, however, it is generally a matter of walking to get through the vast spaces of central Yucatan. In fact, because of difficulties of portages and rapids, the river passages in the south were only usable to the limits of the coastal plains. During the Classic period transportation was improved by the digging of many canals in swamps and the apparent improvement of river beds. Crossing the peninsula was such an arduous task in the sixteenth century for the tough long-distance merchants of Mesoamerica that they preferred to go around Yucatan by canoe, but even this means had its limits. For example, north of Campeche City there is a 12-kilometer-wide (7.5-mile-wide) band of mangrove swamp which is very difficult to penetrate. In ancient and colonial times, canals, which can still be seen today on aerial photographs, were cut through the swamps. In earliest times these improvements had not yet been made.

Mineral resources on the peninsula are scarce, but everything necessary to sustain human life is and was present. Salt was collected on the northwestern corner of the peninsula, the second largest salt-producing area in modern Mexico. Basalt and the harder varieties of limestone were available in various parts for use as food grinders. The forest, animals, birds, and sea life all provided rich resources on which early farmers with primitive techniques could draw. Only one near necessity was lacking: obsidian, the material from which the universal tool of Mesoamerica, the flake-blade, was made. However, deposits of obsidian in the highlands of Guatemala were accessible to lowland peoples through a trade network. It is well known that obsidian lasts a long time and that relatively little was needed. It is calculated that even from the Coban zone of the northern Guatemalan highlands, under good conditions it would take about two weeks to transport goods to Tikal in the central Peten.

Earliest Known Pioneers

The Early Formative is remarkably weak in the Maya Lowlands. As has been seen, there are indications of very ancient hunters and gatherers and of archaic cultures in Northern Belize. The earliest certain agricultural villages date to the Middle Formative, about 1000 B.C. This is the Swasey phase, also of northern Belize. It was formerly thought to be considerably older, but a new series of radiocarbon dates has indicated otherwise (Hammond and Andrews V, in press). Swasey has been defined on the basis of excavations at the small site of Cuello. Carbonized plant remains in the deepest levels there have proven to include maize. The corn farmers of Cuello lived in timber-framed houses set directly on the ground level. Very soon, these early people laid down plaster floors around their houses, probably in order to control the problems of drainage and mud.

The Xe (pronounced "Shay") villages on the Pasión River are nearly of the same age as Cuello but have a somewhat distinctive pottery. Two sites, Altar de Sacrificios and Seibal, have produced pottery and other evidence to indicate that these people are also early agricultural colonists. It is almost certain that there are earlier remains along the coasts of the peninsula which would be in the category of MacNeish's earliest sedentary community. Jack D. Eaton's surveys turned up an amazing number of shell mounds, most of which are Formative in date, but none are as early as the Xe farming villages on the Pasión.

The Xe frontiersmen also built small villages of perishable houses directly on the jungle floor, in contrast to the later Maya, who built their houses on platforms for drainage and better ventilation. This practice may indicate that these early settlers came either from hill country, where there was no need for platforms, or from an area of less rainfall. By that time a full complement of plants was available to the lowland villages, although there is little direct evidence because of poor conditions for preservation. Xe pottery is well developed, although it makes use of the *tecomate* and flat pan forms characteristic of most Middle Formative Mesoamerican cultures. The major functions of pottery are as cooking pots, storage vessels for liquids, serving dishes, and transportation vessels. Water jars are invariably slippery, and in present-day pottery-using communities they last about a year. Part of the solution to the problem of slipperiness was the addition of handles. Another was roughening of the surface of the jar to make it easier to grip. Handles were used on Xe pottery, but the later Maya changed to the roughening solution.

Not much pottery that can be called ceremonial was found in the Xe remains—certainly none that indicates ritual and religious life as do the later informative Maya polychromes. Small, hand-modeled figurines are thought to be items for curing and fertility ceremonies. Presumably, spiritual life was on the level of curing, shamanism, and divination and was animistic, with little community leadership. Judging by similar nonwestern traditional communities, every household was responsible for its own spiritual well-being. No ceremonial structures have been found in either Xe or Swasey sites.

Communities were small and isolated. The two Xe villages now known probably numbered less than a hundred people each. Survival in a world of virtually untouched forest and rivers meant meeting tough daily challenges. At that time, the Pasión was full of tasty fish and turtles but was also full of alligators. The woods contained deer, wild pigs, rodents, and other food animals, but also the formidable jaguar and an awesome tribe of snakes.

We have only hints about the origins of these dauntless groups. A cruciform deposit of jade axes at Seibal is very similar to Olmec deposits. A characteristic Olmec artifact, a jade "letter opener," was found in this cache. Close similarities between Chiapa de Corzo III (Escalera) pottery and that of Xe also indicate that the pioneers may have come into the lowlands from the Gulf Coast zone. However, the ceramics are quite distinct in most respects. Likewise, there is a similarity to simple pottery of the Kal complex used at this time in the Chalchuapa zone of El Salvador, where ceremonial buildings were already being erected. Possible linkages to the Guatemalan highland site of Sakajut near Coban indicate that Xe and the highland peoples may have been in contact or related. Certainly Xe people were in contact with the highlands in some manner; they were obtaining obsidian. However, it is also possible that lowland people had colonized Sakajut, which is just on the edge of the highlands. Therefore, we are left with the probability that Xe people came from one coast or another, or from the highlands, but certainly not as part of a direct colonizing movement.

The Swasey material has not helped at all in solving this problem, inasmuch as it seems vaguely related to Xe and to the succeeding Mamom pottery but shows no similarities to any known outside complexes. These early people had no close links with the great events of the Early Formative, such as the Olmec religious movement or their trading ventures. The Maya Lowlands seem to have been a vast, untamed wilderness which absorbed a great many people and their efforts before their cultures began to evolve from a backwater status.

Slow Evolution

Slow, uneven population growth occurred from 1000 to 500 B.C. (Middle Formative), resulting in the proliferation of small farming communities throughout the peninsula. There are indications that this erratic population growth became an explosion after 550 B.C. The reasons for the apparent jump in numbers of people are obscure. Perhaps larger families became an economic advantage in farming. In any case, there was a filling up of the landscape by ever more numerous villages, presumably colonies from the older communities. In these villages very similar red, black, and cream potteries were made and used throughout the Maya Lowlands during the Mamom period (550–300 B.C.). At Dzibilchaltun in the north, a long occupation begun about 800 B.C. continued in the small hamlets of the zone; platform building began about 500 B.C. Loltun Cave, not far away, has a carved figure which is Izapan in style. The Mani Cenote pottery, once thought to be much earlier, has proven to be Mamom in date. In the Río Bec zone, around the site of Becan, Mamom remains are the earliest. Villages of this date are especially numerous in the southern lowlands, occurring around Tikal, on the Pasión River, and in the lower Usumacinta area.

A computer simulation has been run for this period using population growth and available arable land as the only factors (Koenig, personal communication). The result of the simulation is a nearly random and even scattering of villages, and the actual archaeological samples reflect the same pattern, indicating that the two factors mentioned were probably the most important in the spread and dispersion of population in the Middle Formative.

A noteworthy feature of many of these sites is the beginning of formal architecture and special buildings dedicated to ritual. The architecture is simple and variable. At Dzibilchaltun, packed earthen walls with stucco floors were tried, later developing into packed stone structures. At Altar de Sacrificios, packed lime and ash floors supported the same simple thatch-and-pole buildings lived in by the preceding Xe farmers. Three of the buildings raised on platforms there were grouped around a plaza in what is clearly a ceremonial precinct; the plaza remained a temple zone throughout the remaining fourteen hundred years of the site's occupation. At a small site in Belize, greater sophistication in building techniques appears on the Mamom level: a low, two-stage platform was made of cut stone covered with plaster. Because this is the basic building technique later elaborated on in the Classic civilization, it is clear that experimentation with the idea started far back in the Formative stage.

Small, hand-modeled figurines, most representing human females, indicate the continuation of fertility and curing ideas, but the appearance of mushroom-shaped pots may indicate something more. Hallucinogenic mushrooms occur in this zone of Mesoamerica and are still used as aids to communication with the supernatural in divination, curing, and other ceremonies. Stephen Borhegyi suggests that these mushroom pots reflect the religious use of hallucinogens in that period.

A strikingly different pattern has recently been found by Richard Hansen and his colleagues at the north central Peten site of Nakbe. Hansen found and excavated several large terraced platforms faced with stone, and dating to the Mamom period. A radiocarbon date from one of the structures reads as 620 B.C. The summit of one of the platforms supported a group of three temples, which pattern seems to characterize the later formative buildings at nearby El Mirador (Hansen, personal communication, 1990). The precocity of Nakbe is one of its most interesting features at the moment, but it also seems to show some of the characteristics of later Maya civilization. Nakbe appears to have been abandoned by about 250 B.C., although a Late Formative monument was erected there during a brief reoccupation.

The population explosion, the appearance of ceremonial buildings, however simple, and the uniformity of far-flung Mamom culture at this time all demand an explanation beyond a simple statement of their existence. They reflect a lifeway centered on small villages of pole-and-thatch houses scattered thickly throughout the forested lowlands. An occasional village had one or more elevated structures with more sophisticated features. These were apparently centers of worship. The very large buildings at Nakbe are the exception to this rule.

The uniformity of pottery and other material culture during this period probably reflects a process of extension of settlement based on slash-and-burn agriculture. Later regionalisms of Maya culture grew partly in response to geographic isolation, so we believe that Mamom, because of its peninsula-wide homogeneity, represents a fairly rapid expansion of a population which subsequently did not have time to develop regional distinctions. The use of shifting cultivation in an area of unlimited land would have produced this effect. Since relatively great amounts of land were required for relatively small numbers of people, the population would have had to spread out into previously uninhabited zones as it grew. The Maya transformed their natural environment gradually by cutting down the forests, slowly modifying the watercourses, and leveling many zones. This process of ecological modification accelerated during the next stage.

A similar process took place in the great primeval forests of Europe about 5000 B.C., when the earliest Danubian farmers began to spread into western Europe (Piggott, 1965). Villages were established at a great rate, abandoned, and reoccupied. Slash-and-burn cultivation was used by these early Danubians, and this extensive form of cultivation led to expansion. Transient and shifting communities were characteristic, then, of both the early Maya and the early Europeans, but no connection is implied.

We must note again that there is little or no evidence of significant influence from the startling cultural growth taking place among the Gulf Coast centers.

The Transformation of Maya Culture

A sequence of events occurring over a period of five hundred years transformed Maya culture from a village-centered, more or less egalitarian society to one oriented around formal urban centers containing elite residents presiding over a society of ranked classes. At this moment in our studies, the processes and events are included in a single phase—the Chicanel (250 B.C. to A.D. 250), a Late Formative culture.

There is a clear continuity between Mamom pottery and the later waxy red, black, and cream Chicanel monochromes. Again, in the earlier part of the phase (ca. 250 B.C. to ca A.D. 150) the context is that of village life, with astounding uniformity of ceramics over the entire 251,230 square kilometers (97,000 square miles) of the Maya Lowlands. Slightly accelerated population growth seems to have occurred during this earlier period, creating larger communities and filling up the landscape. About midway through the phase, however, some clearly different things happened. Probably least noticeable to the Maya, but ultimately most important, they had drastically modified their landscape and environment by clearing forests, rectifying watercourses, and leveling land. By A.D. 1 the forests were tamed, and farmers and their families were virtually everywhere.

It is estimated that about fifty small trees are required for a standard rural Maya house today (Wauchope, 1938). This does not include the great amounts of leaves for thatch which are gathered from one species of palm. As noted by Matheny and his associates (1983), a thousand houses, enough to house about five thousand people, would require about fifty thousand small trees. Population was dense enough to force some people in some zones such as northern Belize to use swamp drainage and reclamation techniques as well as hillside terracing. Colha, in northern Belize, became a producer of thousands of high-quality and standardized stone tools, which were used in wetland cultivation in nearby Pulltrouser Swamp.

Meanwhile, many centers were erecting much more elaborate architecture. Yaxuna in far northern Yucatan has a pyramid dating from this phase which is over 18 meters (60 feet) high and which measures about 61 by 128 meters (200 by 420 feet) at the base. Cut stone masonry was used to build this platform, which undoubtedly supported a temple, as did the identical later pyramids. To the west of Yaxuna, at Dzibilchaltun, the use of cut stone masonry was well established, although the buildings were much smaller. The largest Middle and Late Formative center in northwestern Yucatan was Komchen, which covered about 2 square kilometers (0.8 square miles) by A.D. 150, with perhaps three thousand people living around a center formed by five large platforms with their presumed buildings atop them (Ringle and Andrews, 1982). Concentric zoning, a causeway, and other features set Komchen apart as a regional variant of early Maya civilization. Looting has badly damaged this important site, but it is apparent that it subsisted on more than its own agriculture; it may have controlled the nearby salt fields and may have been tied into a trade network which was based on canoe traffic around the peninsula.

The site of Edzna is even more impressive in the efforts expended by its large populations during this period. A huge canal system more than

12 kilometers (7 miles) long was built as a combination reservoir and irrigation source. Irrigated fields, similar to European "water meadows," were created along the canal, and extensions of the canal to the north were made to bring more land into intensive cultivation (Matheny, 1983). A fortress, built into the canal system, was connected with public architecture in the main center by a raised causeway. The immensity of this system of public works may be judged by the fact that the canal system taps water drainage from an area of 220 square kilometers (85 square miles) and has a capacity of at least 220 million cubic meters (7.8 billion cubic feet) of water. The population and social organization needed to build, maintain, and operate such a system were substantial.

El Mirador and the preliminary work there has changed a great many of our ideas about the nature of the Maya Late Formative and its transformation. The work of Dahlin, Matheny, Demarest, and Sharer (Matheny, 1980) all indicates that by A.D. 1, and perhaps earlier, El Mirador was an immense center, calling on thousands of people and controlled by an elite which could plan the construction of an incredibly large and complex system. El Mirador consists of several groups of very large buildings, at least two of which are placed on immense basal platforms. The Danta group terraces and temples alone contain about 2 million cubic meters (70 million cubic feet) of material. Furthermore, the group is surrounded by an impressive embankment 1,300 meters (nearly a mile) long, 20 meters (65 feet) wide, and 6 meters (20 feet) high. This was capped off by high superstructures decorated by large stucco masks of jaguars in various parts and guises. This is not the only large group of temples at El Mirador. It is connected to other centers by a radiating set of causeways that reach out as far as 23 kilometers (14 miles). At the end of the Formative, El Mirador lost its grip and became a secondary center, with no significant public construction thereafter. We will consider this abrupt decline in El Mirador's fortunes when discussing the nature of Maya civilization and its political organization.

At Becan in the central zone (Río Bec region), a large platform 14 meters (45 feet) high was built, and smaller buildings with masonry and stucco platforms and walls topped with thatched roofs were erected. Sometime during the Late Formative, a fortification was built around this and other formal buildings. The defensive system consisted of a dry moat, with earthen ramparts on the inside. More than 126,000 cubic meters (4.4 million cubic feet) of materials were moved in building these fortifications. Further south, at Uaxactun, one of the most elaborate Late Formative structures was built: a pyramid which is decorated with the modeled stucco heads of serpents and jaguars. Twelve miles to the south, Tikal was burying its important dead in formal masonry chambers within platforms. In one of these burials the dead dignitary was furnished with a jade mask with inlaid shell teeth. Red and black monochrome pottery in the burial is distinctive only in form from the general run of Chicanel ceramics. An early temple in Tikal's north acropolis was painted with a procession of human figures dressed in feathers and costumes. The figures are bent around the outside corners of the structure, apparently to give them more dimension. The style of these figures is reminiscent of Izapan art, although probably not derived from it. Fragments of carved stone indicate that the Late Formative inhabitants of Tikal were experimenting with sculpture. Tikal also fortified itself with about 40 kilometers (25 miles) of dry moats and ramparts on both the north and south perimeters of the city. There is no doubt that there was something there worth protecting, and someone to protect it against.

One hundred forty-five kilometers (90 miles) to the southwest, on the Pasión River, the Altar de Sacrificios center possessed three temples and possible residential structures grouped around a plaza. Also at that center, an attempt was made to erect a tomb for a distinguished person. As in the Tikal tomb, the tomb pottery is only distinctive from other red, black, and cream pottery by excellence in finish and form. Small incense burners and the continued use of mushroom pots give us some indication of ritual.

Pendergast's (1981) long-term work at the Belize site of Lamanai has produced evidence of huge structures, decorated with modeled stucco, built during the Late Formative. The center is very large for its time. The not-far-distant site of Cerros is an interesting example of a Maya port complete with canoe basin and jetty. It is also associated with raised fields. The pyramidal structures inside its boundary canal are decorated with symbols of the sun god (Robertson and Freidel, 1986). Freidel and Schele (1988) have interpreted the iconography as reflecting the identification of Maya rulers with jaguar and the sun. The jaguar was thought to be the form taken by the sun when it descended into the underworld at nightfall.

Direct evidence of more elaborate buildings and some ritual parapher-nalia indicates a formalized Maya religion. However, these materials were only the stage and props on which and with which the actual liturgies took place, and we have little evidence of the latter. We have even fewer ideas about the philosophical concepts which underlay the religious practices, although we can draw analogies. Presumably life crises, political community matters, nervous farmers, and a desire to foresee the future determined many of the functions of early Maya religion. These functions are near-universals in human religions. Curing ceremonies and rites to aid in life crises are especially emphasized in village-oriented societies. The more highly organized the society, the more functions are taken on by religion and the more need that exists for specialists. Possibly the dignitaries buried in the early tombs gave not only community direction but also religious leadership. Certainly the early tombs reflect increasingly stratified society and, at least at Tikal, the concentration of some wealth in the hands of a small part of society.

During this same period, Maya writing and the mathematical system were developed and applied to problems of time and astronomy to produce a formal set of calendars. The writing system is closely related to formal art, and there is a good deal of interchange in symbolism between the expressions of intellect and aesthetics. An increasing number of finds now indicate the nature of writing in this early period. An incised glyph on a Chicanel vessel was found at Colha (D. Potter, personal communication, 1982). Nearby and smaller Kichpanha produced a whole text which Peter Mathews interprets as including a personal name (Gibson, Shaw, and Finamore, 1986). These first signs of writing seem to be ownership statements as much as anything, but they may be misleading in that regard because there are so few of them.

The last one hundred years of the Formative seems to have been the initial florescence of Maya civilization. This period, not yet given an agreed-upon name, dates from about A.D. 150 to 250, and in it one can see most of the features of the Early and Late Classic periods of the lowlands.

The Izapa-related art at various points, and other indications of outside contact, hint at some stimulation from widespread Mesoamerican phenomena. However, as nearly as we can determine, the Late Formative Maya world was still largely isolated for most of its inhabitants and penetrated only occasionally by ideas diffused from elsewhere. The rest of their cultural apparatus was evidently developed on their own.

After A.D. 150, it is clear that there were both ceremonial centers with little permanent population in them as well as true cities. In some of these, perhaps all of them, the earliest polychrome painted pottery appeared as a status item for the elite groups. The painted symbols evidently are those of family or larger kin groups and served to set apart the elite families from the rest of society, which continued to use the older types of monochrome pottery for another century or so.

It was once considered possible that Central American elites had intruded into the Maya Lowlands and assumed the leadership roles of Maya society. Indeed, Payson Sheets (1971) has found irrefutable evidence of a violent eruption of at least one volcano in El Salvador which, he suggests, lay down dense blankets of ash about 100 B.C., driving farming populations out of the Chalchuapa zone and possibly into the Maya Lowlands. It now appears more likely that they went into the ecologically and culturally similar highlands of Guatemala. Formative pottery traditions continue largely undisturbed throughout the Maya Lowlands, and the monochrome reds of this period clearly give rise to the later red pottery of the Classic.

Further to the north, slate wares and architectural styles peculiar to the northern peninsula were developed. At Dzibilchaltun we seem to have roughly parallel developments in the full emergence of ceremonial centers and directing elites.

By the beginning of the Classic period (ca. A.D. 250–550), we can define at least five regionalized variants of Maya culture. The northern and central Yucatecan are the most indigenous and least affected by outside influence, except perhaps by example. The flowering of the central Peten zone is clearly derived from regional Late Formative cultures but is distinct in pottery, architecture, and social organization. The centers in the Pasión River zone form a variant different perhaps because of the distinct origins of the population from the Gulf Coast. In northern Belize we have a rather cosmopolitan set of centers which were linked with the north by the canoe trade.

Explanations of the Rise of Maya Civilization

It is easier for us to understand the ultimate collapse of Maya civilization than its rise. We have seen and have had recorded for us the catastrophes and disasters that can overtake human communities, but no records or eyewitness accounts are available concerning the circumstances leading to the rise of any of the world's great preindustrial civilizations. Writing as a necessity and as cultural elaboration is itself a feature of civilized life. History is a still later feature. Even in its earliest forms, writing did not record historical fact as we know it. Linear B of Bronze Age Greece and Crete was used for the accounts of royal households. The earliest Chinese writing records the results of arcane divination important to the elite at the court city of Anyang. In any case, it is unlikely that persons participating in these pristine civilizations understood the evolution and quantum jumps that lead to new orders of society and culture. This is not to say that they did not explain matters, but their later explanations were more in the nature of myth, cosmology, and legend, and there is no reason to believe that earlier explanations were more empirical. No doubt the members of early civilizations had the same confidence in the explanatory power of their theories as we have in our own. However, we do follow the cult of the scientific, which gives us (perhaps unwarranted) confidence that we may be approximating the truth. Be that as it may, the following account combines the best understanding at present of the surge of Maya culture from a village-centered, rural society to the splendor of an exotic tropical civilization.

No single event or theory accounts for the transformation. Faulty as it may be, the evidence indicates that no simple-minded theory of derivation from another culture is the answer. It is equally simple-minded and inadequate to think strictly in terms of in-place evolution, a kind of bootstrap operation on a giant scale.

It has been suggested by Rathje (1971) and Webb (1973) that trade in various guises was a stimulus to the rise of the Maya elite because of the need for managers. Indeed, this seems to be the case in the ancient Middle East (Wright and Johnson, 1975). Rathje suggests that in the southern lowlands the need for salt, obsidian, basalt, and other materials not found there led the Maya to elaborate social organization in order to assure themselves of these materials through trade. It does also seem that the northern center of Komchen may have grown to its large size by reason of the salt trade. Cerros on the Caribbean is clearly a port. However, the quantities of these materials needed are relatively small, and salt is always available through various expedients such as boiling salt-yielding plants. The biggest objection to the trade model is that large and precocious centers such as Tikal do not evidence much early importation of obsidian. Trade does explain the elaboration of various aspects of Maya culture, but after that culture achieves momentum. There are similar problems with other single-factor theories.

The following explanation offered is derived from the model for the rise of Maya civilization developed by a conference of a group of scholars (Adams, 1977a). First, it should be said that the transformation seems to be one of several stages, not a single dazzling event. The initiating factor leading to complexity is probably population growth. Studies have shown that when populations reach certain densities, they disperse. This appears to have happened during Mamom and especially Chicanel. Further population growth will generally lead to structural changes, usually the introduction of a hierarchical principle of organization. This simply means that there will be increasing levels of importance in various parts of the culture, such as economics. In this case, markets in some communities will become larger and handle more variety and volume of goods than lesser towns or villages with their smaller markets or exchanges. In politics, it means that for efficient administration, administrative levels will be developed with increasing centralization of power at the top. The forms that these markets and political arrangements may take will vary according to the civilization, its needs, and the ideological foundation of that culture. Thus, the ancient Middle Easterners in Sumeria, lacking nearly everything, developed markets and trade networks to handle large volumes of materials. Patron deities were protective of the entire city and its population. The ancient Maya, lacking very little of indispensable nature, emphasized trade in high-value, low-bulk commodities, most of which seem to have flowed through the hands of a few people at the top. The Maya religious system emphasized ancestor worship and the divine nature of their leaders, who had distinguished genealogies. Therefore, trade was often used by the Maya to legitimize and reinforce status.

At this point of population growth in the case of the Maya, then, ideology seems to have become the overriding factor in further development of civilized institutions. The Maya elite, deriving their status from having been heads of distinguished lineages or clans, reinforced that status with items of widespread value in Mesoamerica. Trade for jade, obsidian, cacao, and other objects became important. Because of the emphasis on ancestor worship, funerary monuments to important members of the elite were a logical development for the Maya. Large "temple" structures were constructed and embellished through the efforts of the community. Community efforts were also organized to more immediate effect: the drainage of swamps for increased food production, the building of jetties at ports, and the building of fortifications for protection.

Once an elite had emerged, it seems that there was competition between various of these leadership groups. Ultimately, this competition led to warfare. There are probably six major fortresses in the Maya Lowlands dating to the Late Formative; one of them is Tikal and another is Becan. The function of any fortress is to protect a group of fighting men, and it may be to protect an elite as well as a large segment of the general population. The Edzna fortress is relatively small and the Becan fortress of about the same size, but the Tikal fortifications seem to represent an effort to protect a substantial amount of the total population. Warfare, therefore, probably became an accelerating factor in pushing backward Maya centers along the path to increased complexity in social organization.

An additional factor that probably became more important as populations grew in certain waterless zones of the Maya Lowlands was the need to improve and create reservoirs for survival through the annual dry seasons. Robert Carneiro (1970) has developed a theory of the origin of the state that revolves around the growth of population and the intense use of scarce resources. He argues that as population grows, certain resources such as prime farm land and water assume an overwhelming importance and must be managed and enlarged. In addition, he argues that instead of seeking new lands or resources outside the ecological niche already developed, people tend to intensify their use of the resources within their original ecological zone. For the Maya, this "resource circumscription" centered around water. Even in the southern lowlands there are zones with dry-season water problems. Therefore, the people of those regions would modify and build reservoirs which would become the foci for still more people. This situation, in turn, would lead to the concentration of power in the hands of those leaders who could command the manpower to construct and maintain the reservoirs. Immense political power and social control would fall to those able to control the water supplies. It is noteworthy that the major political and religious centers of later times are located near reliable natural or artificially created water supplies. The Late Formative fortress–hydraulic system at Edzna has been noted above.

Thus we see that Maya civilization arose partly from population growth and the consequent need for more social organization, leading to a heredi-tary elite who based their status on genealogy. These elite groups tried to reinforce their exalted status by various symbolic means, such as distinc-tive pottery, costume, and jewelry. They also secured their tools of social control by public works such as monuments to their ancestors and by practical improvements such as enlarged water supplies. Their roles enlarged as directors of trade, administrators, managers, and soldiers. The relatively sudden nature of the transition, during the last century of the Late Formative, is explained by the inherent instability of a transition period. That is, change in a few parts of the culture unbalanced various social institutions and created a need for new developments in nearly all. Pressures from warfare and other forms of competition accelerated the process. Once it had begun, it was irreversible and led to complex cultural systems which could degrade, collapse, and be reformulated but never return to the beginning of the Late Formative.

Summary

At the end of this lengthy review of the Late Formative, a few final words need to be said about the general trends and evolutionary events of the period. In an overall perspective it appears that the following institutions developed in nearly all regions of Mesoamerica before A.D. 250, and in the following order: regional economic centers, elite classes, administrative centers, true urban centers, and, finally, some form of state structure. Looking for a still more reductionist principle, it might be said that this was the period of the application of the organizational principle of hierarchy to nearly all parts of cultural life.

Because nearly every author has a preference about what constitutes a city or a state, these should be defined before going further. The view of a city taken by Julian Steward (1961) was that it heads a hierarchy of settlements and performs unique functions for a regional society and for its time. Most of the famous ten criteria of urbanism of V. Gordon Childe (1950) can be applied to most Mesoamerican regional centers after about A.D. 150. These criteria include relatively higher density of population than the surrounding countryside, a stratified society, non-farming occupational specializations, formalized religions, markets, a bu-reaucracy or civil service supported by a social surplus, and, finally, writing or accounting systems. However, the regional centers clearly preceded city life, as has been seen.

States are political systems with hierarchical organization presided over by a professional ruling class (elite), as Flannery, Marcus, and Kowalewski observe (1981). These rulers are administrators of diverse functions, with propaganda and communication devices (art and writing). States require secure economic bases, although the mix of productive activities may vary. The professional rulers dispose of surpluses of labor and other resources to build public works of various kinds. A state has a monopoly on force, which means that soldiers and police are nearly always present and fortifications are often present as well. Finally, we might observe that strong centralization is not always present.

The characteristics given above deal with two aspects of culture only: a special type of community and a particular type of political structure. This of course, is not the totality of culture, by any means. All cultures have kinship systems, religious and ideological institutions, technology in the broadest sense, social organization, associations or sodalities, and other patterned features. Civilization is not the appearance of city life or state organization alone, but the totality of complex, hierarchically organized institutions. However, because this matrix of complex cultural institutions is required to create and sustain cities and states, the latter have often been used by archaeologists as a kind of "tracer element" in determining the moment and location of civilization's appearance.

Turning back to our record, it appears that regional centers first appeared in the Early Formative in order to serve certain economic needs, perhaps for regional markets, as well as social needs. The social needs might have been only slightly more complex than those of the macro-band activities of the preceding stage. The social context is that of egalitarian societies. The appearance of elites came about variously, based on regional needs. In the case of Izapa, it appears that the elite were truly theocrats who served mainly the philosophical and religious needs of the region. In the case of the much larger and somewhat later center of Kaminaljuyu, there is an emphasis on ranked kinship group leaders giving way to hereditary leaders who had parlayed their special positions into permanently higher status.

These Late Formative cultures of eastern Mesoamerica appear not to be highly centralized. In contrast, the situation of the Basin of Mexico is one which appears to have led to centralization of communities and political systems as well. Planned towns (and probably cities) appear early in this zone and apparently point to the further development of despotic leadership, which seems so characteristic of later Central Mexican civilization.

Thus, in a number of Mesoamerican regions, such as Izapa or Cuicuilco, the elite, or those who aspired to be, learned the proper regional combination of factors that led to higher status. At Izapa it was calendrical ritual, lunar worship, and concern with productivity. At Kaminaljuyu it was an emphasis on kin-group leadership, with ancestor worship becoming a manifestation of that. The Lowland Maya appear to have combined the religious and despotic models in the milieu of their own particular environment. An elite control of all aspects of life seems to have been emerging in the Basin of Mexico. Oaxaca seems to have been developing along a variation of the centralized model, with the additional spur of warfare to accelerate the process. All of these regions either verged on or developed archaic states and cities. Some zones either lagged behind or simply seem not to have aspired to move beyond the village level. Western Mexico is an example of this conservative, rural, and possibly more satisfactory way of life.

CHAPTER 5

CLASSIC MAYA LOWLAND
CIVILIZATION

*Then they adhered to the [dictates of] their reason. There was no sin;
in the holy faith their lives [were passed]. There was then no sickness;
they had then no aching bones; they had then no high fever. . . . At
that time the course of humanity was orderly.*
—Chilam Balam of Chumayel, *1967:83.*

*[Herewith] the history which I have written of how the mounds came
to be constructed by the heathen. During three score and fifteen
katuns (1,500 years) they were constructed. The great . . . men made
them . . . the great mounds came to be built by the lineages.*
—Chilam Balam of Chumayel, *1967:79.*

*Among these high hills which we passed there are a variety of ancient
buildings among which I recognized habitations inside, and although
they were very high and my strength very little, I climbed them,
although with difficulty. These were in the form of a convent with
small cloisters, and many living rooms all roofed, with terraces [out-
side] and whitened with lime inside.*
—Father Avendaño, in Morley, *1937–38:55.*

MAYA CIVILIZATION was not created full-blown in a green flash of Olmec
lightning. As seen in the previous chapter, it is regarded as the result of a
number of factors which interacted, a less spectacular but more interesting
process. Resource concentration, as suggested by Carneiro; population
growth; the demonstrated cultural variability among the farming villages;
development of a powerful set of ideologies; the donation of new ideas
and techniques from outside the Maya area; and the food resources
available to the Maya, all affected the forms of Maya high culture from
about A.D. 200 to 850. Like most of the cultural superstructure in Mesoamerica, Maya Classic civilization was an elite-class phenomenon.
Within its broad patterns there were plenty of variations. This diversity

also operated through time, and, as will be seen, Maya culture underwent serious and drastic changes as a result of several crises in its history. In the background of all this historical action, however, are commonalities and continuities which are connected with the everyday matters of getting enough to eat and drink and of providing shelter. Therefore, the farming and food-gathering patterns of the Maya claim our attention first.

Agricultural Patterns

It was once assumed that the prehistoric Maya practiced agriculture in much the same ways used by their descendants in the sixteenth century and even today. Thus it was thought that the Maya practiced a form of shifting cultivation (*milpa* agriculture), were only able to sustain thin populations, lacked true urban centers, and probably had not developed true centralized states. This assumption led to serious misunderstandings about the agricultural potential of the Maya Lowlands and the possibilities of urban life, and, above all, it misled scholars about the numbers of people involved in ancient Maya societies. It also meant that the Maya could be characterized as a peaceful, noncompetitive, theocratic society, led by philosopher-priests and guided by humane pacific values. It was truly what Hammond has called "the myth of the *milpa*."

Intensive research, beginning about 1968, has led to a drastic revision of these ideas. To put it briefly, it is now known that the Maya probably practiced shifting or swidden cultivation during the pioneer stages of their cultural development (early and Middle Formative), but that during the Late Formative population growth had gradually forced them to more intensive forms of food production. Further, they lived in a large number of true cities, numbered in the millions during the Classic, and were led by secular kings who practiced warfare against their neighbors, often on a large scale. This view of the Maya may make them less attractive than they formerly appeared, but it does make them a great deal more understandable.

The following is a review of Maya agricultural history as it is known at present. It appears likely that the initial agriculturalists, whether colonists from elsewhere or indigenous converts, practiced what may be called localized intensive agriculture. It has been well defined by Warwick Bray (1977), who has suggested that it was nearly universally the first type of plant cultivation. This kind of gardening took place in the zones of best soil moisture, around springs, along river and stream margins, and in the edges of swamps, which probably explains the distribution of Swasey and Xe communities in these very situations.

Mamom (Middle Formative) population growth led to expansive culti-vation, or what has been noted as shifting agriculture. Many studies have been done of the Maya system of shifting cultivation, and although there are variations from zone to zone, a general pattern prevails for the whole area. Corn farming was carried on by a variant of slash-and-burn or swidden agriculture. Typically, in this system a patch of jungle is cleared off and burned and the crop planted in the ashes at the beginning of the rainy season. A family of five needs about 6,600 kilograms (3,000 pounds) of maize (corn) per year, given the diet and food habits of present-day Maya. There is reason to believe that these food habits were the same at the time of the Spanish Conquest and have changed little in the traditional villages since then.

In any period, prehistoric or modern, swidden agriculture imposes its own limitations on Maya life. For one thing, the field must be allowed to lie fallow after about three years of cultivation and given a four- to eight-year rest period. Thus, from four to eight times the amount of land in actual maize cultivation is locked up in fallow ground. Any shortening of the rest period would not allow the land to sufficiently recover its nutrients and would ultimately lead to catastrophic crop declines. The large amount of land necessary for a single family thus imposes one other limitation—the number of people that can live together in one place. If most people wish to live within even a half-day's walk of their fields, then the number of people living together in a permanent farming village is finite. Thus, as population expands absolutely in numbers, it also tends to expand in space, eventually filling up all available land and becoming fairly evenly distributed over the arable parts. This is exactly what the before mentioned study by Koenig seems to show for the Mamom period. Even so, agronomy studies by Ursula Cowgill (1961, 1962), admittedly controversial, indicate that just by using the shifting cultivation system with its dependence on corn as a main crop, the carrying capacity of the land would be about 58 to 77 people per square kilometer (or 150 to 200 per square mile) and therefore capable of supporting a reasonably large urban population in addition to the rural sector (1961, 1962). This is a considerable density, as shown by comparison with France, which averages 33 people per square kilometer (85 per square mile).

The Maya Swidden Cycle

Selection of the piece of land for cultivation takes place sometime during the previous year. Choice is based on the soil, clayey soils being avoided, and drainage. Crops must be drained or they will rot either at the seed stage or later. So the farmer looks for sloping land with enough topsoil and forest on it to guarantee sufficient nutrients for his plants. By planting on the slopes, the farmer also avoids some of the danger of frosts, which occur in the lowest ground. A piece of land is then cleared during the dry season—from January to May for most of the area. This means arduous and difficult work chopping out trees and bushes and dealing with snakes, thorny bamboo, poisonous trees, and other hazards. A man's friends and family may help him, but much of the time he does it alone.

Fig. 5–1. Modern slash-and-burn agriculture. Burning off a patch of jungle at Altar de Sacrificios, Guatemala.

When a sufficient amount of land is cleared, then the cut-down vegetation must dry. On a suitable day, the vegetation is burned (Fig. 5-1). This is a spectacular and dangerous business, and the criteria for a suitable day vary through the lowlands. In the northern lowlands, farmers prefer a windy day which will drive the fire through the field. In the Peten, they wait for a windless day to avoid forest fires in the higher jungle of those parts. In any case, the burning requires cooperation among neighbors, because the fires are set in many places simultaneously to get a "good burn." The field may burn and smolder for several days, although the fire has done most of its work in a few hours. The farmer has now reduced the biomass to usable nutrients for his domesticated plants (Fig. 5-2). Another important decision then follows—when to plant. If the farmer plants too soon before the rains, then the birds may get the seed corn. If he waits too long, he may not be able to get into the field, the seed corn may rot before it germinates, or it may be washed out of the ground.

To plant, the farmer makes a hole in the ash of the burned field with a sharpened stick, drops a kernel in the hole, and with a swipe of the foot covers it up. Once the crop germinates, he needs only occasionally to weed it, but although he has a temporary respite from his labors, his anxieties continue. Hail lurks in the dark, rain-season clouds; high winds may also destroy or decimate the young corn plants. Late rains, insects, birds, and wild animals are an ever-present menace. Where corn fields have been cleared from the jungle, the small Yucatec deer multiply in response, being very fond of corn and quick to take advantage of the tasty meals at hand. Of course the farmer is not entirely the loser; he may hunt the predatory and well-fed deer, thereby balancing his diet with animal protein. Deer may also have been at least partially domesticated as indicated in Spanish accounts of tame deer found in sixteenth-century Maya villages (Puleston, personal communication, 1978).

Several other crops are planted in corn fields among the maize plants. Most common are varieties of beans, squashes, and pumpkins. Kitchen gardens also provide nutritional balance to the Maya diet, adding chile peppers, tomatoes, and other vegetables such as the *huisquil*, with which North Americans are not familiar. Avocados are cultivated, as are the cacao tree and vanilla.

All of this information on Maya diet and farming practices comes from ethnographic and early chronicle sources and fits the present-day as well as part of the prehistoric Indian (O.F. Cook, 1921; Reina, 1967; Sanders, 1973, 1977). Many writers have emphasized the religious aura which surrounds the sacred maize or corn in the mind of the traditional Maya and the ritual which accompanied the varying parts of the agricultural cycle in historic times. The same mystical attachment to the planting and raising of corn still obtains today. There is also the matter of "machismo," which means that a man is not demonstrably "male" unless he wrests a

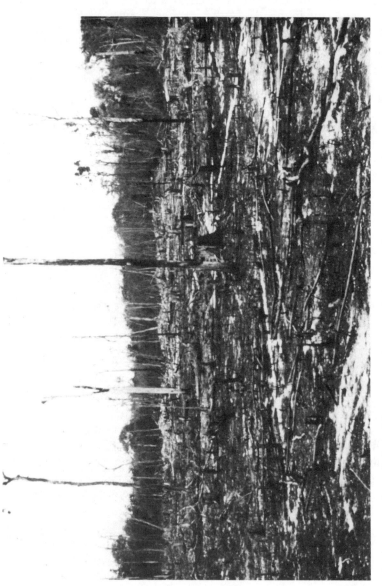

Fig. 5–2. Modern slash-and-burn agriculture. A burnt-over field ready for planting shows ancient house mounds in the background. Although it was a good model for the Formative Maya, this extensive food production system was superseded in the Classic Period by more intensive techniques.

living from nature. This element of prestige probably operated in ancient times also, as we shall see, but for different reasons.

Work by the late D. Puleston of the Tikal project produced data which indicated to him the strong probability that the Maya used the breadnut tree (*Brosimum alicastrum*) in ancient times as a partial substitute for maize. The nut produced by this tree is, in some ways, nutritionally superior to maize. Indeed, when the maize crop fails today, the Maya depend on the *ramon* or breadnut tree as a substitute source of vegetable protein. By experiments, Puleston found that one type of underground chamber (*chultun*) is suitable for the storage of *ramon* nuts, which survive up to eighteen months. However, experiments with smoked maize show that it, too, will last for considerable periods in *chultuns* (Reina and Hill, 1980). Observations by other archaeologists, botanists, and geologists in the field have led to the conclusion that the *ramon* tree is unreliable in the same years that the maize crop fails and that the correlation between *ramons* and ruins is a result of the preference of the tree for well-aerated soil. Because of this, the trees tend to colonize the stony ruins where they obviously were not growing in ancient times.

Marine foods were also quite important in the diet of those people living near the coasts (Eaton, 1978; Ball and Eaton, 1972; Lange, 1971). This is evidenced by large amounts of shell and fish bones in middens near the shores and on the beaches of the peninsula. As a colleague has observed, the peninsula is surrounded by one vast soup, teeming with food. Finally, we do not doubt that many roots, including, probably, yucca roots, *camotes*, and many others that were available for the digging, were used as food. Again, the investment in labor and resources for these foods is minimal and the return is great (Bronson, 1966; Ursula M. Cowgill, 1971; Sanders, 1973).

With all of these supplements and mixes of food production and extraction, by the Late Formative the Lowland Maya were being pressed by population growth to explore new avenues. The third phase of Maya agricultural history began when they were forced to begin wetland cultivation, a phase we might label one of extensive-intensive cultivation. We now know that swamps were being drained and modified in northern Belize by the Late Formative (Chicanel) period. Evidence from Pulltrouser Swamp (Turner and Harrison, 1983) as well as from Cobweb Swamp, 30 kilometers (19 miles) south, demonstrates that raised fields were being constructed and drainage canals, and probably sluice gates and other water control devices, were being built (Fig. 5-3). Huge numbers of stone tools were produced at Colha, located on the edge of Cobweb Swamp, for use in the building, maintenance, and cultivation of the raised fields (Fig. 5-4). Puleston and Siemens were the first to detect and report raised fields, in this case from a river zone in the western lowlands, but it seemed to them that this was a Postclassic phenomenon and limited to watercourse edges. Eaton found extensive field walls and terracing in the Rio Bec zone in 1968, which Turner (1974) later confirmed and estimated at more than 10,000 square kilometers (3,900 square miles) in extent (Fig. 5-5). Much of the Maya Mountains around Caracol were also terraced (Healy et al., 1983). By aerial inspection, the vast Bajo de Morcoy in Quintana Roo was seen by the same two investigators to contain great numbers of canals and raised fields. Turner later confirmed this by ground inspection.

All of this work indicates that by end of the late Formative, the Maya were heavily investing in the labor, planning, and materials needed for major landscape modification for the purposes of agronomy. This process continued through the Classic period (A.D. 250–850), and eventually, it appears, every major swamp in the Maya Lowlands and every watercourse or lake edge was exploited for wetland gardens (Map 5-1). Evidence for this extensive-intensive phase includes radar mapping of a large part of the southern lowlands, a zone of 36,200 square kilometers (14,000 square miles), of which we estimate at least 1,285 square kilometers (496 square miles) were modified by drainage (Adams, Brown, and Culbert, 1981). This is a much larger amount of land than was modified by the later Aztec,

Fig. 5–3. Raised fields in northern Belize at Pulltrouser Swamp. This and many other confirmations of the radar imagery indicate that ancient use of wetland gardens by the Maya was extensive.

Fig. 5–4. Stone tools from Rio Azul, Peten, Guatemala, where they were found in association with ancient raised fields and mounds of stone tool manufacturing debris.

which was about 120 square kilometers (46 square miles). However, as will be noted in more detail in a later chapter, there are differences of scale between the Basin of Mexico (7,823 square kilometers, or 3,020 square miles) and the Maya Lowlands (250,000 square kilometers, or 96,500 square miles). To date at least eight separate confirmations have been made by about that many projects. Thus, it seems that at last we have laid hands upon the economic basis for Maya civilization.

In addition, the wetland developments seem to have made possible the appearance of true urban centers in the Maya Lowlands. The largest Maya cities are located on the largest swamps, which, if we are correct, were the greatest food production zones (Map 5-2).

Settlement Patterns and Population Sizes

The direct evidence of census material for ancient Maya populations does not exist. Therefore, given that we cannot directly count people, we must

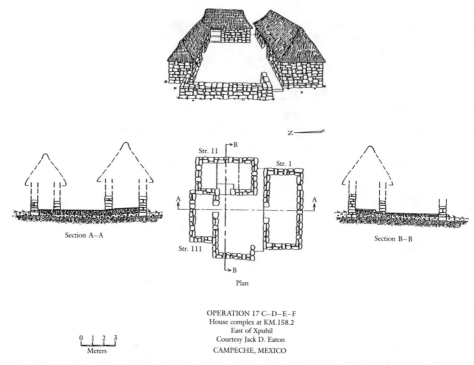

OPERATION 17 C–D–E–F
House complex at KM.158.2
East of Xpuhil
Courtesy Jack D. Eaton
CAMPECHE, MEXICO

Fig. 5–5. Farmstead in the Río Bec countryside, about 5 kilometers (3 miles) east of Xpuhil. Two residences are supplemented by a storage house and a stone wall. This and innumerable other farmsteads are located atop terraced hills in the Río Bec region. Presumably, farmers living in these dwellings worked the terraced gardens and fields. (Courtesy Jack D. Eaton)

use indirect means of assessing population. The traditional means of doing this consists of counting the seemingly countless house mounds that still dot the lowlands. It also, less traditionally, consists of doing volumetric assessments of the masses of formal architecture in the civic centers. The first means leads to estimates based on the numbers of platforms occupied during a given period as well as on an assumption that the ancient Maya had about the same numbers in a household as do present-day Maya. The second means leads to more generalized estimates based on the assumption that the larger a center, the more people it controlled to build and maintain it. Further, because buildings are meant to be used, the larger the center, the more people would be using its marketplace, its reservoirs, its palace buildings, and so forth. Let us consider the implications of studies of house mounds.

House mounds are the small platforms of clay, earth, and stone built to support the domestic housing of the majority of ancient Maya. These

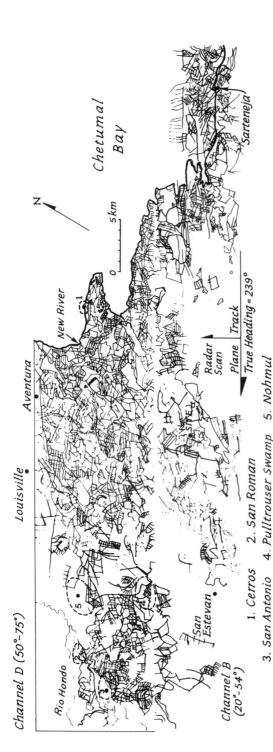

Map 5–1. Overlay drawings made from radar imagery of northern Belize. Indications of zones of raised fields are shown by lattice patterns. Radar imagery is indiscriminate and also shows many other features, such as smugglers' airstrips, hurricane swales, and modern roads.

Channel D (50°–75°)

Louisville

Aventura

Rio Hondo

New River

Chetumal
Bay

N

0   5km

San
Estevan

San Antonio

Channel B
(20°–54°)

Radar
Scan

Plane   Track

True Heading = 239°

Sarteneja

1. Cerros   2. San Roman
3. San Antonio   4. Pulltrouser Swamp   5. Nohmul

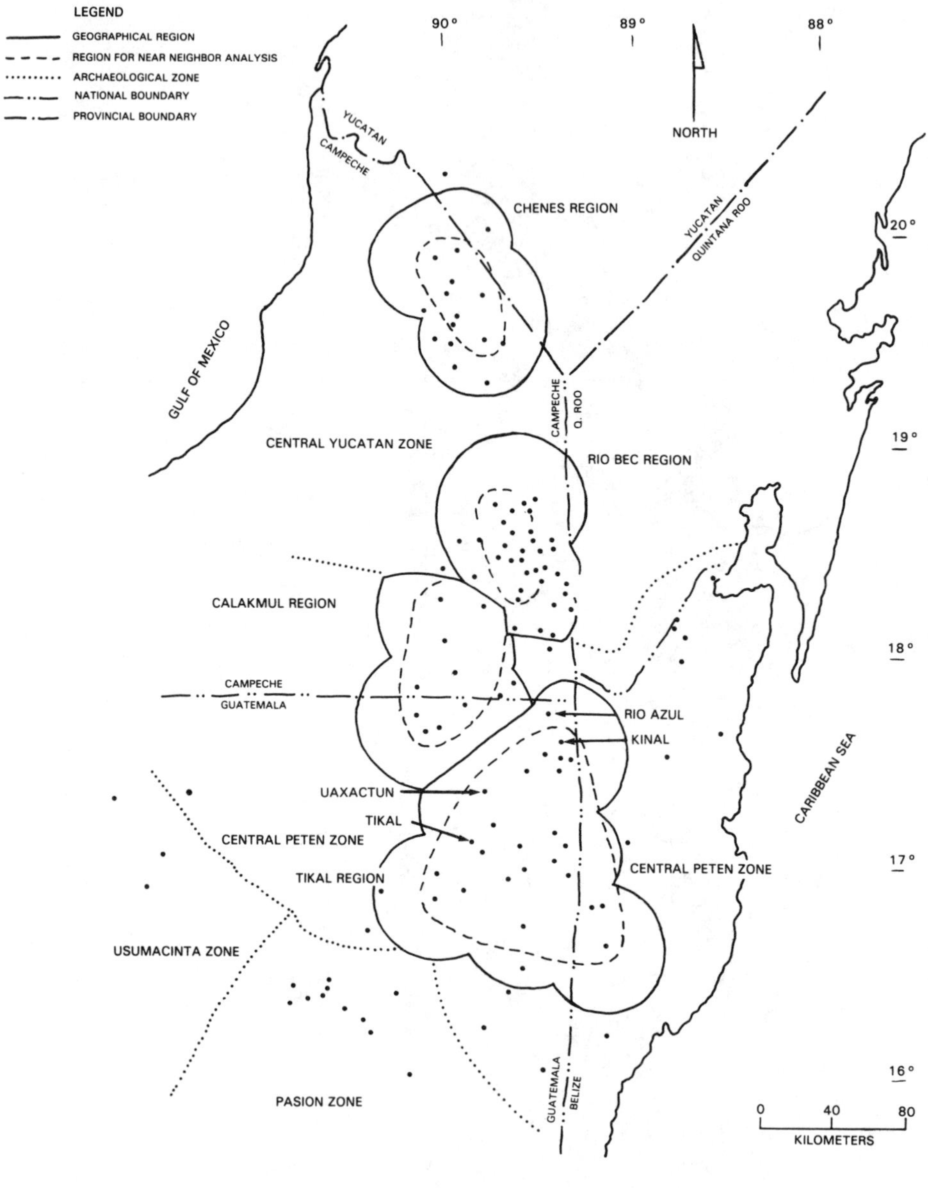

LEGEND
GEOGRAPHICAL REGION
REGION FOR NEAR NEIGHBOR ANALYSIS
ARCHAEOLOGICAL ZONE
NATIONAL BOUNDARY
PROVINCIAL BOUNDARY
90°
89°
88°
NORTH
20°
19°
18°
17°
16°
YUCATAN
CAMPECHE
YUCATAN
QUINTANA ROO
CHENES REGION
GULF OF MEXICO
CAMPECHE
Q. ROO
CENTRAL YUCATAN ZONE
RIO BEC REGION
CALAKMUL REGION
CAMPECHE
GUATEMALA
RIO AZUL
KINAL
UAXACTUN
TIKAL
CENTRAL PETEN ZONE
TIKAL REGION
CENTRAL PETEN ZONE
CARIBBEAN SEA
USUMACINTA ZONE
PASION ZONE
GUATEMALA
BELIZE
0
40
80
KILOMETERS

Map 5–2. The north central Peten, Guatemala, showing some major Lowland Maya sites and their relationships to the terrain and especially to swamps.

small structures supported perishable, thatched-roofed, pole-and-clay-walled (wattle-and-daub) houses; they remain long after the superstructures have gone. The distribution of these small structures is nearly universal over the countryside around the larger sites. One major problem has been to draw boundary lines around the rural sustaining areas and therefore around the house mounds that represent the populations that supported Maya cities, towns, and fortresses.

Studies combining survey and excavation have given us fairly precise estimates of densities and fluctuations through time. For most of the lowlands, the peak population period was the Late Classic. However, it appears that certain restricted zones were also high-density population centers earlier in the Early Classic and in the late Formative. Densities in the Late Formative seem to have reached a maximum of 40 people per square kilometer (104 per square mile) around Dzibilchaltun in the north (Kurjack, 1979), with perhaps as much as three times that amount in the south, which had deeper soils and better water. These high populations seem to have been clustered around their centers and to have formed enclaves of developed farmlands in somewhat the same way the early Sumerian cities did.

Volumetric assessment of early centers such as Mirador indicate a very large number of people involved in the construction (Matheney, 1980). The temple structures at Mirador also indicate a firmly entrenched elite. At Rio Azul, in the northeast Peten, large platforms were built in Chicanel times, and probably a very large temple building (R.E.W. Adams, 1986). At Tikal, the already noted temples of the north acropolis and the huge Mundo Perdido (Lost World) pyramid were built in the Late Formative. The population estimates for these periods indicate that thousands of people were involved in each of these and other cases. In Early Classic times, population growth continued more or less at the same rates, but with a jump in construction activities. At Rio Azul, we estimate not more than thirty-five hundred people in the largely Early Classic city (Adams and Karbula, 1988). However, huge buildings with masses of up to 97,000 cubic meters (3.4 million cubic feet) of fill, such as temple complex A-3, were being built. Again, the implications are of far more people than could be housed at the city, and, in this case, it seems likely that construction crews were imported from the south.

The Late Classic is the period of maximum populations and is the best controlled because the remains of this period lie atop the earlier materials. In the center of the Yucatan peninsula, populations peaked at perhaps as much as 450 people per square kilometer (1,166 per square mile; Eaton, 1975; Turner, 1974; Adams 1977b). In this case, more than 10,000 square kilometers (3,800 square miles) of hillsides were terraced and walled, and farmsteads were located atop hills, with many groups of farmhouses on the flatter ground.

In the Belize Valley it is possible to define segments of the river and associate the house platforms on the valley bottoms with the civic centers of the region. Willey and his associates estimated that as many as 24,000 people were living on about 600 square kilometers (about 232 square miles; Willey et al., 1965). It is estimated that about 6,000 people were associated with each of the major civic centers of the Belize Valley. However, this figure is conditioned by the old assumptions of swidden-maize agriculture, because the evidence for intensive agriculture was not available at the time. Adjusting for the new potentials given by intensive cultivation, it appears more likely that up to 180,000 people, more than seven times the old estimate, may have been present during the peak period of the Late Classic.

It is not possible at the moment to make estimates of total populations for the periods before the Late Classic; but for the latter period, in the eighth century A.D., it is possible that Maya populations peaked at between 9 million and 14 million. That these populations lived a precarious existence indeed is demonstrated by the catastrophic demographic collapse which followed in the next century.

To summarize, the Late Formative seems to have involved regional societies of thousands of people; the Early Classic, of tens of thousands; and the Late Classic, of hundreds of thousands.

Small villages, made up mainly of kinship units, constituted the main settlement pattern during most of the Formative. During the late Formative the picture changed from a landscape dotted with these hamlets and villages to one in which some villages had become regional centers with public architecture. Some of these became very large, and some of the largest masses of material ever piled up by the Maya were assembled at this time, notably at Mirador, a site in the extreme north central Peten. Many other Maya sites show evidence of regional organization into hierarchical patterns made up of at least three, and sometimes four, levels of communities.

Maya Cities and Their Functions

A great deal of scholarly blood has been spilled over the issue of whether or not what J. Eric S. Thompson called ceremonial centers were cities. The results of the past twenty-five years of research have answered that question resoundingly in the affirmative. In present research, we now are concerned with the internal structure of Maya cities, their differing functions from site to site, their population sizes, and their political relationships.

Maya cities varied from region to region and from period to period. By the beginning of the Classic there is little doubt that most of the regional centers of the Late Formative had assumed city status in the sense that it has been defined in chapter 4. However, it has become ever clearer in recent years that the first great florescence of Maya civilization was in the Late Formative. Primary evidence for this conclusion has come from the discovery that many major Maya centers, such as those mentioned before, were already cities in status by the time of Christ or slightly afterward. These communities are associated with tentative or certain evidence of intensive agriculture and high-density rural populations. Early and late, however, all Maya cities had certain constant, formal qualities that were combined in various ways in order to meet the special needs of each case.

There are several major formal classes of public architecture in all major Maya centers: temples, palaces, ball courts, raised road systems (*sacbes*), and reservoirs. In some cases, fortifications were added, but they were not as invariable a component as the other elements seem to be.

By Late Formative and probably earlier, buildings were built of cut limestone masonry covered with a strong stucco plaster to protect the structure from rains. With lines and angles thus softened and smoothed, buildings were more flowing and curvilinear than we see them today. Rubble cores of rough stone, sometimes mortar, earth, and even wood, made up the mass of the structures. The limestone walls often, especially later in the Classic period, formed a sort of veneer over the rough hearting. Generally good-quality mortar was used to cement the stone in place. As pointed out by Laurence Roys (1934), the structural strength of a Maya building is really that of a concrete building tied together by the mortar and rubble mass, with not much integrity given by the masonry skin. Roofs were built using the corbeled arch, which was built by edging stones on opposing walls toward one another, course by course, until the space was small enough to be bridged by a capstone. This form of vault allowed rooms of up to fifteen feet in width, but the usual size was smaller, and Maya rooms tend to be long, narrow, and high.

Temples

Maya temples are generally elevated on terraced substructures (Fig. 5-6). These supporting platforms vary in height and width but generally are solid and without chambers except for tombs and associated passages. The temple structure itself is usually small compared to the mass of the substructure and has relatively little space inside, and even that may be occupied by benches and altars. Very few people could be accommodated within such a building. The rooms are high and narrow because of the use of corbeled vaults, but they were also deliberately made so. The roof of the temple often carries an ornamented wall, called a roofcomb, decorated with modeled stucco. Most temples show remnants of such stucco decoration and red paint, often over most of the building as well as the roofcomb. Burn marks on the floors, masonry altars, and walls indicate the repetitive use of copal, pine resin incense. The fragrant smoke

Fig. 5–6. A very late temple and its stelae at Seibal, Peten, Guatemala. All five stelae and the temple date to A.D. 849 and probably celebrate the accession to power of a new group of Maya rulers, possibly usurpers from Yucatan.

of copal permeates the atmosphere today in Maya communities when religious affairs are being conducted. Other evidence indicates the use of these buildings as ritual structures. Elaborate caches of exotic materials, precious to the ancients, are found beneath floors and in masonry altars. These offerings include items of jade, stingray spines, imported sea shells, and other symbolic materials. At Tikal, such caches are so consistently patterned that archaeologists can predict the nature of the caches and their locations. The traditional interpretation of temples has been that they were centers for the worship of the impersonal deities represented in Maya art. This is partly true, but with new evidence it seems that we can go further.

Carved wooden beams often spanned the doorways of temples. Those that survive are resplendent with florid and symbolic depictions of gorgeously attired persons surrounded with scrollwork, serpents, jaguars, and so on—the panoply of power and authority. Complex texts of hieroglyphs accompany the depictions. As will be seen in the discussion of Maya writing, these texts often include historical information.

Similar subject material is found on a giant scale in the modeled stucco decoration. Super-sized human figures seated on elaborate benches and surrounded with symbolism of divinely attributed authority can still be made out on some of the badly battered roofcombs. Hieroglyphic texts accompany some of the depictions, perhaps all of them. The major key to the interpretation of the function of the temple type of building lies in the sumptuous tombs often found within them and in the nature of the carved stone monuments called stelae.

In 1956, Michael D. Coe suggested that one of the functions of a Maya temple was to be a final resting place for distinguished members of society. Indeed, it seems that if one searches long enough through the often immense mass of rubble of temple substructures, an elaborate burial will often be found. The famous tomb found by Alberto Ruz (1973) in the Palenque Temple of the Inscriptions is one of the most elaborate examples of this sort of mortuary structure. In both this tomb and several others at Palenque there is a feature called a psycho-duct, a small tube leading from the tomb up through the masonry to within a few feet of the floor of the temple building. Several other tombs at Palenque have the same feature. It seems clear that here we have an attempt at maintaining communication with the person placed in the tomb below. This would be something like the *sipapu,* in kivas of the Pueblo Indians of the U.S. Southwest, which allows communication with the spirits underground. Thus, both the common occurrence of elaborate tombs and the psycho-ducts seem to confirm Coe's idea. However, there is more to be said, and we must now consider the nature of the stelae and a little of the content of their texts.

Stelae

Stelae are carved stone shafts which were most often erected in association with temple buildings (Fig. 5-7). T. Proskouriakoff's revolutionary studies (1960, 1961, 1963, 1964) indicate clearly that stelae were historical monuments erected to record the exploits of rulers, their genealogies, the circumstances of their birth, and, probably, justification for their political power. Groups of these monuments were associated with single temples at Piedras Negras, each stelae group dealing with the events of a single ruler's lifetime. The frequent physical association of Maya stelae with temples suggests a ritual and functional association. Indeed, at least one temple on which the stucco decoration was fortuitously preserved, at Rio Azul, seems to duplicate the standard arrangement of texts and depictions found on stelae (Adams and Gatling, 1964). Specifically, the human figures are on the broad surfaces of the roofcomb and building, and the hieroglyphic texts are on the narrow sides of the structure. This physical analogy suggests a functional analogy, and that temples in some way were historical commemorative monuments.

In sum, temples would seem quite often, perhaps always, to be memori-

Fig. 5–7. Seibal Stela 14, very late in style. The ruler may be an intruder from the Puuc area of Yucatan and a member of a military group that took power at Seibal about A.D. 840.

als to the distinguished dead. The implications of this will be further explored when we consider the nature of Classic Maya society.

Palaces

Palace is a catch-all term used to designate what are usually multiple-room, occasionally multiple-story buildings with a nearly endless variety of ground plans. As will be seen, some were truly luxurious residences fitted with service facilities. Others were more suited for administrative functions. Still others include dim and dark rooms which seem only usable as storage facilities. Finally, there is little doubt that many palace rooms have features which fit them for ritual and ceremonial practices.

Many scholars have objected to classification of palaces as elite-class residences. Objections have been made on the grounds that the buildings are dim, dark, slimy, damp, cramped, and unfitted for comfort. This seems an excessively ethnocentric and unimaginative analysis. At the present, palaces indeed deserve all of those opprobrious adjectives, but this is after eleven hundred years of abandonment and neglect. Moreover, judging from their own depictive sources, the Classic Maya elite class had their own idea of what constituted comfort.

In many ways the elite life-style seems to have been something like that of traditional Japanese culture. The commonest sitting position shown is cross-legged. The Maya seem to have made relatively little use of furniture of any size. Most is in the form of low tables, boxes, and other portable items. Most domestic life seems to have occurred either on benches built into the palace rooms or on benches elevated on feet. Rooms with benches are commonly the widest to be found in palace structures, and the benches occupy up to 95 percent of the floor space. With mats, cushions, and a minimum of portable furniture, rooms could be changed in function as need arose. Indeed, the floor plans of what seem to be "apartments" in the A-V palace at Uaxactun provide some evidence that there was relatively little interior space for any single occupying individual or family. Cupboards built into walls presumably stored items needed only at night, such as light blankets. Thus, the multiple use of rooms, the cross-legged sitting position, the use of portable furniture, and the ready availability of outdoor space all would have made the larger rooms with benches quite suitable for living areas. Paved courts and terraces are often found in front of such rooms; with the use of canopies, or temporary awnings, some of which are shown in Maya murals and evidenced by post holes in the courtyards, these pavements would have been supplementary living areas.

Simple maintenance would take care of a great many of the other objections to the use of Maya palaces as residences. Cutting down the present vegetation, restoring paved courts around the buildings, cleaning the walls, and keeping up watertight roofs all would contribute to creature comforts. Under such circumstances, with the major buildings surrounded by acres of heat-reflecting pavements, the dimness and coolness of the interior rooms would have been absolute assets.

Certain palaces have been found with built-in conveniences. It seems clear that the Becan Structure IV palace has an interior drainage system which could have been used with a shower or bath (Potter, 1977). The floor slopes to the drain. In the same building, a built-in fireplace was also found. These features are unusual, however, and it seems that domestic necessities such as kitchens and latrines were most often located in supplementary and even perishable minor buildings. Eaton and Farrior found servants' quarters and cooking facilities built into the Rio Azul palace areas, and Day found a cook shack near a palace at Tikal. At Copan, elite residential groups had small kitchens on platforms on a corner of the compound. At Edzna, Becan, and Piedras Negras, steam baths were available for the use of the inhabitants of the palaces on the other sides of adjacent courts. Not much is known about sanitation facilities, but perhaps some of the more humble types of Maya pottery functioned as chamber pots. There is evidence that the courts, buildings, and rooms were kept swept and clean and that debris was carried to selected dumps.

The question of the sizes of populations resident in palaces is one to which an approximate answer can now be given. By considering the probable function of rooms with benches and making several other assumptions, we can arrive at ceilings on the numbers of people that could have been accommodated. One way to get at this figure is through consideration of sleeping space available. Sleeping quarters are the minimum requirement for residences. Assuming that we are correct concerning the functions of benches as primary living spaces and that these functions included sleeping, then the benches in those spaces were also beds. There is equivocal evidence for the use of the hammock in pre-Hispanic times, and this device, so popular now among the Lowland Maya, seems to have been introduced from the West Indies about the time of the Spanish Conquest. In any case, there is no evidence that the hammock was very popular even if it was present. Protected sleeping space for the inhabitants of the palaces is limited to the benches, and these can be measured for maximum capacity. Assuming also that the proportional mix of ages and sexes in such a palace population was something like that of the ethnographic Maya, one can make certain estimates. For all the palaces at Uaxactun, a medium-sized center, this would mean a maximum population of about 185 persons, which would break down to 125 adults and 60 children. At Uaxactun these people would be perhaps controlling and directing a supporting population of about 18,500. Considering that adult males are most often mentioned in the hieroglyphic texts, and therefore probably were most important politically, it may be that about 20 adult males managed affairs at places such as Uaxactun (Adams, 1974a). Chicanna, to the north, had space in its eighth-century palaces for about 88 people, while one contemporary Tikal palace (5D-46) had a capacity of 34 (Adams, 1981).

Based on their studies at the site of Coba, Folan, Kintz, and Fletcher (1983) came to the conclusion that the city had a minimum population of about forty thousand and a maximum palace population of about four hundred, or 1 percent of the total. This is about the same ratio of elite to total population as at Uaxactun. However, this small directing group at Coba was supplemented by subordinate groups at the tributary cities, which also had their own supporting populations.

Activities of the elite class embraced politics, religion, and economics. Administration was assisted by a kind of civil service, probably made up of members of the minor nobility and perhaps including lower-ranked groups of specialists, such as stewards of elite estates. Properly arranged quarters were necessary for the provision of the ritual and ceremonial context that seems to have surrounded Maya nobility. Many palaces have parts fitted out for religious affairs and perhaps for court protocol. Long, narrow rooms, largely open on one side, with a central throne or altar, probably served these functions (A.L. Smith, 1950). Administration could have been carried out in subsidiary rooms, which are suitable for living but near dead-end spaces suitable for storage. The Group III quadrangle at Holmul might have been such an administrative and storage headquarters. In the center of the quadrangle there is a building with the large rooms and benches characteristic of the living zones. Perhaps a chief bureaucrat lived there. The rooms surrounding the quadrangle are mostly without benches and narrow, and many are interior spaces without ventilation or light. Presumably, there were kept the food surpluses that supported the elite, the servants that cared for them, and the craft specialists that they supported (Adams, 1970). There, too, would be kept elaborate costumes, valuables which gave prestige, and weapons for both war and hunting (Merwin and Vaillant, 1932).

Marketplaces

Institutionalized trade is a longstanding trait of Mesoamerican civilization, going back to the Middle Formative. For most people in Maya societies, Classic-period trade took place within a closed regional system. It seems clear from the distribution of artifacts and from technological studies that certain communities, hamlets, and villages specialized in Classic times in the manufacture of particular items. This would fit with the present-day pattern of conservative Indian culture in areas such as the highlands of Chiapas, where certain towns specialize in crafts such as pottery making. These specialty manufactures are now distributed through a regional market system. However, there is also evidence that in Classic times at least certain crafts, such as the manufacture of polychrome pottery, were done by artisan families attached to noble households.

Textiles, pottery, chert and obsidian tools, feathers, food, drink, salt, raw materials, wooden artifacts, and much else must have circulated through regional economies in Classic times by means of systems based on the local urban centers. Combined with the model of an aristocratically led social structure, the evidence for internal circulation through a region implies both a redistributive and a market system. This is an economic arrangement which is more characteristic of archaic and generalized feudal states than of chiefdoms. Large buildings and controlled paved zones have now been identified as probable markets in Tikal, Rio Azul, and other places. Warehousing has been tentatively identified for some centers.

Open plazas also functioned for public ceremonies of importance to society as a whole. Amphitheaters have been identified at two sites in the Rio Bec region, each of which has a capacity of about eight thousand people (Ruppert and Denison, 1943). Events depicted in Maya art which may have been staged in such spaces and buildings include the judgment of captives after conquest, religious rituals, political rituals, and possibly even sports competitions. No evidence for theater, even in the form of "passion plays," exists for the Classic Maya.

Finally, paved open spaces also functioned as additional living space for palace inhabitants, their retainers, and perhaps even people temporarily come to town. Foundations of ephemeral structures have been found in plaza areas at Becan (Potter, 1977).

Sacbes

Elevated roads or causeways, *sacbes* ("white ways"), often connected important building groups within the civic centers. Especially in northern Yucatan, these roads also form a network of connections among various urban centers (Kurjack and Garza, 1981). *Sacbes* are elevated up to 4.5 meters (15 feet) above the terrain and are up to 18 meters (60 feet) wide. They are made in the usual Maya manner, with a rubble core and cut stone judiciously used to give them a finished appearance. Finally, they were cambered in the center for drainage and paved with a hard plaster. The primary city of Coba seems to have made a consistent effort to connect itself by *sacbes* with its apparent tributary cities (Folan, Kintz, and Fletcher, 1983).

These roads have been suggested to have had commercial, military, and religious functions. Indeed, given the now-known high populations of the Classic Maya, they gave rights-of-way through crowded landscapes. Further, it can be shown that although the roads were intolerably hot and brilliant reflectors of sunlight during the day, they may well have functioned as travel routes during the night. The white ways would have been cool and even visible in the dark and therefore feasible routes for trains of porters, travelers, couriers, and military groups. Ball has argued, persuasively, that an ancient custom of carrying patron deities from one town ward to another in order to visit other patron deities was carried out on the internal road nets of the cities. Indeed, as he notes, in the case of one present-day Yucatecan town (Acanceh) the similar visits of patron saints follow the ancient, and otherwise disused, causeways of the town.

Fortifications: Moats, Walls, and Citadels

In most Mesoamerican centers, the ultimate refuge in war was the chief temple of the town. The weapon systems of the time (spears, spear-throwers, rocks, slings, and so on) made the height and steepness of such buildings a formidable advantage. In addition, the interlocking nature of the buildings would have allowed mutual support by the groups fighting from them. The Maya were probably no exception to this pattern. However, it is now known that the Classic and late Formative Maya built more formal fortifications than nearly any other group in Mesoamerica. Dry moats of formidable length protected Tikal, as already noted. A very large moat and ramparts encircled Becan, and a wide moat filled with water surrounded the Edzna citadel. All of these fortifications date to the Late Formative. Substantial walls were also favored in some sites; at Mirador there is a probable Late Formative example which runs for over 600 meters (1,980 feet; I. Graham, 1967). A probably Late Classic wall at Calakmul is still over 6 meters (20 feet) high and 2 meters (6.5 feet) thick and runs for more than 2,000 meters (6,600 feet; Ruppert and Denison, 1943; Fletcher et al., 1987).

At present, the best-known dry-moat fortress is at Becan, Campeche, where the ditch is about 1,600 meters (one mile) in circumference; it was found by Webster to have originally been about 12 meters (40 feet) deep and some 18 meters (60 feet) across (Webster, 1974). Formidable parapets increase the height of the interior lip of the ditch, and these may have been strengthened by the addition of log palisades. Seven narrow causeways cross the Becan moat; they show signs of having been cut in the ancient past, evidence that the fortifications were not simply built against a contingency. One causeway had been cut again and left open in Late Classic times. In the combination of its isolation in the midst of surrounding swamps, its carefully guarded access to water, and its enclosing ring of fortification, Becan is unique only in the detail in which it has been studied. The Maya Lowlands are littered with fortifications and true fortresses (Adams, 1981).

There are at least two sites which have the characteristics of hill forts or citadels. One is the hilltop fortress of Oxpemul, and the other is Kinal. In both cases, exceedingly steep rises face any hostile approach, and, in the case of Kinal, the rise is partly composed of sheer masonry walls at the top of a 9-meter (30-foot) platform.

Many other Maya sites are potentially defensible in their locations on ridges and next to formidable ravines. Seibal is an example. We have no idea at the moment, moreover, how many sites may have been defended by perishable military works that are detectable only by careful excavation. Deliberately fostered tangles of thorny second-growth jungle in belts around Classic sites could have acted as deterrents to attack. Bolstered by palisades, fields of sharpened stakes, deadfalls, and the occasional features of formal construction, Maya centers would not have been the defenseless, open communities that they seem to be at first sight.

Ball Courts

Another functional class of formal architecture found in Maya sites is the ball court (Fig. 5-8). This is a manifestation of the Mesoamerican ball game played with a solid rubber ball. Although the courts do not bulk large in mass or numbers, they occur frequently at large and small sites. The game varied in style and rules from place to place and through time, as reflected in the bewildering variety of courts from throughout Mexico and Guatemala. However, certain common features probably tie these games together. It seems that either individual players or teams could play, judging by accounts of the conquerors and native sources. Sometimes the idea was to score points on the other side; within an alloted period of play, the highest score won. A variant seems to have been that a single score won the game. This happened when a goal was so difficult that only one score could reasonably be expected.

In Conquest-period Mexico, the game had both recreational and divinatory functions. There is no knowing, at this point, how much of this sixteenth-century data we can extrapolate back in time. The Maya Classic ball courts are so distinct in form and style from later courts that the game may have differed radically. The safest thing we can say is that the game was played in some form, that it was popular, and that it was associated with elite-class life. The courts occur only in the urban centers. This does not mean, however, that play may not have taken place on informal courts away from the centers. Indeed, the game is still played to this day in an impoverished form by peasants on the west coast of Mexico, the court marked only by a few stones at the corners and by lines drawn in the dirt.

Reservoirs and Other Water Storage Devices

Water may not seem to be a vital concern for a people living in a tropical forest. However, because of the peculiar nature of the drainage of much of the Maya Lowlands, water impoundment becomes a necessity. Most of the peninsula of Yucatan is massive, porous, unbedded limestone with little topsoil. These conditions become exaggerated as one goes from south to north. North of Lake Peten Itza in Guatemala there is little permanent surface water in the form of lakes, ponds, or streams. Most of the heavy rainfall goes right through the soil, into the bedrock, and down

Fig. 5–8. Late Classic ball court at Copan, Honduras. An excellent example of the care and planning lavished on ball courts and an indication of their symbolic and possibly recreational importance to the Maya elite.

to the water table. At Tikal the water table is at least 168 meters (550 feet) below the surface. In the northern part of the peninsula the water table is about 20 meters (70 feet) down. During the dry season of three to four months, the small rain catchments often dry up. Modern settlements, even small ones, suffer greatly because of this circumstance, and water often has to be brought from up to 32 kilometers (20 miles) away from the settlement. In the north, sinkholes, locally known as cenotes, give access to water all year around. Caves with permanent springs were used from earliest times, and the remains of thousands of special jars have been found in them, broken while carrying water up to the surface.

Artificial means supplemented the sources in the north and south. In the north, special types of *chultuns,* or underground storage chambers, bell-shaped and plastered, were dug into the bedrock. *Chultuns* holding as much as 19,000 liters (5,000 gallons) of water have been found at Santa Rosa Xtampak (DeBloois, 1970). Some are in use to this day. The one at Kabah has been refurbished and serves the small present-day community. In the south, with less access to groundwater, large reservoirs were favored. At Tikal it is estimated by Carr and Hazard (1961) that the maximum capacity of all the reservoirs amounts to about 151,000 kiloliters (40 million gallons). The permanent population of Tikal is estimated at about seventy thousand people. This would mean that over a long dry period—120 days, assuming a 10 percent evaporation loss—there would still be about 18 liters (4.75 gallons) per person per day, which is quite sufficient. These reservoirs at Tikal, as well as at most other Maya sites such as Rio Azul, were filled partly from the drainage of the great areas of pavement tipped toward them. The runoff must have been extraordinary, judging by the rate at which the reexcavated camp reservoir filled. It was filled nearly to its present capacity of 11,000 kiloliters (3 million gallons) within 70 days after the rains began in 1958.

The matter of water becomes crucial in high-population situations. Impoundment of water means resource concentration, in Carneiro's terms, and, as has been noted, it may be one of the stimuli to the evolution of high culture in a tropical forest zone. Assuming that human population eventually expanded under optimum conditions, and that the needs of the consequent expansion were beyond the capacity of most natural means of water impoundment, then artificial means would have been an absolute necessity at some time early in the Maya settlement of the lowlands. Later, as an elite class developed, the reservoirs and other water storage devices may have become a means of social control.

South of Lake Peten Itza and in certain other regions, such as northern Belize and the southern corners of the lowlands, far fewer problems are involved in providing a dry-season water supply. Permanent lakes, large streams, and rivers there are all dependable. Curiously, none of the largest sites are located in these favorable zones. Perhaps (and this is only a guess) the people with independent means of water and food supply were less amenable to submitting to social control if it were not necessary. This interpretation would fit with, although not confirm, the idea that water was a resource that was concentrated.

Regional and Architectural Variation

Stylistic variation is plentiful among the regions of the Maya Lowlands and among the cities (centers) themselves. These variations undoubtedly reflect in some manner the variations among local social systems and the relative importance of the individual sites. As will be seen, these regional styles, with their associated variations in symbols and decoration, roughly approximate territories of some of the regional states of the Classic period.

Let us consider the technical styles first. There are at least five major Classic architectural regions. The Greater Peten style, characterized by extensive use of polychrome-painted, modeled stucco decoration and an essential conservatism of conception in room dimensions, is the most widespread. The elaboration of relatively few themes and recombination of these architectural elements in a multitude of ways is characteristic of most Peten-style sites, including the outlying city of Coba in the north. Tikal, with its complexities of palace groups and jumbles of temples in groups, typifies this style.

Florid architectural decoration in the form of mosaic facades of carved stone is typical of the two north central styles, the Puuc and the Rio Bec–Chenes (Fig. 5-9). This ornamentation takes the place of and carries the iconographic messages of the modeled stucco in the Greater Peten group. The differentiation between Rio Bec and Chenes styles has been demonstrated to be invalid (Potter, 1976). Chenes facades are typically low, one story high, but with the motif of the earth monster as the primary one

Fig. 5–9. An apartment for an elite family at Becan, Campeche. Structure IV is a palace building with at least four stories of terraced apartments. The regional architectural style is called Chenes. The step is the nose of the sky god, flanked by wall panels of stylized (sky?) serpent faces. The apartments were originally roofed with stone vaults.

Fig. 5–10. Governor's Palace, Uxmal, Yucatan, Mexico, an undoubted palace at this probable capital of a regional state. The Puuc regional style of architecture emphasizes Chac or rain god masks stacked up on the corners of buildings, as in this example. (Courtesy William R. Coe III)

and with the central doorway ornamented as the mouth of the monster. Rio Bec buildings are typically ornamented with large towers which are nonfunctional temples. That is, the staircases are too steep for use, and the dummy temples at the tops are solid masonry. However, there are suitable tomb chambers in the mass of the substructures, although no undisturbed grave has ever been found in them. These towered structures are contemporary with the Chenes style, and indeed, in sites such as Becan and Chicanna, they face Chenes structures across plazas, forming what were undoubtedly functional units. Therefore we shall combine these previously separated styles into one unit.

Puuc structures are baroquely decorated with masks of rain gods and facades of earth monsters (Fig. 5-10). They are also characterized by alternation of carved mosaic zones with severe or undecorated zones (Fig. 5-11). Columns seem to set Puuc apart as well. Both the Rio Bec–Chenes and the Puuc styles are notable for their daring in architectural conception, compared to the Greater Peten style (Fig. 5-12). Rooms tend to be larger and higher, and the massiveness of the structures in general is notable. In other words, the monumentality typical of Maya civic buildings is emphasized in these regional styles, making them possibly the most impressive of Maya architectural groups. The sites of Uxmal, Kabah, and Labna are exemplary of this impressiveness. Care in conception and execution of construction and carving is also typical of these northern styles (Pollock, 1980). Greater Peten architecture often conceals construction faults under the heavy coatings of stucco and plaster.

The two other major style zones are the frontier regions of Maya Classic culture, the Southwestern and the Southeastern. The former is epitomized at the site of Palenque (Fig. 5-13). The use of physical isolation as a means of emphasizing a building, as well as delicacy of stucco ornamentation, set this site and associated centers apart from the rest of the Maya area. Certain other features, such as mansard-style roofs and inner shrines, also distinguish Palenque buildings. Copan is the prototypical site for the Southeastern style unit, although what remains of Quirigua is similar. In the Southeastern style the emphasis seems to be on the temple form and on architectural sculpture nearly in the round, which covers the facades and sides of the buildings. The general emphasis on three-dimensional forms in Copan sculpture is notable, even in the stelae.

Although it has been argued otherwise, it seems quite clear that all of these regional styles are essentially contemporary, and especially during the eighth century A.D. We are not so certain about the Early Classic styles other than the Greater Peten group, since less work has been done to reveal the prototypes of the other regional styles. However, at Palenque and Copan it appears that the styles are essentially Late Classic and the results of generally late cultural florescences in these zones. Rio Bec–Chenes and Puuc fashions appear to go far back in time.

Fig. 5–11. A part of the Nunnery palace quadrangle at Uxmal, with the upper part of the great Temple of the Dwarf visible. The temple's name is an example of the flamboyant and inappropriate names often given to archaeological monuments in a misguided effort to interest tourists. (Courtesy William R. Coe III)

Fig. 5–12. Chichen Itza, Yucatan, Mexico. The round superstructure with a spiral interior staircase is thought to have been an observatory. Its style is Puuc, equivalent to very Late Classic. Human heads sculpted of stone rim the platforms, suggesting that the building fulfilled another function in addition to being a place for star-gazing.

Fig. 5–13. Temple of the Sun and probably the resting place of one of Palenque's Late Classic rulers, Palenque, Chiapas, Mexico. The sculpture in this building shows the accession of Chan-Bahlum to power at Palenque about A.D. 683, according to L. Schele.

Maya Communities and Political Structure

The disputes about the nature of Maya urbanism and especially about the nature of Classic political units have assumed the ferocity of medieval religious wars. I shall attempt to avoid invidious statements in this section and present a balanced picture of the evidence and most probable interpretations.

First, it seems indisputable that by A.D. 150 the Maya had developed urban centers and that these large and small cities became ever more complex through the seven hundred years of the Classic. Examples already mentioned include Tikal, Coba, Edzna, and others.

It is possible to rank Maya cities by size and achieve an idea of their relative importance in the Late Classic. One method of ranking is by count of the courtyards of major architecture in a city (Adams, 1981). Tikal has eighty-five courtyards of architecture (Map 5-3). Calakmul, on the basis of recent mapping, counts about fifty courtyards. These are the largest Maya centers known, and both are estimated to have had large populations as well: 72,000 and 50,000, respectively, in the eighth century A.D. On the next level of size are sites of about forty courtyards,

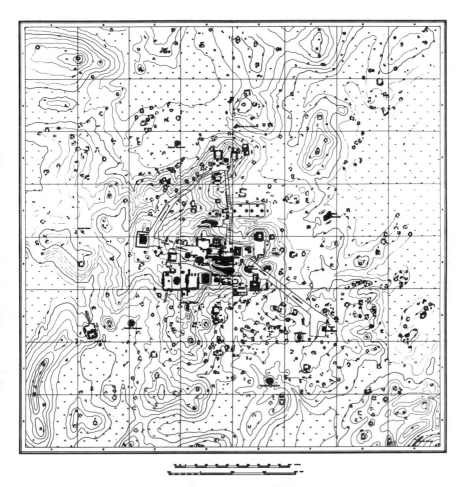

Map 5–3. The central zone of Tikal, Guatemala. Most of the city's major buildings now visible are from the Late Classic. Exceptions are the "Lost World" group and the North Acropolis. The city is defended on the north and south by dry moats and parapets and is estimated by W. Haviland to have had a population of eighty thousand in the eighth century A.D. (Courtesy The University Museum)

such as Naranjo and Rio Azul. Next come sites with twenty to thirty courtyards, such as Uaxactun, Palenque, Copan, Yaxchilan, and a number of others.

Certain patterns emerge from the examination of maps for relative locations and distances. Tikal and Calakmul are about 100 kilometers (60 miles) apart. Each is surrounded by a number of smaller cities, ranging down to sites that have only one courtyard of formal architecture. Further,

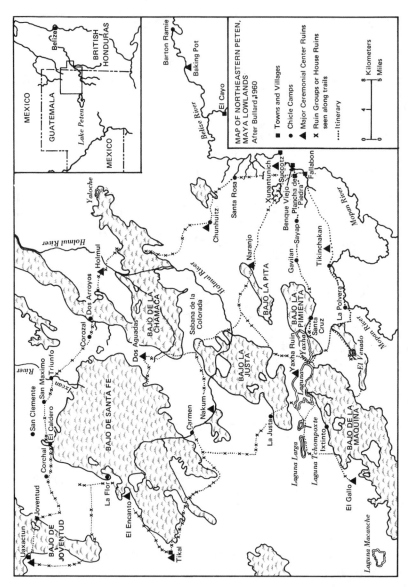

Map 5-4. The Classic Maya Lowlands.

there are some striking features of the Calakmul and Tikal zones, such as the buffer zone between them, at least 20 kilometers wide and 80 kilometers long (about 12.5 by 50 miles), in which no urban centers are to be found (Adams and Jones, 1981). It seems highly likely that places like Uaxactun at twenty-one courtyards, 19 kilometers (12 miles) distant from Tikal, were subordinate to the latter city, which is four times as large.

If one calculates the distance that can be covered on foot or in canoe in the lowlands, it comes to about 40 kilometers (25 miles) per day. Using this figure to draw boundaries around the largest cities and their subordinates, one arrives at a map with the Maya Lowlands divided into groups of cities, towns, villages, hamlets, and farmsteads which appear to have been regional states. In this scheme, Tikal would have been the capital of a regional state that bordered on the Calakmul regional state, with a buffer zone between them. With some adjustments for topography, it can be calculated that during the Late Classic, and probably the Early Classic as well, the Maya were divided into twelve to sixteen regional political units.

The major alternative that is now considered feasible is what may be termed the city-state model. It is based primarily on data from the decipherment of Maya texts. As will be seen in the section on writing, it is certain that the Maya wrote down names that are associated with specific cities. What is not certain is what those names mean. Are they names of places, territories (states), ruling dynasties, lineages, or rulers? All of these possibilities were considered by the discoverer of the glyphs, and the question is not yet answered (Berlin, 1958). At any rate, scholars are now generally in agreement that the distribution of one variety of the so-called emblem glyphs reflects the size of Classic political units. In addition, these scholars, mainly art historians and epigraphers, assume that Maya warfare was largely ritual and ceremonial and not for territorial conquest (Schele and Miller, 1986). Given these assumptions, the conclusion is easily reached that the Maya were organized into small political units defined by territory which averaged a radius of about 25 kilometers (16 miles) around each major city. Occasionally, unusually, and later, larger political units were formed (Mathews and Willey, personal communication, 1986), but these were rare events.

A number of objections can be raised against the city-state model, two of them being that it is dependent on specific and unusual interpretations of the function of Maya art and that it depends on a questionable set of assumptions about the meaning of emblem glyphs. The most serious and fatal flaw in the argument is that it nearly completely ignores the weight of field archaeological data against it. This information is not only the ranking of cities by size, their distributions, and associated patterns, but also the patterning of artifact distributions and of architectural styles and other evidence in the epigraphy. For example, tomb murals and other art at Rio Azul, 45 kilometers (28 miles) northeast of Tikal, indicate that Rio Azul's fifth-century governor was the son of Tikal's ruler. Culbert points out a number of other objections (personal communication, 1988), which indicate that a great number of widespread cities engaged in coordinated activities during the Late Classic. Further, he makes the point that it is unlikely that Tikal, with a population in the immediate area of 360,000, would have been able to govern itself with the rather slim political mechanisms characteristic of city-states. Marcus's recent studies of the Calakmul texts are also incongruent with the city-state model (Marcus, 1987). Finally, the nature of Maya fortifications and the implied extensive patterns of warfare correlate very poorly with the smaller political model.

At this point in Maya research, then, it appears to me that the evidence is heavily in favor of the development of regional states by the beginning of the Classic period.

Variation in Maya Cities

Maya cities varied in composition, pattern, and function. A place like Tikal, probably a capital, had all of the known functions described in the preceding section. It was a very large and complex place. Similarly, Coba, apparently the capital of its region as well, was very complex, but it also seems to have been zoned in a concentric manner (Folan, Kintz, and Fletcher, 1983). The Coba *sacbes* run to important groups within the city which may have been administrative centers for segments (barrios). On the next level of size and complexity, a site such as Rio Azul (Map 5-5) seems to have had a set of special functions, which were military, political, and economic. The city was likely fortified, inhabited by a set of noble families that had military duties, and was located on the frontier of Tikal's regional state. Its location on the river that gives the site its name also allowed for rainy-season canoe traffic, ultimately to the Caribbean. The permanent population in Early Classic times seems to have been not more than thirty-five hundred, which appears to be far too low for the construction of the site. We can only assume that the construction crews were imported. Still smaller sites in the same zone, such as Uaxactun, probably were administrative centers under a local elite reporting to the rulers at Tikal. Dropping to the smallest of centers, such as Uolantun, Haviland has demonstrated that the site was probably a residence for an exiled member of the ruling group.

In the Rio Bec region, medium-sized administrative centers are surrounded by palace residences in the countryside. The latter seem to have been rural "manor-houses" for the local elite.

Farther south, on the Usumacinta River, Yaxchilan is probably a fortified site located within a horseshoe bend, with the remnants of a bridge leading to the north bank, which radar data indicate was probably the

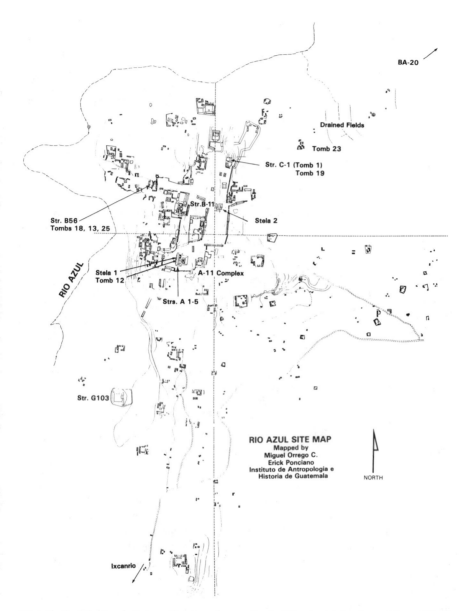

BA-20

Drained Fields

Tomb 23

Str. C-1 (Tomb 1)
Tomb 19

Str. B-11

Stela 2

Str. B56
Tombs 18, 13, 25

Stela 1
Tomb 12

A-11 Complex

Strs. A 1-5

RIO AZUL

Str. G103

RIO AZUL SITE MAP
Mapped by
Miguel Orrego C.
Erick Ponciano
Instituto de Antropologia e
Historia de Guatemala

NORTH

Ixcanrio

Map 5–5. Rio Azul, Peten, Guatemala, an Early Classic city in the southern Maya Lowlands, thought to be part of the regional state whose capital was Tikal, about 45 kilometers (28 miles) to the southwest. Approximately 7,500 people lived in the city in the fifth century A.D.

zone of raised fields (Adams, Brown, and Culbert, 1981). The city was probably a regional capital, dominating sites such as Bonampak, with its famous murals, and Piedras Negras, downstream. In spite of considerable and prolonged work at the site by Mexican archaeologists, very little new data on Yaxchilan have been published on much beyond its sculptures and some formal architecture. It is probable that the city was of considerable size and population.

The site of Palenque on the southwestern corner of the Maya Lowlands has always seemed anomalous. It is a treasure house of Classic Maya art in the form of sculpture, modeled stucco, and even painting. A great deal of restoration archaeology has been done at the site, as well as very intensive studies of the art and epigraphy. The city is about fifteen courtyards in size, about the size of Uaxactun. Clearly, however, it was the dominant, capital city of its region. It is, par excellence, the Maya city of a mainly resident elite supported by a mainly rural population dispersed throughout the surrounding hills and the coastal plain. Isolated as it was, it seems to have gone its own way in cultural evolution from about the sixth century onward and to have assumed some peculiar characteristics. It was not greatly pressured by surrounding, more powerful states and cities, and therefore its apparent city-state development should not be taken as a model for Maya political structure as a whole.

Copan on the southeastern corner of the lowlands is similarly isolated, is also relatively small, but also has an enormous amount of sculptured art. The site dominated its small region, and in its isolation it developed some features which appear to be unique, among them country residences linked to the central core of the city by *sacbes*. These isolated palace establishments are themselves embellished with sculptural emblems of family and dynasty which link them to temples and palaces in Copan. Again, as in the case of Palenque, much of the population seems to have been dispersed through the rural valley. In both Palenque and Copan, the excess of symbolic art everywhere one looks perhaps is related to the fact that they are, in the end, provincial centers and provincial elites. It may be that these isolated noble families felt the need to be more Maya than anyone else, somewhat as the British in India emphasized their English characteristics to set themselves apart.

We should also mention special-function sites such as the burial islands of Isla Jaina and Isla Piedras, off the coast of Campeche. There, especially in the Late Classic, the distinguished and perhaps even the less socially prominent were buried with special ritual and special mortuary figurines that may represent scenes from the lives of the persons with whom they are buried. They have been highly prized for years by the rapacious collectors of pre-Columbian art because of their naturalistic style.

Depictive Media and Communication Systems

The Sacred Almanac. Two major calendrical cycles governed the lives of Mesoamericans. They are analogous in operation to our weeks and months, which are solar and lunar calendars that we use simultaneously. One cycle, which seems to be more ancient than the other, was a sacred almanac consisting of 260 days. Twenty named days were combined with thirteen numbers, with the various permutations of number–day name combinations rotating until they began to repeat after 260 days. Morley's analogy of two unequal gear wheels meshing with one another is probably the clearest analogy to the operation of this cycle. The day names are specific to each region but overlap in meaning. The Maya 260-day round is called the Tzolkin by Maya scholars, but we do not know what the Maya called it. Each day was symbolized by some concept. The second day, for example, was Ik, or "Wind."

As noted elsewhere, the sacred almanac had great ritual significance for all members of a Mesoamerican society. Divination was and still is carried out by means of the omens and gods associated with any particular one of the 260 possibilities, and a person's fate was more or less determined by the circumstance of birthday. The days were conceived of as having lives of their own in the sense that they were divine (Thompson, 1950). The Maya seem to have carried this conception of time to its utmost refinement, using the metaphor of the god of the day carrying the day as a load. Religious festivals falling according to days of the sacred almanac were called "movable feasts" by the early chroniclers, who made the analogy between these native celebrations and the Christian Easter, which also shifts within the astronomical year.

The sacred almanac proved to be the most durable of all calendrical systems in Mesoamerica and is still in use today in many parts. Near Nebaj, in northern Guatemala, for example, Lincoln and Colby recorded the modern version of the almanac and its use in divination. It has been observed that the period of human gestation is about 260 days, and it is possible that this is the origin of the sacred almanac.

The Astronomical Year. The use of the 365-day year was equally widespread among Mesoamericans at the time of the Spanish Conquest. This calendar, an approximation of the "tropical" or astronomical year, was a sun calendar similar to our own. The mathematical arrangements were in the form of eighteen named months, with twenty numbered days in each, and therefore with a short five-day period added on to the end of each year to produce 365. A day in the tropical year was designated by means of its number and month name.

The Fifty-Two-Year Cycle. Obviously, both the systems outlined above can be and were combined. Thus, a particular day among the Maya could be 4 Ahau (according to the sacred almanac) or 8 Cumku (according to the astronomical year). Since these cycles are mathematically indivisible (260 will not divide evenly into 365), then the repetition of any particular combination will come only after the multiplied sum of days: 260 almanac days times 365 astronomical days or 94,900 days, approximately fifty-two years.

The interrelated calendrical systems probably date back to the Formative Period and may be a legacy of the Late Formative cultures. However, when we proceed to more complex calendrical permutations, we apparently leave behind all but the Lowland Maya.

Maya Mathematics, the Long Count, and Supplementary Elaborations

It seems likely that the Classic Maya and certain other Late Formative groups were the only cultures to use an exceedingly accurate system of counting time, called the long count. The day was the basic unit of the long count as it was of the sacred almanac. In fact, the latter was incorporated into the former. An infinite count of days was achieved by the long count. The structure of Maya mathematics is vigesimal, or a progression by twenties, but it was modified at times in order to be able to handle natural cycles. At the calendrical third order of vigesimal progression, the Maya went to a multiplier of 18 instead of 20 in order to achieve a unit of 360 instead of 400. The 360 unit was desired because of its approximation of tropical year length and its correspondence to the astronomical life cycle. Positional notation is also a feature, as well as the use of a bar for five and a dot for one. Finally, the concept of zero or completion was used as a necessary part of the system.

One day was expressed by the lowest dot (1×1). The Classic Maya wrote their numbers vertically, so a dot in the next higher place represented 20 (1×20). The third and highest place indicated one unit of 360 (1×360). Say that the figure desired was 1821. In that case it would be written similarly, except that the third and highest unit would be a bar representing 1800 (5×360), for a total of $1 + 20 + 1800 = 1821$.

An excellent book written by a mathematics teacher, George Sanchez, deals with how the Maya probably handled numbers of all kinds, including fractions and uneven numbers. Sanchez concludes that their system was extremely flexible (Sanchez, 1961; see also Anderson, 1971).

The long count consists of a hierarchy of units which are progressively larger according to the vigesimal system with the modification noted above. Thus we have the following:

1 *kin*	= 1 day	
1 *uinal*	= 20 days	
1 *tun*	= 360 days	
1 *katun*	= 7200 days	(about 20 years)
1 *baktun*	= 144,000 days	(about 400 years)

Special glyphs were developed to designate the various units. As usual, there is a bewilderment of variation, the nature and reasons for which are beyond the scope of this book. For these and other related matters, see J. E. S. Thompson's deceptively titled *Maya Hieroglyphs Without Tears* (1972). Higher orders of time units were probably in use, but most Maya inscriptions begin with the *baktun* number. The Maya began their count with a mythologically determined date of 3113 B.C., and most of their calculations fall within the ninth *baktun*, although dates exist from both the eighth and tenth *baktuns*. There are a few seventh-*baktun* dates, and these indicate that the bar-and-dot system was in use in the old Olmec zone, as well as the Izapa and Kaminaljuyu regions, earlier than in the Maya Lowlands. Tres Zapotes Stela C, dated at 31 B.C., is one of the earliest of these seventh-*baktun* monuments. In fact, no *baktun* 7 texts come from the Maya Lowlands except possibly an altar at Polol in the southern part.

Archaeologists have developed a convention for writing Maya dates in western script. The notation 9.16.3.0.0 means 9 *baktuns*, 16 *katuns*, 3 *tuns*, 0 *uinals*, 0 *kins*. The Maya recorded this date to mean that this amount of time had passed since their zero date (creation?), equivalent to 3113 B.C.

The correlation of the Maya calendar has generated almost as much heat among epigraphers as transubstantiation once did among theologians. With the massive confirmation of radiocarbon dates from Tikal and reinforcement from other projects since 1972, it now appears that the Martínez (Thompson) correlation is correct (Satterthwaite and Ralph, 1960). Martínez was a Yucatec scholar who, unfortunately, died before receiving adequate recognition for his achievement. His is the correlation that leads to the long count starting date noted above.

A lunar calendar and a Venus count were also kept. The former was calculated by the Mesoamericans at about 29.50 days and was adjusted by judicious alternation of 29- and 30-day moon months. The modern astronomical measurement of the moon's cycle is 29.53059+ days. The ancient value for the cycle of Venus was very close to the modern measurement of 583.920 days.

Writing Systems

The Lowland Maya developed the art of writing beyond anything achieved elsewhere in Mesoamerica (Fig. 5-14). It became a true writing system in the sense that it had the capacity to carry a message without the aid of oral explanation or exegesis. Until 1958, nearly all glyphs to which meaning had been assigned were deciphered. That is, they were concoctions of pictorial elements for which meaning had been defined. Translation, the rendering of the glyphs into a Maya linguistic equivalent, was exceedingly rare. It was thought by most scholars that the undeciphered glyphs were mostly additional information about the calendar, math-

Fig. 5–14. A mural from Tomb 12, Rio Azul, Guatemala. The glyphs, which indicate the direction south, were painted on the appropriate wall of the tomb and include a notation of the planet Venus. Early Classic.

ematical permutations, mythological references, liturgical notations, and the like. Even mnemonic functions were thought to be part of the ancient writing. Texts occurring on pottery vessels were considered to be purely decorative (see J. E. S. Thompson's 1950 book, *Maya Hieroglyphic Writing: An Introduction*). All of this has changed drastically, and most of these notions have been discarded.

It is now clear that Maya writing served various purposes dictated by society and its directing elite. These purposes were to record genealogical information about the aristocratic families—the rulers, historical events, dynastic affairs, and marriages—and to place them in the context of the unending cycles of time (Fig. 5-15). The true nature of the script became apparent through a series of insights and studies carried out during the 1950s and '60s. Yuri Knorozov (1958) attacked the script through a phonetic approach. Although he made a number of valid observations and decipherments, these were so hidden in a mass of mistaken assumptions and diversionary errors that the main body of his work was rejected. The major break into the script came first with the discovery by Heinrich Berlin (1958) that there were glyphs which were associated with particular sites. Although Berlin was not sure whether these were rulers' names, place-names, or something else, it became apparent that historical information might be contained in the texts. The truly revolutionary papers of Tatiana Proskouriakoff (1960, 1963, 1964, et passim) demonstrated that rulers' lives were outlined on the carved texts and that these schematic biographies included birthdays, dates of accession to power, notations of conquests of other rulers, marriages, and similar data. These decipherments were rapidly followed by those of other scholars, such as David Kelley (1962; see also 1976), who demonstrated the existence of a dynastic sequence in the texts of Quirigua. Linguists took a hand in the game, and Lounsbury (1973) made a decipherment of a title which read "*ah po*," "lord." It became apparent that Maya script did have phonetic values. A measure of the progress made since the early 1970s is a masterly summary and study by Victoria Bricker, *A Grammar of Maya Hieroglyphs* (1986).

The changes in perspective on Maya hieroglyphs have been profound. As is now known, the nature of the script is that it is both logographic and phonetic. A logogram is a unit of meaning in a given language, equivalent to the linguists' morpheme. An example from English is "-ing," as in "hunt-ing." Maya morphemes usually occur in a consonant/vowel/consonant pattern, such as *bah*. This is a clue to pronunciation but not to precise meaning, because the Maya also used a rebus principle. Therefore, *bah* may mean "pocket gopher," but it also may mean "to pierce, perforate, puncture," etc. (Bricker, 1986). Maya script reflects the structure of Maya languages, mainly of the ancient forms of Chol and Yucatec. Schele, in her studies of verbs (1982), indicates that the basic

Fig. 5–15. Rice paper rubbing of glyph blocks from a palace at the medium-sized city of Machaquila, Peten, Guatemala. The glyphs are not in their original order, but seem to refer to noble individuals and their personal names. Late Classic.

word order for clauses was usually verb-object-subject and verb-subject. Inflectional studies by Bricker (1986) demonstrate the highly technical means of determining meaning through restricting the possibilities.

Colonial and modern Maya texts seem to show certain repetitive patterns in their use of language. Parallelism expressed in couplets is one example. The Maya might say, "There was then no sickness; they had then no aching bones; . . ." Another frequent feature is that of punning, which, on a written level, becomes rebus. An example of this is the use of a fish head for the word *xoc*, a mythical fish, but which also means "to count." As in any language, metaphor looms large in describing the world within which it exists. The Maya had a concept of periods of time as burdens. The ancient script reflects these patterns as well as the structural differences between Chol and Yucatec, which were the two major languages expressed in writing (Thompson, 1950; Bricker, 1986).

All of the above is highly technical, abstruse, and increasingly inaccessible to the nonspecialist. However, it is worth the effort to understand the writing system's general features, because they provide an insider's view of Classic Maya civilization. While much of what we now gain from decipherments remains enigmatic, a great deal can be checked against the patterns of information from field archaeology. Only by a combination of continual checking of one against the other can any substantial and trustworthy understanding be assured.

The Content of Maya Script

For a student or a field archaeologist, the major interest of deciphered texts is the body of insights that they give us on the nature of ancient cultural institutions. The texts form something of a commentary or exegesis on a reconstructed event or pattern. For example, in the case of a highly complex scene on a pottery vessel known as the Altar Vase, the pot was found in a burial (Figs. 5-16, 5-17). The date of A.D. 754 (actually 9.16.3.0.0) is given on the pot, and the six human figures that are in the scene are identified. Only by the archaeological context of stratigraphy, ceramic analysis, and other data is a full understanding of the scene possible. In this case, the combination of data indicates that the painted record is one of a funeral for a middle-aged woman who died at Altar de Sacrificios in A.D. 754. Funeral ceremonies were attended by relatives who came from Tikal, Yaxchilan, and the northern highlands of Guatemala. In the case of Yaxchilan, its ruler was probably present. A young woman was sacrificed and buried near the tomb of the older woman. Both graves were covered by a memorial temple on which was placed a carved monument (Adams, 1971).

There is a great deal more information from this burial, but the point has been made that texts without archaeology are incomplete, and vice versa. The implications here are of a tightly related set of ruling families from important cities (Tikal and Yaxchilan) and a relatively unimportant city (Altar de Sacrificios). This gives something of an idea of the nature of Maya political structure which can be tested against other information. Another point to be made is that the Altar Vase, if it had been found by looters and sold into the New York art market, would be just another pretty vase. It would have lost about 90 percent of the information that came with it because of the careful excavation. Unfortunately, a great deal of interpretation of Maya art and hieroglyphs has been based on illegally excavated ceramics, at least some of which are falsifications.

A tomb found at Rio Azul contained a highly unusual ceramic piece

Fig. 5–16. This roll-out of a scene painted on the polychromed Altar Vase from Altar de Sacrificios, Peten, Guatemala, dates from 9.16.3.0.0, A.D., and shows a funeral ceremony for a middle-aged noblewoman. Among those attending are Bird-Jaguar II from Yaxchilan and the younger brother of Ruler B of Tikal. Bird-Jaguar dances, while a young woman is sacrificed and accompanies her relative into the afterworld. (Courtesy Ian Graham)

Fig. 5–17. Hieroglyphic captions from the Altar Vase (Fig. 5–16) The vertical row is associated with a nobleman from Tikal, and the text ends with the Tikal emblem glyph.

Fig. 5–18. A pot for chocolate from Tomb 19, Str. C–1, Rio Azul. According to David Stuart, the texts on the pot indicate that it belonged to a counselor to "Governor X" and that it was meant to hold chocolate. Analysis by Hershey Food Corporation scientists of the contents of the pot confirmed that it had indeed held chocolate (cacao).

(Fig. 5-18). David Stuart later deciphered the text on its top to say that it was meant for the purpose of containing two kinds of chocolate drink (Hall et al., in press). The decipherment was confirmed by Hershey Food Laboratories, which found that the powdery residue inside the pot was the remains of cacao. The pot also had another text which Stuart read to mean that it belonged to a counselor of a prince ("an heir to power"). Indeed, the person to whom it had belonged had been buried alongside the ruler whom he served. Once more, the combination of decipherment in the context of carefully gathered field archaeology produced results more telling than those that either epigraphy or archaeology alone could have achieved.

The future of decipherment of Maya texts seems promising. Linguistically trained epigraphers are now in a position not only to extract the general meanings of the glyphs, but also to translate them individually and in the form of whole texts.

Ancient Maya Social Structure

There are several models for ancient Maya society. The most traditional but least realistic one is that of the philosopher-kings, who altruistically and humanely led the grateful masses. In this view, the leaders were morally and intellectually superior in the same manner as "gurus" or other religious leaders are in Asian societies. This was more or less the view held by Morley and Thompson (Morley, 1946). It has been resurrected in a new form by David Stuart and other epigrapher-iconographers. Their argument is that the Maya believed the blood of kings sustained the divine and terrestrial balance of the cosmos (Schele and Miller, 1986). The kings therefore were liturgical-political leaders of their small states, and the centers were ceremonial stages upon which the divine dramas were enacted. This seems almost wholly unrealistic. While there is certainly evidence of blood sacrifice, including autosacrifice, the new data from the historical texts, as well as the information on Maya warfare, imply a less benign and more understandable picture of Maya society and its leadership. Other archaeological data indicate a much more secular, worldly, and realistic worldview of the Classic Maya.

Haviland's studies (1968) have indicated that kinship structure was probably patrilineal (descent traced through the father's line), as is the case among all known present-day Maya. The genealogies from the sculpture fall in with this pattern (Haviland, 1977). Tomb patterns, depictive data, and settlement patterns all tend to confirm this conclusion. Furthermore, it appears that most of the ancient populations lived in clusters of houses which were the residences of married sons and their families living near the elderly parents. Becker (1971) found at Tikal that even people on the lower levels of society tried to establish small shrines or mausoleums to the dead members of their lineages. Therefore, it appears that from top

to bottom, ancient Maya society was permeated with an attitude of
ancestor reverence, if not ancestor worship (Fig. 5-19). Among the modern Maya of highland Chiapas, the ancestors are still among the most
important supernatural beings that can be turned to for help and comfort
(Vogt, 1969). The emphasis on genealogical information in the hieroglyphic texts, then, was a kind of legitimization of the right of a ruler to
his or her power. In spite of the patrilineal emphasis, women rulers or
regents appear in the dynastic records of various sites and were certainly
important in creating marriage alliances between cities and states.

Depictive art was a sort of propaganda mechanism which emphasized
the functions of the temples, legitimized the rulers, and glorified the city
and state. The roofcombs were a form of elevated billboard in this sense.
The famous Bonampak murals are undoubtedly historical in nature; the
complex ceremonies, the short war carried out by allied cities, and the
more domestic scenes are all profoundly connected to circumstantial
events and quite distinctive individuals.

*Fig. 5–19. Altar Q, Copan, Honduras. David Stuart thinks that this square throne
shows all sixteen of Copan's rulers, with the two facing one another being the first and
the latest. Late Classic.*

Vogt (1971) has taken some of these data, compared them to ethnographic communities of the Highland Maya, and proposed a model for ancient Maya civilization that is essentially egalitarian. Briefly, this structure centers on a system of rotating religious and civil offices of increasing importance; the fulfillment of the less important offices qualified a man for the more important. Theoretically, every man in Maya society had a chance at the most important offices and the attached political and religious power. Vogt has suggested that this may fit the Classic Maya case and solved their problems of social integration of a dispersed population. The model might well fit the Middle and Late Formative societal picture, with the evidence of ranked social positions rather than class distinctions, but the archaeological data strongly contradict the egalitarian, rotation-of-power model as the prime organizing principle of Classic society. Genealogical data in the hieroglyphic texts used as the justification for assumption of power argue that ascriptive principles were at work in social organization. One's social ranking at birth had a great deal to do with the degree of access to all kinds of things, from sumptuous items and housing to political and religious power.

An increasingly aristocratic principle seems to have been characteristic of Maya society as time went on. Therefore, the best reconstruction that we can now make of ancient Maya society is that of a pyramidal social structure, with a hereditary aristocracy at the top (Fig. 5-20). A careful gradation of rank within the directing elite was also present. In the Late Formative there is evidence that assemblies and councils of lineage heads were the principal governing bodies. By the Classic period, many of the heads of lineages had evidently parlayed their advantages into hereditary superior status. The use of genealogical justification for superior power led to ancestor worship and,ultimately, the claim to divine descent by the elite.

This elite group concentrated their attention on administration of increasingly large aggregations of cities and smaller communities and the dense populations that lived in them. Warfare came and went but was always another interest of the nobility, being the ultimate means of dispossessing other elite families and lineages of their cities and territories. The masses of formal buildings, nearly all at the service of the elite, certainly took up a good deal of time. The constant construction, demolition, and refurbishment of residences, funerary monuments, *sacbes,* and other structures must have absorbed a great deal of the energy of the upper class, even if they were not directly involved with the execution of the plans.

Below this caste of professional rulers were several layers of occupationally defined classes. The tedious and time-consuming tasks of administration, bureaucratic work, may have been handled by minor nobility, but the lower levels, such as those of village headmen or district chiefs, may

Fig. 5–20. Lintel 26, Yaxchilan. Shield-Jaguar and a woman, possibly his consort, who holds his jaguar helmet and shield for him.

well have been filled by commoners. An argument can be made for the existence of a scribal class, which may have been the same as the bureaucratic group just mentioned. The quantity and complexity of the art of writing among the Maya argues for full-time practictioners, scribes. The lack of writing among the few survivors of the collapse of Maya Classic culture also suggests this. Glyphs were drawn on the walls of buildings after the severe population losses of the collapse, but they were of rudimentary and unskilled nature. It also seems unlikely that the most exalted members of the elite class worried over the exact amounts of black beans, squash, maize, chiles, and other mundane items provided periodically by twenty, fifty, or one hundred small villages for the support of the cities.

Sculpture and fine pottery were obvious craft specialties, considering the large quantities of both produced during the Classic (Fig. 5-21). A high degree of knowledge of the canons of art and hieroglyphic writing, as well as of specific skills, all argue this. Manufacturers of elite-class costumes undoubtedly occupied a special place. A wide range of exotic materials and manufactured items were involved, as well as problems of tailoring and fitting. It seems likely that there were specialists something like western culture's couturiers. Weavers were undoubtedly present; cloth is an invariable manufacture and trade item. Pieces of fifth-century textiles were analyzed by Robert Carlsen (1986, 1987) and his colleagues, who found them to be very similar to the sort of "white-on-white," open-weave cotton gauze cloth made today around the north highland town of Coban in Guatemala. It also seems likely that the ancient Maya, like their modern descendants, wove their own clothing for family use and that only a few weavers made the exquisite clothing shown in sculpture and painting.

Musicians and other entertainers are depicted in art, especially in the Bonampak murals, where a full-fledged orchestra tunes up for a ceremony. Servants are also depicted in painting and, rarely, sculpture. Again in the Bonampak murals, servants are shown dressing certain august persons in elaborate costume, adjusting jewelry, and carrying headdresses. Servants are also depicted taking care of elite-class children, and they must have performed many other domestic chores. Maya palace buildings are often quite high and difficult of access, and workers must have been available to carry the necessary water and food to upper apartments. As mentioned before, cooking facilities and servants' quarters have been found at many Maya sites. Large numbers of people, especially sweepers and cleaners, would have been needed to keep the formal buildings, plazas, and other parts of the cities clean. Perhaps this duty was performed on a rotational basis, with the duty going to younger and less important members of

Fig. 5–21. A favorite Teotihuacan ceramic form. Early Classic.

society, somewhat in the manner in which the streets and town headquarters are cleaned in present-day Guatemalan Indian towns.

Construction specialists are only present by inference, but again, the mass of building and complexity of skills involved demand the presence of at least cadres of specialists in matters such as stucco modeling and stone cutting. Much of the work involved with Maya monumental architecture, however, could have been done by part-time specialists. Every Maya man today learns how to build a house without a nail, and such skills can easily be applied to building scaffolding for large-scale construction. The Maya masons from Oxkutzcab, Yucatan, who reconstructed the Temple of the Dwarf at Uxmal covered that immense structure with scaffolding made of poles, planks, and rope in 1968. The directing and supervisory skills may have remained in the upper class, or there may have been foremen and master masons who ran things.

Judging by R. L. Rands's work in the Palenque region (1973), there seem to have been various specialist communities, and thus there may have been specialists, as suggested above, in satellite communities around the cities as well as in special quarters. Rands's data also suggest that the local craft products seldom went beyond the bounds of the individual city's domain; in Palenque's case, that was an area of about 125 square kilometers (about 85 square miles). However, Palenque was relatively isolated on the southwestern corner of the lowlands, and other regions seem to have distributed craft products widely. Colha, in northern Belize, furnished thousands of high-quality, standardized chert tools to a regional economy. It may be that these tools even reached the Rio Azul zone, about 60 kilometers (38 miles) to the west, and perhaps farther. Colha is documented as a specialist community which probably produced its own food but which also exported its manufactures (Shafer and Hester, 1983). Given the political structure outlined previously, it is likely that these manufactures were controlled and distributed within the regional states. There is also evidence at Colha and elsewhere that craftsmen such as flint knappers were attached to noble households. The famous polychrome pottery of the classic period appears to have been manufactured on demand by such attached artisans and with the motifs dictated by the noble families. It would have been something like the nobility of the ancien régime of France ordering a set of dinnerware from Sevres.

The above information and patterning lead to the conclusion that the fundamental structure of Maya society was one in which there were reciprocal obligations between the classes, vertically, so to speak. To put it another way, there appear to have been patron-client relationships between noble households and commoner families. On the level of classes, we can rank them from the highest nonelite, who had intimate and continual contact with the aristocracy, down to those people who rarely interacted with the elite or even saw them. The former would have been those who practiced skills most needed by the rulers, and the latter would have constituted a mass of farmers, many in isolated districts of the regional states. Viewed in this way, Maya society probably had at least five classes; elite, petty administrators and stewards, skilled artisans, commoner-farmers, and the ever-present dispossessed.

Judging by Haviland's evidence for ranked patrilineages at Tikal (1968), and confirmatory studies from elsewhere, it appears that relationships within classes were primarily based on kinship.

Control of land seems to have been nearly completely in the hands of the elite by the beginning of the Classic. The manor houses and palace structures in the countryside of the Río Bec region, and other zones as well, indicate control of the general terrain and particularly of the zones of intensive cultivation. However, these lands would have been cultivated by the commoners bound to noble families by reciprocal obligations (protection by the elite and production by the commoners). These features generally characterize social systems which have been called feudal (Coulborn, 1956). Feudal systems are known not just from Europe, but also from medieval Japan (pre-Shogunate) and from ethnographic situations—Rwanda-Burundi, for example (Adams and Smith, 1981). The model has been criticized because some archaeologists have maintained that feudal structures are only characteristic of disintegrating social structures, particularly in Europe of the eighth century after the fall of the Roman administrative system. However, as can be seen, feudal systems are found in other circumstances, the features fit the Maya well, and such a model explains the universal problems of control of land and manpower. It is without doubt the case that many Maya regional societies went beyond the rather loose feudal system, and particularly Tikal, Calakmul, and perhaps Seibal became centralized, bureaucratic systems. However, it appears at this point in Maya studies that these most rationalized structures developed from a generalized feudal base.

Arthur Demarest has suggested that a concept derived from Southeast Asian studies, that of "pulsating galactic polities," is a good model for Classic Maya social and political structure. He argues that the uncoordinated decline and rise of the most important Maya cities cannot be explained by coordinated events such as climatic shifts. Therefore, the shifts in political fortunes should be in some manner connected to cultural institutions, and probably to the nature of Maya leadership. The "pulsating galactic polity" notion is that strong individuals at the head of kinship-oriented states surround themselves with subordinate chiefs that ally themselves to the larger cities on the basis of the realpolitik of outstanding personal leadership. Because this type of leadership is, by its nature, ephemeral and shifting, it accounts for the relatively rapid patterns of rise and fall in the Maya Classic.

These ideas, while attractive, fly in the face of the increasing evidence for the importance of territoriality and regional state organization in the Maya Classic. Dynastic continuities at Tikal are at least as stable as those of ruling houses in Europe. Furthermore, it seems to me that the concept of "pulsating galactic polity" leans too heavily on the "great man" theory of history in only a thinly disguised form and ignores the stability given political organizations by cultural institutions such as ancestor veneration. The Demarest model is nonlinear, but it is also nonevolutionary, ahistorical, and functionalist. In the end it explains little except the internal working of societies already in being. It may also be noted that the functional parallels between Southeast Asian and Maya societies were first pointed out by M. D. Coe (1957).

At this point we have passed from social structure and returned to political systems as they may have been transformed through time. We must now examine a reconstruction of Maya history and cultural evolution.

A Political and Cultural History of the Late Formative and Classic Maya

The following is one archaeologist's reconstruction of the major events that we now see as crucial in Maya cultural history, from both the political and the anthropological points of view. It is built on the work and ideas of many colleagues and predecessors, some of whom may not recognize their brain-children in their new forms.

In the Late Formative, it appears that a number of hitherto independent villages were aggregated into coalitions which supported certain regional centers. I have avoided the use of the term *chiefdom* here because of our uncertainty about the real nature of Late Formative leadership. We have no idea at the moment how many of these coalitions there may have been in the lowlands. Some were based on development of trade, of which the port of Cerros is an example, and possibly Lamanai as well. In the north, Komchen was probably also trade-based, exploiting the nearby salt fields. Leadership was by heads of ranked lineages, who, we may speculate, were governing councils for zones and villages and focused on regional centers. Mirador, with its gigantic structures, was surely one of the largest in terms of available population, but Tikal was nearly as big. Edzna in the west central zone and Becan in the center were also this kind of center. Altar de Sacrificios in the south was yet another zone, as was its neighbor on the Pasión River, Seibal. These interior and southern communities seem to have based their growth more on population mass than on development of commerce. Sanders suggests that these centers were either centers of, or parts of, enclaves and that there were thinly populated zones between. Ideological differences can be seen among these various centers and regions. Competition took the more frequent form of organized warfare, and fortresses appeared at nearly all of the centers mentioned above.

In Early Classic times, population growth evidently continued, and competition among these centers heated up. The centers were converted from regional market and administrative centers to cities. Likewise, social structural changes took place which converted the old lineage heads to hereditary aristocracy with client commoner families. A basic feudal system developed with an aristocracy based on control of land and water and the labor to work it. Stated in another way, the shift was from a kin-based to a tributary mode of production.

Mirador failed at the beginning of this period. It may be that some kind of soil/water failure through drought drove people away from the great center, although there is evidence for a substantial Early Classic population. It seems more likely that this fortified center was overcome by another defensible city, Tikal. The thrusting elites of the Early Classic seem to have consolidated as many cities and lesser communities as they could under the leadership of a single dominant city. Tikal certainly falls into this category, and the replacement regional capital for Mirador, Calakmul, seems to do so as well. A well-defined boundary buffer zone developed between Tikal and Calakmul and their regional coalitions. However, at that moment, about A.D. 350, an outside intervention seems to have transformed the situation.

Teotihuacan is mentioned at Tikal several times in connection with a date which corresponds to about A.D. 360. It appears that connections between the two great cities existed before, probably on a commercial trade basis. Teotihuacan was apparently a despotic and extraordinarily well organized city and capital of an empire—probably for the purpose of trade as well as other benefits. Tikal was one of the largest and certainly best organized Maya cities by that time. Commodities that certainly interested Teotihuacan included cacao, salt, honey, and beeswax as well as medicinal herbs. All of these were sixteenth-century exports from the lowlands. Tropical woods and bird feathers were also of great value to the highlanders. Many of these items, especially herbs, require a well-organized population which, in this case, knows exactly what plant part is to be used in what form for what ailment. At any rate, Teotihuacan displaced the ruler of Tikal, a certain "Jaguar-Paw," at about A.D. 360 and placed on the throne a more amenable ruler—one we have nicknamed "Curl-Nose" from his name glyph. Apparently, this gave Tikal an edge over other Maya cities, and it expanded still further. Part of the benefit it received from the alliance was military advice. According to Coggins, whose reconstruction this is, Curl-Nose married a woman who may have been a daughter of Jaguar-Paw.

Tikal expanded in several directions, but certainly to Rio Azul about A.D. 380. The Rio Azul rulers were executed, as shown on a set of altars found at that city, Rio Azul was transformed into a frontier fortress, and the boundary with the Calakmul state was consolidated. Curl Nose's son, "Stormy Sky," is shown on Tikal Stela 31 as a Maya ruler, but he is flanked by Teotihuacan warriors. One of his sons was born in A.D. 417 and was eventually appointed governor of the district dominated by Rio Azul. This governor also was provided with military and other sorts of advice (Adams, 1987b). It appears that during this period Tikal probably moved far beyond the basic feudal political system and became much more of a centralized and bureaucratic state, somewhat along the lines of Teotihuacan. Such a drastic reorganization and probable displacement of powerful families created an eventual backlash.

Teotihuacan, for reasons discussed in the next chapter, began to withdraw from its far-flung contacts in the late fifth century. This left the usurping rulers without outside support. Coggins suggests that the older ruling families tried to make a comeback. Ultimately this attempt failed, but apparently it created a series of civil wars and internal revolts in the southern region, especially in the Tikal region state. Rio Azul was overrun and destroyed during this period. This is the period of the hiatus in Maya texts, which lasted from about A.D. 534 to 593.

It was during this time of troubles that the relatively small city of Caracol in southern Belize claimed a battlefield victory over Tikal (Chase and Chase, 1987). While this is probably correct, the implication that Caracol replaced Tikal or took over its territory is almost certainly not. The massed demographic power of a regional state like Tikal far outmatched anything that Caracol could muster. We must remember the propagandistic function of the texts as well.

In the north, Teotihuacan seems not to have made such an impact. Coba was certainly an important regional center during the Early Classic (Folan, Fletcher and Kintz, 1979; Folan, Kintz, and Fletcher, 1983), but it may be only toward the end of this period (ca. A.D. 500) that it reached city and city-state levels of organization. Folan and others (1983) have postulated that a dry period inhibited growth at the end of the Late Formative, especially in the north with its relatively marginal rainfall. Komchen was abandoned at the end of the Late Formative, and Dzibilchaltun seems to have collapsed as well (Andrews, 1981). It is possible that the coastal trade route collapsed as Friedel has suggested, but there seems to be no evidence to support this idea. Teotihuacan's presence and contact is suggested by a *talud-tablero* platform at an outlier group of Dzibilchaltun, but Andrews (1981) is not sure if this presence is connected with the collapse. Perhaps Teotihuacan traders moved into a zone disorganized by drought problems and established a salt administration center.

Meanwhile, the political perturbations of Teotihuacan's intrusion and withdrawal apparently upset the development of various sites. Altar de Sacrificios and Seibal were very weak centers during this period.

The even more devastating events of the hiatus and the suggested civil wars and revolts in the south required a lengthy recovery. It was not until about A.D. 650 that Maya civilization began to function again, and then it was somewhat different than before. This seems to have been a period of cooler, more humid climate (Folan et al., 1983), with the consequent rapid development of more regional states than previously. Coba became a capital in the northeast, as Dzibilchaltun apparently did in the northwest, with populations of about 40,000 and 25,000, respectively. Becan and many sites of the Río Bec zone flourished, with rural populations reaching up to 450 persons per square kilometer (1,166 per square mile), supported by 10,000 square kilometers (3,900 square miles) of terraced hillsides and drained fields in swamps (Adams, 1981). Calakmul to the west seems to have been a large city of about 50,000, supported by surrounding wetland cultivation and extensive hydraulic works (Fletcher et al., 1987). Huge palaces were built in all zones. On the southwestern and southeastern corners of the lowlands, the remarkable sites of Palenque and Copan flowered with strong rulers who are known to us by name. One of these is Pacal, whose extraordinary tomb has been found (Ruz, 1973). We know in great detail of his accomplishments and those of his descendants, thanks to the work of a group of dedicated scholars. Pacal was mainly a great builder and organizer, and the site that can be seen today is largely as he designed it.

It appears that the southeastern center of Quirigua had been established by a dynasty linked to the Tikal ruling families. After an immense flood in the sixth century, the location of the major public architecture was shifted to its visible present site. After that move, the center flourished as never before, constructing an acropolis of palace and temple buildings and erecting immensely tall and finely carved monuments to its rulers (Ashmore, 1984). It has been suggested that the evident wealth to pay for all this conspicuous consumption came from the large-scale production and export of cacao. The basic economic structure was probably that of aristocratic extraction of tribute from the regional population.

The larger nearby city of Copan also had a series of great rulers, and only encountered difficulties at the end of the Classic when the neighboring site of Quirigua captured Copan's ruler, Madrugada, who may have been executed. Copan languished after that disaster, and the valley apparently lapsed back into a state of "balkanization."

It is to Tikal and its regional state that we must finally turn, because of the immense amount of detail that has been produced by several generations of work there. Ruler A at Tikal came to power about A.D. 682 and began a great deal of the building program, which included the giant temples (Jones, 1977, 1987) (Fig. 5-22). He was a descendant, or made claim to be, of the Curl Nose dynasty, so the Teotihuacan-linked usurpers won in the end after all. Ruler A's name has been translated to read Ah Cacau, or Lord Cacao, a title appropriate to a ruler who was buried with an incredibly rich amount of jade. We know that it was Ah Cacau in the

Fig. 5–22. Central Acropolis at Tikal, Guatemala. The Late Classic residences of Tikal's rulers, including, probably, Ah Cacau, who is buried under Tikal Temple I in the left middle ground.

Fig. 5–23. Late Classic Temple I at Tikal, Guatemala, during the process of excavation. Built by the eighth-century ruler Ah Cacau, it proved also to be his burial place. Much of presently apparent Tikal is the work of this king and his two successors. (Courtesy William R. Coe III)

tomb of Temple I at Tikal because his name is monogrammed on his hair-tweezers, a mosaic pot placed with him, and several other objects (Fig. 5-23). Altar de Sacrificios revived and was linked by blood and marriage with more important cities such as Tikal. Tikal had about 72,000 people by A.D. 750. Rio Azul was not much larger; it was somewhat rebuilt after the catastrophe of the hiatus, but it never regained its splendor. The site of Kinal was selected as a citadel and probable administrative center for the district during the Late Classic.

One general characteristic of Maya culture wherever one finds it during the Late Classic is the immense increase in the size and numbers of the buildings. There was an implied increase in the size of the resident elites as well (Willey and Shimkin, 1973). The labor burden on the commoners must have increased something on the order of ten times. Wetland cultivation was increased to its maximum, and other forms of intensive agriculture were expanded. Deforestation was undoubtedly a problem. Firewood simply for cooking and heating would have been scarce, but immense amounts were also required to produce the high-quality slaked lime for the building programs practiced by rulers like Ah Cacau. Yet the Maya rulers seemed to have had no more heed for this problem and others than our present-day politicians do for the rapid destruction of modern tropical forests. The expansion of all parts of Maya society made it vulnerable to many internal and external stresses, leading to increased military competition and ultimately to the sudden and final catastrophe of the ninth century. Before we consider this event and its implications, however, we should examine the other polarity of Mesoamerica in this period, the great and very different city of Teotihuacan.

CHAPTER 6

TEOTIHUACAN, MONTE ALBAN, AND OTHER EARLY CLASSIC CIVILIZATIONS

. . . There at Teotihuacan, as they say, in times past, when yet there was darkness, there all the gods gathered themselves together, and they debated who would bear the burden, who . . . would become the sun.
—*Sahagún, 1963, Book, 3:1.*

And there [Teotihuacan] all the people raised pyramids for the sun and for the moon; they made many small pyramids where offerings were made. . . . And when the rulers died, they buried them there. Then they built a pyramid over them. . . . For so it was said: "When we die, it is not true that we die; for still we live; we are resurrected. We still live; we awaken."
—*Sahagún, 1961, Book 10:191.*

MOTECUHZOMA II, worried by events of ill omen, is said to have made a pilgrimage to the dead city of Teotihuacan a few years before the arrival of the Spaniards (Vaillant, 1962:65). There he made sacrifices and communed with the gods. As it turned out, his prayers were futile, but his worries were justified. Motecuhzoma was following a long tradition of pilgrimage established in a past so distant to the Aztec that they had lost the history explaining the enormous fossil metropolis. Even in ruins, Teotihuacan was so impressive that the sixteenth-century people of the Basin of Mexico thought the city had been built by direction of the gods. The myth of the successive suns tells that the gods assembled at Teotihuacan in the primordial darkness to bring light to the cosmos. Two of the gods were believed to have sacrificed themselves in a fire and thus became the sun and the moon. After that, humanity gathered at the place and built the great city (León-Portilla, 1961:23–27).

A major and sustained effort at understanding Teotihuacan began with Manuel Gamio's 1917 project and continues today with a fifth generation of scholars. Fortunately, the work of excavation and study has focused on the entire Valley of Teotihuacan and not just on the city.

Chronology

A series of phases divides the cultural history of Teotihuacan into several periods lasting from about 200 B.C. to about A.D. 650. The terminal date is still in dispute, and it may be that the city lasted until about A.D. 750. The important point is that even if this latter date is correct, Teotihuacan had lost its imperial and dominant status by 650, surviving as a large regional state and delaying only its physical destruction until 750. On the other hand, there is no dispute over the major features of Teotihuacan's rise and cultural apogee.

It seems quite likely that the giant Pyramid of the Sun was built about A.D. 100 (Fig. 6-1). Just before this construction feat, the population of the urban area rose sharply, from about 2,000 at 200 B.C. to about 60,000 at A.D. 100 and finally to about 150,000 or more at A.D. 600. There is strong evidence that this growth resulted from the concentration at Teotihuacan of most of the population of the Basin of Mexico and not from a population explosion. It is clear that Teotihuacan must have had political and social control of the basin to be able to accomplish this aggregation. Further, it is now clear that this immense population was physically reorganized in the fourth century A.D. by construction of most of the two thousand apartment compounds that make up the bulk of

Fig. 6–1. The Pyramid (or Temple) of the Sun, Teotihuacan, viewed from the Pyramid (or Temple) of the Moon, with lesser platforms in the foreground. All of these structures once supported brightly decorated temple buildings.

residences at Teotihuacan. To understand this overwhelming dominance by one city not only of the basin but also of great areas of Mesoamerica (See Map 6-1), it is easiest to begin with an examination of the city at its height. This will indicate the functional relationships of the parts of the city and show some of the imperatives that drove Teotihuacan to its position of preeminence.

The Urban Capital: A Survey

According to the mapping project directed by Rene Millon (1970, 1973, 1981), Teotihuacan at about A.D. 600 sprawled over a huge irregular area of about 20 square kilometers, about 8 square miles (Map 6-2). The space was occupied by avenues, markets, plazas, temples, palaces, apartment compounds, a grid system of streets, slums, waterways, reservoirs, and drainage systems. The city ultimately was laid on a north-south axis of about 15¼ degrees east of north. This orientation was also typical of other contemporary centers on the central plateau under the domination of Teotihuacan. The major north-south avenue is now known as the Street of the Dead. This is a name, like all others at Teotihuacan, applied by the Aztec and archaeologists at best or by tourist guides at worst (Fig. 6-2). Another major avenue is on an east-west axis, and the axes intersect at the location of the administrative, religious, and market center of the city, the "citadel" zone.

Along the north-south main street are clustered sumptuous and lavish elite residences which jostle with large and small temple platforms. The street is also the location of the two gigantic Pyramids of the Sun and Moon as well as of the Citadel and the Great Compound. Away from the north-south street and arranged on a grid system of smaller streets are one-story apartment houses. Most of the population ultimately lived in these formal structures. On the edges of the city, less formally planned clusters of rooms built of poorer material are found, including one- and two-room houses which resemble those built today in the valley. These were probably Teotihuacan's slums.

Springs rise from the ground in the southwest section of the city, and their waters were led away to fields and *chinampas*. Some still-extant canals are oriented to the Teotihuacan grid. The location of the ancient city was determined by these springs, which were evidently more widespread in ancient times. The sources of the San Juan River are separate and derive from runoff and tributary streams some distance up the valley. In Teotihuacan times, this river was channeled and fed through the city, winding down its eastern edge and then turning west to run north of the Citadel and Great Compound zone. Ultimately the river gave access to the great sheet of lake water that lay to the southwest of the city. Reservoirs were built and side channels dug which gave more of the city's inhabitants

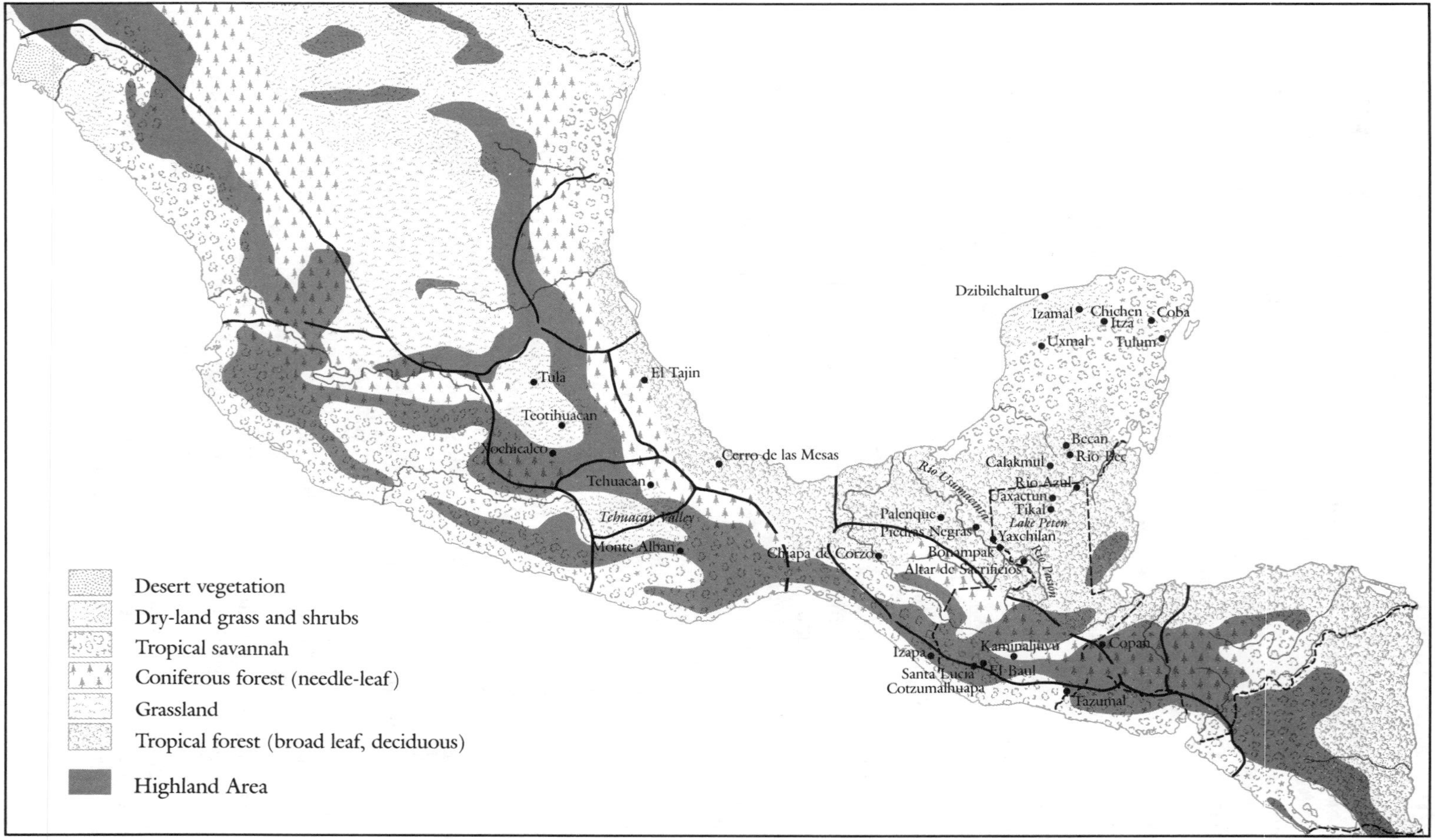

Map 6-1. Classic Mesoamerica, showing the distribution of early civilizations over its

Desert vegetation

Dry-land grass and shrubs

Tropical savannah

Coniferous forest (needle-leaf)

Grassland

Tropical forest (broad leaf, deciduous)

Highland Area

Dzibilchaltun

Izamal · Chichen · Coba
Uxmal · Itza
· Tulum

Becan
Rio Bec
Calakmul
Rio Azul
El Mirador
Tikal
Lake Peten
Uaxactun

Río Usumacinta
Río Pasión
Palenque
Piedras Negras
Yaxchilan
Bonampak
Altar de Sacrificios

Copan

Chiapa de Corzo

Tazumal

Kaminaljuyu
Izapa
El Baul
Santa Lucia
Cozumalhuapa

Cerro de las Mesas

El Tajin

Monte Alban
Tehuacan Valley
Tehuacan

Tula
Teotihuacan
Xochicalco

access to river and spring water. Wells have been found within the city, sealed under later floors (Cowgill, personal communication).

One of the many significant findings of the Teotihuacan mapping project was the discovery of walls which are at least partitions and may be defensive. Such walls set off large parts of the city from one another and define their boundaries. Examples are the east-west walls located just north of the Pyramid of the Moon. These walls tie in with another which runs north-south, protecting or delimiting the western city limit until this function is taken over by the Barranca de Malinalco. Millon notes that the *chinampa* district in the southwest would also slow any attacker, and on the east the San Juan River would serve the same purpose, the latter being more than 80 meters (260 feet) across and 20 meters (65 feet) deep in places (Rattray, 1987). Millon (1973) makes a convincing case that Teotihuacan may have been a clumsy giant but was certainly not a defenseless city. If belts of cactus were added to the other features, the defenses would have been strengthened.

The oldest part of the city is in the northwestern quarter, where architecture dating to Tzacualli times (about A.D. 100) has been found. This section also became the most densely populated part of the city. Everything noted above except for the slums points to urban planning and controlled growth from at least Tlamimilolpa times (A.D. 200). Whether the entire city followed a master plan or simply grew by accretion within the quadrants formed by the avenues is unknown but is also somewhat irrelevant. From the point of view of urban definition, Teotihuacan shows every evidence of having been a sophisticated and gigantic center, with its growth following a general and perhaps very detailed plan.

Construction Techniques, Materials, and Style. The most common building material at Teotihuacan was a kind of pudding made of chunks of porous volcanic stone (*tezontle*) set in a matrix of clay, gravel, and mortar. Walls, ceilings, and floors were covered with heavy coats of plaster and finished by polishing, which made them both attractively glossy and impermeable. Large amounts of wood were used to construct roof beams, vertical supports within walls, centers for masonry pillars, and door lintels. Huge tree trunks were incorporated into platforms to transmit weight to the ground. It has been suggested that deforestation probably resulted and led to erosion of agricultural lands (Millon, 1967). At first sight then, Teotihuacan architecture might seem concrete enough to satisfy the most demanding fire marshal, but it concealed within the plaster and mortar highly flammable materials. Add to these the equally flammable textiles, wood, feathers, and mats in the buildings, and the fire rating would probably have been very high (Margain, 1971; Marquina, 1964). The fire hazards were similar to those at Casas Grandes, where a fierce conflagration also incinerated the town (DiPeso, personal communication). When Teotihuacan was finally destroyed, an enormous fire left a blanket of ash and debris that is found nearly anywhere one excavates.

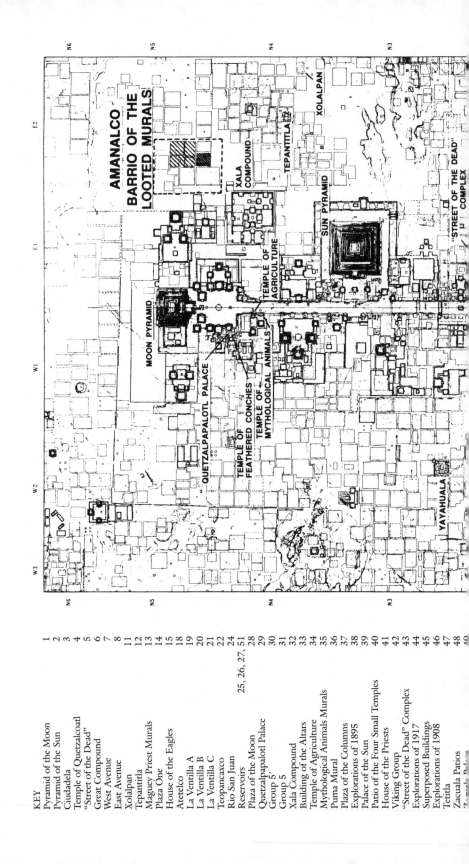

KEY

Pyramid of the Moon	1
Pyramid of the Sun	2
Ciudadela	3
Temple of Quetzalcoatl	4
"Street of the Dead"	5
Great Compound	6
West Avenue	7
East Avenue	8
Xolalpan	11
Tepantitla	12
Maguey Priest Murals	13
Plaza One	14
House of the Eagles	15
Atetelco	18
La Ventilla A	19
La Ventilla B	20
La Ventilla C	21
Teopancaxco	22
Rio San Juan	24
Reservoirs	25, 26, 27, 51
Plaza of the Moon	28
Quetzalpapalotl Palace	29
Group 5'	30
Group 5	31
Xala Compound	32
Building of the Altars	33
Temple of Agriculture	34
Mythological Animals Murals	35
Puma Mural	36
Plaza of the Columns	37
Explorations of 1895	38
Palace of the Sun	39
Patio of the Four Small Temples	40
House of the Priests	41
Viking Group	42
"Street of the Dead" Complex	43
Explorations of 1917	44
Superposed Buildings	45
Explorations of 1908	46
Tetitla	47
Zacuala Patios	48
Zacuala Palace	49

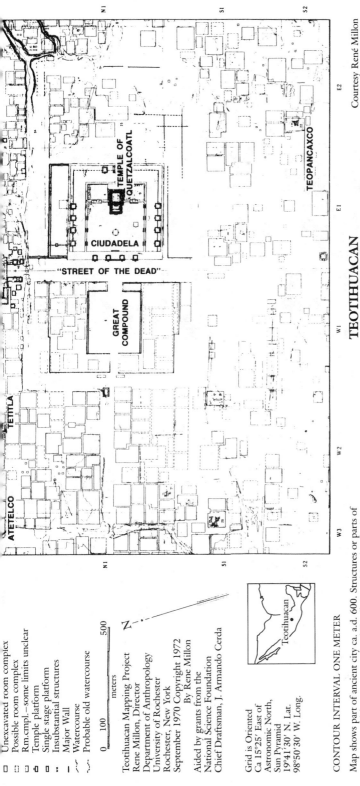

Map 6–2. *Central sector of Teotihuacan. Note the distinctive grid pattern oriented to the cardinal points and around the two major avenues. Most of the 2,600 buildings in the city are apartment compounds, and most of them are unexplored.*

TEOTIHUACAN

Courtesy René Millon

CENTRAL PLATEAU OF MEXICO
ARCHAEOLOGICAL AND TOPOGRAPHIC MAP
OF THE NORTH CENTRAL ZONE

CONTOUR INTERVAL ONE METER

Map shows part of ancient city ca. a.d. 600. Structures or parts of
structures which are excavated and Teotihuacan Mapping Project
test excavations are shown. Reconstructions based on the project
survey of surface remains of unexcavated and partially excavated
structures are also shown. Note canalization of watercourses.

Grid is Oriented
Ca 15°25' East of
Astronomic North,
Sun Pyramid
19°41'30" N. Lat.
98°50'30" W. Long.

Teotihuacan Mapping Project
Rene Millon, Director
Department of Anthropology
University of Rochester
Rochester, New York
September 1970 Copyright 1972
By Rene Millon

Aided by grants from the
National Science Foundation
Chief Draftsman, J. Armando Cerda

0   100   500
    meters

□   Unexcavated room complex
░   Possible room complex
▨   Rm.cmpl.–some limits unclear
▤   Temple platform
▥   Single stage platform
▦   Insubstantial structures
—   Major Wall
⌒   Watercourse
⌒   Probable old watercourse

ATETELCO

TETTLA

"STREET OF THE DEAD"

TEMPLE OF
QUETZALCOATL

CIUDADELA

GREAT
COMPOUND

TEOPANCAXCO

Fig. 6–2. Teotihuacan, Mexico. The Temple of the Moon viewed from the Temple of the Sun. The moon structure sits on the north end of a great avenue now called the Avenue of the Dead, certainly not its ancient name.

Teotihuacan developed a characteristic architectural style on which archaeologists depend in the detection of the city's influence on other cities of the time. Buildings were single-story and flat-roofed, whether placed directly on the ground, on low platforms, or elevated. Edges of roofs were decorated by large ceramic elements. Spouts from the roofs and underground drains from the patios carried off rainwater and sewage. Large and small interior courtyards allowed fresh air and sunshine to penetrate the windowless structures. Porches, arcades, and wide doorways relieved the otherwise faceless exteriors. As in later Tenochtitlan and much other traditional Mexican architecture, the most attractive features of the buildings are concealed within.

Pyramidal platforms supported both temples and some elite dwellings. These platforms are distinctively styled into a set of terraces using what has been named the *talud-tablero* (terrace–recessed panel) form. The concept is best grasped visually; it consists of a slanting terrace wall topped by a vertical framed panel. The terrace top recedes to the base of the next terrace wall, and so the *talud-tableros* continue to the top of the platform. Decorative and symbolic painting is often found in the panels.

Civic and Religious Structures. The largest buildings at Teotihuacan are the Pyramids of the Sun and Moon. Both platforms undoubtedly supported temples. The discovery of an ancient tunnel leading to a cavern under the Pyramid of the Sun suggests one of the functions of the huge piles. Water was led through the now dry cavern by a channel (Millon, 1981). Therefore, the cavern may have been conceived of as the house of Tlaloc, the principal deity of the city. Millon also suggests that in accordance with the ancient chronicles, the cavern may have been thought of as the birthplace of the sun and moon (see the epigraph at the beginning of this chapter). Tombs of distinguished persons may also be located within the mass of the two large structures. The two pyramids both have frontal platforms similar to those used as locations for burials at the Teotihuacan-influenced city of Kaminaljuyu.

To the south of the Pyramid of the Sun (home of the sun and moon?) and across the artificially channeled river is the famous and fortunately named Citadel (Ciudadela) complex (Fig. 6-3). The major part of this complex consists of a huge platform surrounding a great square. The base platform once also supported an encircling wall which would have been defensible. On the eastern edge of the square is located what must have been one of the major temples of Teotihuacan, perhaps dedicated to the rain god, Tlaloc, or to the feathered serpent, Quetzalcoatl. Two building phases are now visible. The outer structure is plain and relatively unadorned, consisting of severe *talud-tablero* terraces, though in ancient times it was probably decorated brightly with painted stucco. The inner and earlier temple is a spectacular example of Teotihuacan architectonic sculpture. Great feathered serpent bodies writhe across the *tablero* panels, punctuated regularly by projecting heads of serpents and what is perhaps goggle-eyed Tlaloc (Fig. 6-4). A grand staircase with balustrades decorated by toothy serpent heads leads to the top of the pyramid. The sculpture is highlighted by painting in greens, reds, and white. Seashells and other water symbols strongly suggest that one is in the presence of Tlaloc. The temple atop this glorious structure is long since gone, no doubt destroyed in ancient times during the refurbishment of the square or in the ultimate catastrophe that overtook the city. Enough of its floor remained to show that it had the two-room arrangement typical of most Mesoamerican temples.

Clusters of rooms like those found in the apartment compounds and palaces were found on the terrace abutting both sides of the main Citadel temple. Millon suggests that this was the double palace of Teotihuacan (1967:43). If there was an emperor in Teotihuacan or even a region-state ruler, then probably this was where he lived and administered.

The Great Compound, across the road from the Citadel, is thought by Millon to have been the central market of the city. Today it is covered by a modern parking lot, tourist shops, museum, and restaurant. Thus this complex continues to function somewhat as it did in ancient times. The compound is the largest in the city, reflecting its importance. Millon notes

Fig. 6–3. The Ciudadela, or Citadel, Teotihuacan. A part of the richly ornamented terraces of the Temple of Quetzalcoatl, which was covered by later construction and thereby preserved. Feathered serpents and Tlaloc (rain god) faces and bodies writhe among seashells and other water symbols.

that apartment compounds are to be found around the Great Compound and suggests that the second level of society was housed in these residences.

Referring to Map 6-2, one sees clutches of "lesser" temples oriented around small courtyards in groups of three. Many of these temples—

more than seventy-five—are along the Street of the Dead. The smaller courtyard groups are also found in other parts of the city. Low platforms often located in the patios and courtyards served as places for public ritual and dances. These dances were not simple entertainment. A mural from the Atetelco apartment compound shows gaily clad but armed warriors whose dance steps are diagrammed by footprints on the platform floor in true Fred Astaire style. More soberingly, these warriors carry elaborate curved knives on the ends of which are stuck bleeding human hearts.

Murals and models found at Teotihuacan depict single-story temples highly decorated with feathers, paintings, and cloth on the walls and roofs. A mural fragment shows such a small temple sitting by a road on a single-terraced *talud-tablero* platform. All such depictions of temples show what are apparently wooden armatures on the roofs supporting feathers and other decoration (see Sejourne's reconstruction of Zacuala in 1966: Fig. 28). The green feathers waving and swaying in the breezes perhaps symbolized the bright green corn leaves stirred by the wind in the vast fields around the city.

If they followed what seems to be a common Mesoamerican pattern of the time, these temple groups were dedicated to gods associated with specific kinship groups. Excavations in such buildings should produce

Fig. 6–4. Detail, Temple of Quetzalcoatl, Teotihuacan. The Tlaloc faces seem to be crocodilian, with pebble-grained skin. The serpent heads with ruffs possibly represent Quetzalcoatl, whose name means "Feathered Serpent."

the remains of tombs with ancestral burials in them, if such was the case. Indeed, founders' burials may be associated with the construction of many apartment compounds, as in the case of Xolalpan (Millon, 1981). However, it also seems certain that the greatest of these temples attracted worshipers from outside the city. The remains of offerings from other parts of Mesoamerica have been found at Teotihuacan. Pilgrimages from far-flung places, as well as those from the basin and other nearby locations, no doubt provided people with some of the needed means of ideological identification with the city. Millon argues that such an identification was needed to provide an incentive besides force and economics to build and maintain such a highly structured city and society.

Palaces. The famous Quetzalpapalotl (Quetzal Bird–Butterfly) Palace is incompletely excavated but shows the magnificence in which the elite lived. A set of deep porches lead to a central courtyard which is surrounded by an arcade and three large rooms. This part is altogether unsuitable for habitation and seems to have been an administrative audience area. The rear of the audience area gives into several room clusters which were for living purposes. These rooms are similar to those found in the not-so-elaborate apartment compounds. The Quetzalpapalotl Palace is located on the edge of the courtyard in front of the Pyramid of the Moon and therefore is probably one of the most important and elaborate of such structures. If this palace is more or less typical, however, the pattern of porches giving access to an audience area with adjacent and secluded living quarters may be repeated elsewhere in the city. Certainly these palace buildings are distinguished from the apartment structures by larger size, complexity, and special features not found in other residences (Acosta, 1964*a*).

Apartment Compounds. Of the twenty-six hundred known buildings in Teotihuacan at the end of the mapping project, over two thousand of them are apartment compounds. As of 1988, only twenty-five or thirty of these had been even partially excavated. These buildings are highly consistent in general pattern. Clusters of rooms are arranged around several patios, and a common outer wall surrounds the whole maze. The structures are arranged on a grid system of streets which averages about 60 meters (197 feet) from street to street. However, both the grid and the sizes of the houses are variable. The latter vary from 625 to over 6,000 square meters (6,750 to over 64,500 square feet) in extent. There are probably a few larger and smaller examples. Millon estimates that about 100 people lived in the largest compounds and about 20 in the smallest. From these figures he estimates the total population at about A.D. 600 as at least 75,000 and perhaps more than 200,000, with a mean figure of 125,000 (Millon, 1970:1080).

There is no doubt that these buildings were residential. Each apartment apparently had its own kitchen, within which have been found cooking places and large amounts of cooking, serving, and storage pottery (Fig. 6-5). Most cooking was apparently done on three-prong braziers (similar to those used for cooking at nearby Chalcatzingo about 700 B.C.). Sufficiently careful excavations to detect such evidence have been made in only a few cases. The apartment compound named Tetitla perhaps had a cistern for storing rainwater which was fed by roof drains, according to Laurette Sejourne (1966), but the evidence is puzzling and not at all certain. There were also sanitary facilities in the forms of patios or blind alleys where the results of visits were available to turkey buzzards. Fortunately, the high altitude and strong sunlight helped promote rapid sterilization of effluents. Below-floor drains carried the rains away from the patios and into the streets.

Each apartment compound varies in number of rooms and patios, but most have at least fifty, Tetitla over one hundred, and Tlamimilolpa an estimated three hundred. All apartment houses thus far excavated have

Fig. 6–5. A black-brown cooking pot, probably used in a kitchen of one of the hundreds of apartments in Teotihuacan.

their own temples or shrines. In many ways the apartment houses were self-contained units. Even burials, presumably of former inhabitants, were made inside the structures. Not all were buried in this way, however, as cremation seems to have been a favored means of disposal of the dead.

Tlamimilolpa is apparently an apartment structure, but more extensive than most and without discernible outer walls. Its rooms are smaller, but its plan and orientation conform to the standards of the compounds along the Street of the Dead. According to recent excavations by Evelyn Rattray, Tlamimilolpa went through three phases of construction, beginning about A.D. 300. The building materials of the earliest phase were mainly adobe and mud, possibly indicating a relatively low status for the inhabitants. However, the compound does contain a possible founder's burial which was well made and full of fine pottery; more than twelve hundred artifacts were placed in this tomb, and the body was cremated in place. By A.D. 400, the fortunes of the group in Tlamimilolpa had markedly improved, and they rebuilt the compound with the higher-quality concrete materials used in most other compounds. It is possible that the inhabitants were porters and warehousemen for the nearby Merchants' Barrio. However, they may also have been craftsmen engaged in the manufacture of the fine textiles and processing of hematite for export that was done in the Merchants' Barrio (Rattray, 1987; Iceland, 1989).

The social groups occupying these compounds were probably a form of kinship unit which traced descent from both the mother's and the father's lines, but with a bias toward the father's. Spence's studies of skeletal materials from apartment compound La Ventilla B showed that the males were genetically more closely linked than the females buried there (Millon, 1981).

Millon writes of these buildings: "The residential areas of Teotihuacan must have presented a somewhat forbidding aspect from the outside; high windowless walls facing on narrow streets. Within the buildings, however, the occupants were assured of privacy. Each patio had its own drainage system; each admitted light and air to the surrounding apartments; each made it possible for the inhabitants to be out of doors yet alone" (1967:43). Millon has also commented on the defensive nature of these structures. It is worth noting that the apartments provided a far higher quality of housing for most of the city's populace than that available in the valley since the Spanish Conquest (Sanders, 1965).

Summary. Obviously, our classifications of palaces, apartment houses, and so forth are artificial separations. The city grew almost organically, and the functions of these buildings overlapped and melded into one another. For example, consider the great double palace wrapped around the temple in the Citadel; the fact that apartment houses have their own temples and shrines; palaces that combine many functions, even including sumptuous burial places; some apartment compounds that are nearly palaces in elegance and appointments; and the Great Market, which was probably involved with religious activities as well. The Tlamimilolpa compound group seems to show that though it might have been under-privileged in its earlier phase, the fortunes of the kinship unit occupying it later shifted for the better. Barrio divisions in Teotihuacan are clear, with status differences within each city ward as well as between them, yet each of these neighborhoods had its own temple center.

Art and Religion

No one source gives us as much information about the Teotihuacanos and their lives as the brilliant murals to be found on the interior walls in practically every building of the city. As sculpture and modeling were preferred by the Maya for architectural decoration, so was mural painting at Teotihuacan. Nicholson (1971b) notes that Teotihuacan sculpture is cubistic, massive, and stylized. It is typified by the giant and blocky sculpture of Tlaloc outside the National Museum of Anthropology of Mexico. Sculpture found within the city itself can be viewed in the form of the bas-relief columns of the Palace of Quetzalpapalotl, where repetitive and unexciting depictions of quetzal birds and butterflies are worked into intricate patterns. However, whatever their stone sculpture lacked in vitality the Teotihuacanos made up for in their mural art. Over 350 examples of painting are known from only thirteen locations. Because there are over 2,600 buildings in Teotihuacan, and most are as yet unexcavated, there must be an unparalleled treasury of art still unrevealed.

Clara Millon (1972, 1973), Esther Pasztory (1974), George Kubler (1967), and Kubler's student Arthur Miller (1973) have made the principal studies of mural art. According to Kubler, there are at least forty-five images of life forms in the painting, and these are far surpassed by the number of geometric and stylized motifs. There are also about fifty elements which are probably glyphs. Kubler characterizes Teotihuacan murals as being strongly liturgical, especially in the early phases. That is, religious symbols and graphic obeisances are arranged and repeated in a kind of polychrome litany.

The liturgical murals fall into five thematic clusters, which probably correspond to specific religious cults. The Raingod Cluster is the most common (Fig. 6–6). An example of it is the speech scroll of the singing priest of the Maguey Mural. In the scroll are richly various signs for water, and the scroll's edges are trimmed with a Tlaloc headdress, a serpent's eye, and a possible lightning symbol. Avatars and variable manifestations of the rain god occur in the forms of feathered serpents (recall the Citadel Temple), starfish, jaguars, flowers, and warriors.

In an extraordinary tour de force, the porticos of the three temples in Atetelco apartment house are covered from floor to ceiling with the life-giving figures of the rain god. The human face in the Tlaloc costume is

Fig. 6–6. Mural from an apartment compound in Zacuala, Teotihuacan, showing one of the versions of Tlaloc. In this case the god or an impersonator stands in full front position with a large feathered hat. From his hands flow a number of beneficial and desirable items: food, pottery, and seashells, among others.

replaced by coyote and eagle heads in some murals, while water-drooling jaguars prowl at the bases of the walls. Tlaloc in a full front view is shown at Tetitla with water flowing from his hands (Lothrop, 1964). Symbolically, within the water streams are pieces of jade, human heads, animal heads, and perhaps grains of corn.

In the fascinating Paradise Mural from Tepantitla, Tlaloc, grasping Tlaloc dolls, presides over a scene which Caso (1942) has interpreted as a depiction of Tlalocan, the afterworld of the rain god. A great waterspout gushes upward in the center of the mural, spewing people into paradise. The spout seems to result from two rivers flowing from springs guarded by jaguars in the corners of the mural. Interestingly, the rivers are bordered by neatly divided and irrigated fields. Paradise is indeed a happy place, and speech and song scrolls issue from the many that have arrived. One man is so happy to be there that he weeps and makes a magnificent utterance, judging by the ornate speech scroll issuing from his mouth. Tlaloc's goggle-eyed butterflies flit through the scene, which shows humans engaged in games and other pursuits. This promised afterlife no doubt gave the Teotihuacan priesthood a powerful moral and psychological tool to use for social control. This unitary view of the "Tlaloc" figures has been challenged by Pasztory (1974), who thinks that several gods are represented by these figures.

The Butterfly Cluster of themes is often found on incense burners used in funeral rites, suggesting that the butterfly may be a symbol for the soul. Owls, darts, and shields are members of a third complex and are probably the symbols of war. Kubler suggests that the combination of owl and quetzal birds in the Quetzalpapalotl Palace designates a specific dynasty and its association with war. It is worth recalling that the Maya glyph for the Teotihuacanos at Tikal is a hand with a spear-thrower.

A fourth complex of paintings centers around the depiction of a cult object and its worshipers. In a mural discovered in 1889 in the Temple of Agriculture and since destroyed, chanting worshipers look at two smoking altars, which they offer pottery, what may be a quail, food, and bundles of what may be incense. Cremation was one way to dispose of the dead, and this scene may show just that sort of funeral with the symbols of the presiding deity.

The fifth cluster of themes is grouped around rain, groundwater, lightning, and fire. In many scenes, jaguars, symbols of the underworld, prowl, blowing shell trumpets which drip water and which produce thunderous sounds, as indicated by noise scrolls (Fig. 6-7).

Changes through time in mural subject matter and style indicate both

Fig. 6–7. A jaguar blows a trumpet from which drops of water fall in a mural from an interior structure at Teotihuacan. Starfish and feathered headdress (?) designs frame the scene.

changes in basic cultural values and more subtle aesthetic trends. Clara Millon's important work has been oriented toward these diachronic matters, as contrasted to Kubler's essentially synchronic approach. Millon (1972) has sorted the trends in painting into six major periods. Specific qualities which persist through all these periods include (1) a use of flat colors, (2) a general absence of spatial depth, and (3) a prohibition against portrayal of human sexual characteristics.

Period 1 painting seems to have been largely supplementary to sculpture, which was more important than painting early in the city's history. A few ancillary depictions on the Quetzalcoatl pyramid-temple typify this art.

Period 2 murals include the Mythological Animals painting and those from the Superposed Structures building. The general characteristics are small bodies combined with large heads, increased polychromy, and complexity of composition.

In Period 3 a more monumental style was developed. The giant jaguars painted on exterior walls of the Street of the Dead are good examples. Much experimentation in style is in evidence, indicating that many painters were at work in a period of canonical flux. Millon comments that "among the paintings we find artistic disasters and magnificent successes" (1972:9).

Period 4 is one of a fully developed art style with a realized potential. The famous Tepantitla Tlalocan mural is from this period, as is the sequence of "kneeling jaguars" at the Tetitla apartment compound. Millon sees Maya and Zapotec influences in the Tetitla paintings. Again, the style is rich and varied, but it is tied together in its concern with the transcendental. Brilliant polychromy is characteristic.

Period 5 painting is distinguished by the trend toward painting almost entirely in tones of red. The netted design in the Atetelco Patio Blanco (White Courtyard) is an example of one thematic development. Clara Millon has recently interpreted a motif from this mural and others as representing temporal and sacred power combined. This grapheme is a tassel attached to a *tablero* (C. Millon, 1973). As will be seen, this tassel motif is also used as symbol for Teotihuacan in Monte Alban.

Period 6 is the final period and seems to feature a narrower color range than preceding periods. The upper painting of the Quetzalpapalotl Palace exemplifies this period. Ornateness and simplicity exist side by side, continuing the divergent traditions established long in the past.

In my opinion there may be a distinct shift in cultural values through time reflected in these thematic changes. From an emphasis on the exaltation of nature, the Teotihuacanos, late in their history, shifted to glorification of warriors and rulers. As noted above, Teotihuacan religion seems to have been strongly animistic in its earliest phases and then to have moved to a focus on humanized deities and even deified humans. The Mural of the Mythological Animals is thought by Millon to represent the myth of cyclical creation and destruction and is early in date (C. Millon, 1972). Another example of this earliest cosmology is on a decorated pot found at Las Colinas, Tlaxcala, but probably made in Teotihuacan. In a fascinating analysis, Hasso von Winning (1961) demonstrates that the figures on the pot represent Tlaloc in four aspects: serpent, coyote, quetzal bird, and water. The four may symbolize the four kinds of rain associated with the four world directions. Later murals show armed figures with spear throwers, darts, and shields and even depict symbols of human sacrifice.

Teotihuacan Society

From data on settlement patterns which show differences in housing, we can recover something of the structure of Teotihuacan society. By supplementing our knowledge with depictive data and information from artifacts, a surprisingly detailed picture emerges. Evidence for occupational specialization indicates considerably more than just a two-part stratification—rulers and ruled. Rene Millon has defined at least six social classes. In spite of this, at present we can see only the outlines of the fully developed and sophisticated system in the latest period; the earlier periods are even hazier. The correctness of the following survey of social classes depends on the correctness of the functional interpretations that we have made of the various city structures, murals, artifacts, and other information.

Farmers. The support of the more than 125,000 people living in Teotihuacan about A.D. 600 was based on farmers who lived both in the city and in nearby communities. It also depended on tribute from satellite cities and on the control of large zones of the central plateau. The huge market in Teotihuacan was the redistribution mechanism for the urban center. Farmers living in the apartment houses and small shacklike houses managed the surrounding irrigated farmlands shown in the murals. Rural towns such as Maquixco provided specialized agricultural products. Satellite cities must also have contributed foodstuffs and acted as regional collectors in the immemorial way.

Maquixco (technically known as site TC-8) is located on the northern slopes of the Teotihuacan Valley a few kilometers west of the city. It is in the piedmont zone and therefore in an area of poorer soil and less water than the valley-bottom settlements. This rural community consists of about fifteen houses similar to the Yayahuala apartment complex in the city. The apartments of Maquixco are quite different in detail from those in the city, however. The building materials are inferior, being mainly of adobe as contrasted to the concrete of the urban dwellings; the apartments are smaller; and there are fewer rooms within each building; twelve to fifteen versus the fifty to more than one hundred rooms in most of the urban houses. At Maquixco, because there is a much greater expanse of vacant terrain, a grid plan is lacking and, instead, the apartment compounds are grouped around plazas. Murals at Maquixco are uniformly dull geometrics and lack the lively, variable forms of city art. Five hundred to six hundred people lived at Maquixco at its height (Sanders, 1965)

Today the area is exploited for the production of maguey, which provides fiber and pulque to the region. Beans are another important crop. Maquixco performed the same functions from about A.D. 400 to 600. Special obsidian blades used for processing maguey are found in large numbers over the site. The Fat God, the god of pulque, is the most common type of figurine in the village. Maquixco produced very little else for itself, however. Pottery and obsidian and other stone tools are identical to those found in the city and were undoubtedly made there. In other words, the town was firmly tied into a trade network and probably marketed its products in the central market of the city, exchanging them for obsidian, fine ceramics, stone corn grinders, and other necessaries. Undoubtedly Maquixco also depended on the city for religious reassurance in its agricultural activities (Sanders, 1965). A mural, now unfortunately in the Cleveland Museum, shows a singing priest striding over a nicely cultivated field into which are stuck unmistakable maguey leaves. A spiny crocodile-serpent, symbol of the earth, frames the scene.

Maquixco may be typical of the towns of the near hinterland which were tied into the subsistence base of the city. There were relatively few of these communities during the great period of Teotihuacan. Jeffrey Parsons's surveys of the eastern and southern basin have shown that most of it was thinly populated during this time. The implication is that most of the people were congregated in the city (Parsons, 1968, 1974).

It has been suggested that *chinampa* agriculture was developed by the sixth century A.D. and helped to support the city. Armillas's work (1971) has shown that the great period of *chinampa* farming came when water in the lakes fell to relatively shallow levels in the Postclassic period. However, the *chinampa* technique may well have been instituted during the Classic. Certainly the area just outside the southwest part of the city seems to have been so exploited, not to speak of any lake activity farther south.

Craft Specialists. Although most of the farmers lived either in Teotihuacan or in small farming villages like Maquixco, perhaps 25 percent of the city's population, tens of thousands of people, were craft specialists. Rene Millon and his colleagues found a tendency for people living in the same compound to engage in the same occupation. They also found over five hundred workshops, the vast majority of which were obsidian workshops. Considerable doubt exists as to whether all of the obsidian surface finds represent real full-time craft zones.

Other specialized craftsmen made other stone items such as the famous stone masks, while still others manufactured elaborate and exquisite pottery (Fig 6-8). Stuccoed, slab-footed tripod vessels were a Teotihuacan specialty, as distinctive as Wedgwood pottery is today. Much utilitarian pottery was also made (Fig. 6-9). The murals indicate that there were also couturiers, who fabricated the elaborately feathered and bedizened elite costumes. Leather sandals for the elite and probably woven grass sandals were made. The huge amount of formal architecture and some specialized tools indicate that there were full-time masons, plasterers, quarrymen, and other construction trades workers. Painters of murals were certainly a specialist class. As with the Lowland Maya, painters had to command not only technical aspects of fresco painting, but also the sophisticated iconography which gave meaning to their efforts.

As has been done for the Classic Maya, one could construct a complicated and stratified model of these specialties. The most prestigious presumably would be those involving arcane knowledge largely shared with and derived from the elite classes. If this were the case, then the construction trades and common implements crafts were probably the least prestigious. Producers of luxury and sumptuary items with ritual significance, such as the stucco-coated tripod ceramic bowls and the sophisticated murals, would have been highest on the craftsman's social scale.

Fig. 6–8. Luxury pottery ornamented with a "serpent's eye" design from Teotihuacan. This pot once stood on three cylindrical legs, now broken off. The motif is one of the few glyphlike elements in Teotihuacan art.

Fig. 6–9. Red on brown pottery, of a highly standardized form and decoration, from Teotihuacan. Probably used for food service, this type was traded widely and mass produced.

Presumably there were also merchant-craftsmen who dealt with the transactions of the city's marketplace. There were also long-distance merchants who handled the transport and exchange of goods to far-off areas. These antecedents of the Aztec *pochteca* class were probably of higher status than the resident craftsmen merchants.

If we make analogies to the earliest cities of Mesopotamia and the protohistoric cities of Mesoamerica, we find that there was probably a group of specialties that were the province of a bureaucracy. These civil servants may also have been the elite, but they were ranked according to their responsibilities. Teotihuacan had a more complex arrangement and was larger than the later Aztec capital, although Tenochtitlan may have had more people. It is therefore unlikely that Teotihuacan was any less complex in social organization.

Sanders (1965) has suggested that kinship units consisting of groups of related families or lineages lived in the apartment compounds. This arrangement is analogous to that of the Aztec "small ward" (*barrio pequeño*), which was probably the residential area of a lineage. Therefore, patrilineal clans or similar units may have existed in Teotihuacan and performed the functions that similar familial groups did later for the Aztec. Social organization and kinship structure are probably the most conservative parts of human culture, aside from the values that produce them. Assuming that the Aztec-period peoples inherited much of their cultural apparatus from Teotihuacan, it may also be that social forms came from this period.

Foreigners in the City. One of the most interesting findings from the work of Rene Millon and his colleagues was that of the presence of at least two barrios set aside for foreigners. One zone was apparently occupied by people from Oaxaca. Excavations in this ward on the western edge of the city produced one genuine Oaxacan-style tomb, which had been looted. However, the ancient tomb robbers left in place a stela carved with a Oaxacan glyph. Bones of several individuals suggest that the tomb may have been a crypt reopened from time to time for burial of a newly deceased person. In addition, two Monte Alban–style funerary urns were found in other nearby excavations.

The Merchants' Barrio was so named by Millon because of the high percentage of foreign pottery found in it, much of it from the Gulf Coast and the Maya Lowlands. Rattray (1987) later excavated it and found that the barrio dated from about A.D. 400 and was composed of at least fifteen round houses. In addition, tens of thousands of obsidian blades were found there, at least some of which were used in the processing of cinnabar (Iceland, 1989). Fine weaving implements for the production of cloth were another common artifact. Some 15 percent of the ceramics were Gulf Coast and Early Classic Maya, mainly of fine wares. Rattray suggests that this barrio housed people from the origin zones of the pottery and that they were merchants importing feathers, cotton, and cinnabar, the first two of which were important as materials for warrior uniforms. Although the form of the houses in the barrio changed from time to time to conform with the Teotihuacan norms, the zone was occupied by foreigners right up to about A.D. 650.

One implication is that Teotihuacan supplemented the income from its tributary areas by long-distance trade with Oaxaca, the Veracruz lowlands, and the Maya Lowlands. The nearer Huastec area may also have been represented by a resident group of people in the city, as evidenced by a round temple in the northwest section of the city. The Quetzalcoatl-Ehecatl wind god cult and its round temples were particularly strong in the Huastec region.

Teotihuacan Elite. Elite-class specialties included religion, politics, and warfare. As indicated above, long-distance trade may also have been an elite activity.

Formal religion had changed in response to other cultural evolution, and began as animism and ended as a complex religion with great similarities to that of Aztec times. That is, the latest manifestations of Teotihuacan cosmologies and ritual practices seem to glorify humans who were historical personalities and who were eventually identified with the supernatural.

Among the thousands of figurines produced through the several hundred years of the city's life are depictions of gods or godlike humans known from later times. The flayed god (Xipe), the rain god (Tlaloc), the feathered serpent (Quetzalcoatl), and the fire god (Xiuhtecuhtli) were all present. Sanders argues that the same association of religion with warfare and ritual cannibalism was present in the final stages of Teotihuacan as in Aztec times. Maquixco, for example, produced large quantities of split and splintered human bone fragments in general garbage and trash heaps, indicating that humans were being used for food during the A.D. 400–600 period. The murals showing human hearts brandished by Teotihuacan warriors suggest the same. Jaguar and eagle deities shown in late Teotihuacan murals were later patrons of Toltec and Aztec warrior societies. Large numbers of projectile points are found in late Teotihuacan debris at Maquixco. All of this may indicate an aggressive Teotihuacan, able to move against its neighbors with military force partially rationalized by religious ideology sanctioning and demanding human sacrifice (Sugiyama, 1989).

Among other motivations for aggressive warfare was the one familiar in our own day—that of the demands of a large and growing population. Conquered areas could be made to yield valuable tribute of food. The role of the warrior became increasingly important to Teotihuacan, and Rene Millon (1988) thinks that a powerful military organization existed by the beginning of Teotihuacan's rise. Teotihuacan had the organizational jump on most Mesoamerican cultures during its first centuries, but as time went on, the gap narrowed, and the great city finally came into peril.

Teotihuacan and the Rest of Mesoamerica: Empire or Alliances?

Bernal (1966) suggests that Teotihuacan was an empire along lines initially invented by the Olmecs. He distinguishes between the metropolitan culture of Teotihuacan and Teotihuacan influences found in regional cultures. Metropolitan culture was as has been defined above. The distribution of this culture certainly includes the valleys of Mexico and Puebla and possibly the Valleys of Toluca and Morelos. One other large city within this metropolitan zone was Cholula.

Cholula, in the Valley of Puebla, is pitifully little known, considering its pre-Hispanic importance and the size of the site and in spite of forty years of intermittent excavation. From nearly any point in the valley one can see the vast bulk of the great pyramid glowering over the small provincial town that now occupies the site. Most investigations have concentrated on the pyramid. Tunnels into the structure have revealed some earlier pyramids, which date from the Teotihuacan period. These earlier platforms have *talud-tablero* features. Painted in the panels around the terraces are various polychrome motifs: black, red, and blue stripes with seashells; insects which may be a Cholulan version of the sacred butterflies of Teotihuacan; and geometrics.

Some extraordinary murals were discovered in 1965 painted on the panels of a Teotihuacan-style structure adjacent to the inner pyramid. These are the so-called Drunkard Murals (Marquina, 1971). Groups of rather elastically formed persons vigorously enjoy themselves drinking cups of what is probably pulque. These people roister, gesture, and pour pulque from jugs into larger jugs while dogs bark and run. All in all, the scene gives the impression of a carefree gaiety unusual in somber central Mexico. Marquina suggests that the scene is that of a harvest or planting celebration like those described by Sahagún.

Other examples of Teotihuacan-style architecture have been discovered at some distance from the main pyramid group. Clearly, during Teotihuacan times, Cholula was not the major center that it later was. The great pyramid had not yet been built. Yet the area of its location was occupied by a group of Teotihuacan-style buildings. What sort of a settlement surrounded those buildings is unknown, in spite of the thorough work of the German Puebla Scientific Mission. Teotihuacan-period pottery is quite standard in style and was probably locally made.

Xochicalco, near Cuernavaca, may have been another such city. Sanders has noted cell-like residential structures at Xochicalco similar to those found at Teotihuacan. However, these are not necessarily grouped into apartment compounds. Beyond the Central Plateau the evidence is of strong regional cultures which were more or less influenced by Teotihuacan. For example, two stelae, carved in Teotihuacan style and depicting male and female rain gods, have been found in northern Guerrero on a route that leads to the Balsas River (Díaz Oyarzabal, 1986). Using the model of protohistoric empires, we find it likely that any empire built by Teotihuacan had large geographic holes in it. That is, there were undoubtedly zones in Mesoamerica controlled by alliance, intimidation, or isolation, with only the most crucial zones and routes physically occupied and controlled by Teotihuacan. Patterns of Teotihuacan's influence and control indicate that it fits the classic model of empire in many world areas, and, more to the point, so does the Aztec case. An examination of the most important cases in point will demonstrate this analogy.

Maya Highlands: Kaminaljuyu. Sanders's work at Kaminaljuyu shows a dramatic change about A.D. 300 from the scattered plaza settlement pattern we have seen in the Late Formative (Sanders and Michels, 1969). The lineage-temple groups were abandoned. Teotihuacan's presence is marked by a shift to a single massive acropolis in Teotihuacan style (Kidder, Jennings, and Shook, 1946; Sanders and Michels, 1977). *Talud-tablero* temples, oriented about closed courtyards, were built in adobe. Frontal platforms on these temples concealed and protected successive elaborate tombs. Within the tombs are masses of pottery, carved bone, and other materials, much of which is clearly within the stylistic canons used at Teotihuacan itself. Stuccoed, slab-footed tripods, with scenes featuring Tlaloc, and thin orange effigy vessels are examples of items exported to Kaminaljuyu from Teotihuacan. However, much of the painting on the stuccoed tripods is in Maya style, and recent studies by Jacinto Quirarte have shown that many of the tripods themselves were manufactured in the Maya Highlands. In other words, Maya craftsmen at Kaminaljuyu made their own versions of the tripods and exported them back to Teotihuacan.

The strength of Teotihuacan influence at Kaminaljuyu was so strong that A. V. Kidder, Sr., who dug out the famous tombs, suggested that it is an example of a military takeover by Teotihuacanos and the subsequent exploitation of a native population (Kidder, Jennings, and Shook, 1946). This idea fits the later pattern of military takeover of the Maya Highlands by small Mexican groups who established ruling houses in Late Postclassic times.

The size of Kaminaljuyu was about 240 hectares (600 acres), and the population in and around the center was at least ten thousand. The limitations on any archaeological work in the zone now make it impossible for us to know the true extent of the center during this period. Rural population also increased at about this time. By about A.D. 500 three subordinate towns had been established along the route between Kaminaljuyu and the south coastal plain of Guatemala, a distance of only about 40 kilometers (25 miles).

Coastal Guatemala: Cotzumalhuapa, the Middle and Late Classic. The Pacific coastal plain was in contact with the Olmec in earlier times. Later, it was also an important zone to the Aztec because of its cacao (chocolate) bean production. Modern bulldozing operations on the coast have destroyed dozens of mounds and produced immense quantities of Teotihuacan-influenced pottery (E. Shook, personal communication, 1972). Most of this pottery is made of a local ware called Tiquisate ware, which has also been found in Teotihuacan itself. Many Teotihuacan-style incense burners have been found by divers in Amatitlan Lake, less than 16 kilometers (10 miles) from Kaminaljuyu.

Sanders and Price (1968) say that the motivation for a Teotihuacan takeover of Kaminaljuyu was control of the coastal plain and the trade route out to the Maya Lowlands. Kaminaljuyu evidently acted as a major outpost of Teotihuacan's power and had connections with the important center of Tazumal in El Salvador as well as with Tikal and other Maya Lowland centers to the north. Teotihuacan undoubtedly extracted more than just chocolate beans from the Maya area. For one thing, the Pacific coastal zone produces high-quality cotton today and may have done so in the past. The attractive native brown cotton grows in the highlands as well. Manufactured goods of great variety, including high-prestige items such as green quetzal feathers, could have been exported from the Maya area.

The present explanations of the nature of Teotihuacan's influence in both the highlands and the adjacent coastal zones are clearly inadequate. Investigations in progress and unpublished data indicate a much more complex situation, and no new consensus has been reached yet on this important question (Marion Hatch, personal communication, 1988).

Around the present-day town of Santa Lucía Cotzumalhuapa are a number of ancient regional centers, including Bilbao, El Castillo, and El Baúl. El Baúl was occupied at least as early as Late Formative times, and handsome examples of sculpture have been found there which are contemporary with but distinct from the sculpture of Izapa. El Baúl Stela 1 dates to either A.D. 11 or 37. Later sculpture at the three sites has been interpreted in terms of two different models.

Lee A. Parsons and S. F. de Borhegyi worked for some time at Bilbao, and Parsons has developed the concept of the Middle Classic (L. Parsons, 1967–69). Briefly, he thinks that the period of Teotihuacan's influence over all of Mesoamerica was so pervasive that a separate time period should be set aside for it. The Middle Classic period was thus one of rapid and widespread distribution of Teotihuacan ceramics and other cultural forms. It lasted from A.D. 400 to 700 and is divided into two phases. The earliest phase (A.D. 400–550) was that of the establishment of commercial and military colonies throughout Mesoamerica. In Parsons's view, Bilbao was one of those colonies. The later phase (A.D. 550–700) was the period during which Teotihuacan influence was assimilated into the regional art styles and new styles were synthesized. In this period the great city's outposts abandoned their ties with it and became independent.

Parsons sees the art of the Cotzumalhuapa region as a result of the above process. In his view, if Teotihuacan controlled the Cotzumalhuapan region, it was probably through a group from Tajin. Tajin was either an ally or under the domination of Teotihuacan at that time. Even in terms of Mesoamerican art, its style is somewhat bizarre and unrelieved by much aesthetic merit. Its subject matter falls into narrative and portrait categories. Human busts, full seated human figures, and very large heads make up the second category. Stiff, awkwardly portrayed people engage in the sacred ball game, human sacrifice in a multitude of forms, and various symbolic acts such as climbing ladders and offering human hearts to a diving figure, which is probably the sun. A preoccupation with death is pervasive, and there are many death's heads and skeletal figures. Many of the large scenes are carved on gigantic boulders, and among the figures twine vines on which are human heads, birds, and leaves. The art style, the ball game scenes, and the game equipment (stone yokes, thin stone heads, and "*palmas*") all link the Cotzumalhuapa style to that of Tajin, in Parsons's interpretation.

Hatch (1987) has developed a more economical and more convincing reconstruction based on more precise dating and the historical approach to Mesoamerican art. The ceramics associated with the Cotzumalhuapan style are now known to be Late Classic. Further, the carbon 14 date depended on most heavily by Parsons can also be interpreted as Late Classic. Repetitions in the subject matter of the boulders and stelalike stones at the three sites of Bilbao, El Castillo, and El Baúl lead to an interpretation in which three governors can be identified by costume and glyphs. Each sequence of scenes shows one of the governors as he ascends to power and receives symbols of authority and as other legitimizing events occur. Each person also is associated with symbols of special kinds. Governor 2, for example, was apparently greatly involved in human sacrifice and death. Governor 3 seems to have been more interested in matters associated with the sacred ball game. Hatch thinks that the time span represented by the sculptures is no more than one hundred years and falls into the early part of Late Classic. Continuities in sculptural symbolism and style occur between early El Baúl Stela 1 and the later Cotzumalhuapan style. This indicates to Hatch a strong regional culture that underwent various permutations and transformations and which is probably the originator of both the Formative and Late Classic sculptures. Finally, it should be noted that examples of Cotzumalhuapan sculptures are known from the adjacent highlands (Valley of Almolonga; Hatch, personal communication, 1988).

Today the zone around Cotzumalhuapa is occupied by sugar cane fields and coffee plantations. The Pacific coastal plain is hot and sticky, and the vegetation is a dense, intense green. The huge volcanoes of the nearby highlands are always in sight. At Bilbao, one plunges into the shady coffee groves and walks on soft, damp, springy earth accompanied by the constant sound of small streams. Two Tlaloc figures carved from a boulder nestle in the mossy bank of a stream at Bilbao. The huge boulder sculptures with their grotesque figures rest on the terraced zones among the earthen mounds of the ceremonial center. Altogether, it is a fascinating, repellent, and exotic place for either Mesoamerican highlanders or modern travelers. The coastal sculptural style and hieroglyphic system are distinct from that of either the Maya Lowlands or the Mexican Highlands. Cotzumalhuapan culture is an excellent example of the sort of regional cultural development which took place over and over again in Mesoamerican prehistory.

Maya Lowlands: Tikal, Uaxactun, Becan, Rio Azul. The facts, nature, and interpretations of the relationships of Teotihuacan with the Classic Maya are dealt with in detail in the preceding chapter. To briefly recapitulate, Teotihuacan apparently established commercial ties with several parts of the Maya Lowlands, including the salt zones of the northwest peninsula and Tikal in the south central region, in the fourth century A.D. By about

A.D. 360, an alliance or a takeover of Tikal and its regional state was engineered by Teotihuacan through a collaborationist ruler at Tikal who apparently had military and political advisors from Teotihuacan. Uaxactun was in Tikal's orbit by this time, and Rio Azul was conquered. The fortress of Becan apparently fell under Teotihuacan's control at about the same time, although it is not certain what connection it may have had with Tikal. It may have been simply a fortified redoubt on the cross-peninsular trade route leading from the Gulf of Mexico to the Caribbean.

The Teotihuacanos probably exercised an influence out of proportion to their numbers, bringing ideas, statecraft, and sophistication in military and political matters which caused an initial shock to Maya society and then a transformation of it. In other words, the Teotihuacan groups and their legacies may have been the stimuli by which the Lowland Maya continued their evolution toward centralized and urbanized states. W. R. Coe (1965b:35–37) sees the Tikal evidence as also reflecting a later Teotihuacan period, one which may have been tied more to Gulf Coast variants than to the culture of the great city itself. After the fall of Teotihuacan there may have been a diaspora of craftsmen and other refugees, some of whom landed in the Maya Lowlands. This second wave of Teotihuacan's influence dates about A.D. 700.

Classic Veracruz Centers: Cerro de las Mesas and Matacapan

While Tajin in the north was still a small and undistinguished center, Cerro de las Mesas in the south became the most important regional center in the Veracruz plain after the epi-Olmec episode. The site underwent great expansion, and some dozens of platforms (and buildings) were built. Although little of the site has been dug, there is no doubt that it was of great importance, if only because of the fifteen stelae and eight other monuments found there. These Early Classic sculptures echo some Izapan traits but are largely distinctive. Stiff human figures stride or stand on the stelae in poses which are reminiscent of early Maya styles. These persons are accompanied by hieroglyphic texts, some of which include long-count dates written in the Maya Lowland system or a parallel system (Fig. 6-10). There are also many unread texts which seem to deal with names, places, and conquests.

Tlamimilolpa-Xolalpan (A.D. 200–550) pottery is found at Cerro de las Mesas together with a locally developed set of gigantic clay sculptures. The latter include gods also represented in the figurines and murals at Teotihuacan—the old fire god (Huehueteotl), for example. Even so, a majority of ceramic types are of strictly local tradition. The accumulated wealth of the elite at Cerro de las Mesas is shown by the enormous cache of about eight hundred items which Drucker found there (1943a). The cache included such things as Olmec heirloom pieces, other jade carvings, jewelry of calcite and serpentine, and much other paraphernalia. Perhaps

Fig. 6–10. *Stela 5 from Cerro de las Mesas, Veracruz, Mexico, an Early Classic site probably extant during the Late Preclassic. Note the use of dot and bar numeration, shared with the Lowland Maya but not with the Central Mexican Highlands.*

this represents a burial of the ritual equipment of a great person. It seems significant that when Teotihuacan influence disappeared in the Gulf Coast plain, Cerro de las Mesas was abandoned. It is into this power vacuum that Tajin expanded.

Matacapan is a large center consisting of some seventy mounds located in the Tuxtlas Mountains by the sea. The one mound excavated by Valenzuela was a typical *talud-tablero* Teotihuacan platform. Ceramics include Teotihuacan pottery along with the locally made wares. M. D. Coe (1965a) believes that Matacapan will prove to have been as intensely reflective of Teotihuacan influence as is Kaminaljuyu. A project under the direction of Robert Santley has reportedly confirmed this prediction. Indeed, Matacapan may have been the way station established and used by Teotihuacan groups on their way to the coastal plain of Guatemala and thence to Kaminaljuyu.

Late Classic Centers in the South: Nopiloa and El Zapotal

While Tajin dominated matters on the Gulf Coast to the north, Nopiloa was apparently the prime center of the south. It is not as large or impressive as Cerro de las Mesas. Indeed, M. D. Coe (1965a) thinks that the culture of the area may have stepped back to essentially a village-style, Late Formative state. This seems unlikely, given the evidence of widespread uniformity of complex religious practices that are now available. A Pan-Coastal art style was developed and mainly expressed in clay sculpture and small stone sculpture. The Yoke-palma-hacha small sculpture complex is widespread. The Smiling Figure complex developed in parallel with the sculpture. These famous figures, with their unwarrantedly broad grins, are found throughout the area.

A recent excavation at the Mixtequilla site of El Zapotal, not far from Nopiloa, has produced some evidence of their function. A mound was found at El Zapotal which contained many burials in association with a remarkable shrine made of modeled clay. The shrine included a large and bony image of a death god. One nearby multiple burial was guarded by Smiling Figures brandishing knives in their hands as if warding off the many hazards of the afterlife to which Mesoamerican souls were subject. An ossuary in the same mound consists of a stack of eighty skulls about 3 meters (10 feet) high buried in a pit. It is difficult to know if these were burials of persons who died normal deaths or the remains of victims of ritual sacrifice. The fact that late Teotihuacan pottery was found with the burials indicates that Teotihuacan may have been a power in the plain after A.D. 550, but likely no later than A.D. 650.

Early Civilization in Northern Veracruz: Tajin

The coastal plain of Veracruz is divided into compartments by rivers which flow to the Gulf of Mexico from the highlands. As one proceeds north from the old Olmec heartland,the climate becomes progressively drier. However, even in the northern compartment where Tajin is located, mists and rain prevail much of the year, but a longer dry season occurs than in the south. This was apparently the case in ancient times and caused problems for the inhabitants. Water is scarce during the dry season, and even the sea is 30 kilometers (19 miles) from Tajin.

The Preclassic Background

Long sequences of ceramic complexes have been found by Ekholm (1944) and MacNeish (1954) to the north of Tajin at Tampico. These sequences begin about 1500 B.C. and continue to a period linked with the earliest Tajin occupation, about A.D. 100. Ceramics and figurines of great variety have been found throughout Veracruz, one of the most famous stylistic groups being the Remojadas sequence. This pottery is derived from the zone around the mouth of the Tecolutla River. Although the excavator has divided the pottery into lower (early) and upper (later) periods, it is apparent that both complexes represent enormous spans of time and varieties of materials. Lower Remojadas includes Middle and Late Formative items, and Upper Remojadas is made up of Early and late Classic pottery and figurines. There are practically no published data on settlement patterns for the central and northern Veracruz Formative period. Some Late Formative house mounds from Chalahuites, found by García Payón (1971a) to be made of river cobbles, are an exception. We must assume that village-level life was the rule during most of the Formative period, but we have no idea whether or not there were Olmec-influenced towns of greater sophistication. Neither do we know if there was an indigenous development of regional centers and emergent elites. Finally, there are few data on the nature of the transition from village-level society to civilization. Few of the many Formative sites were used in the Classic period. There are no indications of epi-Olmec influence or centers of any great importance during this transition period. Presumably there was a pattern of population growth similar to that in the rest of Mesoamerica, accompanied by cultural elaboration and then a shift from dispersed villages to more concentrated centers. At least toward the end of the Formative stage, the non-Olmec area of Veracruz shows distinct regionalization. Carved stone yokes, large figurines with smiling faces, and special ceramic forms such as chile grinders were all well developed. Some scattered finds in the Tajin zone show that it was thinly occupied during the Formative.

The Classic Florescence

Tajin itself has been excavated for over thirty years, but detailed architectural or pottery descriptions have yet to appear in print. Fortunately, syntheses by Wilkerson (1987) and Kampen (1972) aid in making sense of the site. Some of the chronology which follows is my own interpretation of García Payón's work.

Chronology. There are two major periods in the city's history. During the first period (A.D. 100–550) Tajin was a minor center with relatively small pyramids and a few elite residences. Ceramics from this era show great Teotihuacan influence, especially that which links it to the Early Classic (Middle Horizon) phases of the great city. Trade wares from the Valley of Mexico are present, as well as thin orange materials which are probably from northern Oaxaca. Teotihuacan may have established Tajin as a commercial-military colony. It will be recalled that there probably was a Classic-period Veracruz quarter at Teotihuacan itself.

Teotihuacan's influence began to wane about A.D. 500, and it is after this date that Tajin reached its greatest development. This second phase (A.D. 550–1100) was one of dynamic expansion of Tajin culture through the coastal plain and possibly even as far as Cotzumalhuapa in Guatemala. The spectacular architecture and sculpture that the visitor sees today at Tajin is nearly all from the second period (Marquina, 1964).

Building and Site Function and Sculpture. Tajin is situated among dramatically abrupt hills, with much of the 5 square kilometers (1.9 square miles) of the site laid out on relatively flat ground in a valley. An adjacent hillside has been terraced and otherwise modified for an enormous mass of structures. There are more than two hundred mounds (Krotser and Krotser, 1973). The basic plan is made up of a series of courtyard groups. The plan is thus more like that of Classic Maya centers than it is like that of more highly organized Teotihuacan. Buildings fall into the familiar categories of temple, elite residence, and ball court. There are eleven ball courts at Tajin, reflecting the extreme ritual importance of the game in the lives of these ancient Veracruzanos. Architecture is decorated by a baroquely elaborate style in both sculpture and modeled stucco. A hallmark of the building style is the common use of a jutting cornice on terraces.

The center is dominated by a large temple-pyramid about 18 meters (60 feet) high which is fantastically decorated by 365 niches. It has been suggested that these niches represent the days of the tropical year and that originally small stucco figures were set in them. Other smaller temples dot the site. Large, elaborate, palatial residential buildings imply an enlargement of the elite class at Tajin from earlier times.

Sculptural style reaches its fullest expression in ball-court and temple slabs, which show human sacrifice, warriors, and the ball game. All of these elements seem to be tied together into one ritual activity. M. E. Kampen (1972) says that the one major theme in Tajin art is human sacrifice. Wilkerson (1987:64–66) outlines a plausible ritual cycle as reflected in the ball court sculptures; this pattern parallels that of the Cotzumalhuapan sculpture some nine hundred miles away. Other subjects include the watering of maguey plants with sacrificial blood. Hieroglyphs which accompany the sculpture refer persistently to a 13 Rabbit, possibly the calendrical name of a great ruler. This putative ruler is shown sitting on a throne surrounded by important captives who are in the process of being sacrificed (Wilkerson 1987:71–72). Particularly interesting are depictions of what appear to be Eagle Knights, a military order later widespread over Mesoamerica. A sculpture in the Museum of Xalapa from Tajin shows a ritual involving a cacao tree.

Enormous amounts of small sculptured objects were produced, most of which had either a ritual or functional use in the sacred ball game. Yokes, thin stone human heads, turkeys carved into the "palma" form, and other attractive items are known. Palmas were stuck into ballplayers' belts, while yokes were worn around the waist. These items were widely traded during this period and are found in highland Guatemala.

Based on the Krotsers' work (1973) and that of Wilkerson (1987), it seems clear that a large population was scattered about the center in house lots which contained gardens and fruit trees, as was the pattern at Tikal. Using the Tikal density of 600–700 people per square kilometer (1,500–1,800 per square mile), and accepting the Krotsers' estimate of Tajin's extent as 5 square kilometers (2 square miles), an estimated population of 3,000 to 3,500 can be calculated. Tajin dominated much more territory, of course, and total population must have been at least three times the core population, or about 13,000 in total. Wilkerson (1987:73) surmises that this population was likely sustained by intensive raised-field irrigation systems found nearby.

Given the above information, incomplete as it is, we do not find it difficult to think of Tajin as one of the more militaristic allies or colonies of Teotihuacan, and one which went on to establish tributary colonies of its own, one of which may have been Cotzumalhuapa. It is particularly significant that Tajin expanded and underwent a florescence only when Teotihuacan influence was removed. It is also clear from pottery found at the site that the great period of Tajin corresponds with an important period at Monte Alban in Oaxaca and at Xochicalco and Cholula. The abandonment of Tajin about A.D. 1100 meant the lapse of the zone back into a condition of fragmented social and political units. Tajin had politically dominated the coastal plain, but when it declined, new centers arose along the central coast which controlled the region until the arrival of the Spaniards.

Summary. Veracruz clearly had a crucial role in transmitting Teotihuacan's influence throughout eastern Mesoamerica during the Classic period. The sites of Cerro de las Mesas and Matacapan may have been Teotihuacan's colonies or allies during the Early Classic. Tajin was a small, unimportant center in the north during this time. When Teotihuacan's influence and power were withdrawn, the Early Classic centers deflated.

Tajin then began a rapid cultural and military florescence and probably dominated the coastal plain and perhaps the transisthmian zone, including the former Teotihuacan colony in the Cotzumalhuapan district.

The Oaxacan Late Formative and Early Classic

The consideration of the Late Formative material from Oaxaca has been reserved to this point in order to give it the continuity it deserves.

During the period from 700 to 500 B.C. (Rosario phase), San José Mogote reached its apogee as a regional center. As noted before, it was probably only one of a number of such centers. In spite of this status, it seems not to have had more than fourteen hundred people supporting it. Public architecture was accumulated into a small "acropolis," which included an elite residence. The appearance of sculpture and the use of the sacred almanac (260-day calendar) reinforces the impression of an increasingly stabilized social structure with a hereditary elite at the top. The sculpture includes a depiction of a sacrificed human captive. Undoubtedly, warfare in some form was present.

However, as impressive as all of these matters may be, it remains the case that Monte Alban as well as other sites of later importance were occupied by 500 B.C. Flannery, Marcus, and Kowalewski (1981) do not see any sign of state institutions in this phase. They consider that Monte Alban I (500–200 B.C.) was the period of development of such institutions, given that a fully developed state was present by 200 B.C. They think that an elite class developed on the basis of a religious and ritual leadership which also redistributed obsidian and patronized certain craft specialties. To this set of elite functions should be added that of military leadership and some general administrative duties such as settlement of disputes within the communities. Legal functions are a nearly invariable duty of any sort of community leadership, even on the simplest level.

How leadership became hereditary is still an unsettled issue unless one grants that the separate creation myths of the later Zapotecs and Mixtecs were present. Such myths justified the later hereditary rulers, partly through genealogy and partly through putative ties to the supernatural. Such ties, emphasized and established through ritual position, would have been reinforced by the development of a cult of ancestors as intermediaries for mankind with the gods. If such intermediaries had been religious leaders in their lifetimes, then their descendants would have a better claim to means of communication with them.

In any case, it is now certain that the Zapotec state was in existence by the end of Monte Alban I (200 B.C.), and it is to the sequence largely centered on the great site of Monte Alban that we must turn.

The Oaxacan Classic: Monte Alban

The major periods of civilization in Oaxaca are named after phases defined by work at Monte Alban and modified by later investigations. Thus, we have periods denominated Monte Alban I to V, although the best information on the last two periods is actually not from Monte Alban itself. The following chronology summarizes the phasing and gives equivalent Christian dates:

Monte Alban Period	Christian Dates
I	500–200 B.C.
II	200 B.C.–A.D. 250
III	A.D. 250–700
IV	A.D. 700–1000
V	A.D. 1000–1500

Transition to Civilization and Preeminence

By about 400 B.C. Monte Alban began to outstrip its competitors and eventually rose to preeminence. The reasons for this success are still obscure. Developmental theories such as the Palerm-Wolf hypothesis explain the enabling circumstances. No doubt the massed demographic and economic power of the valley within which such historical events take place was important, but not the whole story. In the specific case of Monte Alban, terrain was also a factor.

Topographically and scenically, Monte Alban's ridge system dominates the Central Valley of Oaxaca (Fig. 6-11). The valley is divided into three arms. The Etla branch runs northwest to southeast and then splits at the ridge. A southeastern branch runs off to Tlacolula and beyond. The southern arm reaches down to the area of Zaachila. Any community wishing to physically, politically, and militarily control the entire valley had to control the ridge system at its crux.

Flannery's research group has concluded that the site of Monte Alban was chosen partly because of the factors of terrain described above, but primarily because it was neutral ground where elite groups from several communities, including San José Mogote, could reside (Flannery, Marcus, Kowalewski, 1981). Blanton (1978; Blanton and Kowalewski, 1981) further argues that Monte Alban was established because it was the logical place to locate the headquarters of a voluntarily formed confederation.

Ignoring the principle of original sin and considering only the archaeological data, it seems most unlikely that the unification of the valley took place solely on a voluntary basis. Flannery, Marcus, and Kowalewski (1981) note that there was warfare during the period 700–500 B.C. and that it escalated through Monte Alban I and II. The presence of dozens of sculptured monuments depicting captives at Monte Alban in the period 500–200 B.C. as well as formal fortifications at the city by about 100 B.C. suggest that unification was not a matter of an establishment of a "peaceable kingdom."

Some of the most interesting work of recent years has been done by

Fig. 6–11. View north from the main ridge at Monte Alban toward the Cerro del Gallo in the middle ground and Atzompa in the background. In the far distance are the mountains of the Mixteca zone, from whence came intruders into the Zapotec region.

Richard Blanton (1978), whose research group surveyed the slopes of Monte Alban's ridge and located over two thousand terraces, which were used for both agricultural and housing zones (Map 6-3). Excavations by Marcus Winter (1974) have shown that at least some of this terracing and housing dates back to the earliest part of Monte Alban I. Blanton estimates that five thousand people resided at the site and that this concentration of population amounted to about 50 percent of the total in the valley. A settlement hierarchy is already apparent, with at least six secondary administrative sites outside the Monte Alban zone. The boundaries which appear in analytical operations are interpreted as falling between administrative districts. However, it appears equally likely that they were boundaries between independent political units, some of which were resisting amalgamation into a unified state. The *danzante* figures at the top of the ridge possibly represent the leaders of the failed resistance.

Monte Alban I and II (500 B.C.–A.D. *200).* The entire top of the Monte Alban ridge was artificially sculptured into a series of flattened and filled plaza areas around which was arranged the formal architecture of the center. Later massive construction has covered the earliest buildings, but there is no doubt that large-scale building was done in period I. The only

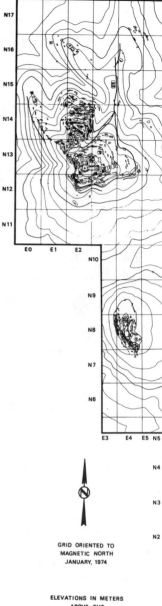

GRID ORIENTED TO
MAGNETIC NORTH
JANUARY, 1974

ELEVATIONS IN METERS
ABOVE THE
VALLEY FLOOR

CONTOUR INTERVAL 25 METERS

Map 6–3. The urbanized zone of Monte Alban, Oaxaca, Mexico. This very large site was located on a ridge above the present-day city of Oaxaca. Blanton and his colleagues found that the entire ridge had been terraced and was occupied by apartment compounds faintly similar to those of Teotihuacan. (Courtesy Richard E. Blanton)

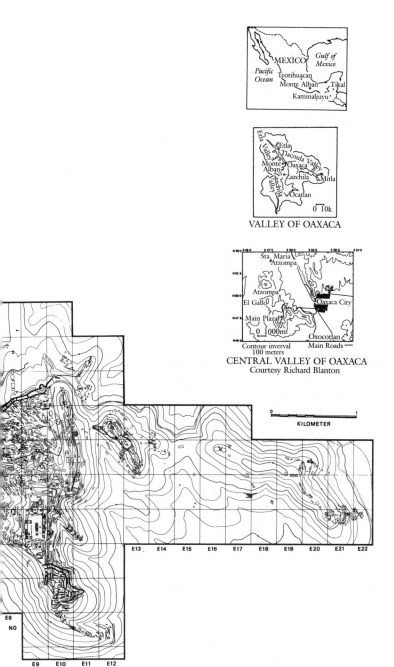

MEXICO

Gulf of
Mexico

Pacific
Ocean

Teotihuacan
Monte Alban
Tikal

Kaminaljuyu

Etla Valley
Etla
Tlacoula Valley
Monte Alban
Oaxaca
Zaachila
Zaachila Valley
Mitla
Ocatlan

0 10k

VALLEY OF OAXACA

Sta. Maria
Atzompa

Atzompa
El Gallo
Oaxaca City

Main Plaza

0 1000m

Oxocotlan

Contour inverval   Main Roads
100 meters

CENTRAL VALLEY OF OAXACA
Courtesy Richard Blanton

0   1

KILOMETER

E13   E14   E15   E16   E17   E18   E19   E20   E21   E22

E8
NO

E9   E10   E11   E12

major piece of architecture known from this phase is the Danzantes structure, a stone platform on the edge of the main plaza (Building L). A small inner platform some 3 meters (10 feet) high was the first built on the spot and may have supported wood and thatched buildings.

The most interesting feature of the platform is the sculpture which is set into the walls. These are the famous sculptures the *danzantes,* or "dancers" (Fig. 6-12). The so-called *danzantes* are boneless-looking humans depicted by grooved lines incised on slabs of rock. Many appear to be lifeless, all are nude, and many are sexually mutilated, leading M. D. Coe to suggest that they represent dead and tortured enemies (1968). Many of the three hundred known *danzantes* have hieroglyphic names, probably indicating that they were persons of importance.

Monte Alban I ceramics were surprisingly complex, making up by a wide variety in form what they lacked in color. Human and animal effigies began their long-lasting popularity. Gray wares were especially typical, and a popular bottle form with attached spout was traded as far south as Chiapa de Corzo.

Hieroglyphic texts on stone include dates in the 260-day sacred almanac and the 365-day year. Other notations are probably personal and place names. A two-column text from this period lays out what is probably a date with a verb and possible name (Marcus, 1980). Simple stone tombs ("box tombs") are found within the center. All of these features imply a fair level of sophistication among the elite class at Monte Alban. By the end of the period, the population at Monte Alban had risen to about sixteen thousand.

Contemporary Centers: Monte Negro and Dainzu. In the Tlacolula branch of the valley there is a very large site called Dainzu, the main structures of which are backed against a large butte. It may be significant that this position is also militarily defensible, although not as strong as that of Monte Alban.

Ignacio Bernal has excavated at the site and found a very large stone platform which supported a masonry building. Set into the walls of the platform and its stairway are sculptures similar but not identical to the *danzantes.* A great many (forty-seven) of the Dainzu sculptures show ball players (Marcus, 1983a). Bernal (1965a) also found nearby a large ball court which dates to the same period as do the platform and much of the sculpture: Monte Alban I. Similar tombs with that date occur at both centers. Dainzu was likely the capital of one of the competing petty states eventually incorporated into a larger state headed by Monte Alban.

The Monte Negro (Black Mountain) site is of special interest. It is located north of the central valley in an area later occupied by the Mixtec. The top of a ridge was modified, as at Monte Alban, and a town with thatched-roof houses was erected. The ceremonial buildings were grouped around an open courtyard. One of these civic structures had the

Fig. 6–12. Early Oaxacan sculptures at Monte Alban are carved in a style known as that of the danzantes, *or dancers. Actually, these are portraits of dead enemies whose bodies have been mutilated. They reflect a period of considerable warfare at the beginning of the great period of Monte Alban—one in which a unified Zapotec state was created.*

unusual feature of large columns carved from single pieces of stone. In general, Monte Negro represents a paler and less developed version of Monte Alban I culture. No writing or sculpture has been found there, and the pottery is poorer in variety. It possibly represents a provincial version of Monte Alban I culture and one which may be ancestral to the Mixtec. On the other hand, it may also be an outlier of Monte Alban I culture which was later displaced (Flannery, 1983a).

Some 307 Monte Alban I sites were found by Blanton's group in the central valley, but many of these finds are based solely on samples of surface pottery. It is estimated that the total valley population amounted to about thirty thousand by 200 B.C. With nearly 50 percent of the total population, if Monte Alban was not the dominant site at the beginning of the period, it became so by the end of it.

Monte Alban II (200 B.C.–A.D. 250). In period II we see an enlargement and development of complexity which signals the accession of Monte Alban to fully civilized and sophisticated status. The full-scale sculpturing of the Monte Alban ridge tops into flattened and terraced areas took place during period II (Flannery, 1983b). The scale of this effort indicates that

Monte Alban could call on resources of manpower not available to it before. Certainly the period of political unification of the central valley was necessary in preparation for this effort.

Within the great plaza at Monte Alban, the arrowhead-shaped observatory (Building J) was built; apparently its peculiar plan was dictated by its function in making astronomical observations. Other platforms appear which have the characteristic Oaxacan balustrades with a decorative feature reminiscent of the *talud-tablero*. These platforms supported temples with two rooms and thatched roofs. Presumably the elite class which directed these construction activities lived in the center, but no palaces have been excavated from this period.

Stelae and bas-reliefs with hieroglyphs were carved and displayed. Many of the bas-reliefs show human heads hanging downward from glyphs which are apparently place names, and Caso (1965) has suggested that these are records of conquests, an opinion with which Marcus (1983*b*) concurs and which she amplifies. There are more of such records than before, indicating a relatively violent era.

Blanton and Kowlewski (1981) note several interesting features in period II. The valley in general, Monte Alban included, suffered a population decline: 30,000 to 20,000 for the valley and 16,000 to 14,500 for the city. Fortifications were built around Monte Alban, as noted before, and it appears that defensible sites were the ones that thrived. All of this, again, implies warfare within the valley itself. Probable correspondences between sixteenth-century Aztec name glyphs and those found on Monte Alban II monuments suggest that Monte Alban was also engaged in military expansion outside the valley (Marcus, 1980). Forty such name-place glyphs occur on period II conquest monuments. In the vicinity of one of the identified places, Cuicatlan, excavation revealed an edifice of skulls which resembled those built by the Aztec of skulls of sacrificed victims (Redmond and Spencer, 1983).

Tombs of period II are more elaborate, and some of them show features which lasted until the Spanish Conquest. Under the courtyards were stone burial chambers with steps leading down to antechambers. These were used for sepulchers in which only one person might be buried. In other tombs retainers and servants accompanied their masters into the afterlife. Some of the period II tombs are decorated with wall frescoes. The Tomb 72 mural is of glyphs which refer to the Zapotecan version of the 260-day sacred almanac (Miller, 1988). Large incense burners or burial urns were placed with the dead. Caso and Bernal (1952) thought that these urns represent various gods, with one of the most popular being Cocijo, the local god of rain. However, Marcus (1983*c*) argues that they are portraits or apotheosized depictions of ancestors or contemporary relatives, some wearing masks of gods in the same manner as that of some figures on contemporary sculpture. Most urns carry a calendric name derived from the 260-day calendar, arguing that they indeed depict humans and not deities.

Other ceramics became more complex, with delicately painted stucco applied to some vessels. As in so much of period II development, the major changes were in the elite sector of Oaxacan culture. Much of the elaborate pottery seems to be linked with ceramics of Veracruz and Chiapas. It is very difficult to detect any significant changes in the folk culture of the villages away from the centers, indicating that for most people, daily life went on much as before.

Apogee: Monte Alban III (A.D. 250–700). The two major cultural and linguistic groups occupying Oaxaca at the time of the Spanish Conquest were the Zapotec and Mixtec. The culture fully developed during period III was undoubtedly Zapotec. The features of Zapotec civilization as known from the Conquest period are so similar in both general features and in detail to that of period III that there is little doubt that Monte Alban periods I to IV represent Zapotec culture. Thus, we probably have a Zapotec state established by A.D. 200, developing during period II, and expanding during period III.

The major historical features of period III are (1) the final establishment and expansion of a unitary Zapotec state in the Central Valley of Oaxaca and beyond; (2) the expansion and enormous size of both city and population at the capital, Monte Alban; and (3) the independence of Monte Alban from Teotihuacan.

Chronology. The end of Monte Alban is now placed at about A.D. 700, or roughly at the same time as the collapse of Teotihuacan. The period is divided into two phases, III*a* and III*b*. Trade, pottery, and other influences from Teotihuacan are present in III*a* but are missing from III*b*. This is a principal distinction between the phases. The late phase seems increasingly inward-looking and isolated. At the end of III*b*, Monte Alban was abandoned as a city. However, cultural continuity beyond this event is indicated by the fact that pottery from III*b* and the following phase IV can be distinguished only by close study. The Zapotecs had lost their ancient capital about A.D. 700 but were as culturally distinctive as ever.

The City of Monte Alban. Bernal (1965*a*) defines Monte Alban during period III as a true city. Formal, public architecture and surrounding terraces covered over 40 square kilometers (about 15 square miles). Density was not nearly as high as at Teotihuacan, but Blanton's surveys have shown, as noted before, that more than two thousand terraces, all with one or more houses, occupy the slopes of the main ridge system. Many small ravines were dammed for water. The whole ridge was probably dotted with these small ponds used by the households.

Population growth was spectacular during period III. It began slowly at the city itself, but by the end of period III*b*, 24,000 people lived at Monte Alban and perhaps 31,000 more in 356 other communities (Blanton and Kowalewski, 1981). Jalieza in the southern arm of the valley became a large preindustrial city with about 12,000 people. It is thought that it was the administrative center for its district. Several other large centers handled the administrative tasks for the rest of the central valley. As an indication of the difference in order of magnitude of urbanism, it can be noted that Jalieza had only about 45,000 cubic meters (1.6 million cubic feet) of public architecture, whereas Monte Alban's public buildings had about 600,000 cubic meters (21 million cubic feet) of mass. This also ignores questions of quality and detail, such as plans, decoration, and so forth.

Monte Alban had developed into a splendid center by this time, and it was during III*b* that it assumed its most complex form. It is this architecture that the modern visitor sees when at the site (Figs. 6-13, 6-14). Monte Alban is arranged on a north-south axis, with two enormous platforms at either end of a very large plaza. The platforms support complex arrangements of pyramid-temples, palaces, patios, and tombs. The east side of the great plaza is lined with six residential buildings and a small ball court (Figs. 6-15, 6-16). The middle of the plaza is occupied by three buildings jammed together into one unit. The ancient observatory–conquest monument (Building J) sits detached in front of the grand

Fig. 6–13. System IV, Monte Alban, a temple complex dating from about A.D. *450. It is one of fifteen temples on the top of the ridge which possibly correspond to the fifteen barrios of the city.*

Fig. 6–14. *View of Monte Alban east from System IV with a part of that complex's forecourt visible in the foreground.*

Fig. 6–15. *Monte Alban ball court in the central (upper) civic complex. Ball courts with an I plan appear early in Oaxaca.*

Fig. 6–16. Monte Alban. View of an interior courtyard in the possible palace zone of the northern great platform, main civic complex.

staircase leading to the south platform. The west edge of the plaza is occupied by three units: two more or less symmetrical architectural complexes, called System M and System IV, which flank the ancient *danzantes* structure (Building L). The south platform may date entirely from period III*a*, but most of the other buildings mentioned were modified or enlarged during III*b*. Ancient sculpture was retained, moved around, and reused. Thus, some of the *danzante* sculptures were shifted. New stelae and carved slabs commemorated new conquests and other events of dynastic importance (Figs. 6-17, 6-18). One stela on the south platform shows a conqueror symbolically driving his lance through the name glyph of a town. Other stelae in the same zone show bound captives standing on the name glyphs of their home towns.

The architectural style of Monte Alban was characterized by something called a *doble escapulario,* or double recess, which has something of the appearance of a World War II artillery embrasure. Some 90 percent of the public buildings at Monte Alban have this feature, which is very regional. It is not clear whether Monte Alban architecture was painted and elaborated by modeled stucco, but certainly most of it was plastered.

One hundred seventy formal tombs have been found at the site. Most of these date from period III and have a characteristic form. They are built of masonry slabs and are placed below the courtyard floors. Some have been found in the great plaza and many more under the patio floors of apartment houses on the upper slopes of the ridge. Most period III tombs are entered by a flight of stairs leading down below ground level to an antechamber. The facades of the tombs are nearly identical to the facades of temples once extant at Monte Alban. Above the doorways there is often a niche within which rests an elaborate incense burner (funerary urn). Carved and plain slabs close the tombs off from the antechambers. The interiors of the tombs are mainly rectangular, with deep wall niches within which rest pottery and other offerings to the dead. Most often the tomb was occupied by a single person surrounded by ceramics and other items which presumably belonged to him during his lifetime. Again, the remarkable incense burners are highly characteristic of these offering groups.

Occasionally murals decorate the tomb walls. Some of the most interesting of these paintings were found in Tombs 104 and 105. In each case, Caso and Miller both have noted certain similarities to the mural art of Teotihuacan in the lines of gaily costumed figures with speech scrolls who parade around the walls. Miller (1988) has analyzed the Tomb 105 scene, which shows four couples exiting from the tomb, and believes that one of the women is Maya. Taken as a body, the mural art seems to show an

Fig. 6–17. Classic-period stelae at Monte Alban showing conquests. The left-hand monument shows a captive figure standing on top of a glyph which indicates the person's home town.

Fig. 6–18. Classic-period stela at Monte Alban showing a captive. A date in the Zapotec calendar is noted in front of the person, perhaps indicating the date of conquest.

indigenous regional Mesoamerican style. It is surely Oaxacan in origin, although it may share certain ideas and conventions in common with other Mesoamerican cultures.

A hint of the elaborate ritual which surrounded the lives and deaths of the elite at Monte Alban is given by a remarkable group of figurines found above Tomb 103 (see Paddock, 1966b: Fig. 151). A dead man is represented by a mask set on a miniature pyramid. An orchestra and five priests surround the mask, while another person impersonates the old fire god. This figurine group is probably a record of a memorial ceremony for someone of great importance already buried, perhaps for the person interred in Tomb 103 below. As is the case of the group of Olmec figurines from La Venta and the village figurines from Nayarit it is as close as we will ever get to a "snapshot" of the culture in action.

Crafts and Specialists. The amounts of ceramics found around Monte Alban are enormous even by Mesoamerican standards. Much of the material was made for household use, but a great deal of specialty pottery was also produced. A polished gray ware is the most characteristic pottery of period III. Teotihuacan flower vases (*floreros*) and other forms appear in III*a* along with significant and persistent amounts of a trade ware called thin orange. Studies have shown that thin orange was probably made in an area which lies between Puebla and Oaxaca. Other Teotihuacan forms were also made from local clays. The baroquely elaborate incense burners were almost certainly made by craft specialists. Aside from these urns, III*b* represents a simplification of III*a* ceramics. During the late phase, similarities to Teotihuacan ceramics disappear entirely from the Monte Alban ceramic complex.

Other crafts are not particularly well developed, especially when measured against the exquisite productions of the later Mixtecs. Some carved jades from tombs are relatively simple in technique and motif. The best were imports from the Maya Highlands.

Social Structure and Religion. The sumptuous palaces and what are apparently dynastic records at Monte Alban imply a hereditary elite. Ancestor worship in some form is indicated by the funeral complex and the nature of the tombs. The reinforcement of social status by religious sanction seems to have been in operation among the Zapotec as it was among the Classic Maya. Zapotec rulers are clearly shown as receiving divine aid in their activities, and their burial places under and near temples indicate that when they died they assumed their places in the supernatural order.

Very specific ideas about the nature of Monte Alban III religion can be gained from a study of the incense burners and murals (Fig. 6-19). This has been masterfully done by Caso and Bernal (1952). Some thirty-nine gods have been identified, most with calendar names derived from the sacred almanac. Eleven of these gods were female. Nearly all of them are grouped around several major themes which are strikingly similar to those defined for Teotihuacan. One theme is that of the rain god–lightning complex. The jaguar is associated with this group and is at least partly symbolic of Cocijo, the rain god. Another cluster of deities is organized around the maize plant. The maize god himself, Pitao Cozabi, took the form of a bat. A number of serpent gods include Quetzalcoatl in his guise as the wind god. Bird-masked gods; goddesses; the "flayed god," Xipe Totec; and an opossum deity make up the rest of the period III Zapotec pantheon. Nearly all of these deities were still worshiped at the time of Spanish contact, so a certain amount of information about them comes down to us from the early Christian missionaries. It is again clear that there is an extraordinarily strong continuity between the culture of Monte Alban III and that of the contact-period Zapotec. On the other

Fig. 6–19. Classic-period glyphs, mainly from incense burners, at Monte Alban.

hand, there are also enough distinctions to make clear that period III culture may have been somewhat more elaborate than that of 1521.

Relations with Teotihuacan or the Ñuiñe? The fact that there were two powerful and culturally vigorous states coexisting in Mesoamerica is of interest. Even more interesting is the question of their relationships.

It used to be thought that the influences in ceramics of Monte Alban II and IIIa indicated a very powerful general influence on Monte Alban from Teotihuacan. In reviewing the nature of the contacts, however, it is remarkable to us how few and ephemeral they were. Principally, outside influence assumes the aspects of Teotihuacan ceramic forms made from local wares, the import of thin orange pottery, and reminiscent stylistic links in architecture and mural art. These links and influences are quantitatively small. Furthermore, John Paddock (1966b) has noted that the thin orange ware came from a zone intermediate to Teotihuacan and Monte Alban, a zone called the Ñuiñe, or "hot land." Thin orange was exported from about A.D. 200 to 500. Paddock has defined a style named after the origin area of the pottery. It is also intermediate to both Teotihuacan and Monte Alban in its style of sculpture and in its glyphic system. Paddock argues that the traits noted above were most likely not transmitted directly from Teotihuacan but through the intermediary culture of the Ñuiñe. This zone was apparently a buffer area under the control of Cholula.

This still leaves us with the problem of the "Oaxacan Barrio" at Teotihuacan (Paddock, 1983a). Apparently the Oaxacan group was of relatively high status, and represented an essentially autonomous political and cultural zone. Cowgill comments that although Monte Alban may have been independent of Teotihuacan, the two states were certainly not on a par. Teotihuacan undoubtedly prevented Monte Alban from extending its area of influence much beyond the Central Valley of Oaxaca (Cowgill, personal communication).

A study by Joyce Marcus has clarified the situation considerably. Stone monuments at Monte Alban define something of the relationship between the two cities from the Oaxacan point of view. Four sculptures show the probably diplomatic visit of persons from Teotihuacan to Monte Alban sometime during period IIIa (Marcus, 1980, 1983d). In the scenes, the envoys travel from a Teotihuacan-style temple, confer and burn incense with Zapotec leaders, and are identified by their personal names and by special tassels (Fig. 6-20). Relationships thus seem to have been on the basis of an uneasy alliance or detente rather than dominance and subordination.

Period III is the apogee of Monte Alban and also of Zapotec culture. The city existed and grew in the midst of ever-extending populations and subordinate centers. The nature of the probable relationships between the rulers and the mass of the population has been very well described by Paddock:

> Monte Alban was a place electric with the presence of the gods. . . . Every temple stood over half a dozen temples of centuries before. Buried in the great temples were ancient high priests of legendary powers, now semi-deified; centuries of accumulated mana in ceremonies, centuries of power and success lay deep inside that masonry. But with their own humble hands, or those of their remembered ancestors, the common people had made the buildings. No whip-cracking slave driver was needed. The satisfaction of helping to create something simultaneously imposing, reassuring, and beau-

Fig. 6–20. A very late (ca.A.D. 600) monument at Monte Alban showing a conference between two personages seated on their respective glyphs (personal or locality names?).

tiful is enough to mobilize endless amounts of human effort. [Paddock, 1966*b*:153]

And yet at the end of period III*b*, about A.D. 700, Monte Alban was abandoned by rulers and ruled.

Summary

Teotihuacan, Cholula, and Monte Alban were the urban centers of early highland civilizations. Later cities such as Xochicalco and Tula were small and provincial places at the time of Teotihuacan's greatness. Teotihuacan, in this view of things, was probably not the overwhelmingly dominant city some have portrayed. It exerted enormous influence, but strong regional cultures outside its homeland resisted or assimilated its influence.

Cholula was most susceptible to this influence, being physically close. Monte Alban was apparently safe from domination behind its mountain walls. The relationship between the Oaxacan city and Teotihuacan must have been an alliance at the most. The outposts of Teotihuacan, such as Kaminaljuyu, depended largely on the good will of the states of the gulf region and the Oaxacan highlands. In the Maya Lowlands, Teotihuacan apparently took more of a direct hand in the regional politics and operated through a collaborationist ruler at Tikal as well as through traders. However, even this intervention did not place Teotihuacan in absolute control of a Maya regional state. Perhaps this is the explanation for the foreigners' quarters at Teotihuacan. They were in the nature of embassies and trade missions rather than delegations from subservient states. In short, impressive as it was, Teotihuacan had rival centers which were beyond its power to dominate. The time came when Teotihuacan, weakened by whatever factors, found itself threatened by new states near and within its homeland. This situation set the stage for the sequence of collapses and transformations that attended the ends of these first highland civilizations.

CHAPTER 7

TRANSFORMATIONS: EPI-CLASSIC CULTURES, THE COLLAPSE OF CLASSIC CULTURES, AND THE RISE AND FALL OF THE TOLTEC

And they left behind that which today is there . . . the so-called serpent column. . . . And the Tolteca mountain is to be seen; and the Tolteca pyramids, the mounds, and the surfacing of Tolteca [temples]. And Tolteca potsherds are there to be seen. And Tolteca bowls. . . . And many times Tolteca jewels. . . .

—Sahagún, 1961:165.

Then there was a change of the katun, *then there was a change of rulers. . . . Whereupon a numerous army was seen, and they began to be killed. Then a thing of terror was constructed, a gallows for their death. Now began the archery of Ox-halal Chan. Then the rulers of the land were called. Their blood flowed, and it was taken by the archers.*

—Chilam Balam of Chumayel, 1967:76–77.

APOCALYPTIC visions are more convincing and easier to sell then they used to be. Even in the recent past, however, when archaeologists talked of the great disasters of prehistory, the spectacular catastrophic aspects tended to be emphasized, and those features which illuminated the events as transformations were given short shrift. The remarkable successes of ancient cultures tended to be overshadowed by the sense of impermanence lent by the foreknowledge of their doom. It is significant that many of the disasters of the past led also to cultural reformulations and ultimately to new heights of cultural and social success. On the other hand, there is no question that some collapses led to a kind of devolution which resulted in drastic simplifications of cultural forms. Therefore, to truly understand what happened, it is necessary to take each of the events on its own terms.

Simply stated, Mesoamerican civilizations collapsed when they became overdeveloped in unbalanced and inefficient directions. Cowgill (1979) comments that, like ancient China, at least some Mesoamerican cultures expanded to produce "ever larger and ever less efficient bureaucracy, higher taxes (especially for peasants), increasing diversion of tax revenues into the pockets of local officials, and decreasing availability of revenue for state purposes. . . ." Whatever the specifics, these civilizations became fatally vulnerable to various stresses exerted by natural or cultural factors, or combinations of the two. Prehistorians have been too prone to attribute these rapid cultural transformations to single causes. For example, at one time or another it has been fashionable to attribute the fall of Maya civilization to the single factors of soil exhaustion, moral collapse, climatic change, grass invasion of farmlands, military invasion, disease, or earth-quakes. In recent years, however, archaeologists have fortunately been exposed to the revivifying effects of systems theory, feedback models, general model building, and multiple causation. At the same time, infor-mation about cultural and social collapses has become more complex and sophisticated. It has been increasingly clear that multiple factors were involved in all of these events. Therefore, the latest explanations tend to be complex and multifactored. With these points in mind, let us approach the subject of the fall and transformations of the Classic Mesoamerican civilizations.

The Collapse of Teotihuacan

The explanation that one advances for a collapse is obviously affected by the perspective one assumes about the nature of that society. An older view of Teotihuacan and its sociopolitical nature is advanced by Wigberto Jiménez-Moreno (1966a). This distinguished scholar argued that Teoti-huacan was less an empire, as we historically know this form, and more a religious confederation like traditional Tibet. He drew an analogy between the chief priest of Teotihuacan (an incarnation of Tlaloc?) and the Tibetan Dalai Lama, who is continually reincarnated. The dominance of Teotihuacan in this view, then, was a result of its moral force, which dissipated with the erosion of the religious enthusiasm that had originally proselytized Mesoamerica. This erosion of moral primacy led to vulnera-bility. Jiménez believed that Teotihuacan was ultimately overthrown in its weakened condition by a group of militaristic barbarians from the north known as the Otomi. However, Jiménez clearly admitted that such an invasion would have been only symptomatic and that the ultimate causes of the fall remained unidentified.

Teotihuacan, with the aid of recent research, looks increasingly like a gigantic regional state expanded to an empire, with other regional states bound to it by tribute and alliance systems. Its heartland was the central Mexican plateau and especially the Basin of Mexico. The social and political structure at the final point of supreme crisis seems to have been a somewhat secularized form of divine kingship bolstered by considerable military power. A noble administrative class controlled highly organized kinship groups, which were the basis of the society, living in city wards. These kinship units were probably occupationally specialized, with most of them including farmers. Teotihuacan's power was largely derived from this highly organized and large mass of about two hundred thousand people and from the control that they exerted over various economic resources outside the heartland. In Sanders and Price's terms (1968), the Teotihuacanos had put together the Central Mexican Symbiotic Region within the context of a single political and social system. The gradual withdrawal of Teotihuacan's influence from outlying parts of Mesoamerica, about A.D. 550, would indicate that the great city had more pressing problems nearer home than the maintenance of an imperial system.

Recent work at Cholula, around Monte Alban, and especially in Garcia Cook's "Teotihuacan Corridor" (1981) demonstrates that Teotihuacan was not entirely alone in its sophistication during its terminal phase of A.D. 500 to 650. However, it now appears that Tula, the later capital of the Toltec, was not in existence, even as a small town, until about A.D. 800. Therefore, we can discard the notion that the ancestors of the Toltec had much to do with the demise of Teotihuacan. Similarly, the suggestion that Xochicalco to the southwest was powerful and (ultimately) hostile enough to block Teotihuacan's access to western Morelos, and to the Balsas River area beyond, is no longer viable (Hirth, 1984). This fortified city was not an urban center before A.D. 650. Therefore, we must regretfully discard the suggestion by Sanders (1965) that an early "triple alliance" among Tula, Xochicalco, and Cholula may have cut off Teotihuacan. As we have seen, Monte Alban was certainly independent of Teotihuacan, although in contact with it. Garcia Cook reads the Tlaxcala data for the period immediately before A.D. 650 to mean that there was a move toward autonomy by several important regional states of the region. The dominant cities of this "Teotihuacan Corridor," the major commercial route to the gulf and to the south, dominated and cut it. He further suggests that the "Olmeca-Xicalanca" of the later chronicles took over Cholula and established Cacaxtla as a capital. Fortresses and fortified cities were established (Garcia, Cook, 1981).

According to this perspective, Teotihuacan's world may have ended with both a bang and a whimper. Post-collapse Oxtoticpac-Xometla–phase materials of Teotihuacan are found within a much shrunken and perhaps devastated city. Although Millon interprets the evidence otherwise, the four hundred instances of fire in structures along the Street of the Dead, and the two hundred occurrences in other parts of the city, tie together with other data to suggest the systematic looting and destruction of the city. A recent addition to this evidence is that of the Instituto Nacional de Antropología e Historia, which found a dismembered skeleton in a room of the burnt-down main palace in the Citadel (Cabrera, Rodríguez, and Morelos, 1982). Millon (1988) notes other examples of dismembered bodies in the Citadel palaces. Much of the destruction has the characteristics of an "inside" job. Caches of sacred and valuable items were dug from their hiding places, and tombs were systematically looted.

Both of these hidden depositories yielded luxury pottery, perhaps textiles, and certainly the carved jade jewels which were the highest form of Mesoamerican wealth. Deliberate destruction of religious symbols and of other artifacts bespeak a violent end to Teotihuacan. More important, and more basic, were the losses of commercial wealth beforehand and, later, the loss of prime farmland in and around the basin.

Ultimate explanations of Teotihuacan's downfall still elude us. It may be that the very success of Teotihuacan in developing and spreading a new urban order of society and politics led to the rise of rivals. These rivals, newer and less tradition-bound, may have had the edge on the older, more ponderous regional-imperial capital. Their motivation to overthrow the mother city may have been a drought, as suggested by Armillas. Further, the foreigners in the city may have intrigued with dissident factions against the ruling groups. In any case, it seems clear that a few hundred dusty barbarians from the north would have had a very difficult time making a serious impression on a well-organized city of two hundred thousand. It is also clear that internal weaknesses and rival military powers of equal sophistication were necessary to bring down Teotihuacan and to result in its looting and destruction.

The lack of urban bases and forts would not necessarily have been a handicap to professional military groups that could have operated from camps and groups of small villages. The idea of such groups operating during the period of collapse and establishing themselves in the Epi-Classic states afterward is developed in the following section.

The collapse of the city and its political system had several important effects. One of the most important was the release of inhibitions on regional centers which had previously been suppressed by Teotihuacan. Jeffrey Parson's surveys (1974) in the Texcoco and Chalco sides of the basin show a dramatic resurgence of population after Teotihuacan's fall. Texcoco was established shortly thereafter. Reciprocally, within the Valley of Teotihuacan, population fell from two hundred thousand at A.D. 650 to about thirty thousand at A.D. 900. During this time the large center of Azcapotzalco, on the western side of the lake, showed a growth spurt. The expansions of Tajin, Xochicalco, and Cholula have already been noted.

Another effect was that of a diaspora of Teotihuacan craftsmen over Mesoamerica. It is no coincidence that a second, late injection of Teotihuacan influence appears in the Maya Lowlands at this time. A small temple, possibly dedicated to Tlaloc, was built near the most important precinct in Tikal. Along with the craft technologies that no doubt were spread in this manner, political expertise may also have been carried by former civil servants and nobility of Teotihuacan. In any case, the period immediately following the central Mexican collapse was one of reverberating clashes and military competition among expanding and elaborating city and regional states. It was also a time of opportunity for groups which had heretofore been on the fringes of the major cultures and major states. Groups such as barbarians from the north penetrated southward into the basin and beyond. Jiménez-Moreno's Otomi would have come in at this time. Within the jumbled and locked-up valley of northern Oaxaca, Mixtec states were being formed and reformed. Certain groups located in the Gulf Coast zone were in contact with the Classic Maya and began to press them, perhaps as early as A.D. 750. It now seems that the use of military mercenaries became widespread, that central Mexican groups were brought in by the Maya, and that Maya–Gulf Coast groups penetrated the Central Mexican Highlands. There is no doubt that the Classic Maya lasted longer than Teotihuacan. The wonder is not that they eventually fell, but that, given their internal weaknesses, they lasted as long as they did in the unsettled conditions after Teotihuacan's collapse.

Epi-Classic States in Central Mexico

Following the collapse of Teotihuacan as a supraregional capital, a number of regional states arose whose capitals were usually fortified cities. In reality, Teotihuacan remained a very large center of population itself, although without the political dominance it had exercised before. Without the restraint of a superpower, regional elites established themselves in strategic positions and engaged in expanding their power bases. These regional states and cultures represent both a transitional and a new type of society: the predatory conquest state, the form of which was ultimately developed by the Aztec into an empire. The Epi-Classic, as Hirth (1984) and others have defined it, is focused mainly on Central Mexico, and especially the sites of Xochicalco, Cacaxtla, Teotenango, Cholula, and several others less well known. The concept might logically be extended to include the Tajin state, as well as the city of Tula in its first stages, and the regional states of the Puuc and the northern plain of Yucatan. Here we will only consider Xochicalco and Cacaxtla, for which we have new information. The other, contemporary sites and regions are considered under other headings.

Xochicalco

This city is located in some rather grim terrain of western Morelos and, in fact, on some of the worst agricultural land available. However, it appears that this may have been one of the reasons for the choice of location; its availability in a situation of powerful neighbors who already occupied the best lands. Hirth's report on his project at Xochicalco has developed and synthesized his own work and that of his predecessors (Hirth, 1984). The following account depends largely on his published material.

The substantial Classic-period population around the hilltops of what was later Xochicalco did not support an urban center or public architecture other than a few temples. After A.D. 650 a fortress city was built on top of that series of adjacent hills, eventually covering a zone of 4 square kilometers (1.5 square miles). A series of five extensive terrace systems sculpted the main hill for human occupation. The topmost zone, with the famous Pyramid of the Plumed Serpent, was a very private place with limited access. An extensive palace there was the residence of the governing elite (Figs. 7–1, 7–2). Three stelae were found in this group with apparent depictions of Quetzalcoatl in an art style reminiscent of that of Tajin on the Gulf Coast. The second level down was evidently a public zone. It had a large temple and several public, perhaps administrative, buildings. A formal road net apparently tied the surrounding countryside to the city as well as parts of the urban center together and ends at the public zone. Below this zone were three more broad terrace systems which supported residential compounds as well as some small gardens. The whole city was surrounded by a defensive wall and moat. Population estimates are not given by Hirth, but it seems likely that no fewer than fifteen thousand people were present by A.D. 800. An indication of the precarious times in which the city existed is at least one refuge, made defensible by moat and wall, on an adjacent hilltop.

Fig. 7–1. Sculptured base of the Temple of Quetzalcoatl at Xochicalco, Morelos, Mexico, on the highest hill within this fortified city. The hybridized style is characteristic of civilizations of this period of transition from Classic to Early Postclassic.

Fig. 7–2. A drawn rendition of part of the sculpture of the Temple of Quetzalcoatl at Xochicalco. The feathered serpent writhes among seated human figures and hieroglyphs which may designate the rulers of the zone and name their seats of government.

Eventually, Xochicalco dominated nearly all of western Morelos, with smaller administrative centers tributary to it. The nature of the elite may be indicated by the art style of the uppermost architecture and stelae, which both have some Maya and some Gulf Coast features. By A.D. 900, Xochicalco had been mostly abandoned, possibly because of the intrusion of groups from both north and west. Litvak-King has suggested that the large center of Miacatlan replaced Xochicalco, but lack of work at the former leaves us without much notion of the nature of the ruling groups there.

Cacaxtla

This fortified hilltop city, established after A.D. 650, was the capital of a regional kingdom ruled by a people called the Olmeca-Xicalanca in the later chronicles (Garcia-Cook, 1981). Situated as it was in the "Teotihuacan Corridor," this fortress-capital may have interrupted Teotihuacan's commercial and communication route to the Gulf Coast. The Olmeca-Xicalanca are said to have come from the Gulf Coast area—specifically, the Chontal Maya region of Xicalango—and to have been in the eastern Mesa Central considerably earlier (Garcia-Cook, 1986). Thus, they may have been military opportunists who seized a strategic place and advantage at the moment of disorganization created by the fall of Teotihuacan. They apparently also took control of the much older city of Cholula.

The site, as presently known, consists of a hilltop modified to accommodate ten massive platforms which sustained palace and temple structures as well as food storage facilities. The latter are of a biconical shape and adobe construction (*cuexcomates*) still in use by present-day farmers of the region (Sánchez del Real, 1987). All but one of these platforms are on a north-south axis in the site. The platforms, in turn, are protected by a series of dry moats which are up to 24 meters (80 feet) wide and 9 meters (30 feet) deep; at least one of the moats is backed up by a rampart. The schematic map of Cacaxtla also shows terracing down the hillsides, but the levels apparently are not connected in the manner that made Xochicalco so formidable.

The now-famous paintings of Cacaxtla, located on Platform II, were found by archaeologists exploring a looter's tunnel. The murals are, in a word, extraordinary (Fig. 7–3). The brilliance of the well-preserved colors and figures indicate what we have lost in so much of Mesoamerican civilization. The style combines central Mexican style, reminiscent of the sculpture of Xochicalco, with features of Classic Maya painting as known from Bonampak. Dancing, pirouetting figures dressed in jaguar, bird, and other costumes are framed by elongated feathered serpents, jaguars, and marine animals. Glyphs reminiscent of those of Xochicalco embellish and, presumably, explain the action. A ghastly battle scene between "bird-men" and "jaguar-men" shows all too graphically exposed intestines,

Fig. 7–3. A figure from the murals at a palace in Cacaxtla, Tlaxcala, Mexico, a fortified city to the east of Xochicalco. This particular figure seems to be Maya, although there are human figures from both highlands and lowlands in these paintings.

severed heads, blood, and other results of violence. Garcia-Cook (1986) suggests that this scene may record a battle which gave the rulers of Cacaxtla control over the area.

Modeled stucco bas-relief has an even greater appearance of Maya art, and one fragment could be taken entire from a Maya stela (portico of Edificio E). Further, Sánchez del Real illustrates a modeled stucco human portrait head which is startlingly like those found in the Maya Lowlands. A seated human figure has a great resemblance to one found at Yaxchilan from about the same period. A "jalousie" window made of stucco is nearly a duplicate of one recently found at the Maya site of Uaxactun (Sánchez del Real, 1987).

Evidently Cacaxtla fell on evil days about A.D. 900 and was abandoned by A.D. 1000. Garcia-Cook (1981) thinks that the Olmeca-Xicalanca were driven out and concentrated in the southern zone around Cholula for another century or so.

New World Condottieri?

These and other Epi-Classic states lasted a considerable time and evidently were partly the result of the intrusion of new ideas. We suggest that the groups from the Gulf Coast, the Olmeca-Xicalanca for one, may have been military predators and mercenaries something like the condottieri groups of fourteenth-century Italy. Sometimes they were employed by central Mexican states, and perhaps Teotihuacan began the practice, what with the presence of trading groups in its capital city. At other times, as during the disorganization of the collapse of Teotihuacan, they may have tried to achieve legitimacy (always a problem for mercenaries) by establishing themselves as intrusive elite at places such as Xochicalco and Cacaxtla. Perhaps some of the raids into the Classic Maya Lowlands were simply long-distance predatory strikes launched by these centers. Certainly, as we shall see, the probable mercenary status of the Toltec in Yucatan was converted by them into full-blown permanent power. In this case, the mercenaries may have turned on their presumed employers, the Epi-Classic Puuc cities, and overthrown them. The political fragmentation and general social chaos following the A.D. 650 Teotihuacan collapse, and then the A.D. 850 southern Maya collapse, gave these opportunists plenty of chances to improve their own statuses and positions. It is to the second great catastrophe, that of the Classic southern Maya, that we now turn.

The Classic Maya Collapse

If we accept the idea of a forced dispersal of Teotihuacanos throughout Mesoamerica in the late seventh century, then the first inklings of trouble for the Maya are in the appearance of the god Tlaloc on a Late Classic polychrome plate and on a stela at Copan. Pushing this line of thinking too far implies that the fall of Maya civilization was the result of external causes, which is probably not the case at all. A conference on the Maya collapse has developed an explanation which combines external and internal stresses with known historical events (Culbert, 1973). Culbert has recently brought the model up to date (1988).

According to what we now know, Maya civilization began to reach a series of regional peaks about A.D. 650. By A.D. 830, there is evidence of disintegration of the old patterns, and by A.D. 900, all of the southern lowland centers had collapsed. An understanding of the Maya apocalypse must be based in large part on an understanding of the nature of Maya civilization. During the Terminal Classic period, A.D. 750 to 900, cultural patterns of the lowlands can be briefly characterized as follows. Demographically, a high peak had been reached at least as early as A.D. 600 and perhaps earlier. This population density and size in turn led to intensive forms of agriculture and the establishment of permanent farmsteads in the countryside. Hills were terraced, swamps were drained and modified, water impoundments were made by the hundreds, and land became so scarce that walls of rock were built both as boundaries and simply as the results of field clearance. These masses of people were also highly organized for political purposes into region-state units, which fluctuated in size. These states were more than simple aggregations of cities and were characterized by hierarchical and other complex relationships among them.

Society was organized on an increasingly aristocratic principle by A.D. 650. Dynasties and royal lineages were at the top of the various Maya states and commanded most of the resources of Maya economic life. Most of the large architecture of the cities was for their use. Groups of craft specialists and civil servants supported the elite, with the mass of the population engaged in either part-time or full-time farming. Trade was well organized among and within the states. Military competition was present but was controlled by the fact that it had become mainly an elite-class and prestige activity which did not greatly disturb the economic basis of life. Thus, Maya culture at the ninth century A.D. seems to have been well-ordered, adjusted, and definitely a success. Yet a devastating catastrophe brought it down.

Characteristics of the Collapse

It sometimes seems that the accumulation of weighty theoretical formulations purporting to explain the collapse of Maya civilization will eventually, instead, cause the collapse of Maya archaeology. A refreshingly skeptical and clear-sighted book by John Lowe (1985) reviews the major theories and tests them as well. We will not be as thorough in the following section but, it is to be hoped, just as convincing. A brief characterization of the collapse includes the following features:

1. It occurred over a relatively short period of time: 75 to 150 years.

2. During it the elite-class culture failed, as reflected in the abandonment of palaces and temples and the cessation of manufacture of luxury goods and erection of stelae.

3. Also during the period there was a rapid and nearly complete depopulation of the countryside and the urban centers.

4. The geographical focus of the first collapse was in the oldest and most developed zones, the southern lowlands and the intermediate (Río

Bec–Chenes) area. The northern plains and Puuc areas survived for a while longer.

In other words, the Maya collapse was a demographic, cultural, and social catastrophe in which elite and commoner went down together. Drawing on all available information about the ancient Maya and comparable situations, the 1970 Santa Fe Conference developed a comprehensive explanation of the collapse. This explanation depends on the relatively new picture of the Maya summarized above. That is, we must discard any notion of the Maya as the "noble savage" living in harmony with nature. Certainly, the Maya lived more in tune with nature than do modern industrial peoples, but probably not much more so than did our nineteenth-century pioneer ancestors. As we shall see, some dissonance with nature was at least partly responsible for its failure. More than this, however, data have been further developed since the conference which strengthen some assumptions and weaken others. Therefore, the explanation which follows is a modified version of that which appears in the report of the Santa Fe Conference (Culbert, 1973).

Stresses. Maya society had a number of built-in stresses, many of which had to do with high populations in the central and southern areas. Turner's and other studies (Turner, 1974; Adams, 1977b) indicate that from about A.D. 600 to 900 there were about 168 people per square kilometer (435 per square mile) in the Río Bec zone. The intensive agricultural constructions associated with this population density are also found farther south, within 30 kilometers (19 miles) of Tikal. They are also to be found to the east in the Belize Valley, and there are indications elsewhere to the south that high populations were present. According to Saul's studies (1972 *et passim*) of Maya bones from the period, the population carried a heavy load of endemic disease, including malaria, yellow fever, syphilis, and Chagas's disease, the latter a chronic infection which leads to cardiac insufficiency in young adulthood. Chronic malnutrition is also indicated by Saul's and Steele's studies (Steele, 1986). Taken altogether, these factors indicate the precarious status of health even for the elite. Average lifespan in the southern lowlands was about thirty-nine years. Infant mortality was high; perhaps as many as 78 percent of Maya children never reached the age of twenty. Endemic disease can go epidemic with just a rise in malnutrition. In other words, the Maya populace carried within itself a biological time bomb which needed only a triggering event such as a crop failure to go off.

With population pressing the limits of subsistence, management of land and other resources was a problem, and one which would have fallen mainly on the elite. If food were to be imported, or if marginal lands were to be brought into cultivation, by extensive drainage projects, for example, then the elite had to arrange for it to be done. There were certain disadvantages to this arrangement. Aristocratic or inherited leadership of any kind is a poor means to approach matters that require rational decisions. One need only consider the disastrous manner in which seventeenth-century European armies were mishandled by officers whose major qualifications were their lineages. There is a kind of built-in variation of the Peter Principle in such leadership: one is born to his level of incompetence. Maya aristocracy apparently was no better equipped to handle the complex problems of increasing populations than were European aristocrats. There were no doubt capable and brilliant nobles, but there was apparently no way in which talent could quickly be taken to the top of society from its lower ranks. Lowe's model of the collapse of Maya civilization emphasizes the management-administrative aspects of the problem and essentially considers the collapse as an administrative breakdown (Lowe, 1985).

There are also signs in the Terminal Classic period of a widening social gulf between elite and commoners. At the same time, problems were increasing in frequency and severity. The elite class increased in size and made greater demands on the rest of Maya society for its support. This created further tensions. Intensive agriculture led to greater crop yields, but also put Maya food production increasingly at hostage to the vagaries of weather, crop disease, insects, birds, and other hazards. Marginal and complex cultivation systems require large investments of time and labor and necessitate that things go right more often than not. A run of bad weather or a long-term shift in climate might trigger a food crisis. Recent work on tree rings and weather history from other sources indicates that a Mesoamerica-wide drought may have begun about A.D. 850. In addition, there are periodic outbreaks of locusts in the Maya Lowlands.

These stresses were pan–Maya and occurred to a greater or lesser degree in every region. No matter whether one opts for the city-state or the regional state model, competition over scarce resources among the political units of the Maya resulted from these stressful situations. The large southern center of Seibal was apparently taken by a northern Maya elite group about A.D. 830. Evidence is now in hand of military intrusions from north to south at Rio Azul, at the Belize sites of Nohmul, Colha, and Barton Ramie, and at Quirigua in the Motagua Valley. At least at Rio Azul and Colha a period of trade preceded the raids, presaging the later Aztec *pochteca* pattern. The patterns and nature of the intrusions indicate that the raids were probably from the Puuc zone and that a part of the motivation, as suggested by Cowgill (1964), was to capture populations. Warfare increased markedly along the Usumacinta River during the ninth century A.D., according to hieroglyphic texts and carved pictures from that area.

There are also hints that the nature of Maya warfare may have changed during this last period. A lintel from Piedras Negras appears to show numerous soldiers in standard uniforms kneeling in ranks before an officer. In other words, organized violence may have come to involve many more people and much more effort and therefore may have become much more disruptive. Certainly competition over scarce resources would have led to an increasingly unstable situation. Further, the resultant disorganization would have led to vulnerability to outside military intervention, and that seems to have been the case as well.

There were also external pressures on the Maya. Some were intangible and in the form of new ideas about the nature of human society as well as new ideologies from the Gulf Coast and Central Mexico. The northern Maya elites seem to have absorbed a number of these new ideas. For example, they included the depiction of Mexican Gulf Coast deities on their stelae as well as some Mexican-style hieroglyphs. Altar de Sacrificios was invaded by still another foreign group from the Gulf Coast about A.D. 910. These people may have been either a truly Mexican Gulf Coast group or Chontal Maya, who were non-Classic in their culture.

A progressive pattern of abandonment and disaster in the western lowlands is suggestive. Palenque, on the southwestern edges of the lowlands, was one of the first major centers to go under; it was abandoned about A.D. 810. The major Usumacinta cities of Piedras Negras and Yaxchilan (Bird-Jaguar's City) were the next to go. They put up their last monuments about A.D. 825. Finally, it was Altar de Sacrificios's turn about A.D. 910. Clearly, there was a progressive disintegration from west to east, and it seems likely that it was caused by pressures from militaristic non–Maya groups. These peoples, in turn, were probably being jostled in the competitive situation set up after the fall of Teotihuacan and may have been pushed ahead of peoples such as the Toltecs and their allies. Perhaps the Epi-Classic states discussed above were involved, as well as some mercenary groups. In any case, it appears certain that these groups were opportunists. They came into an area already disorganized and disturbed and were not the triggering mechanism for the catastrophe but part of the following process.

At any one Maya city or in any one region, the "mix" of circumstances was probably unique. At Piedras Negras there is evidence that the elite may have been violently overthrown from within. Faces of rulers on that site's stelae are smashed, and there are other signs of violence. Invasion finished off Altar de Sacrificios. Rio Azul was overrun by Maya groups from the north, perhaps including Toltec allies, as were a number of Maya centers along the Belize coast and down to Quirigua. At other centers, such as the regional capital of Tikal, the elite were apparently abandoned to their fate. Without the supporting populations, remnants of the Maya upper classes lingered on after the catastrophe. At Colha and Seibal, northern Maya acting as new elites attempted to continue the southern economic and political systems, but they abandoned these attempts after a relatively short time. The general demographic catastrophe and disruption of the agricultural systems were apparently too great to cope with.

In short, ecological abuse, disease, mismanagement, overpopulation, militarism, famines, epidemics, and bad weather overtook the Maya in various combinations. But several questions remain. What led to the high levels of populations which were the basis of much of the disaster?

The Maya were much more loosely organized politically during the Late Formative than during the Classic period. The episodes of interstate competition and of Teotihuacan's intervention seem to have led them to try new, more centralized political arrangements. These seem to have worked well for a time, in the case of the Early Classic expansion of Tikal. After the suggested civil wars of the sixth century there seems to have been a renewed and still stronger development of centralized states, which were probably monarchical.

Using general historical and anthropological experience, Demitri Shimkin (1973) observed that village-level societies approach population control very differently than do state-level societies. Relatively independent villages are oriented plainly and simply toward survival. There are many traditional ways of population control, female infanticide being a favorite practiced widely even in eighteenth-century England. Use of herbal abortion, late marriage, ritual asceticism, and other means keep population within bounds for a village. A state-level society, on the other hand, is likely to encourage population growth for the benefit of the directing elite. The more manpower to manipulate, the better. In the case of the Maya, we have noted a certain megalomania in their huge Late Classic buildings. Unfinished large construction projects at Tikal and Uaxactun were overtaken by the collapse. Such efforts required immense manpower reserves and a simultaneous disregard for the welfare of that workforce. The Maya appear to have shifted gears into a more sophisticated and ultimately maladaptive state organization.

Another question to be considered is, Why did the Maya not adjust to cope with the crises? The answer may lie in the nature of religiously sanctioned aristocracies. Given a crop failure, a Maya leadership group might have attempted to propitiate the ancestors and gods with more ritual and more monuments. This response would have exacerbated the crisis by taking manpower out of food production. Inappropriate responses of this sort could easily have been made, given the ideology and worldview that the Maya seem to have held. On the other hand, if the crisis were a long-term drought, with populations dangerously high and predatory warfare disrupting matters even more, perhaps any response would have been ineffectual.

The rapid biological destruction of the Maya is an important aspect of the collapse. From a guessed-at high of 12 million, the population was reduced within 150 years to an estimated remnant of about 1.8 million. The disease load and the stress of malnutritional factors indicate that a steady diminishment of Maya population probably started by A.D. 830 and rapidly reached a point of no recovery. An average increase of 10 to 15 percent in the annual mortality rate will statistically reduce 12 million to 1.8 million in 75 years. Obviously there was not anything like a steady decline, but the smoothed-out average over the period had to have been something of that order, or perhaps the decline began earlier, at A.D. 750, when Maya civilization reached its peak.

The disruptive nature of population declines can be easily understood if one considers the usual effects of epidemics. In such catastrophic outbreaks of disease, those first and most fatally affected are the young and the old. Even if the main working population survives relatively untouched, the social loss is only postponed. The old take with them much of the accumulated experience and knowledge needed to meet future crises. The young will not be there to mature and replace the adult working population, and a severe manpower shortage will result within fifteen to twenty years. Needless to say, much more work on population estimates and studies of the bones and the general health environment of the ancient Maya needs to be done to produce a really convincing statement on this aspect of the collapse.

A last, although not by any means final, question concerns the failure to recover. This feature may involve climatic factors. If shifts of rainfall belts were responsible for triggering the collapse, then the answer might be the persistence of drought conditions until there were too few people left to sustain the Classic cultural systems. As now seems probable, the Maya were confronted with the situation of having overcultivated their soils and having lost too much surface water. Temporary abandonment of fields would have led to their being rapidly overrun by thick, thorny, second-growth jungle, which is harder to clear than primary forest. Thus, a diminished population may have been faced with the problem of clearing heavily overgrown, worn-out soils, of which vast amounts were needed to sustain even small populations. Second-growth forest springs up overnight and is even today a major problem in maintaining archaeological sites for tourists.

Another possible answer to the question of recovery is that the Maya may have been loathe to attempt the sort of brilliant effort that had ultimately broken them. Just as they preferred to revert to swidden agriculture rather than maintain intensive techniques, they probably found it a relief to live on a village level instead of in their former splendid but stressful state of existence.

The above is an integrated model of the Maya collapse. It explains all the features of the collapse and all the data now in hand, but it is not proved by any means, and in some respects is more of a guide to future research than a firm explanation. If the model is more or less correct, however, it should be largely confirmed within the next ten years of research. Indeed, this process of confirmation has already begun. The 1970 conference which developed the model could explain certain features of the archaeological record only by assuming much higher levels of ancient population than were otherwise plausible at the time. The 1973 Río Bec work of Turner (1974) and Eaton (1975) turned up a vast amount of data which indicate that higher levels of ancient populations indeed had been present. Recent work at Colha (Eaton 1980) and Rio Azul has indicated the importance of militarism in the process (Adams, 1987*b*). All of these findings lend credibility to the model.

Delayed Collapse in the North

The vast and very densely distributed centers of the Puuc area survived for a time. These Puuc cities, possibly a regional state with a capital at Uxmal, appear to have turned into predators on the southern cities. As noted before, part of the motivation may have been for the capture and enslavement of southern populations. Even so, it seems that large centers such as Uxmal, Kabah, Sayil, and Labna lasted only a century longer than the southern cities. Northern Maya chronology is much more disputed than that in the south, but it now seems likely that outsiders, including Toltec, were in Yucatan by A.D. 900 and perhaps earlier, and there are clear indications that Uxmal was absorbing Mexican ideas much earlier. Certain motifs, such as eagles or vultures, appear on Puuc building facades late in the Classic period.

We are now faced with at least three possible explanations of the Puuc collapse: they may have succumbed to the same combination of factors that brought down the southern Maya centers; the Toltec may have conquered them; or a combination of these factors may have been at work (Pollock, 1965; Potter, 1977). At this time, it appears that the northern florescence was partly at the expense of the southern area. As will be seen, evidence for Toltec conquest now appears even stronger, and this is presently the favored explanation for the Puuc collapse.

Chichen Itza, in north central Yucatan, is a center which was culturally allied with the Puuc cities in architecture and probably politically as well. Puuc centers have been found even in the far northeast of the peninsula. At Chichen Itza, Puuc architecture is overlaid and succeeded by Toltec architecture. Unmapped defensive walls surround both Chichen and Uxmal. The data available now make it likely that the Toltec and other groups may have appeared in Yucatan by A.D. 800 and thereafter, perhaps brought in as mercenaries, as so often happened later in Maya history. In whatever capacity they arrived, they appear to have established themselves at Chichen Itza by A.D. 950 as the controlling power. As has happened in history elsewhere, the mercenaries became the controlling forces. Toltec raids, battles, and sieges, combined with the internal weaknesses of Classic Maya culture and perhaps with changing environmental factors, brought about a swift collapse in the Puuc.

The aftermath of the collapse was also devastating. Most of the southern Maya Lowlands have not been repopulated until the last fifty years. Eleven hundred years of abandonment have rejuvenated the soils, the forests, and their resources, but modern man is now making inroads on them. Kekchi Maya Indians have been migrating into the lowlands from the northern Guatemalan highlands as pioneer farmers for the past century, and the Mexican government has colonized the Yucatan, Campeche, and Quintana Roo area with dissatisfied agriculturists from overpopulated highland areas. The forests are being logged and cut down. Agricultural colonies have failed in both Guatemala and Mexico, and some zones are already abandoned. In other areas, the inhabitants have turned to marijuana cultivation. Vast areas have been reduced to low scrub jungle, and large amounts of land are now being converted to intensive agriculture. One looks at the modern scene and wonders. Fortunately, in 1988 a movement began to set aside the remnants of the once immense monsoon forests, and it may be that a series of protected zones in the form of contiguous national parks will soon be in existence in Guatemala, Mexico, and Belize.

The Legendary and Historical Toltec

Itzcoatl, the fourth Aztec emperor (1427–40), did no one any favors, least of all when he ordered a purge of the state archives and the burning of all of the most ancient history books. In that particular act of antiintellectualism perished the documents which could have unscrambled the history of the Toltec. As it is, Toltec traditions and history are a mass of contradictions, conflicting dates and king lists, overlapping and telescoped events, and plainly fraudulent rewriting on the part of the Aztec to support their claim that they were descended from the Toltec. Fortunately, Wigberto Jiménez-Moreno and other distinguished scholars have been able to make sense of the major features of Toltec history and to inject a good deal of convincing documentary detail into the archaeological record.

There are two major lists of Toltec rulers. One is derived from Ixtlilxóchitl's *Historia Tolteca-Chichimeca*, which is an account of the origins and history of Texcoco written by an educated Texcocan after the Spanish Conquest. The other source is the *Anales de Cuauhtitlan* (1945), a generalized history of a city-state in the Valley of Mexico whose inhabitants claimed that their ancestors had come from Tula; its author is unknown. The two lists are different but overlap. G. C. Vaillant and others (Sanders, 1965:182) believe that the two lists are of different dynasties but that they overlap with Topiltzin-Quetzalcoatl, who is named in both. Table

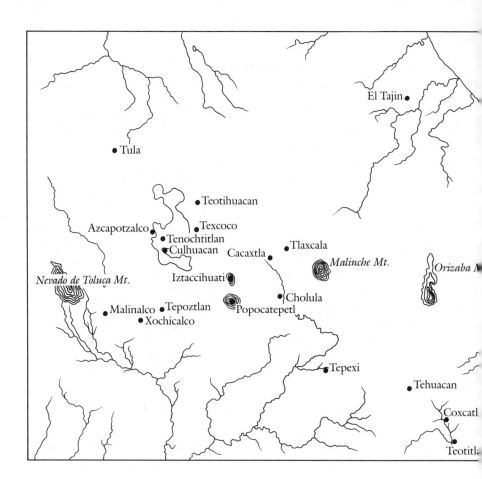

Map 7–1. Central Highlands of Mexico and lowland Veracruz, showing locations of Epi–Classic- and Toltec-period sites.

7–1 summarizes the lists and their correlation as presented in Sanders (1965). The numbers in parentheses are the lengths of reigns.

Of the nine dated reigns from Ixtlilxóchitl's list, six are of fifty-two years each. This corresponds to a complete cycle of the sacred almanac and inspires less than complete confidence in the accuracy or even the truth of this list. The very irregularity of the reigns and their lesser lengths in the *Anales de Cuauhtitlan* (1945) lend somewhat more credibility to it. Huemac, an extraordinarily important figure as the last Toltec ruler, had a reign of seventy-five years, somewhat suspect by its length. Notice also the conflict in the length of reign assigned to Topiltzin in each list— fifty years' difference.

By checking one document against another and the historical information against the archaeological material, Jiménez-Moreno has developed a framework for Toltec history and prehistory (1941, 1966b). What follows is largely his synthesis. There are other reconstructions, notably that of Paul Kirchhoff (1961).

During the period of Teotihuacan's dominance, peoples of Mesoamerican culture from in or around the Valley of Mexico colonized to the north, penetrating even into Durango and Zacatecas. Jiménez-Moreno suggests that the great fortress of La Quemada may be the Tuitan of the chronicles. This expansion took place during the period of A.D. 100 to 300, and colonial centers thus established lasted until about A.D. 600,

Table 7.1.   Summary and Correlation of the Lists of Toltec Rulers.

Ixtlilxochitl List		Anales de Cuauhtitlan	
Huemac, a migrant priest leader			
Chalchiuhtlanetzin	A.D. 510–62 (52)		
Ixtlilcuechahauac	562–614 (52)		
Huetzin	614–66 (52)		
Totepeuh	666–718 (52)		
Nacoxoc	718–70 (52)		
Mitl Tlacominhua	770–829 (59)		
Xihuiquenitzin (Queen)	829–33 (4)	Mixcoamatzatzin, a migrant military leader	(?–?)
		Huetzin	869–? (?)
Iztaccaltzin	833–85 (52)	Totepeuh	?–887 (?)
		Ihuitimal	887–923 (36)
Topiltzin (Quetzalcoatl)	885–959 (74)	Topiltzin (Quetzalcoatl)	923–47 (24)
		Matlacxochitl	947–83 (36)
		Nauhyotzin I	983–97 (14)
		Matlaccoatzin	997–1025 (28)
		Tlilcoatzin	1025–46 (21)
		Huemac	1047–1122 (75)

when many of them were abandoned. The expansion was in many cases connected with extensive mining activities.

The first major period of Toltec history began when, after the fall of Teotihuacan, people from the northern colonies flowed back south into the central mesa zone. Barbarian groups from the northern deserts also moved south. Jiménez-Moreno would see the Toltec as a Mesoamerican group led to the Valley of Mexico by their legendary leader Mixcoatl (Cloud Snake), who established their capital at Ixtapalapa.

The second and greatest period began when, pressured by the historic Olmec who controlled Cholula, the Toltec moved to Tula and placed their capital there. Tula was already a town and had been established in the period of Teotihuacan's dominance, possibly as a colony of the main city. Tula is the most frequently mentioned Tollan of the chronicles, although there are other places which were also called Tollan. The Toltec move was made under the leadership of Topiltzin, also known as Quetzalcoatl. He was also called Ce Acatl, or 1 Reed, after his birthday. This move was probably made about A.D. 960, according to the chronicles (Carrasco, 1971b).

During this period, Topiltzin, the high priest of the Quetzalcoatl cult, became involved in a power struggle with another religious and political faction. In the chronicles, a series of events is mentioned in which Quetzalcoatl and Tezcatlipoca are pitted against one another, and Quetzalcoatl is defeated by treachery and is exiled. Jiménez-Moreno argues persuasively that this is historical truth—that Quetzalcoatl was actually the high priest of a religious cult and that his faction was defeated and sent into exile. According to the legends, Quetzalcoatl abhorred human and blood sacrifices and urged that flowers, fruits, and some animals be offered to the god he represented. The Toltec-Chichimec followers of Tezcatlipoca, the lord of darkness, wished to promote human sacrifice and all of the bloody terror that went with it. Sanders (1965) suggests that the faction of Tezcatlipoca represents newcomers from the barbarian north.

Walter Krickeberg (1956:209) has compared Topiltzin-Quetzalcoatl with the Egyptian heretic king Akhenaton. Like Akhenaton, who also sought to reform a dominant state religion, Quetzalcoatl seems to have had a relatively ephemeral effect. In any case, Topiltzin–Quetzalcoatl, with his followers, the Nonoalco, moved off the Toltec stage at about A.D. 987 and reportedly went to Cholula and then to Yucatan. The great period of Tula continued, and Aztec chronicles speak with unvarnished admiration of these Toltec.

Sahagún's informants said, "The Toltecs were wise. Their works were all good, all perfect, all wonderful, all marvelous; their houses, tiled in mosaics, smoothed, very marvelous" (1961:Book 10, 165–66). The Toltec were righteous, not deceivers. Food, especially maize, was produced in abundance. "They were tall; they were larger [than the people today].

Because they were tall, they ran much and so were named [the tireless runners]" (1961:Book 10, 169). It is also claimed that they spoke Nahuatl.

Paul Kirchhoff (1961) has attempted to define the extent of the Toltec empire using material from the chronicles. It is clear that the main focus of the empire was north and west of the Valley of Mexico, with major centers at Tula, Tollanzinco, and Tenanco and with parts of the Bajío of Jalisco included. Thus, most of the Valley of Mexico and all of the Valley of Puebla were excluded. Those two central valleys were controlled by the historic Olmec Uixtotin, who apparently ruled with an iron hand from Cholula. The chronicles speak of an "Olmec tyranny."

Tula dominated its large political unit until about A.D. 1156, when it was overthrown. The third and last period of Toltec history began when Huemac, the last Toltec king, transferred the capital south to Chapultepec, where he died in about 1162. This is the end of an independent Toltec dynasty, and by this time new waves of barbarians were again breaking through the northern frontiers and penetrating even into the Valley of Mexico. The breakup of the Toltec empire meant that again Mesoamerican refugee groups and newer, rawer barbarians began a series of intrusions against the cities of the central zone.

The Archaeological Record at Tula

Very little direct information about the Toltec pertains to the first period of their history. The second period is reasonably well documented by Acosta's work at the main acropolis of the civic center (1956, 1964*b*, 1974). Thirteen seasons' work in the civil architecture has given us a basic sequence upon which to build. This is supplemented by Matos's excavations and area surveys (1974) and by Diehl's excavations in residential structures (1974, 1983).

Tula is located about 65 kilometers (40 miles) northwest of Teotihuacan. It is laid out along one major ridge, with groups on adjacent spurs. The Tula River, which is a tributary of the Río Panuco, flows north past the ridge, giving easy access to water. It also forms a route of communication to the Veracruz coast. Generally rolling countryside broken by sharp ridges characterizes the zone inhabited by the Toltec. To the east lies the ancient Teotlalpan or "Land of the Gods," and still further to the east and north was Huastec country. Teotlalpan contains the important Pachuca obsidian mines and was also an extremely important agricultural zone at one time. Both Teotlalpan and the immediate Tula area were ravaged during the colonial period by the destructive effects of overgrazing by sheep, goats, and cattle, continuing a drastic decline in fertility begun in the fourteenth century through erosion and overcropping. What are now exhausted, eroded, deforested lands were fertile, well-watered, and extensive croplands and forests at the time of Toltec domination (S. F. Cook, 1949).

Work by Robert Cobean (1974) indicates that there were at least six ceramic phases in the Toltec area. These phases fall into three major time periods. Two early ceramic groups correspond to a period of contemporaneity with Teotihuacan. Settlement for this period indicates no large communities. Communities consist of small Tlamimilolpa-, Xolalpan-, and Metepec-phase groups of house mounds scattered over the countryside between Tepeji del Río to the south and the present Endho Dam of the Tula River to the north. While no significant architectural remains from this period have been found at Tula itself, it is possible that a large, unexcavated ceremonial precinct at the center of the ridge (Tula Chico) dates to this period. The pottery shows certain Teotihuacan affinities, and a good deal of it belongs to a ceramic group called Coyotlatelco.

The second ceramic period correlates with the major architectural period of Tula and is characterized by orange-colored pottery decorated with multiple wavy red lines, the Mazapan style. Various monochromes and dichromes make up most of the complex, with the major forms comprising chile bowls, water jars, and simple bowls with nubbin legs. A few shards of Late Classic Maya polychrome have been found. By far the most important imported pottery, however, is plumbate, from the Pacific Coast of Guatemala. Plumbate, a lead-colored and glazed pottery widely traded about A.D. 1000, is found in great quantity and variety. Nicoya polychrome from Costa Rica and fine orange from the Maya Gulf Coast were also imported (Diehl, Lomas, and Wynn, 1974).

The third ceramic period dates from after the fall of Tula from its status as a great power center. Black-on-orange potteries similar or identical to those from the Basin of Mexico are found over the site. Aztec 2 material is clearly from a widespread occupation, whereas Aztec 3 ceramics are limited and sporadic in distribution, indicating more of a squatter occupation. It may have been during the Aztec 3 period that the main occupation center shifted from the ridge to the modern location of Tula. The modern town probably rests on the site of the sixteenth-century community, which was sizable. Chalco-Cholula polychromes appear in this later complex, as do quantities of black-on-white pottery from the Huastec area (Huastec 6 period).

At about the time that Tula became the capital of the Toltec, the archaeological records show a great expansion of the center. The city grew to cover about 14 square kilometers (about 5.4 square miles) by A.D. 1000. Some one thousand mounds are scattered over the zone. However, there must be at least as many more undetected low structures, many residential. Present estimates for Tula's maximum population are that it fell between 32,000 and 37,000 (Diehl, 1981). The Tollan phase, about A.D. 950–1200, is associated with this expansion. Mazapan pottery from this period shows some stylistic affinities to later "Aztec" black-and-orange wares.

R. A. Diehl and his colleagues have excavated a group of fifteen houses located northeast of the Tula Chico zone in the center of the ridge (Diehl, 1983). The houses are grouped into what Dan Healan (1974) argues are corporate residential groups built for extended families. The houses are rectangular and arranged around central courtyards, with restricted access to each group. The architecture is of small stones set in mud in the lower parts of the walls and adobe block above. Beam-and-mortar roofs finished off the rooms. Food processing areas have been located in many of the houses, and other areas were used for textile manufacture and processing of maguey fiber. The diet of the Toltec of Tula was probably more varied than that reflected in the record; only six food plants are mentioned as having been locally cultivated (Diehl, 1981). However, food remains indicate that many small animals were hunted and eaten, with a heavy emphasis on deer and dogs. Extensive evidence of irrigated fields where food plants and other products such as cotton were raised can be seen on aerial photographs of the zone (Mastache and Cobean, 1985).

In this same group of houses a kiln was found which seems to have been used to produce the subfloor drain tubes so common throughout Tula. Healan suggests that the houses are big enough and arranged in such a way that they imply the accommodation of about 4.5 persons per house. A temple-type structure has been found in one group. Altars, one with a burial inside it, were found within all courtyards. The skull was missing from the burial, and whether this implies human sacrifice or ancestor worship is presently impossible to say. What is certain is that the housing groups at Tula are quite different from the great apartment compounds at Teotihuacan. The terrain at Tula would have made a gridded arrangement difficult, but more important is the fact that, as Rene Millon (1973) points out, there was apparently no social necessity, either at Tula or later, for the apartment compound developed at Teotihuacan. A spectacular cache of plumbate and Nicoya polychrome vessels was found in one house.

Near these residential structures is a civic center group, Tula Chico, or El Corral. Acosta's excavations there have revealed a two-stage temple structure, part of which was round, suggesting that the temple may have been dedicated to Quetzalcoatl in his guise as Ehecatl, the wind god. An attached altar carried a frieze that shows skulls, crossed bones, and Toltec warriors. Associated with the temple was a platform which contained the only Tula artifact that lives up to the reputation of the Toltec for fine craftsmanship. The piece is a plumbate jar covered with mother-of-pearl carved to represent feathers. The motif is that of a coyote with the mouth open to reveal a man. Apparently it represents a Toltec warrior with an animal headdress. Acosta argues that this is an actual representation of

Quetzalcoatl. The coyote is known to have been Quetzalcoatl's *nahual*, or animal soul, and therefore the symbolism would be appropriate.

The main group of late civic architecture is elevated, acropolislike, on the southern end of the ridge, with artificially terraced slopes. It contains about 35 percent of the one thousand mounds at Tula. Diehl reports terrace walls 15 to 18 meters (50 to 60 feet) high on the north and west sides, and these were certainly defensible. Other, smaller civil plazas, such as Tula Chico, are known within the city, but the main temples, those of the sun (or White Tezcatlipoca of the East) and Quetzalcoatl, are in the acropolis group. The group is oriented 15½ degrees east of north, as is Teotihuacan (Diehl, 1981).

The focus of the southern, late, and most important civic group is Structure B, or the Temple of Quetzalcoatl in his form as the morning star (Tlahuizcalpantecuhtli). Structure B, facing south onto the square, is a squat mass of masonry built with *talud-tablero* features (Figs. 7–4, 7–5). It was enlarged and renovated at least six times. In its latest phase, the whole platform was encased in sculptured panels depicting prowling, slavering jaguars and pumas, heart-devouring eagles and buzzards, and Quetzalcoatl himself (Fig. 7–6). Toltec warriors and more abstract designs are also shown. The motifs of these panels were emphasized with bright greens, reds, blues, and white. Most of the paneling has been destroyed or removed since the city fell, and only a few zones remain intact.

Fig. 7–4. Structure B at the capital of the Toltecs, Tula, Hidalgo, Mexico. This building is evidently one which was copied by the Maya at Chichen Itza (the Temple of the Warriors).

Fig. 7–5. Structure B, Tula, viewed along its colonnaded forecourt, the columns of which once supported beams and a flat roof. Projecting stones are the structural ties to the cut stone veneer that once covered the platform.

Fig. 7–6. Structure B, Tula, with a section of original sculptured panels and stone veneer. Prowling Jaguars and crouched eagles gloat over human hearts. Both the animal and the bird were symbols of the sun.

The superstructure was entirely missing when excavated, but judging by Toltec architecture in Yucatan (Chichen Itza), a large, two-roomed temple probably stood on top of the platform. The temple was approached by a broad staircase, at the top of which were banners held by human and jaguar figures of stone. A stone *chacmul,* or reclining human figure, sat in front of the doorway. The main door was framed by the columns formed from stiffened serpent bodies, the heads of which rested on the floor. Inside, gigantic human figures in the form of caryatid columns held up the flat roof in the front room, while square, carved columns supported it in the rear chamber. Also within was probably a large, flat stone table altar supported by small columns carved in the shape of men who raise their hands to carry the table—the famous Atlantean figures, so named from their posture of burden-bearing. Alternating wooden columns and adobe brick sections made up the walls, if the temple followed the general pattern of construction at Tula. Elsewhere in Tula walls were plastered and painted with bright murals, and it is likely that the major temple was decorated similarly. Perhaps Structure B shows us in somewhat diminished form what the greater temples at Teotihuacan looked like.

Altogether, the effect of the theoretical reconstruction of the Temple of Quetzalcoatl is bizarre, magnificent, and powerful to our minds. It must have been at least as impressive to the Toltec and their contemporaries, who also vested the building with the supernatural power of an important god.

The major temple on the square, Structure C, faces west and is possibly a temple to the Sun, or the White Tezcatlipoca of the East. In later times, the White Tezcatlipoca was sometimes a manifestation of Quetzalcoatl. So much of Structure C was destroyed at the time of the city's downfall that nothing is left but the immense platform, which was apparently undecorated. A feature reminiscent of Teotihuacan is the large subsidiary platform attached to the centerline front of the main platform. Atlantean figures were found in the debris of this building.

An elaborate wall, called the Coatepantli (Serpent Wall), is, curiously, located to the rear (north) of the Temple of Quetzalcoatl. A row of lively serpents, shown apparently devouring skeletal figures, is set into a panel between frames of forests. The frets are the same as those that appear as part of the name glyph for Tula in the Mixtec codices (Codex Bodley, 9–11:Caso, 1960:38). The wall is capped with shapes like capital Gs or shell cross-sections, which are also found on the edges of Tula's palace roofs. The serpent wall closed off the northern zone from access to the sacred precinct. A similar wall performed the same function in Aztec Tenochtitlan.

Jammed among and against the temples were colonnades and palaces. The large main square was marked off on two sides by such colonnades.

Structure 3, west of Temple B, is largely formed by a row of three patios, within which are altars, daises, and benches all placed under arcades. Built-in plastered fire pits and huge pottery incense burners were found in the palace. Enormous masses of burned debris were found on the patio floors, giving Structure 3 the name of the Burnt Palace. It is noteworthy, however, that other than deliberate burials, no skeletal remains were found within the structure. Everyone evidently escaped when the palace burned down, or they had abandoned it long since.

The interior of Patio 1 was sumptuously decorated around the edge of the courtyard's roof with a carved stone frieze made up of slabs similar to those found on nearby Structure B. Reclining human figures, sacred green stone symbols (*chalchihuites*), capital G forms, and the depiction of a blood and heart receptacle make up the major motifs. Within an altar in Patio 1 was a closed stone box which contained, among other things, a carved jade plaque, one of the few precious items recovered from the site.

Scratched into the plaster of the floor of Patio 3 of the Burnt Palace are what were probably boards for the playing of the popular Mesoameri- can game *patolli*. The boards vary somewhat among themselves, but generally look like modern game boards marked with squares around the periphery and an additional cross of squares in the center. The game was played by advancing counters around the board using bone dice. One can imagine that the end patio may have been the zone where the palace guard or other permanent functionaries were stationed and that the *patolli* games were a means of whiling away the endless hours. The later Aztec gambled on the outcome of the games.

An altar or dance platform was placed in the middle of the main plaza. A cache found in its masonry consisted of thirty-three ceramic vessels, many of which were precisely like early (Aztec 2) black-on-orange pottery from Culhuacan in the Valley of Mexico. It is interesting to note that when Tula was abandoned and part of its population settled in Culhuacan, the later Aztecs attempted to legitimize themselves by taking a ruler from that city. Three hollow female figurines were also found in the platform cache; these also are greatly similar to contemporary figurines from the Valley of Mexico.

A very large ball court located on the west side of the main square is similar in its closed plan to one at Xochicalco. It is about 110 meters (361 feet) in overall length. Another ball court lies north of the Coatepantli. At least three more are known from elsewhere in the site, making a total of five at Tula.

Acosta comments that the site of Tula and its principal buildings show meticulous and excellent planning, but that execution of those plans was careless and characterized by poor workmanship. Many or most of the features of the civic architecture and the building groups were present at

Teotihuacan, but the Toltec added their own contribution in their use and conceptualization of those elements. One innovation which took hold and lasted until the Spanish Conquest was the use of masses of columns around open courtyards. These columns, usually carved, supported roofs and sheltered stone benches. A comparison of the great market of Aztec Tenochtitlan with the central square of Tula shows great similarities in this regard. The emphasis on the ball game and the ball court as a formal structure begins in this period, and the lavish use of architectonic sculpture in place of or supplementing mural art was another change in emphasis from Teotihuacan times.

Sculpture and Other Art

Most of Tula's Toltec art survives in the form of sculpture. Apparently, however, all of the sculpture was colored, and unsculpted surfaces were painted. Most of the fragments of painted walls are geometric in motif. Bands of red, blue, yellow, and black decorated the walls of a passage between Temple B and the Burnt Palace. The only life scene recovered from Tula so far is that of a sketchily drawn deer hunt, but it is from a much earlier structure which may date back to Teotihuacan times.

A hallmark of the Toltec horizon in much of Mesoamerica is the *chacmul* sculpture. These stiff and ungainly reclining human figures were probably always placed in front of temple doorways to receive preliminary offerings. Free-standing sculpture at Tula included four stelae, long since removed from the site, that may have depicted rulers of the city (Fig. 7–7). Certainly to be included in the inventory of sculpture is a petroglyph on a rock of a nearby mountain which shows Quetzalcoatl and which includes his calendrical name, Ce Acatl (1 Reed). Production of a great mass of small sculpture which supplemented architectonic sculpture is highly characteristic of the cultures of the Tula Toltec and the later Basin of Mexico.

However, most Toltec sculpture was architectonic, consisting of stone slabs designed to be fitted into continuous bands or friezes or of columnar sculptures, the other major group. Many of the motifs have already been noted, but an important feature not yet mentioned is that of hieroglyphic writing. Several panels include bar-and-dot and day-sign notations: "2 Serpent Eye," for example. The distinctive features of writing at Tula seem to be closely related to the system found at Xochicalco, according to Acosta (1964), as well as to that of the murals of Cacaxtla. The glyph for *cipactli* ("alligator") is often found at the top of columns.

One of the most interesting sculptural scenes at Tula is that found on a dais in the antechamber of a palace between Temples B and C. Quetzalcoatl himself is depicted against the background of a feathered serpent. He faces a file of Toltec warriors, and a line of feathered serpents undulates

Fig. 7–7. A rather smug-looking ruler depicted in full-front position on a stela at Tula. He holds a spear thrower (atlatl) in his left hand.

above the whole scene. This scene and sculpture and dais are practically duplicated at the Temple of the Warriors in Toltec Chichen Itza, Yucatan.

Trade, Metallurgy, and Northern Expansion

Tula was said by Sahagún's informants to have been a place where lived a number of distinct peoples who spoke different languages. Certainly it was large enough to be an ethnically diverse city. Comparing its size with those of better-known Mesoamerican cities, its 37,000 compares favorably with populations of other capitals. As did Teotihuacan, Tula had craft specialists, many of them obsidian workers. Also like Teotihuacan, Tula had ties with the rest of Mesoamerica through long-distance trade. Diehl's project detected a cache of ceramic vessels located in an apartment compound. The pottery was plumbate and Nicoya poly-chrome, both styles made outside Tula. Plumbate was made in the Izapa and Tajumulco areas of southern Guatemala, which also produced cacao, and the Nicoya polychrome was from the Pacific coast of Nicaragua and Costa Rica.

These long-distance trade connections are of more than ordinary inter-est, because they may indicate the means by which metallurgy was intro-duced into Mesoamerica. Metalworking in western Mexico appears at about A.D. 800 at the earliest, but it is much older in South America and dates back to at least 800 B.C. in the Andean area. It has long been thought that metallurgy was introduced to Mesoamerica from South America. The intermediate zones of Central America, Colombia, and Ecuador also had a longstanding tradition of metalworking. Although it is not by any means clear at this time, it may be that fairly sophisticated metallurgical techniques were learned from Central Americans and trans-mitted by Mesoamerican traders. It may also be that long-distance voyages from South America introduced the craft through West Mexico.

The Toltec era was one in which metallurgy spread over Mesoamerica. Yet it is also frustratingly true that not a single shred of metal has been reported from Tula. Superior examples of Toltec-style metalworking are known from Yucatan, but these probably were produced by Maya craftsmen. However, these Maya had to have learned the technique from the Mexicans, inasmuch as metalworking is not present in Classic Maya culture. Thus, at present we can only make the most circumstantial sur-mises: that metallurgy was probably introduced into Mesoamerica by way of the Pacific Coast and, ultimately, from South America through Central America, and that the Tula Toltec probably had a great deal to do with the development and spread of the craft throughout Mesoamerica by means of their long-distance trading activities.

A line of outpost settlements of Mesoamericans was established through expansion into the frontier areas of Durango and Zacatecas during Teotihuacan times (J. C. Kelley, 1971:768). These peripheral and frontier Mesoamerican cultures are grouped together generally as the Chalchihuites culture. The earliest penetrations were made about A.D. 100, during a period of greater rainfall which encouraged agricultural expansion. There is evidence of conflict between these cultivators and the more nomadic groups of the zone, and many of the Mesoamerican sites are fortifications protecting agricultural communities or mining areas. Hematite, weathered chert, flint, and possibly jadeite and turquoise were the principal objects of mining operations. Vast areas of churned-up gravels as well as the ancient mines themselves indicate that mining was an expansive and considerable operation (Weigand, 1968). Withdrawal of Mesoamericans began about A.D. 600, and by A.D. 850 the Suchil and

Colorado drainages of the Chalchihuites area had reverted to their original inhabitants, who had absorbed much Mesoamerican culture themselves. The Toltec expanded into the northern frontier zone, or Gran Chichimeca, about A.D. 900, this time to both the coastal and eastern sides of the western Sierra Madre. Contact was apparently made with the cultures of what is now the southwestern United States. Metal objects were transmitted to the northern regions, but not the craft (Meighan, 1974). Charles Di Peso thought that about A.D. 1050 Casas Grandes was converted from a small village in Chihuahua to a major Mesoamerican trading center (Di Peso, 1968, 1974, 2:290–309). From this and other centers such as Zape, *pochtecas,* trading expeditions, made trips into the Hohokam and Anasazi areas of Arizona and New Mexico trading copper bells and other items for turquoise, slaves, peyote, salt, and other commodities that the northerners provided. Cultural influences followed commerce, and it is believed that many traits in ethnographic religions of the U.S. Southwest derive from Mesoamerican influence. Murals from Awatowi in the Hopi area seem to show regional versions of Tlaloc, Quetzalcoatl appears in several areas, and Chaco Canyon in far-off northwestern New Mexico shows impressive architectural parallels with Toltec building.

A more detailed examination of the debated and complex cultural history of western and northern Mexico and the role of those regions in Mesoamerican relationships with the U.S. Southwest is outside the scope of this book. Suffice it to say that several northern Mexican trading centers were built after A.D. 1050. "Each appears to have [had] its own internal history and each collapsed due to a combination of local factors and pressures, triggered in part by unrest within the Mesoamerican governments, their main consumers" (Di Peso, 1968:54). These centers, as will be seen, outlasted the Toltec and, in some cases, the Mexican trading connections on which their existence largely depended.

Toltec Intrusion to Yucatan: The Background

Within this segment of Maya prehistory we again consider an era on which ethnohistory and archaeology bear and within which they sometimes conflict. Fortunately, several excellent minds have considered the problems and produced syntheses that are more or less convincing in their major features (Ball, 1974, 1985; R. Roys, 1965, 1972; J. E. S. Thompson, 1966; Tozzer, 1957). The scheme followed below owes much to all these scholars, but especially to J. W. Ball's attempt to reconcile all pertinent data (1974, 1985).

With the simultaneous collapse of Maya civilization in the intermediate and central lowlands there were intrusions of northern Maya elite to such places as Seibal on the Pasión River. These northerners already had absorbed significant influence from Mexican Highland cultures. As early as the eighth and ninth centuries, new motifs in sculpture at centers like Kabah show the influence of Mexican religious concepts. At Dzibilchaltun a stone platform for use as a skull rack (*tzompantli*) for sacrificial victims dates to this period. Both giant and not so large phallic stones appear at Uxmal. Censers with Tlaloc faces applied to them show up in a rain-god shrine deep within Balankanche Cave near Chichen Itza; the censers were dated by carbon 14 as having been placed there about A.D. 860 (E. W. Andrews IV, 1970).

One major question has always been whether the northern Maya centers went under with those of the Peten or survived for a longer time. E. W. Andrews IV (1965) has argued forcefully that the Río Bec, Chenes, and Puuc areas all survived the southern centers for a number of centuries. He seems to have been partially right. The Río Bec sites, including the Becan fortress, appear to have weakened as major military-political centers by about A.D. 750. As was the case farther south, diminishing populations held on in the hinterlands and even in the centers for as much as another century, but the intricate social and political arrangements deteriorated and finally disappeared. The Chenes area seems to have suffered the same collapse. The Puuc area, however, is the exception to Andrew's argument.

At the archetypal Puuc center of Uxmal is a Chenes-style building which was later buried under the gigantic platform of the purely Puuc-style Governor's Palace. This and similar physical evidence at Uxmal indicate that Puuc outlasted Chenes and Río Bec architectural styles and therefore also survived the general disaster to the south. It also seems likely that Puuc was a style which spread over the entire northern plains area and was not just confined to the hill zone from which it takes its name. Indeed, the center of Chichen Itza has a Puuc-phase building. Yaxuna, to the east of Chichen Itza, also is known to have Puuc building, and other sites in that same area also have Puuc features.

J. W. Ball (1985) ties these events of the late eighth and early ninth centuries to the first coming of the Itza, a ruling group of Mexican derivation which settled at Chichen Itza. Various chronicles give dates around A.D. 800 for this event. It is possibly through these ruling families that Mexican ideas were introduced to Yucatan and that some of the subsequent predatory raids and intrusions to the south (Seibal) took place. The Puuc cities may also have joined in this predation. Calakmul has a set of very late Yucatec-style stelae which may reflect a takeover of the same nature as that at Seibal. Raids on other cities to the south may have followed. It is also possible, as has been seen, that a group of Toltec military mercenaries were involved in these raids.

Yucatan is an unprepossessing place for exploitation, being mainly barren rock, and we are puzzled at first as to what would motivate such a political and military intrusion to the area. Ceramic linkages and hints from the chronicles seem to show that the Itza and their colleagues were probably Chontal from the lowland Tabasco area at the bottom of the Gulf Coast. In such a location, they traditionally were probably middlemen in trade relationships between the Maya area and Mexico and would have been familiar with the resources of the peninsula. The largest salt fields in Mesoamerica were and are located at the northwestern corner of Yucatan, and as such were a prize worth risks. Another principal resource of Yucatan for an exploitative group might have been its dense population. Even Yucatan can be a very comfortable place with enough servants. Ball suggests that the "abandonment" of Chichen Itza mentioned in the chronicles is really the departure of some of the Itza for Seibal, where they established themselves about A.D. 830. Ball identifies the archaeological Seibal with one of the historical Chakanputuns mentioned in the Maya chronicles.

It will be recalled that about A.D. 910 there was an invasion of Altar de Sacrificios downriver from Seibal. This invasion was probably made by another group of Chontal from the Tabasco region. Seibal and Altar de Sacrificios both were subsequently abandoned by A.D. 950. These events would correlate with the attack of one Itza group on another mentioned by the chronicles. If one accepts Ball's identification of Chakanputun as the archaeological Seibal, then its abandonment is mentioned in the chronicles.

All of the material in the above paragraph goes over events already discussed, but with the addition of detail to the historical process outlined before. This material is important because it leads to an explanation of one of the most interesting episodes in Mesoamerican prehistory: the establishment of a Toltec center in northern Yucatan.

Relationships between the native Maya and the early intrusive Chontal-Itza seem to have been relatively harmonious. Ball notes that an early Mexican-influenced building at Chichen has a wall relief showing what is apparently a peaceable meeting between Maya and probably Chontal leaders (Tozzer, 1957:33). These amicable relationships did not last.

Toltec Intrusion to Yucatan: The Event

According to the above reconstruction, then, the superb Puuc variant of Classic Maya civilization was still thriving on the northern plain of Yucatan about A.D. 987. The chronicles mention that in that year the Itza returned and that Kukulcan (Quetzalcoatl by his Maya name) arrived. It was a result of this intrusion and takeover that the great and magnificent Toltec center at Chichen Itza was established. A great many of the Toltec-period ruins at Chichen have been excavated, and it is to that archaeological evidence that we now turn.

Chronology and Trends. As usual in the Maya area, the chronology is in part based on a ceramic sequence and on Maya dates, thirty-four of them at Chichen Itza. No reliable carbon 14 dates are available, although the

Fig. 7–8. The remains of a frontier fortress at La Quemada, Durango, Mexico, on the trade routes north to the Indian cultures of the U.S. Southwest. Trade lapsed at various times, finally leading to the abandonment of these way-station cities. (Courtesy Margaret N. Bond and Franklin C. Graham)

above-mentioned Tlaloc censers found in the nearby Balankanche Cave contained twigs that have been processed. Three major periods may be derived from a consideration of all the evidence.

Period A lasted from about A.D. 692 to 968, with nearly all the Maya dates falling into the short span from A.D. 869 to 889. This is the already discussed period of Puuc-related Late Classic culture. Toward its end the period brought an infiltration of influence from Mexican sources. Chichen at this time consisted of widely scattered groups of civic architecture which included the "Old Chichen" zone, with its famous round Observatory, and the Monjas Palace structure, with its elaborate annexes. These groups are connected by *sacbes,* of which nine are known. Other groups include the Temple of the Phalli and a number of other small but elegant Puuc-style residential structures. According to Roys, Chichen's name at this time may have been Uucil Abnal (Seven Bushy Places).

Period B was a transitional Maya-Toltec style represented by the inner Temple of Kukulcan and the Temple of the Chacmul under the pyramid of the Temple of the Warriors. It would overlap in time between Periods A and C and possibly represents no more than one hundred years.

Period C was about two hundred years long and lasted from about A.D. 987 to 1187. It was the period of the Toltec–Maya and the phase of construction of the most magnificent of Chichen's buildings. Tohil plumbate and Silho fine orange potteries were introduced at this time through trade.

Location. A functional description of the Toltec center must take account of the natural water sources which attracted settlement in the first place. There are many cenotes (sinkholes) in the Chichen vicinity, most of which are now choked with naturally fallen debris. In ancient times, however, many of these may have been open and furnished water. If so, then Chichen was indeed a favored spot, with a much more secure water supply than that of most of the northern plains, and it might have been looked on as specially favored by the rain god. Two large cenotes were the foci for major architecture. One cenote (the *xtoloc,* or "iguana") was the main water source. The other, larger, and almost sheer-sided sinkhole was apparently used exclusively as the focus of a rain-god (*chac*) cult (Fig. 7–8). According to Landa, the first Spanish bishop of Yucatan, "Into this well they have had, and then had, the custom of throwing men alive as a sacrifice to the gods, in times of drought, and they believed that they did not die though they never saw them again. They also threw into it a great many other things, like precious stones and things which they prized" (1941:179–81). Indeed, dredging the well has produced an immense amount of valuable material as well as human bones. Legend has embroidered fact by stating that the sacrificial victims were beautiful young virgins. A. E. Hooton, who analyzed the bones, acerbically observed that it was difficult to tell from them if their owners had been either beautiful or virgin. What he did find, however, was that most of the victims (21) were children or adolescents, with a minority of adults (maybe 15; Hooton, 1940).

Much of the valuable material found in the well, especially dozens of extraordinary pieces of carved jade, is Late Classic in date (Proskouriakoff, 1974). A considerable amount had been imported from other parts of the Maya area or from outside of it, including Cocle goldwork from Panama (Lothrop, 1952). It therefore seems likely that the Toltec simply took over an established center of religious pilgrimage which drew people from much of eastern Mesoamerica. This would partially explain the location chosen by the Toltec for their colonial capital. Finally, Chichen is geographically located in the center of the northern plains and is well situated for military and political control of that area.

Architecture. The major Maya Toltec structures are built on a vast platform in the middle of which is set the most important temple, that of Kukulcan-Quetzalcoatl (Fig. 7–9). This structure is more or less in line with a *sacbe* leading out of the civic precinct and north some 300 meters (980 feet) to the sacred well. Another *sacbe* leads south to another large plaza with a large temple in its center, the so-called High Priest's Grave.

Fig. 7–9. The Sacred Well (Cenote) at Chichen Itza, a center of pilgrimage for Mesoamericans because of the belief that it was the home of the rain god. It is 20 meters (70 feet) to the water and 20 meters more to the bottom. Valuable objects anciently thrown in as offerings have been recovered from it.

Fig. 7–10. The Temple of Kukulcan (Feathered Serpent) at Chichen Itza is the largest Toltec-period structure at the city. A causeway leads from this temple to the Sacred Cenote.

"Dance platforms" and a *tzompantli* (Fig. 7–10) are scattered about the Kukulcan plaza. The northwest corner of the precinct is occupied by a monumental ball court, the largest in Mesoamerica. It measures about 150 meters (490 feet) long and is magnificently adorned by small temples and ornamented by sculpture. The eastern side of the Kukulcan plaza is occupied by a row of three temples, one of which, the Temple of the Warriors, is much larger than the others. A very large colonnade closes off the rest of the eastern plaza. Behind this colonnade is the Group of the Thousand Columns, a subsidiary plaza surrounded by large structures built nearly at ground level something like the palaces at Tula. Another large ball court lies to the east of this group, with a jumble of structures around it which includes a sweatbath.

If Tula suffered from shoddy workmanship, such is not the case at Chichen. This colonial capital of the Toltec is magnificent in both conception and realization. No doubt the availability of Maya masons who were used to produce the superbly cut and fitted stone of Puuc structures made a difference. The stonework there is excellent. Toltec Chichen is clearly central Mexican in plan and many features, but Maya building practices of long standing are also apparent. In short, the architecture is a blend of two strong and distinctive cultural traditions.

The introduction and use of multiple columns for roof support at Chichen Itza allowed vastly greater spaces to be enclosed within buildings. The Maya arch was combined with the columns. Although the Temple of Kukulkan (the Castillo) is somewhat Maya in plan, with an inner sanctuary, most of the other buildings consist either of one large room or of two rooms, one behind the other. As at Tula, long and spacious roofed colonnades furnished with benches afforded vast cool areas for large numbers of people. The great numbers of columns were decorated with stiff Toltec warriors and priests, invariably framed between the sun god above and Quetzalcoatl below, on all four sides. Also, as at Tula, one major temple, the Temple of the Warriors, was decorated with bas-reliefs set in panels around the terraces of its platform (Fig. 7–12). These panels depict the heart-devouring eagles and jaguars also to be found on the "dance platforms." Stiffened feathered serpents frame the temple doorways, and *chacmul* figures rest outside the doors, waiting for offerings (Fig. 7–13). Banner holders carved in human form have been found. Atlantean figures hold up large table altars in several temples. By analogy with later and similar central Mexican buildings, there are buildings in the eastern group suitable for use as palaces, barracks, and a marketplace.

Fig. 7–11. The Skull Rack (tzompantli) near the Great Ball Court, Chichen Itza. The sculpted human skulls are depicted as stuck onto vertical posts. This platform presumably once supported an ancient skull rack similar to that described by the Spaniards in late Aztec Teotihuacan.

Fig. 7–12. A section of carved panel on the Temple of the Warriors, Chichen Itza, Yucatan, Mexico. Human figures with Tlaloc and other symbolism alternate with jaguars holding (offering?) human hearts. Note the conceptual and physical similarities to sculpture on Structure B, Tula (Fig. 7–6).

The so-called High Priest's Grave is a somewhat smaller version of the Temple of Kukulkan. Feathered-serpent doorway columns and all of the other Maya-Toltec features are to be found on it. E. H. Thompson lifted the stone floor and found a stone shaft penetrating the platform, with several burials on various levels within the shaft. Ultimately Thompson found that he was on bedrock, where a stone cover concealed the entrance to a natural cavern that had been used for the burial of an important person. Years later, J. E. S. Thompson analyzed the burial furnishings and concluded that the person buried there was probably a member of the ruling class at the time of Toltec or Itza domination (E. H. Thompson, 1938). Functionally, then, at least one of the major temples at Chichen was a funerary temple.

Architectonic sculpture is a strong feature at Chichen Itza. Bas-relief covers large areas in several monumental structures. In the great ball court (Fig. 7–12), scenes of sacrifice accompany the ball game scenes, indicating that it did not pay to have a losing team. Bas-relief skulls decorate the platform, which eventually supported a wooden frame with real skulls (Fig. 7–11). Scenes of conquest decorate some buildings, the Temple of the Tigers, for example. The Toltec memorialized their conquests in some

Fig. 7–13. Temple of the Warriors, Chichen Itza, with stiffened feathered serpents serving as the supports for lintels (now absent) which once bridged the doorway. Again, note the mixture of sculptural styles with long-nosed Chac masks on the wall and a chacmul in the foreground.

superb mural art found in the Temple of the Warriors and other places. An infinity of detail makes it clear that Tula and central Mexico are the sources of derivation of the new ideas. Roof frets occur in the form of the Toltec glyph for war, for example. On the other hand, the Maya rain god, Chac, decorates panels and corners of the Temple of the Warriors (Fig. 7–13). Toltec Chichen Itza was truly the seat of a hybrid culture.

Art. Sculpture, murals, and small portable objects make up most of known Toltec–Maya art. As seen above, the style is definitely a synthesis of two distinctive traditions. The subject matter is also definitely weighted toward the martial and toward ritual violence. The hundreds of columns in the buildings and colonnades are carved with hundreds of warriors and priests, each distinctive and unique. Could these be portraits of the individual invaders? There are over nine hundred known human figures carved on the walls and columns. Depictions or impersonations of gods emphasize Quetzalcoatl-Kukulkan along with his old antagonist, Tezcatlipoca, and Tlachitonatiuh, the sun god. Scenes of battle are found in murals, in sculpture, and on the repoussé-decorated gold disks from the Cenote of Sacrifice. Toltec and Maya warriors are quite distinctive, with the Maya usually wearing individualized feathered headdresses and car-

Fig. 7–14. The Great Ball Court at Chichen Itza, the largest ball game court in Mesoamerica. Several of the small temples associated with the court have intensely interesting sculpture. One shows an assault on a walled city with siege towers. This and other scenes are perhaps from the conquest of Yucatan by the Toltecs.

ing flexible shields and feathered back frames. The basic Toltec hat is a cylinder set with feathers and sometimes with ear flaps. Round shields, loincloths, and sandals rounded out the basic Toltec uniform. Battle scenes show raids on seacoast villages, combat within villages, and fighting on lakes and along the shoreline. The gold disks are the most explicit in showing the Toltecs as conquerors throwing spears at fleeing Maya, interrogating prisoners, sacrificing a human, pursuing in canoes Maya who are escaping on rafts, and other variations of those themes. Sky deities, including the feathered serpent, attend the battle scenes. Disks L and M from the Cenote of Sacrifice show Tula-Toltec eagles attacking the Maya. A carved and painted dais shows lines of warriors who face each other in the center. It is noteworthy that each of these figures is backed with a feathered serpent. At Tula the strikingly similar dais has only one person with a feathered serpent behind him, leading to his identification as Quetzalcoatl. At Chichen, all are protected by the feathered serpent.

Much of the mural art is lively, informative, and interesting. Fragments from the excavation of the Temple of the Warriors show a jaguar crouched on a masonry pyramid, cactus and other plants in bloom, gorgeously clad elite-class people, tantalizing scenes of combat, a humble man offering burning incense in a bowl at the foot of a pyramid, birds and bees, and much else. A magnificent scene reconstructed by Ann Morris shows a peaceful seacoast village with people at their daily tasks. Porters carry burdens, a woman attends a boiling pot, and three canoes loaded with warriors cruise just offshore through waters filled with fish, stingrays, snails, and other shellfish. The local elite discuss matters in a building over which the feathered serpent writhes (Morris, 1931). Grimmer subjects are depicted in the north temple of the great ball court. In scenes fraught with symbolism, prisoners are interrogated, houses and a temple burn, a sleeping person's throat is cut, and two Toltecs perform an act of phallic worship. Some small-scale Faberge-quality turquoise mosaics tend to confirm the Toltecs' legendary reputation as craftsmen. These mosaics, which depict the feathered serpent, were used as dedication offerings in temples.

Social and Political Implications

The chronicles say that the Itza and their Toltec colleagues ruled at Chichen Itza for about two hundred years. Ralph Roys believes that they dominated nearly all of the peninsula. At some point during this period, probably fairly early, the last variant of Classic Maya culture, the Puuc, was extinguished. Very little is known of this delayed part of the Maya collapse, but it may have been that the new order at Chichen, with its superior military organization, was too much competition. It is a fact that no plumbate or Silho fine orange potteries, hallmarks of the Toltec period, have been found at Puuc sites, and therefore those sites must have been off the trade routes and then soon disappeared. At present we know practically nothing else about the Puuc collapse, although it would not be surprising if its general nature were the same interrelated downward spiral of decreasing populations, disrupted agricultural systems, health problems, social disorder, and military activity.

Trade Patterns and the Itza Port of Cerritos

Explorations of the artificial port of Cerritos on the northeast coast of Yucatan have given a good deal more information on the nature of Toltec-Itza control (A. P. Andrews et al., 1988). The island is small, barely 200 meters (650 feet) in diameter, and is largely artificial. It possesses port facilities in the form of a breakwater, still visible, with at least two piers. A large number of platforms (29), most of which may have supported perishable warehouses, have been mapped. The port was apparently constructed in the local Terminal Classic period (A.D. 750–900) and enlarged during the Early Postclassic (A.D. 900–1200). Andrews and his colleagues think that during the latter period Cerritos became the principal port for Chichen Itza, 90 kilometers (56 miles) distant. Most of the obsidian tools found on the island came from central Mexican sources controlled by Tula. A major portion of the salt trade was possibly controlled through this port.

The End at Chichen Itza

The later Maya had scant respect for the intruding Itza, magnificent as the Chichen capital may have been. The Itza were considered to have been those who introduced lewdness (phallic worship?), promiscuity, incest, and other perversions to Yucatan. They were also said to have spoken Maya brokenly, which would fit the Chontal, who spoke a distinct dialect of Maya.

The chronicles give us a puzzling account of the end of Chichen Itza. Apparently, the ruler of Chichen stole the bride of the ruler of Izamal. Hunac Ceel, head of Mayapan, who was an ally of Izamal, avenged the abduction and led the sack of Chichen Itza. The Itza abandoned their capital and journeyed south to Lake Peten, their historical location. Apparently, this all occurred about A.D. 1187. It is probably not coincidental that Tula had fallen shortly before this date. The Chichen center had been set adrift without the Mexican support it had once enjoyed. Hunac Ceel then turned on Izamal, defeated it, then at Mayapan rapidly put together the short-lived urban center and small conquest-state which lasted until A.D. 1446 (R. Roys, 1966).

In terms of broad historical perspective, it is certain that any ruling class remaining two hundred years in the midst of an alien people must have become highly acculturated. The Chontal were Maya speakers to begin with and by the end of Chichen's domination must have handled Yucatec well. Altogether, Chichen's fall is more to be explained by external competitive politics and the internal stresses of a weakening dynasty than by any grand cultural-historical theory. As will be seen, Mayapan represents a renaissance of the native Maya tradition, although in a transmuted form.

The Collapse at Tula

Heumac's departure with his followers for Chapultepec about A.D. 1156 signals the end of Tula as a capital. Actually, the center had probably been hard-pressed for some time. There is evidence from the U.S Southwest that a series of droughts affecting the whole Gran Chichimeca began about the middle of the twelfth century. The northern frontier areas of Mesoamerica were so marginal in rainfall that minor shifts in precipitation would have had major effects. It seems likely that colonial and frontier Mesoamerican settlements were abandoned and that the populations began flowing back to the south, creating pressures on the cities there. As will be seen, the invading groups were all called Chichimecs, but there were varieties of them. Some were the frontier Mesoamericans, and others

Fig. 7–15. Maya rain god (Chac) mask carved on a corner of the Temple of the Warriors, Chichen Itza. Both central Mexican (Toltec) and Maya styles are represented on this building.

were acculturated peoples from the northern deserts and mountains. Still others drifted south who were genuine unacculturated barbarians from the Gran Chichimeca. The Toltec chronicles mention dissensions and conflict among factions within Tula as well as external wars. In any event, Tula was abandoned, and the city was savagely destroyed.

As in the case of Teotihuacan, the destruction has the marks of being an inside job. Huge trenches were put through the major temples, perhaps in search of tombs and their valuables but also clearly for the purpose of extirpating Toltec symbols. The giant caryatid columns of Quetzalcoatl's temple were thrown down and battered. The sun god's temple (Building C) was so thoroughly trenched that it was exceedingly difficult to make much architectural sense out of it later. Adjacent palaces were burned; hence the name for Structure 3, the Burnt Palace. No extensive excavations have been done in other parts of Tula, and so it is unknown whether or not they were burnt out along with the civic buildings.

After the destruction of Tula, various Tula-Toltec groups joined the general drift south into the Basin of Mexico, where they settled in several communities.

A kind of golden haze fell over the Toltec in after years, and great prestige accrued to those who could claim descent from them. A diaspora of people from the broken Toltec state throughout Mesoamerica seems to have taken place. The noble houses of several regions, including the Valley of Mexico and the highlands of Guatemala, traced their ancestry back to the illustrious Tollan.

More than social prestige was involved, however. For the Aztec, the age of Tollan represented something of a lost golden time which filled them with nostalgia, in somewhat the same way that the era before World War I is regarded in our own day: "And they were also very rich—of no value were food and all sustenance. . . . And these Toltecs enjoyed great wealth. They were rich; never were they poor. Nothing did they lack in their homes. Never was there want. And the small ears of maize were of no use to them. They only [burned them to] heat the sweatbaths" (Sahagún 1952, Book 3:14).

CHAPTER 8

THE MIXTEC, TOTONAC, MAYA, TARASCANS, AND OTHERS

Before the Spaniards had conquered that country [Yucatan], the natives lived together in towns in a very civilized fashion. They kept the land well cleared and free from weeds, and planted very good trees.

—*Landa, 1941:62.*

Now in those days when Mayapan was captured in battle, they confronted the katun of affliction. . . . Although after the days of shooting down the multitudes we pleaded for mercy, they then kindled fires over the whole province. The heavens were sealed against us. When they had succeeded in reducing the population, the compassion of heaven set a price upon our lives. Should we not lament in our suffering, grieving for the loss of our maize and the destruction of our teachings concerning the universe of the earth and the universe of the heavens?

—*Chilam Balam of Tizimin, 1951:3–4.*

The first [ruin] that attracted my attention was a massy pile of building apparently designed for the defense of some interior structure. . . . It stands on the projecting angle of rock surrounded by vast precipices, [and protected by] innumerable serpents, fostered by a climate so intensely hot as that of the lower Misteca.

—*G. Dupaix in Gorenstein, 1973:18.*

BY THE THIRTEENTH century, civilization within Mesoamerica had a history of some twenty-six hundred years. It had assumed certain patterns of ebb and flow, rise and fall, and reformulation. In some ways, the situation resembled the ancient Middle East in pre-Islamic times. A. L. Kroeber (1963:761–825) has pointed out the cyclical nature of patterns and cultural reformulations which occurred in the late prehistoric period of Middle Eastern civilization. That this was the case in Mesoamerica, and that it was somewhat recognized by Mesoamericans, is hinted at by the myths of cyclical creations, the endless cycles of time, and the belief among some of them that history literally repeated itself in accordance with the calendrical rounds. This was the "insider" view of what was happening. In the short run, the cyclical manner of viewing things does explain some events. Our "outsider" view, however shows us a different reality, at least over the longer perspectives of time given us by archaeology. We will now resume the stories of various parts of Mesoamerica, bringing them down to the terrible event of the Spanish Conquest, which truncated all of their culture histories, cycles or not.

This chapter covers the final three hundred to four hundred years before European contact. In some areas, such as western Mexico, we will cover more time, but topically the focus is the same: the development of the formal and dynamic qualities of the civilizations encountered by the Spaniards (Maps 8–1, 8–2). The Aztec are excepted from this consideration and given a chapter to themselves.

The Maya Lowlands

At some point about A.D. 1200 the Toltec episode came to an end in a manner not at all well understood. It seems likely that intermarriage and long residence over several generations had assimilated the Toltec rulers into the Maya mainstream. It also may be that the lapse of contact with the Toltec cities of central Mexico made the colonial capital at Chichen vulnerable in the always fierce competition among Maya political units. In any case, Chichen and its Mexicanized elite, the Itza, lost their primacy.

E. W. Andrews IV (1965) has suggested that the east coast of Yucatan, with its isolated location, preserved the more strictly Maya traditions, and that after the Toltec colony's fall, these influences flowed back into the northern plains area. The reestablishment of this more native tradition took most vigorous form at Mayapan. As noted before, Hunac Ceel, having overthrown Chichen and Izamal, made the previously insignificant center of Mayapan the capital of a unified Maya state.

The Mayapan Period

Diego de Landa wrote, "In that guardiania [Mani], near a mission-town called Telchac, a very populous city once existed called Mayapan in which (as if it were a court) all the caciques and lords of the province of Maya resided and there they came with their tribute" (R. Roys, 1962). A substantial body of historical information that survives about Mayapan has been sifted and organized by Ralph Roys (1962). Prophecies for the twenty-year *katun* periods contain historical material in accordance with the Maya penchant for mixing prophecy with reality. The *Relaciones de Yucatán,* written in the sixteenth century, are replete with data. The Hunac Ceel episode is related in these sources as an explanation of the intrigue by which that ruler, as the head of the Cocom family, gained ascendancy over the rest of the Maya ruling lineages. A unified govern-

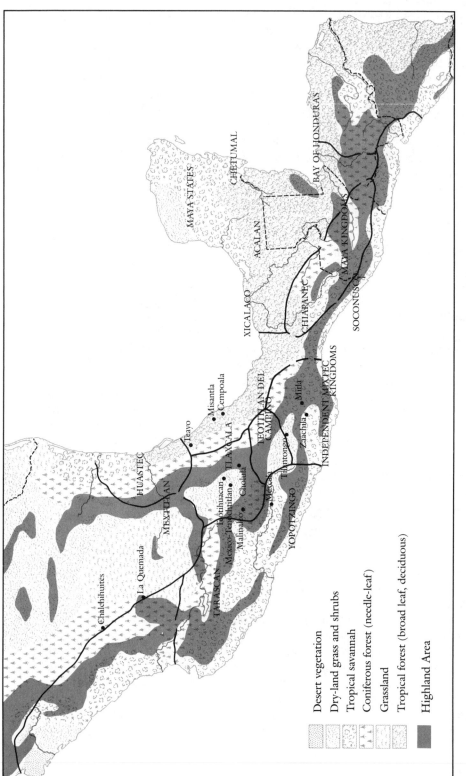

Map 8–1. Protohistoric Mesoamerica, showing the approximate placement of the historic-period (Late Postclassic) native civilizations at the time of the arrival of the

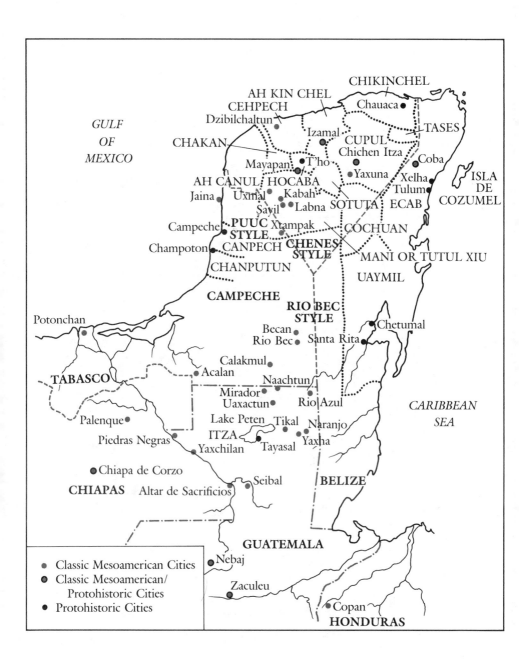

GULF
OF
MEXICO

CHIKINCHEL

AH KIN CHEL
CEHPECH
Dzibilchaltun
Chauaca
TASES
Izamal
CHAKAN
CUPUL
Chichen Itza
Coba
Mayapan
T'ho
Yaxuna
Xelha
AH CANUL HOCABA
Tulum
Jaina
Uxmal
Kabah
ISLA
DE
COZUMEL
Sayil
Labna
SOTUTA
ECAB
Campeche
PUUC
STYLE
Xtampak
COCHUAN
Champoton
CANPECH
CHENES
STYLE
MANI OR TUTUL XIU
CHANPUTUN
UAYMIL
CAMPECHE
RIO BEC
STYLE
Becan
Chetumal
Rio Bec
Santa Rita
Potonchan
Calakmul
Acalan
TABASCO
Naachtun
Mirador
Uaxactun
Rio Azul
CARIBBEAN
SEA
Palenque
Lake Peten
Tikal
Naranjo
Piedras Negras
ITZA
Tayasal
Yaxha
Yaxchilan
Chiapa de Corzo
Seibal
BELIZE
CHIAPAS
Altar de Sacrificios

GUATEMALA

● Classic Mesoamerican Cities
◉ Classic Mesoamerican/
   Protohistoric Cities
● Protohistoric Cities

Nebaj

Zaculeu

Copan
HONDURAS

Map 8–2. The Maya Lowlands in the sixteenth century, showing the various regional states and major centers. This map is mainly based on Ralph Roys' study of the sixteenth-century Maya.

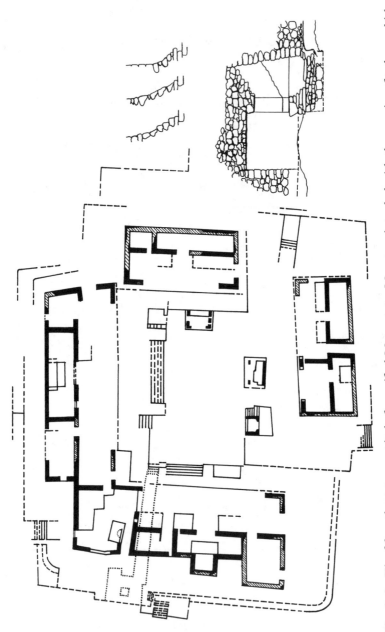

Fig. 8–1. The fifteenth-century capital of a unified Maya state, Mayapan is packed with the remains of palaces which were residences of hostage regional rulers. These complexes include apartments, shrines, and family crypts.

ment was established, with the local rulers required to reside at Mayapan in order to guarantee political order and control (Fig. 8–1).

Landa in his *Relación de las cosas de Yucatán* (1941) says that Quetzalcoatl (Kukulcan) himself was the founder of the city and that he ordained the political arrangements. It is true that the principal temple at Mayapan is dedicated to Quetzalcoatl-Kukulcan. However, it seems likely that the god was the patron deity of the ruling family and unlikely that the actual historical personage of the Quetzalcoatl myth was involved. Myths of Quetzalcoatl's doings are too far-flung, demand too much accomplishment, and take up too much time for any single historical individual to have been referred to. According to accounts, all was well ordered and harmonious at Mayapan for a while. Lords lived in Mayapan with stewards who attended to their needs, arranging for their support by their native provinces. Mayapan, however, was rent by dissension under a later Cocom ruler, who brought in Mexican mercenaries from Tabasco (more Chontals?) to tyrannize the rest of the people. A conspiracy among the other lords was set in train which finally exploded with the systematic killing of the Cocom family, the destruction of their houses, and the abandonment of the city of Mayapan. Only one son survived; his descendants later took a terrible revenge in the sixteenth century.

With this revolt the league of Mayapan dissolved into its component parts. According to R. Roys (1957), there are hints that the sixteen independent states found by the Spaniards represented the various former provinces of the Mayapan league. However, the correspondence is certainly not exact, because some of the former provinces had expanded at the expense of others during the ninety years or so after the fall of Mayapan.

Archaeology. Mayapan is an unimpressive set of stone heaps located in some of the poorest agricultural land in the northern lowlands. A number of cenotes located in and around the site seem to be its only natural advantage. A low stone wall fortifies the city, enclosing 4,140 buildings, large and small, within an area of about 4 square kilometers (1.5 square miles). Two major periods are to be found at Mayapan, the earliest corresponding to the Toltec phase of Chichen Itza. Mayapan was apparently a small and unimportant center at this time, probably established for the worship of Kukulcan and as a subsidiary administrative center for the Toltec. This phase is dated about A.D. 1100 to 1250.

The second period is that of the city's political importance, about A.D. 1250 to 1450. Nearly all of the construction now visible dates from the second period. Study of the detailed map of Mayapan yields no evidence of central planning except for the general features of an enclosing wall, the location of the public buildings near the center of the city, and the siting of the major houses on natural rises to catch the breezes.

The civic-ceremonial precinct of the city constituted about 121 buildings arranged in functional assemblages which more nearly resemble the central Mexican patterns than those of their Classic Maya predecessors. A basic ceremonial group at Mayapan included a colonnaded hall, a shrine, an oratory, and associated service buildings. Temple groups included the temple itself, along with colonnaded halls which may have been used either by pilgrims to the temple or by young men being trained for the priesthood. The colonnaded halls are reminiscent of the later *calmecac* buildings (bachelors' quarters) to be found in Tenochtitlan. In many ways Mayapan is also reminiscent of Toltec Chichen in that its principal temple is a smaller version of Chichen's Kukulcan temple. There are also contrasts. Mayapan lacks a ball court, skull racks (*tzompantli*), and sweatbaths. On the other hand, it shows distinctively Maya patterns, such as the survival (or revival?) of the stela cult, with at least twenty-five sculptured and plain monuments. This is an astounding number considering the short period of time Mayapan was the seat of government. Altogether, however, as Proskouriakoff (1962) points out, the public center of Mayapan is much reduced in proportion to the other construction at the site.

Of the 4,140 buildings in the city, about 2,100 were used as dwellings, housing an estimated maximum population of twelve thousand (thirty persons per hectare, or seventy-four per acre). These houses, as noted, were sited to be cooled by the wind and therefore are scattered at random. Stone property walls surrounded each house or group of houses, resulting in a maze of alleyways instead of planned and formal straight streets. House plans varied from the simple two-room structure, which was most common, to more elaborate structures, the homes of the nobility. The latter are quite interesting in several ways. They show a clear emphasis on home worship, with nearly every house having its own shrine. The larger houses also had what appear to be family tombs. This evidence for ancestor worship is a continuity from the Classic period. All houses, large and small, are furnished with built-in benches, which we have earlier interpreted as sleeping, eating, and general living places.

In nearly every way, and by nearly any criterion, Mayapan represents a cultural decline from the Toltec or the Classic period. The masonry work is poor, with defects covered by heavy coats of plaster; the buildings are smaller and less well planned; and the sculpture is crude compared to even the ordinary productions of Classic times.

Mayapan pottery is overwhelmingly utilitarian and mainly lacks the elaborate decoration of earlier periods. An exception to this are the incense burners, which are very elaborate indeed. These censers are often massive pottery cylinders with attached molded heads, hands, arms, legs, and costumes of various deities that are overwhelmingly related in form to those of central Mexico. That is, the iconographic symbols and colors are quite similar to those found in central Mexican codices. On the other hand, Itzamna, the sky serpent–creator deity of the Maya, is quite a popular subject on the incense burners, as is the Pinocchio-nosed Yacate-cuhtli (god of merchants), known among the Maya as Ek Chuah.

Mayapan then, although not a large city, was a tribute-based urban administrative city in all formal senses. It contains many signs of dissolution of unifying cultural features which heretofore had held the Maya apart from the rest of Mesoamerica and had kept it internally linked. Its culture represents not so much a resurgence of Maya tradition as an incomplete fusion of Toltec and Maya, according to Proskouriakoff. Perhaps this ideological fragmentation was one reason that Mayapan could only be held together by force. Provincial lords were virtually captive in the city, and finally, outside mercenary troops were called in to maintain order. The successful conspiracy of 1446 is evidenced in the archaeological record by the fact that the ceremonial center was torn apart; deliberate destruction and burning are evident in the excavations. The city was abandoned and had become a ruin at the time of the Spanish Conquest, about one hundred years later.

The Sixteenth-Century Maya States

In 1517, when Francisco Hernandez de Cordoba first sighted Yucatan, the peninsula was divided among sixteen separate regional states. Most of these were dominated by a capital city or center which was the seat of a provincial ruler called the *halach uinic*, the equivalent of the *tlatoani* in central Mexico. The ruler was supported by tribute. Lineages of these rulers and nobles were important in determining success. Roys notes that "the upper class also had a secret lore handed down from father to son, a sort of ritual in which many words had a concealed meaning not understood by any except initiates. The knowledge of this code was an important evidence of noble descent" (Roys, 1972:33). Each town was ruled by a *batab*, who was administrator, judge, and commanding officer and was supported by a farm allocated to him (Roys, 1957). Records were kept in the hieroglyphic books. Chief exports from Yucatan were cotton, cloth, salt, and slaves, with honey and beeswax also shipped. Nobles, commoners, and slaves made up a three-class social structure. There are indications in several documents that hint at a preferred position for the nobles in regard to land ownership (Roys, 1957).

An example of a Maya province is Chikinchel, or Chauaca, located roughly in the north central coastal zone of the peninsula behind a long lagoon which yielded the highest production of salt in Yucatan. In 1605 the yield was stated to be 2.8 million to 3.2 million liters (80,000 to 90,000 bushels). Copal was also exported from the province. The Spaniards reported very high populations for the area, where subsistence was based on *milpa* farming and on fishing. The province was one of those ruled not by a *halach uinic*, but by a council of the town rulers, or *batabs*. R. Roys quotes the Spaniards to the following effect: "The people of

Chikinchel are more precise in their reasoning and more polished in this language, although the latter is the same all over Yucatan" (1957:104).

The sixteen states occupied most of the northern plains and stretched down both coasts to Champoton to the west and to Chetumal in the east. To the interior and south of these states were the Cehache, about whom we know little more than their name. The Itza inhabited the interior around Lake Peten, but, as with the Cehache, their territory was not considered one of the sixteen northern provinces.

East Coast Yucatan: Tulum, Xelha, and Santa Rita

Although the site of Tulum was probably occupied during the Classic, its major period of construction is Late Postclassic. Its sixteenth-century name was Zama, according to R. Roys, and the Spaniards reported it as early as 1518. Juan Díaz, expedition chaplain for Juan de Grijalva, wrote, "Towards sunset we saw from afar off a town or village so large that the city of Seville could not appear greater or better; and in it was seen a very great tower" (R. Roys, 1957:147).

Tulum is a fortified town enclosed by a wall on three sides and by the sea on the fourth (Figs. 8–2, 8–3). It is today a somewhat better example of Late Postclassic Maya architecture than Mayapan, which was deliber-

Fig. 8–2. Tulum. The principal temple palace is set on the edge of a cliff. It was poorly built, like all construction at Tulum, and the defects were covered over with heavy plaster.

Fig. 8–3. View of the principal building of Tulum and its location. The shallow lagoon protected by a reef allowed canoes to enter this area with relative safety. Tulum's lifeblood was the east coast canoe trade.

ately destroyed. Again, if we judge from a technical point of view, the buildings are inferior to those of the Classic centers. Sloppy construction techniques led to the slumping and leaning of walls so that certain buildings have a drunken appearance. Then, too, the architecture is not massive or tall. Defects, as at Mayapan, are covered by heavy coatings of plaster. Withal, the site has a certain charm beyond that given by its exquisite natural setting on the edge of the sea. It has an architectonic unity which is readily grasped and which the more grandiose centers such as Toltec Chichen lacked.

Mural art is one of the most interesting features of Tulum; one building, the temple of the frescoes, preserves several nearly complete scenes. Although they are more hieratic and less lively than those dealing with daily life found at Chichen, there is nonetheless a great deal of information in them. Gods are shown that are readily identifiable as those seen in one of the Maya books, the Codex Madrid. These deities engage in various ceremonial activities, and in one scene, according to the interpretation of J. W. Ball, they visit one another using the sacred roadways, the *sacbes*.

Modeled stucco motifs embellish the Tulum buildings at the corners and especially in niches over the doorways. So-called diving gods in these doorway niches are actually depictions of the bee gods, the Ah Muzencabob, according to R. L. Roys (Fig. 8–4). Wings and antennae are clearly modeled, and the resemblance is great to depictions of honey

Fig. 8–4. A principal export from Yucatan in the sixteenth century was honey. This damaged example of a "Diving God" from over a Tulum doorway in reality represents the Ah Muzencabob, the bee gods.

bees in the Codex Madrid. Indeed, the importance of bees at Tulum and the fact that the Codex Madrid has an entire section devoted to a beekeeper's almanac suggest that the manuscript may have been made on the east coast, possibly at Tulum. Honey was probably an important export, as noted, and Tulum lies along the traditional trade route around the peninsula to Honduras. The pilgrimage island of Cozumel lies off the coast from Tulum, and the latter could have served as a port of embarkation from the mainland, although other places are more convenient.

Tancah, another nearby and contemporary site, though smaller, also acted as a port, as did Xelha farther up the coast from Tulum. Arthur Miller (1982) found murals at Tancah resembling those at Tulum. A series of lighthouses and watchtowers is stretched at intervals along the east coast. Tulum is in sight of two of these, one to the north and one to the south; they are not only convenient to navigation, but also outposts for the city. All of these centers and ports are within the old province of Ecab, but it is not understood what hierarchy of authority existed among them, if any.

To the south of Ecab was the province of Uaymil. Peter Harrison (1981) has done extensive archaeological reconnaissance in the zone and has found large numbers of crude house platforms which date to the fourteenth and fifteenth centuries—to the Late Postclassic period, in other words. No masonry structures are found on these platforms, and the only ceramics are Mayapan-style censers, which were in use long after the fall of Mayapan. It has been suggested that in the general simplification of culture during the Late Postclassic period, utilitarian ceramics were replaced by gourd vessels, *jicaras,* and indeed, fragments of Late Postclassic wooden vessels have been found in caves in Belize (Harrison, 1974).

Chetumal province, which includes the modern town and bay of the same name, was Uaymil's southern neighbor. The famous site of Santa Rita is located near the bay and within the old provincial area. Thomas Gann (1900) found on a stuccoed wall there some extraordinary Late Postclassic murals which are clearly related in stylistic detail to Mixtec art. In this sense, Santa Rita shares in what Donald Robertson (1970) calls the "international style" of late prehistoric times in Mesoamerica. However, as Jacinto Quirarte (1982) points out, there are distinctive Maya treatments of the subject matter. Many gods or god-impersonators engage in sacred actions. A Yacatecuhtli (merchant god) figure taps a drum, while another personage faces him with a severed human head in hand. Both stand on what may be fields planted with various crops. Chac, the rain god, and others show great resemblance to their images as depicted on the incense burners. Mayapan-style incense burners were found in association with the murals, as were small ceramic figures depicting motifs characteristic of Mayapan.

Lamanai, on the large lagoon of the New River, is unusual in that it seems to have survived the southern collapse and to have continued into the Late Postclassic and right up to the 1670s. Pendergast (1981) has developed a long sequence at this center, which includes a great many Early and Late Postclassic materials. Sheetgold, copper ornaments, and ceramics affiliated with northern wares were found in Postclassic burials there. Other pottery is very similar to that produced in the Peten-Itza zone of the interior, and still later, Mayapan-style censers appeared. Tulum-style pottery marks the final prehistoric periods at Lamanai. Through the Early and Late Postclassic, building activities sank to a much lower level than during the Classic or Formative. The ceramics and other artifacts suggest that Lamanai may have survived only because it had been taken over during the Terminal Classic by northern Maya who became a new elite. Thereafter, the center became steadily less important, although it was clearly linked into the east coast trade routes. Hammond's work at Nohmul (1982) and that of Diane Chase (1985) at Santa Rita in the same zone of Belize have also indicated a southward intrusion of Maya from Yucatan.

Fragmentary as the archaeological record is, there is every evidence of a well-organized, culturally and economically linked series of centers along the east coast of Yucatan reaching down to Honduras, which was the major source of cacao. Columbus, on his fourth voyage, encountered a Maya sailing canoe out of sight of land in the Bay of Honduras. The reason that one son of the Cocom family escaped from the Mayapan massacre was that he was on a trading expedition to Honduras. Sabloff and his colleagues have argued that after the Toltec fall, the new Maya rulers were a merchant class, their power ultimately based on long-distance trade (Sabloff and Freidel, 1975).

On the west coast were the plains of Tabasco, the homeland of some of the greatest traders of sixteenth-century Mesoamerica, the Chontal Maya, including the Acalan. These Chontal were ultimately related to the Itza and to those groups which had broken into the Classic Maya area. In the sixteenth century they acted as middlemen between the other Maya groups and the rest of Mesoamerica. The dominant group among the Acalan was the merchant class. No doubt much of the canoe traffic that went past the east coast centers originated in Xicalango and Potonchan, the "free ports" near Acalan. Both places were neutral ground where normally hostile groups could meet in peaceful trade. Cozumel Island acted in the same way, bolstered by its status as a pilgrimage shrine. It is interesting that Cozumel even today is a free port. Acalan is a symbolically appropriate name, meaning "canoe land." The area is crisscrossed with the estuaries of a number of major rivers. A. H. Siemens and D. E. Puleston (1972) found a series of short canals along the Candelaria River which J. E. S. Thompson (1974) suggests were fish ponds. There is some ethnohistorical evidence for this. Raised-field techniques were also used in the Candelaria bottoms. These techniques are tied to the high populations reported for the zone by the Spaniards. It was no accident that Cortés contacted the Acalan people when he proposed to march across the peninsula to Honduras. These far-ranging traders knew the major and minor routes of the area intimately. Enclaves of Nahuatl-speakers from the highlands occupied several towns in Tabasco, and Xicalango itself had Nahuatl rulers. Commerce was indeed the chief motivation for many features, events, and characteristics of the Late Postclassic.

The Itza Remnant: Tayasal, Topoxte, and Macanche

It is ironic that the last surviving remnant of Maya culture was that of the Itza, who had been expelled from Yucatan in the thirteenth century and who were not considered Maya enough to be included in the list of Late Postclassic states. The historic center of the Itza was a town called Tayasal located on an island in the large lake of Peten Itza. Cortés himself visited the Itza, and he was received by them in 1526 on his epic march to Honduras. He was in straitened circumstances and did not attempt to conquer them. We have his description of them as well as those of several Spanish priests who visited Tayasal during the sixteenth and seventeenth centuries. It was not until 1697, however, that the Spaniards made a serious effort to reach Tayasal with military power enough to destroy the

Itza state. When they did, it took only a one-day battle to bring an end to the last fragment of native American civilization.

Tayasal's site is today occupied by the town of Flores, which effectively blocks much excavation (Jones, Rice, and Rice, 1981). The best hope of information on the Itza comes from historical sources and from William Bullard's work at contemporary sites (1970*b*). George Cowgill's work in the area sets the archaeological stage for such information (1963). Using combined data, the sequence and nature of events from the end of the Classic to the arrival of Martín Ursua, the conqueror of 1697, can be traced.

Tayasal was only one of a number of Postclassic settlements around the favored ecological zone of the central Peten Lakes, including Lakes Peten, Macanche, and Yaxha. Evidently surviving populations concentrated around these lakes after the disasters of the ninth and tenth centuries. Small Tulum- and Mayapan-style centers were established. One of the earliest of these was Macanche. Later, in the thirteenth century, Topoxte was developed as a small, compact capital of a petty state containing about half a dozen temples and a like number of open halls. The halls are like those found at contemporary Mayapan. Architectural similarities to the Tulum group of sites are so striking that they are clear indications of contemporaneity and of the same specific cultural tradition. Bullard (1973) thinks that Tayasal must have had much the same appearance as Topoxte, judging by Spanish descriptions. Topoxte and Tayasal evidently overlapped in their occupations, although Topoxte was abandoned by 1697, whereas Tayasal obviously was not. Bullard notes that ceramic and architectural continuities indicate that when the Itza moved south in the thirteenth century, they did so as an elite group, and took over an already developed resident population around the lakes.

The Itza were only following a pattern established long in the past, one which they apparently had practiced with success several times in their own history. During the whole of the Postclassic period, the large Classic centers of the area remained abandoned but not forgotten. Stelae were moved about, and at Tikal, Late Postclassic people in the thirteenth century put a grave in the inner rooms of Temple I, leaving burnt copal, incense burners, and characteristic pottery. But Tikal and other Classic sites were mainly left to molder. Today, the Maya of the northern and central lowlands burn incense to the "kings" and "queens" on the stelae to propitiate their spirits. The Lacandones until recently made prayers and burned incense in special burners in the Classic temples at Yaxchilan, which still have special status and the power to awe.

The Maya Highlands

The chronological definition of the culture histories of the various regions of the Maya Highlands is Early Classic, A.D. 300–600; Late Classic, A.D.

600–900; Early Postclassic, A.D. 900–1250; and Late Postclassic, A.D. 1250–1540.

Although useful for schematic purposes, this chronological control is highly unsatisfactory for other things—measuring culture process, for example. Continuous sequences have been defined for only two valleys in the Guatemalan highlands, those of Las Vacas (Guatemala) and the Cotzal, the latter as yet unpublished. To the west, the Chiapas highlands do have a long sequence, defined mainly by ceramics, which has been worked out by T. P. Culbert (1965), but that was a distinctly marginal region even within the Maya Highlands. Eventually, chronologies will be worked out for each small region, a complex job but rewarding in the variety of cultural events that they will reflect.

In the fragmented and broken topography of the Maya Highlands, small Classic states arose about which we know little. We know that they consisted of a number of small ceremonial and elite residential centers surrounded by relatively dense populations. These centers consisted of temples, palaces, and burial places of the elite, along with a number of ball courts which later were very popular (Figs. 8–5, 8–6, 8–7). These Classic sites were generally located on valley floors and were more or less open and unfortified (Kidder and Smith, 1951). After about A.D. 1000 there was a striking transformation, with the dominant centers in each zone relocated to defensible ground, usually on the tops of ridges or mountain spurs. These sites were bolstered with defensive ditches, high terraced walls, and free-standing walls. The sites of Río Blanco, located on a river bottom, and Chutixtiox (Fig. 8–8), located on a high ridge, exemplify the change and contrast in a single region. Both are in a zone later dominated by the Quiche, and it is possible that these centers represent the Classic and Postclassic Quiche.

In certain isolated and no doubt backward areas, such as the Cotzal Valley, life continued more or less undisturbed. No perturbation of the basic patterns laid down in the Early Classic can been seen until the Spanish Conquest smashed the cultural structure. The religious focus in these areas was on ancestor worship, as reflected in family tombs used for several generations and accompanied by several phases of pottery offerings (Fig. 8–9).

Small ceremonial centers were built around the tombs of the more important lineages. In the sixteenth century these lineages were known as *tinamitl,* and Pierre Becquelin has excavated several such centers in the Acul zone (1969). In one tomb near Ilom, Early and Late Postclassic pottery was found along with a clay figure of a horseman from the early colonial period. Many of the old lifeways survived in the sixteenth century in isolated and marginal areas.

Certain of the larger fortified centers in the largest and most populous regions became the nuclei of the Late Postclassic Highland Maya states. The Cakchiquel had a capital at Iximche and the Quiche at Utatlan. Like

Fig. 8–5. An "owl" god sculpture at El Baúl, Guatemala. It is still worshiped today by Indians who come to this Pacific coastal plain site to work in the sugar and coffee plantations.

the Itza state centered around Tayasal, these groups were directed by ruling houses which were Mexicanized in certain ways, especially ideologically. These houses claimed descent from the Tula Toltec and documented such claims after the Spanish Conquest in manuscripts like the *Titulo C'oyoi.*

Perhaps a hundred years before the Spanish arrived, the Quiche, under

Fig. 8–6. *Zaculeu, Huehuetenango, Guatemala, capital of the sixteenth-century Highland Maya Mam. The site was excavated and restored by the United Fruit Company.*

a ruler named Quicab, were actively engaged in a series of aggrandizing moves which had greatly enlarged their territories. Their capital at Utatlan was a somewhat larger version of the usual temple–open hall groups (Carmack, 1973). Excavation and settlement pattern studies have added immense amounts of detail to the record (Carmack and Weeks, 1981). Based on both documentary and archaeological data, Carmack's group was able to suggest former locations within Utatlan for the major lineages. Lineage residences were defined, along with ritual and political (council) zones. These residences were called by a term which means "big house" in Quiche Maya, a term similar in meaning to that of the Aztec *calpulli*, as will be seen in the next chapter. On the other hand, the Quiche term for "king," *ajpop*, is nearly the same as the translated term for "lord," *ah-po*, in Classic Maya hieroglyphs, indicating the mix of Mesoamerica-wide elements in these late cultures.

The Cakchiquel revolted against the Quiche and established their own state. About 1524, the Cakchiquel king was in dire straits because of plagues of the newly introduced European diseases, revolts, and wars with the Quiche. He made the fatal error of sending to the Spanish for help. They came and promptly, under the cruel Gonzalo de Alvarado, conquered Quiche, Cakchiquel, and all.

The Cakchiquel capital of Iximche has been excavated and partially stabilized by George Guillemin (1966). The site is located on a defensible and beautiful spur of land. Large temples, dance platforms, ball courts, and multiple-roomed structures, presumably palaces, make up the center (Fig. 8–10). Guillemin has found some excellently preserved fragments of polychrome murals, which show skulls, hearts, and other motifs reminiscent in subject matter and style of central Mexico.

Utatlan and Iximche were the capitals of monarchically centered states. Zaculeu in the west was the capital of the Mam (Woodbury and Trik, 1953), and Mixco Viejo to the east (Lehmann, 1968) was the chief town of the Pokomam. There were others. Bolstered by their fortresses, which acted both as frontier security and regional places of refuge, these states were continually in contention with one another. In political organization, size, and warlike nature they resembled the Mixtec states.

Most of the Highland Maya groups were conquered by Alvarado in 1524, and their descendants live, in many cases, near their ancestral centers. The remnant of the Pokomam inhabitants of Mixco Viejo, conquered in blood and fire, were settled in present-day Mixco, now a suburb of the city of Guatemala.

Fig. 8–7. The restored ball court at Zaculeu, typical in being an enclosed zone in the shape of a capital I.

Fig. 8–8. Reconstruction drawing of the fortress city of Chutiztiox, Quiche, Guatemala. The Quiche were the most powerful of the Highland Maya groups and were in the process of military expansion when the Spaniards arrived. (After Proskouriakoff)

The Chiapas highlands show a set of interesting trends. Like much of the northern highlands of Guatemala, this area was sparsely settled or vacant during the Formative. During the Classic a pattern of small, open centers was established. Late in the Early Classic a considerable growth in population took place, followed in the Late Classic by the development of large, nucleated fortified towns. R. McC. Adams (1961) argues that independent communities were the dominant political form at this period. During the Early and Late Postclassic periods, the trend was toward larger centers which forcibly organized large numbers of people and the most productive lands into larger political units. These never reached the size of those to the east or north, however, and Chiapas remained a backwater area until the Spanish Conquest and, in fact, to the present day.

The Basin of Mexico

Within this richest of all the central plateau zones, a confused period (ca. A.D. 1175–1425) followed the collapse of the Tula Toltec. In a period of about 250 years several events documented by the chronicles occurred. There was a major movement of peoples from north to south. Some were civilized remnants of the cultured groups at Tula itself, others were regional Mesoamerican peoples from the outskirts of the Toltec empire, and still others were fierce barbarians from the northern desert steppes. All were called Chichimec with notable lack of discrimination in many of the chronicles.

Pedro Carrasco (1971*b*) has masterfully separated these various groups and traced their fortunes. The Nonoalca were a group present at Tollan-Tula and settled in the Itzocan region of Mixteca-Puebla. Another group

Fig. 8–9. Lid for a funerary urn from the Quiche zone of the Maya Highlands. The divine face below and the jaguar above are the symbols of the sun and of rulership. Possibly the urn was made for a member of a ruling family.

Fig. 8–10. Iximche, Chimaltenango, Guatemala, one of the several capitals of regional Highland Maya states in the sixteenth century. Temples and platforms for perishable palaces are to be found in this fortified city of the Cakchiquel Maya.

from Tula came to rest at Culhuacan, in the northern Valley of Mexico. The Mexica (Aztec) were a part of the least civilized groups. Xolotl, a legendary leader of some of these hunting tribes, reputedly established the ruling dynasty of Texcoco on the eastern lake shore. A famous codex records the wandering of the various subgroups.

After the fall of Teotihuacan, various city-states that had been established in the Basin of Mexico, although evidently under the domination of Cholula and Xochicalco, had maintained the traditions established by Teotihuacan. Azcapotzalco, on the western edge of Lake Texcoco, is especially noteworthy for its epigonal forms of Teotihuacan traditions in figurines, pottery, and presumably architecture. Carrasco suggests that at some point fairly soon after the fall of Tula, Culhuacan and Coatlinchan may have formed an alliance with Azcapotzalco. However, Azcapotzalco came to dominate the alliance and the rest of the valley, especially under a redoubtable leader named Tezozomoc. The final reformulation of these shifting alliances came in 1428, when the Aztec-Mexica of Tenochtitlan formed the Triple Alliance with Texcoco and the small state of Tacuba and overthrew Azcapotzalco. After that, the Acolhua from Texcoco and the Aztec came to dominate the alliance. After the death of the great Texcocan ruler Nezahualcoyotl, the Aztec moved gradually into the position of major partner in which they were found when the Spaniards arrived.

The chronicles of various city-states in the basin are replete with dynastic details and ethnic migration stories which rival the tangled affairs of European principalities in their Byzantine intricacy. In many cases, however, not a great deal of culture history of any significance is to be found in the tales of intermarriages and lineage rivalries. The Aztec, being brash and barbarous outsiders, however, depended for their very existence on the alliances that they could make with more powerful neighbors. In these arrangements, until 1428, they were like many other petty Mesoamerican states. Their great leap forward in social organization and ideology led irreversibly to a new order. This transition, which occurred under the great Tlacaelel, made possible the spread of an empire beyond the basin.

West Mexico: Classic to Protohistoric

Present evidence based on carbon 14 dates indicates that West Mexico can largely be correlated with the rest of Mesoamerica using the Early Classic, Late Classic, and Early and Late Postclassic rubrics. However, these are strictly chronological in utility and do not by any means explain the cultural rhythms of the west, which were quite distinct from those of central Mexico. The distinctions between western Formative cultures and those of the Early Classic period are minimal in many regions, although Teotihuacan items do appear in horizons in the period of A.D. 350 to

600. The Late Classic is again a matter of detailed chronological and technical distinction in the main, except at a few sites.

Amapa in Nayarit is one of those centers which takes a quantum jump in the Late Classic stage or just at the end of it. Early Postclassic dates there are from about A.D. 900 to 1200; this was a time of more general disturbance and development than had been seen before. Most of the metal from Amapa, which may indicate Central American and even South American contacts, dates from the Early Postclassic period. Tula-related items show up in many western sites in the Postclassic period, perhaps distributed through a *pochteca* network. Conjumatlan in Michoacan was occupied at that time.

The date of Tarascan culture's emergence as a distinguishable entity is uncertain; Borbolla's date of A.D. 1000 as early Tarascan is strictly an estimate. It seems likely that Tarascan culture had to have been in existence at least by A.D. 1250 in order to have developed to the extent of complexity that it did before the Spanish Conquest. Therefore, A.D. 1000 as a starting date may not be far off the mark. According to documents, A.D. 1390 represents the beginning of Tarascan expansion through the west.

Classic to Postclassic (A.D. 300–1200)

By the end of the Formative period, as seen in chapter 4, West Mexico had generally achieved the level of village-centered, regional cultures. Special burial modes, particularly the shaft-tomb complex, seem to indicate that ideologies related to the proper disposal of the dead had developed there. These religious cults, if that was what they were, began to die out during the Classic period, and by the beginning of the Late Classic, shaft tombs were no longer being built. Small regional centers continued, but with some rearrangement of settlement. Red-on-brown ceramics became a generally distributed group of styles during the Late Classic period. Again, Amapa provides a crucial sequence for understanding what happened (see Pendergast, 1962; Grosscup, 1961; Meighan, 1976).

Amapa is located between two large rivers only fifteen miles from the sea on the coastal plain of northern Nayarit. Thus, it had easy access to the ocean. The site itself is 1.5 square kilometers (0.6 square miles) in area and consists of some two hundred mounds, large and small and of all shapes. Apparently, during its Early Period (A.D. 250–700), Amapa was only a large village consisting mainly of wattle-and-daub houses After a period of abandonment, the site was reoccupied, and dramatic changes took place. Most of the large construction at Amapa was built during the Early Postclassic period (A.D. 900–1200). Many small mounds supported only wattle-and-daub houses, but large platforms of dirt and river stones supported temples of perishable materials, and an I-shaped ball court was built.

Perhaps the most interesting thing to happen at Amapa was the introduction of metals about A.D. 900. A cemetery which largely dates from this period provided many of the metal items found, 205 in all: needles, awls, tweezers, fishhooks, wire, pins, and many types of bells. Mazapan-style figurines like those found at Tula and throughout Mesoamerica on the Toltec horizon are associated with metallurgy at Amapa. Also found in the metal-yielding graves were finely decorated incised bowls and many handsomely painted polychrome vessels. The chile-grinder, *molcajete*, form is characteristic of this period.

Both forms and motifs at Amapa show close affinities with Postclassic central Mexican cultures, and there is little doubt that West Mexico was more fully integrated into Mesoamerica at this time than at any time before. For example, many of the animals painted on the polychromes are very similar to some of those found in the Codex Borgia group from the Mixteca-Puebla area. At least one Amapa monochrome vessel has a plumbate form. At the same time, acting as the undoubted agency for the introduction of metallurgy to Mesoamerica placed the west in an unaccustomed and innovative role.

In addition to metals, *molcajetes,* and Mazapan figurines, Robert Lister has also used the appearance of *malacates,* or spindle whorls, to define the Postclassic. It may be that superior strains of cotton from South America were introduced at the same time as metals, but in any case spinning (and presumably weaving) became a widespread western activity after A.D. 900.

In Michoacan during the Early Classic period, red-on-brown pottery appears at the cemetery of Apatzingan. *Molcajetes* and *malacates* both appear at Apatzingan in the succeeding phases, and many other sites show this sequence of events, confirming the widespread nature of these horizon markers.

The general picture of Classic and Postclassic West Mexico is one of regionalized cultures, mostly centered around villages but occasionally with a larger ceremonial center as a focus. Ixtepete and Ixtlan del Río, large sites in Nayarit, are examples of the larger centers. These small regions responded differentially throughout the period A.D. 300 to 1200 to influences from central Mexico that were transmitted possibly from South America and probably from Central America. The northern part of the zone was involved in the expansion of Mesoamerican cultures northward in Teotihuacan times and, later, during the Toltec period. Internal motivations to cultural complexity may have been largely based on population growth. All indications are that during the Classic and Postclassic periods population increased and that elaboration of sociopolitical arrangements was one sign of increasing complexity. At the time of the Spaniards' arrival, most of the area was either dominated by regional centers, such as Cojumatlan, or incorporated into the Tarascan empire (Chadwick, 1971; Meighan, 1974).

The Tarascans (A.D. 1000–1521)

The Tarascans are anthropologically famous for having a language that is unrelated to any other known Mesoamerican language and for having developed an "empire" that successfully resisted the aggressive advances of the Aztec. The *Relación de Michoacan* (Craine and Reindorp, 1970) gives considerable information about the Tarascans, and the Tarascans themselves are still around to be consulted, at least on their language and other surviving matters of interest. Swadesh, with characteristic daring, has linked Tarascan to Zuñi in the Gran Chichimeca and to Quechua in South America (Chadwick, 1971). J. Greenberg has suggested that Tarascan belongs to Macro-Chibcha, another large South American linguistic family. This connection fits somewhat with the possibility of West Mexican contact with South America, as evidenced by the introduction of metalworking. A bit of possible additional archaeological evidence is in the form of a two- or three-story adobe building with a trapezoidal doorway, found near Arcelia, Guerrero, according to reports. Trapezoidal doorways and multiple-storied buildings are characteristic of the Inca area, which is also Quechua-speaking. However, Arcelia is possibly outside of Tarascan territory. This is still a question of great complexity and one on which too little evidence bears.

Fortunately, Shirley Gorenstein and Helen Pollard have done a great deal of work in the Tarascan area and among its documents and have enlightened us considerably about the nature of the Tarascans. The following depends on their accounts (Gorenstein and Pollard, 1983; Pollard, 1980).

The Tarascan state occupied about 65,000 square kilometers (25,000 square miles) and included within its boundaries various ethnic and linguistic groups. Thus, it fulfills the formal qualifications required of an imperial system. The *Relación de Michoacan* relates that the Tarascans were ruled by a priest-king-god who governed a large political unit. In terms of area, it seems to have been the largest political unit in Mesoamerica at the time of the Spanish Conquest. The empire was administered by a wide variety of officials who handled matters such as taxes and censuses.

Although 340 settlements are mentioned by the *Relación de Michoacan*, only four of them qualified as cities, and they were located within the Lake Patzcuaro basin. The largest was the capital of Tzintzuntzan, which had been founded about A.D. 1000 as a center for the worship of two important deities. By 1350, the center had been transformed into an urban area sprawling along the lake shore, with a population of between twenty-five thousand and thirty-five thousand people. Archaeological survey has detected four districts that are the probable residence zones for four classes: upper and lower elite, commoners, and ethnic foreigners. Wards (barrios) for the various social and occupational groups survived in modern Tzintzuntzan into the twentieth century. The residence of the king was near a set of burial-temple platforms, the famous *yacatas* (Figs. 8–11, 8–12). The king was buried with great pomp, and several retainers went with him to the afterlife. The shrine of the major Tarascan god Curicaueri was also located nearby. The king's palace was set on a large platform and included offices where councils met, civil and criminal courts, and storehouses where tribute was stored and allocated. Workshops, mainly having to do with the production of stone tools, have been found within the city. We also know that there were specialists in the production of ceramics, featherwork, bronze, copper, and gold objects in Tzintzuntzan. These artisans were organized into craft guilds, each with a patron deity. There were also weavers, bureaucrats, priests, medicine men, palace custodians, storytellers, merchants, spies, messengers, and couriers.

Burials found in the *yacatas* contain exotically shaped ceramics, including many "foreign vessel" forms, decorated by negative painting. Also found in the burials and elsewhere are examples of virtuoso metalwork in gold, silver, and copper. Excellence in metallurgy is matched by many fine productions in obsidian, turquoise, and other stone. Stone sculpture emphasized coyotes, but seated human figures and *chacmuls* were also common.

Tzintzuntzan and its court presided over an exceptionally clear hierarchy of settlements. Three of them were nearby and had populations of about five thousand each. One of them, Ihuatzio, was a kind of fortified country capital to which the court apparently repaired at times. Three *yacatas* are present there, and it is mentioned in the chronicle that in 1520 Ihuatzio was the royal treasury.

The settlement pattern of the Tarascans was essentially rural, however, and most people lived in hamlets, villages, and towns. In fact Gorenstein and Pollard contrast the Tarascans with the Aztec in the degree of political and administrative centralization that they achieved. They attribute this to the fact that the Tarascans had no previous complex societies to deal with or to incorporate within their empire. They therefore were able to devise a highly rationalized administrative structure which included professional soldiers. Society was integrated by making lucrative offices available to nearly all of society.

Economically, there were the usual local and regional markets, which also were hierarchically tied into a system with Tzintzuntzan at the top. The state derived great amounts of tribute on a regular basis; a great deal of that was used to support various governmental activities, including the

Fig. 8–11. The rounded part of a keyhole-plan platform, (yacata) in the former capital of the Tarascans, Tzintzuntzan, Michoacan, Mexico. These platforms were the burial places of the rulers and the sites of temples dedicated to a local variant of the wind god. (Courtesy Margaret N. Bond and Franklin C. Graham)

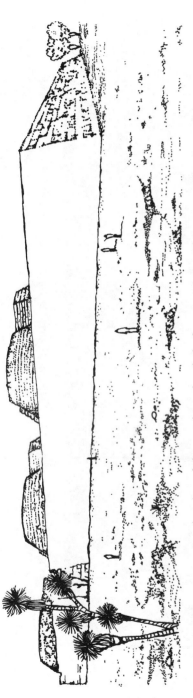

Fig. 8–12. A reconstruction drawing of the very large basal platform supporting the yacatas at Tzintzuntzan.

Fig. 8–13. A stucco relief found on an elite residential platform at the fifteenth-century Zapotec site of Lambityeco, Oaxaca, Mexico. The relief shows a married couple and gives their names. They were buried below their former house in a tomb.

army. War was waged after the harvest was in, in good Mesoamerican manner. Spies (perhaps *pochtecas*) were employed for intelligence purposes. The Tarascans resisted the Aztec with a chain of fortified cities and with a professional army.

Oaxaca: The Zapotec

The Postclassic Period or Monte Alban IV (700–1000)

In the Valley of Oaxaca, three major sites dating from the period after the abandonment of Monte Alban have been at least cursorily examined. These Monte Alban IV sites are Lambityeco, Yagul, and Mitla, all in the Tlacolula arm of the central valley. Further surveys by Blanton and his colleagues have added more data (Blanton and Kowalewski, 1981).

Lambityeco (Paddock, 1983*b*) is an open site on the valley floor. It is dated within Monte Alban period III*b* and early IV. The site was occupied by at least A.D. 600, judging by some early types of fine orange pottery found there. Over two hundred mounds constitute the site and cover an extensive area. Its site plan is similar to that of Monte Alban III*b* culture, with the same style of patio arrangement of large buildings and the same sort of subpatio tombs. One large tomb at Lambityeco has the usual antechamber with a formal facade over the entrance to the burial room. The facade includes finely done stucco heads which may be portraits of the persons buried inside (Fig. 8–13). The building immediately above the tomb carries a stucco decoration including the figures and calendrical names of persons who may have been the parents of the man buried below. Celebration of distinguished and ruling lineages continued, therefore, from Monte Alban III times and certainly into the historic period.

John Paddock, the excavator (1983*b*) sees in Lambityeco a reflection of the decadence and decline of Monte Alban culture. It does appear possible that differences between Monte Alban and Lambityeco could simply be those between a metropolitan center and a county seat. In early Monte Alban IV, Lambityeco was one of several large centers surrounded and supported by large populations, and Blanton and Kowlewski (1981) feel that there were ten or twelve such communities after the dissolution of Monte Alban, each representing a petty state. However, many of these political units were amorphous and decentralized, especially as reflected at Jalieza, with its sixteen thousand people but no central civic precinct. Lambityeco seems to have been abandoned well before the end of period IV. Perhaps the population moved to nearby and more defensible Yagul.

Yagul is located on a flat spur running away from a large butte or mesa. It was apparently occupied as early as Monte Alban I, but this earlier material is so heavily covered by IV and V deposits that it is difficult to say anything about it except that the early settlement was small. Excavations at the site have revealed evidence of a "building boom" at the beginning of period IV and coincident with the abandonment of Lambityeco.

Period IV sculpture and ceramics reveal the same sorts of attitudes toward the distinguished dead as in earlier periods. The burial tradition continued (though with a notable decline in technical and aesthetic quality) through the valley and no less at Yagul. Effigy vessels with "bat-claw" feet are particularly characteristic of the period. Carved rectangular stones are finely detailed and carry scenes of what are apparently married couples seated facing each other. Marcus (1980, 1983e) notes that sculptural subjects shifted in periods IV and V from state visits and conquest monuments to depictions of royal marriages and other genealogical matters. Even so, this class of monuments retained its original function to the end—that of political history. A tomb mural from this period at Monte Alban (Tomb 125) also seems to show the same shift in subject and includes a genealogical register (Miller, 1988).

Mitla is located about six miles farther east in the Tlacolula arm of the valley on a small river. Traces of the Guadalupe phase and of Monte Alban I and II occupations have been found there, but no information of substance is yet available. Two groups of major structures dominated by temple buildings and several tombs and burials represent the IIIa and IIIb periods. However, the modern town of Mitla surrounds these buildings, and the site may have been much more extensive than it seems. The location of these two temple groups is open and undefended. Period IV pyramids are located in a fortified zone above the river but have not been explored. The shift is important, however, and reflects more disturbed times.

All of the above sites date from a time during which the Mixtec were pushing into the central valley from the north, down the Etla arm. According to Ronald Spores, the major period of Mixtec aggression was in the Late Postclassic, but certainly the fragmentation of Early Postclassic Zapotec cultures and the breakup of the Monte Alban centralized state indicate considerable pressure during Monte Alban period IV. Note, however, that Blanton and Kowalewski (1981; Blanton, 1978) and Marcus (1980) argue for a collapse of Monte Alban based on the overwhelming costs of maintaining such a center. In any case, this is a period of political "balkanization."

The Late Postclassic Period (A.D. 1000–1521)

In some ways, the mysteries of quasars and black holes in space are easier to explain than Monte Alban periods IV and V and their relationships. The work of Donald Brockington (1973, 1974), Ronald Spores (1972), John Paddock (1966c, 1974a, 1974b, 1983b), and Richard Blanton and Stephen Kowalewski (1981) has made the situation somewhat clearer. The difficulty lies in the history of Oaxacan archaeology. The site of Monte Alban was the first to be intensively excavated. Its periods were naturally thereafter "stretched" to apply to the whole valley. However, ethnic terms were then applied to the valley-wide periods. Monte Alban IV became, ipso facto, Zapotec, and Monte Alban V became Mixtec.

It is very difficult to determine the ethnicity of the ancient owner of a piece of pottery. Paddock, Brockington, and Spores have pointed out that trade of luxury (elite) goods can distribute them far beyond their origin points. Some documentation indicates that Mixtec products were distributed by means of an elite trade network that stretched throughout central Mesoamerica. Further, it is known that Mixtec and Zapotec elites were intermarrying as early as A.D. 1250. Brockington found that in the Mixtec area of Miahuatlan, south of the main valley, the "Mixtec" gray common wares were distinct from those of Nochixtlan-Yanhuitlan and other still undefined parts of the Mixtec area, indicating that there was a great deal of variation within Mixtec culture itself. Finally, a conference of Oaxacan specialists in 1970 found that "Mixtec" gray ware distribution in the Valley of Oaxaca during periods IV and V was nearly identical to the distribution of the Zapotecs immediately after the Spanish conquest. Ignacio Bernal some time ago suggested that Mixtec and Zapotec culture fused in some respects during the later periods and offered some evidence for this having happened in period V (Bernal, 1965b).

Considering all of the above, we shall use the following principles to deal with late prehistoric Oaxacan culture. Elite cultural material found in formal tombs, and particularly Mixtec polychrome pottery, may indicate either Mixtec or Zapotec elite culture, and the decision must be made on other grounds. Documents such as the local relaciones and Fray Francisco de Burgoa's writing have proven to be quite accurate and can be used to make such distinctions. Tribute networks in Late Postclassic times included towns containing foreign ethnic groups, and therefore different cultural products could show up in elite contexts. Brockington's Miahuatlan work shows that Zapotec and Mixtec cultures varied widely within themselves. In other words, as we have known for many years, linguistic uniformity does not mean cultural uniformity. On the other hand, there was apparently a considerable uniformity of culture among the common folk of both linguistic groups in single geographical regions, especially during the final prehistoric period.

The main cultural-historical process of the last two periods therefore seems to have been the progressive fusion of Zapotec and Mixtec cultural variants in the Valley of Oaxaca. The period of maximum differentiation between Mixtec and Zapotec cultures seems to have been IIIb. Even in that period some "Mixtec" traits show up in the ceramics, however. Therefore it seems reasonable to deal here with Monte Alban IV and V as they were probably originally intended to be treated, as purely chronological blocks of time against which we can draw the major features of prehistoric events. In these terms we may define Monte Alban IV as A.D. 700 to 1000 and Monte Alban V as A.D. 1000 to 1521, the date of the Spanish Conquest. I have adjusted the Monte Alban IV and V dates to take account of Blanton and Kowalewski's latest published estimates (1981).

Stratigraphic evidence from Yagul and Mitla developed by Bernal indicates that period V can be subdivided (1965*b*). The earlier phase is characterized at Mitla by the appearance of stone mosaic decoration and fine gray pottery in tombs. Monte Alban's period V tombs, except for Tomb 7 and its great treasure, date to this earliest phase. The dating of this phase is then A.D. 1000 to 1400. The later phase in period V is represented by Mixtec polychrome pottery and the latest palaces at Mitla and Yagul, as distinguished by their room plans. Zaachila Tombs 1 and 2 and Monte Alban Tomb 7 date from this period. The second phase started about A.D. 1400 and ended in 1521.

During Late Postclassic times, Mixtec penetration of the Central Valley of Oaxaca reached its maximum and then receded under a Zapotec reassertion. Apparently the Mixtec had practical political control of most of the communities of the valley at one point. According to Bernal's survey data, this occupation may have constituted as much as 75 percent of the two hundred sites in his sample. However, by the time of the Spanish Conquest in November, 1521 the Tlacolula and Zaachila arms of the valley were under partial Zapotec control, and Bernal's conclusions may be biased by factors discussed at the beginning of this section. This comeback was consolidated and expanded by the Zapotec in the early colonial period. Cuilapan in the western valley, perhaps having as many as 13,500 inhabitants, represented the major Mixtec outpost in 1521. In 1519 the total valley population was a maximum of 52,000, according to Blanton and Kowalewski's estimates (1981). This population is much less than former rough estimates, which were about ten times as great. Population was also widely dispersed throughout innumerable (at least 867) communities, most of which were hamlet-sized. As in the Basin of Mexico, Zapotec and Mixtec communities were organized into tributary networks typical of the Late Postclassic city and regional states. For example, Macuilxochitl was tributary to Zaachila. Thereby, a loose political control was exercised by Zaachila (originally named Teozapotlan) over the continually bickering communities. Valley towns were often multiethnic, having Mixtec barrios in Zapotec areas and vice versa.

Major centers of Monte Alban V (or the Late Postclassic period) were fortified or had fortified refuges. Mitla and Yagul are the best known. At Yagul, an extensive palace complex has been excavated, with six patios very similar in design to those of nearby Mitla. A formal fortress was built on top of the mesa. A large and impressive ball court was located near the palaces. Several T-shaped major tombs have been found at Yagul which are not similar to the rectangular tombs at Monte Alban. Again, similarities may be noted with structures at Mitla. For example, the door to the burial chamber of Yagul Tomb 30 is closed by a stone slab which is carved with the same "running fret" motif so common in the Mitla palaces. Bernal points out some near identities in plan between palace groups at the two sites. Yagul apparently was occupied at the time of Spanish Conquest, and its population was moved to Tlacolula, where their descendants still live.

Mitla's period V aspect is that of a town built near a river, with a nearby fortress on a defensible mesa. Work by K. V. Flannery's group indicates that the town was 1 to 2 square kilometers (0.4 to 0.8 square mile) in area, with a sustaining area of about 20 square kilometers (7.7 square miles). The latter includes dry-land terracing of the hillsides up to the 1,800-meter (5,900-foot) line. The major civic construction known from period V is represented by the three large and famous palace groups so often visited today, as well as by the Adobe Group of palaces. These palace groups consist of rectangular buildings arranged around the four sides of spacious patios. The buildings themselves emphasize the horizontal, with their facades broken by mosaic-decorated panels. The interior upper walls are dizzyingly covered with continuous and repetitious frets of various sorts: running, interlocking, and stepped. Bernal suggests that these decorative motifs and others indicate a fusion of Zapotec and Mixtec cultural ideas.

Fragments of extraordinarily fine murals are still to be seen in the Church Group at Mitla. In images, techniques, and coloration, these are quite close to designs of the Codex Borgia, as pointed out by the great scholar Eduard Seler (1904; see also illustrations in Miller, 1988). Personified versions of the planet Venus and of the sun are to be found as principal themes. Huge monolithic columns supported the roof in a palace today called the Hall of the Columns. Lintels are massive and stones of the same size supported the roofs of tombs which lie beneath the plaza in front of the palaces. Father Burgoa, a seventeenth-century priest of Zaachila, records that these chambers were the traditional burial places for the priests at Mitla and that they smelled abominably (Paddock, 1966c). A hill 2 kilometers (1.2 miles) distant was fortified with massive walls that closed off the gaps in the naturally rugged terrain.

Mitla held a religious primacy over other Zapotec communities and was apparently a center for the worship of a certain Coqui Bezelao and Xonaxi Quecuya (Lord and Mistress of the Underworld). Spores characterizes valley Zapotec religion in the early sixteenth century as using stone and wooden idols and requiring a trained priesthood, with ritual sacrifices of dogs, birds, and human beings. Liturgical matters included blood offerings from body parts as well as fasting, penance, feasting, intoxication, and ritual cannibalism. This religious complex involved the underworld as the place of death and of ancestors. In keeping with the religious focus of Mitla, a priest, instead of the usual local lord, ruled the center (Spores, 1965).

Zaachila or Teozapotlan is located at the entrance to the arm of the valley of the same name. Until recently the site was little known because of the incredible hostility of the inhabitants toward outsiders in general and archaeologists in particular. They had run the latter out of town twice in the past. The rather extraordinary finds of Mexican archaeologists Roberto Gallegos (1962) and Jorge Acosta (1972) have begun to fill this void, albeit under the unusual circumstances of military protection. The ancient site is evidently extensive but is partly covered by the modern town, as at Mitla. Major architecture is located on natural and man-made elevations and consists of patio groups of the usual sort. A ball court may be included in the site. All of the visible material is evidently of period V. Mound B is the largest at the site and is high enough to enable one to see Monte Alban 15 kilometers (9 miles) to the north-northeast. This complex structure consists of several terraces leading to at least four elevated patios. Elevation would have given defensive advantages.

Mound A is the location of the two tombs which have been the focus of most of the work at the site. It is lower than adjacent Mound B but still elevated some 9 to 12 meters (30 or 40 feet) above ground level. A sunken patio on the top of Mound A is surrounded by the usual set of stone and adobe rooms. Tombs 1 and 2, both with antechambers, are located under the north building. Tomb 1 contained one principal individual and nine others crumpled along the walls. Eight pieces of some of the most magnificent pottery ever found in Mesoamerica, all of the famous Mixtec polychrome, with its glossy, lacquerlike finish in brilliant colors, were found in the antechamber. The individual pieces are extraordinary. A small blue hummingbird perches on the edge of a gloriously colored drinking cup. A howling coyote's head forms the mouth of a pitcher, with the spout being the animal's red tongue. Turquoise mosaic disks and masks and gold rings were included with the offerings.

On the walls of the tomb are modeled stucco figures of humans with calendrical names attached to them by a line, codex-style: 5 Flower and 9 Flower. Before each of these figures marches the modeled figure of the death god, Mictlantecuhtli, or Coqui Bezelao. It is possible that both 5 Flower and 9 Flower are mentioned in the Mixtec codices as rulers in the dynasty of Mixtec Yanhuitlan. By a complex and tortuous genealogical argument, Alfonso Caso thought that the person buried in Tomb 1 was probably 8 Deer "Fire Serpent," a ruler known to have been born about A.D. 1400. The figures 5 Flower and 9 Flower were ancestral to 8 Deer "Fire Serpent" (Caso, 1966a), but his argument depends on the assumption that there was a recording mistake in one of the codices.

Tomb 2 contained another sumptuous burial, with twelve persons in the latest interment, the prior occupants' bones having been carefully stored in the niches of the tomb. Mixtec gray ware, a well-made plain pottery, was used for the ceramic offerings but this plainness was offset by some superb pieces of gold work and carved bones. In quality, these items are quite the equals of any found elsewhere.

Two other tombs found at Zaachila, with less spectacular offerings but which nonetheless give information, are located in a small mound under the ruins of a colonial Catholic chapel. It is known that early sixteenth-century chapels were often placed on the razed sites of former native shrines. The two tombs date from Monte Alban V and contained 124 pieces of pottery, some of it very fine indeed.

Several other burials also were found, one with an exceptional combined gold and turquoise-jade disk. The gold was beaten thinner than tissue paper and is exquisitely decorated with Mixtec codex-style seated human figures. Relying on the documentary evidence, which states that Zaachila was the Zapotec political capital but fell to the Mixtec late in the prehistoric period, it seems probable that the persons in these tombs were Mixtec. However, even if they were Zapotec, marital connections to Mixtec elite families would explain Mixtec luxury goods in the tombs and burials.

Monte Alban Tomb 7 is famous as a great treasure house of Mixtec art. As interpreted here, the evidence is as good that the occupant was Zapotec as Mixtec. However, considering the documentary evidence that the Mixtecs controlled the nearby zones in the sixteenth century, the tilt now seems to be toward a Mixtec tomb.

Tomb 7 is located in a small architectural group of the usual sort with stone buildings facing inward upon the courtyard. The tomb entrance is in the patio, and the burial chamber is under one of the structures. The occupants of Tomb 7 were literally mixed up, and the count of individuals is seven to nine adult males with the remains of two women and one infant thrown in for good measure. The discrepancies and uncertainties in numbers can be explained by the possibility that body parts of various individuals were included as part of the funerary offerings. The principal occupant was a human monster with a cerebral tumor. Caso suggests that he might thus have represented in life an incarnation of the god Xolotl, god of monsters. A skull among the parts had a turquoise mosaic overlay and a flint knife in the nasal opening—a symbol of Tezcatlipoca.

The offerings were extraordinary and comprehended 337 separate items of gold, silver, copper, carved bone, jade, and other materials. The quality of the jewelry work is notable. Ten gold pectorals were in the tomb, one with a calendrical date. Another is a composite example, with sections showing a ball game in progress, a sun symbol, and other scenes;

it was hung with delicate golden rattles. Rings, brooches, fan handles (one of jade), a gold diadem with a gold feather, earplugs, bracelets, and a copper axe were included in the inventory.

The carved human bones are extremely complex and rich in iconography. They are nearly identical to those found in Zaachila Tomb 2. The gold objects also show great similarity to Zaachila Tomb 1 material. So complex is the tomb and its implications that Caso needed four hundred pages in a sumptuous volume (1969) to completely describe and analyze it. The implications of wealth, craftsmanship, and economic networks are all enormous. The legendary skills of the Mixtec as artificers of the sixteenth century are confirmed. Brockington (personal communication) points out that Mixtec were imported to Tenochtitlan in Aztec times to practice their skills in the great capital (Fig. 8–14).

The Zapotec spread and expanded into the coastal plain of Oaxaca and into the Isthmus of Tehuantepec during the late prehistoric period. In point of fact, they may have been refugees. The *Relación de Cuilapa* says, "Finally these [Mixtec] had a war with the people of Teozapotlan, who, recognizing that they were at a disadvantage fled to Teguantepec" (after Paddock, 1966a:375). Spores (1965) goes so far as to say that the major center of Zapotec political power may have shifted completely away from Zaachila to the Tehuantepec center of Guiengola a few years before the Spanish Conquest.

Guiengola is little known, having only been incompletely investigated by Eduard Seler in 1896 (Seler, 1960, 2:184–199) and remapped later by Peterson and MacDougall (1974). It is a large and imposing fortress located on a ridge. Paddock (1966b) comments that the site has the typical Zapotec arrangement of major buildings around patios. However, David Potter points out that the style of the buildings at Guiengola is very different from that of Lambityeco (personal communication, 1976). It also contains a ball court and a curious and complex palace area. The rugged hillside is ringed with two massive walls, evidently for defensive purposes. The pottery on the site is all Late Postclassic. We know from historical accounts that in about 1497 Guiengola was the location of one of the most resounding defeats suffered by the Aztec in their expansion of empire. For once, the Zapotec and Mixtec made peace and joined in resisting the common enemy. A Zapotec ruler called Cocijoeza led the resistance during the four-year siege and then turned on the Mixtec. Brockington (personal communication, 1976) notes that the name means simply "rain god worshiper" and therefore could be a title carried by any or many rulers. Paddock (personal communication, 1976) notes that a real person, despite these questions about his title, occupied the throne in the early sixteenth century.

The suggested Zapotec comeback after Mixtec aggression may have been accomplished mainly after the Spanish Conquest. The Zapotec invited the

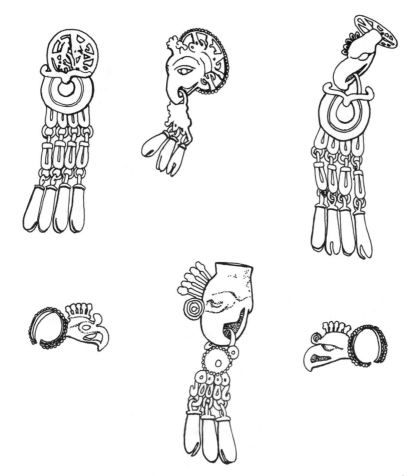

Fig. 8–14. Gold jewelry made by Mixtec artisans of the fifteenth century. Renowned for their craftsmanship in gold, a group of these specialists resided at Aztec Tenochtitlan.

Spaniards into Oaxaca to help them against the Mixtec, seemingly an act of desperation. In any case, the Spaniards and their allies came and conquered both Mixtec and Zapotec in a one-month campaign in 1521.

The Zapotec and Mixtec (both of their original names roughly mean "cloud people") survive today. They have suffered the trauma of the Conquest, the worst blows of the colonial period, a steady erosion of their economic and biological base, and the continuing assault of the modern world on their cultural traditions. In their fierce independence and cultural persistence they are something like the Highland Maya and the Zuni of the southwestern United States.

The Mixtec

Ronald Spores (1969, 1972) has commented on the diversity of cultural groups which constitute the Mixtec language family. These regional variants are usually grouped into the Mixteca Alta (Highland Mixtec), Mixteca Baja (Lowland Mixtec), and Mixteca de la Costa (Coastal and Coastal Range Mixtec). Brockington's work in the cultural fracture zone, which is the Oaxacan coast, will be treated separately; it includes Mixtecan groups but probably also archaeological remains from other linguistic groups. The only regional variants of which we know anything of archaeological substance at present are those of Coixtlahuaca and the Nochixtlan Valley (Bernal, 1949). Spores's Nochixtlan sequence is as follows:

Phases	Dates
Convento	A.D. 1520–35 to 1820
Natividad	A.D. 1000 to 1520–35
Las Flores	A.D. 500 to 1000
Ramos	200 B.C. to A.D. 500
Cruz	1300 B.C. to 200 B.C.

In terms of many of the regional sequences of Mesoamerica, these are fairly long periods of time, but the sequence is continuous and shows considerable internal development. For these reasons, and others that will become clear, we will review the sequence from beginning to end.

Preclassic or Formative: Cruz Phase

Nochixtlan developed a fairly standard highland Formative culture during the Cruz phase—one which was mainly village-oriented but with contacts both inside and outside the region. Ceramics of the phase reflect ties with adjacent valleys and farther away, as do its ubiquitous figurines. Housing within the small communities evolved from houses with packed-earth floors to some with plastered floors. Block adobe walls were favored from the earliest times. One probable elite residence was found at Inityu, and an immense platform from a nearby site indicates that the general Mesoamerican Formative trends towards social complexity and associated civic architecture were in medias res in the Nochixtlan Valley. Parallels with the Central Valley of Oaxaca are striking.

Early Classic: Ramos Phase

An urban center first appeared about 200 B.C. at Yucuita. Several hundred structures, including ten major civic groups, are concentrated in an area of 1 to 1.5 square kilometers (0.4 to 1.2 square miles). Spores thinks that Yucuita probably dominated the whole valley. There was considerably more to dominate than in the Formative period. Population had doubled (twelve thousand to fourteen thousand people) and communities had grown both in size and in complexity. Some ten towns and at least twenty hamlet-sized sites were in the valley, most of them clustering around the developing urban center.

Yucuita seems to have been internally specialized, with a number of different kinds of craft and social groups living together. Yucuita itself probably had only about seven thousand people, but they were supplemented by people in the subordinate communities, themselves specialized. Spores feels that the consistency of pattern between the settlement complexes of historic times and of the Ramos phase allows him to infer that the pattern of the Mixtec petty state ruled by an aristocratic family was already in existence. This inference is reinforced by the fact that the sequence shows no significant breaks and indicates that the same cultural tradition is involved throughout at least two thousand years. That tradition is reflected in the gradually changing gray wares, which lasted from Cruz up to Convento times.

Late Classic: Las Flores Phase

Total valley population reached an estimated thirty thousand during the Las Flores phase. Less desirable lands were developed, particularly those higher up-slope, probably as a result of population pressures. Again the region was dominated by a single large center, this time located in a defensible position on one of the highest mountains in the valley. This capital, Yucuñudahui, covering about 2 square kilometers (0.8 square mile), was a planned urban area. Sculptured monuments found there have a system of writing similar to that in use at Monte Alban in period III. The center existed within a context of an increased number of communities.

The larger centers were composed of a number of palace complexes surrounded by humble housing of the one- or two-room type. The smaller centers had one or two palaces surrounded by many small and inferior houses. Spores finds in this pattern great similarity to the settlement pattern which accompanied the distinctive Late Postclassic social organization. Ruling families in the latter days occupied the main centers, while outlying settlements were administered by a network of loyal nobility. All nobility maintained two or more homes, one in the administered communities and one in the capital. There, the historically known social organization would fit the Las Flores settlement pattern quite well. Nobility would have been supported by the service and tribute system well known from the Late Postclassic period. It is also noteworthy that the same Late Classic shift from open to defensible locations which took place in the Guatemalan highlands also occurred here.

Early and Late Postclassic: Natividad Phase

The Nochixtlan Valley has relatively sparse evidence of the famous Mixtec polychrome during the Natividad, a late prehistoric phase, although

Coixtlahuaca has it in abundance. On the other hand, a diagnostic red-on-cream type is exceedingly common in this period. We must, therefore, look elsewhere for the origin of the Mixtec polychrome tradition, perhaps to another valley such as Coixtlahuaca or to the Mixteca de la Costa area. Paddock suggests that Maya polychrome tradition may be the ultimate origin. Gray pottery, of the kind that appeared in the Oaxacan central valley, continued its gentle but persistent modulation throughout the period.

The population of the Nochixtlan Valley reached its maximum during this long phase. One hundred and fifty-nine Natividad sites have been found thus far, and an estimated fifty thousand people occupied them. An intensive form of agriculture based on terracing (*lamabordo*) of the upper slopes was developed. The even distribution of valley population of the preceding period shifted to a pattern of concentration in the northern end of the valley, around Yanhuitlan. Spores correlates this shift with the rise of the kingdom of Yanhuitlan, although it was only the largest of seven kingdoms in the valley. Most population was located in indefensible positions, and therefore it seems that this phase was a time of peace and tranquillity. According to the codices and *relaciones,* the Yanhuitlan petty state was fairly stable for the last four hundred or five hundred years before the Spanish Conquest. However, there were outside pressures on the valley, among them aggressive moves by neighboring Mixtec states, especially the Pacific coastal kingdom-empire of Tututepec. Late in the period, the major aggressor was the Culhua-Mexica (or Aztec) empire, which rather easily overran the area in 1486 and in 1506. To the internally generated stresses of growing population and growing elite classes, then, were added the external stresses of tribute demands from outside political systems.

It is clear that the Nochixtlan Valley had less demographic potential than did the Basin of Mexico, simply on account of its smaller size. In addition, its subsistence base was poorer. The city-states of the basin averaged about fifty thousand people each, whereas that figure was shared among seven kingdoms in the Nochixtlan area. Spores thinks that eventually the stresses would have led to conflict within the valley in spite of the stability afforded by elite alliances and economic interdependence. For other parts of the Mixtec area, the main period of upset and conquest was in the eleventh and twelfth centuries. Perhaps these regions had still less demographic potential than Nochixtlan and reached their limits more rapidly, triggering predatory competition.

Ethnohistoric Yanhuitlan

Using documents from the sixteenth century, Spores has reconstructed late prehistoric Mixtec society in the region of Yanhuitlan (1967; also Spores and Flannery 1983). Social organization was based on a four-class system. The first class was the ruling family with its privileged relatives. They were supported by a tribute system that yielded goods and services. A second group was made up of supporting nobility, who were the civil service for the small kingdom; they were also entitled to support from the tribute system. Together with the ruling family, the nobility made up a caste. A third class was made up of commoners who carried a large part of the burden of the tribute system. A special-status group may have been formed by merchants. Tribute included items not available in the valley, such as "Guatemala (quetzal) feathers," and therefore these traders ranged fairly far. The lowest class was made up of tenant farmers, servants, and slaves and was smaller than the commoner class. Kinship ties were important at all levels of society, although not beyond the community, except in the case of the elite. The elite maintained their caste exclusiveness by carefully recording genealogies, which appear in the pre-Conquest codices in the colonial documents as well. This system was in use throughout the Mixteca, of which the Valley of Nochixtlan was only a part and of which the kingdom of Yanhuitlan was one among many. It is to these fascinating prehistoric picture books that we now turn.

The Mixtec Codices: Content, Decipherment, and Characteristics

There is only one topical group of pre-Columbian manuscripts from the Mixteca area. Anawalt (1981) has demonstrated by analysis of the costumes depicted that the "Borgia group" is a mixed bag of documents, three from Puebla and two from the Gulf Coast. They are no longer to be considered as Mixtec and will be referred to elsewhere. The group of pre-Hispanic documents which interests us most here is genealogical-historical in content. It consists of eight surviving manuscripts. Bishop Burgoa tells us that the painted books of the Mixtec give us the day and year signs, name and god hieroglyphs, marriages, ceremonies, sacrifices, and military events (M. E. Smith, 1973). A few codices, the Codex Vienna, for example, combine information from both categories.

The major decipherment of the manuscripts was done over a fifty-year period. Zelia Nuttall in 1902 first suggested that the Codex Nuttall (Nuttall, 1975) contained historical information (Fig. 8–15). James Cooper Clark in 1912 put together the story of the great Mixtec conqueror 8 Deer "Tiger Claw," which though inaccurate in many respects was a major step forward. Interest in the manuscripts then lapsed except for commentary by Long and Spinden. The latter defined the genealogical-historical category. The great breakthrough came in 1949 with the publication of "El Mapa de Teozacoalco" by Alfonso Caso. In that study, Caso dealt with a pictorial document which shows the genealogies of the Mixtec ruling families of Tilantongo and Teozacoalco. The record was carried back into the prehistoric past and overlapped with pre-Columbian manuscripts such as the Codex Nuttall. Further, "El Mapa de Teoza-

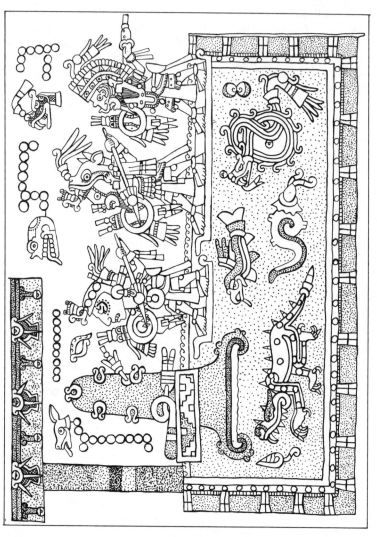

Fig. 8–15. Codex Nuttall, from the highland Mixtec area. Page 75 from this history and genealogical record shows the attack on an island city by Mixtec warriors in canoes. An alligator swims in the water, possibly indicating a location in the lowlands.

coalco" carried European dates corresponding to the Mixtec hieroglyphs as well as a commentary in Roman script. Using these keys, Caso proceeded to a series of brilliant commentaries on the various codices of the genealogical-historical group. With this extraordinary work, and those of his colleagues, we now have elite-class histories available for a great part of the Mixtec area running continuously from A.D. 692(?) to 1642. The colonial documents overlap, and we are thus able to carry the record up to modern times in some cases.

A group of revisionist scholars has made the claim to having accomplished a drastic overhaul of Caso's chronology and therefore his interpretations (Troike, 1978), but nothing substantial has been heard of that revision since its initial announcement, so it will be assumed here that the majority of Caso's work is sound and that his interpretations stand substantially as published.

The following is a summary of some of the most interesting information produced by Caso and others from the codices. With it we are able to construct (at times) amazingly detailed historical records for regions that are as yet archaeologically unknown. Our perspective, therefore, is more than that which is given us by the still small archaeological sample. The whole picture is still incomplete, but the basic outlines of historical events comprehend most of the Mixteca. Social structural features contained in great detail in the colonial documents supplement and continue the prehistoric records. Thus, we can infer these same features onto the framework provided by the prehistoric manuscripts and archaeology.

Most of the codices are painted in bright colors on deer or other animal skin sized with a plaster coating. The codices are screen-folds and usually are to be read in a zigzag fashion. Reading is helped by the use of red lines which divide the codices into registers, and one usually reads until a break in the red line is found and then shifts up or down to the next register. Multiple colors are used, and the superficial appearance is like that of our Sunday comics. However, the resemblance ends with the surface stylistic features. Several codices are extremely pleasing in an aesthetic sense and, indeed, Burgoa says that the nobility also used them as room decorations.

Walter Krickeberg said about the codices that "Gods and mythical figures continually intervene in human destiny and the beginning of a genealogy in particular always depicts a 'Prologue in Heaven,' and presents the primal ancestors emerging from the centre of the earth and out of the trees" (1956:277). Burgoa favored the theory that the elite class had come from the northwest and over the mountains. He also mentions two other theories current in the seventeenth century. One story had the Mixtec settlers coming from the west. Another myth was that the Mixtec came from trees on a river bank near the town of Apoala. In the Codex Bodley (Caso, 1960), an extraordinary scene early in the manuscript seems to show the birth of an ancestress of the Tilantongo rulers from the Apoala trees. This origin myth, however, seems only to apply to the aristocracy. Commoners had come from the center of the earth.

All persons shown in the codices are named after their birthdays in the sacred almanac system. Thus the ancestral female shown in the Codex Bodley had the name 1 Death. However, to distinguish among all persons born on the same day, at the age of seven each was given a nickname. Thus, we have the famous conqueror 8 Deer "Tiger Claw" to distinguish between him and later rulers such as 8 Deer "Quetzal Cobweb" and 8 Deer "Fire Serpent."

Each small city-state kept such records, usually in the temple or in the palace buildings. These genealogies constituted the validation of the right to rule, of the patrimony and the rights and privileges that went with the position, and a record of how things went during a reign. Only a few of the presumed many documents have survived to this day, most in European libraries and museums. Fortunately for us, the historical circumstances of the Mixtec were such that at one point most of the records overlapped through the activities of 8 Deer "Tiger Claw."

According to the amalgamated story pieced together by Caso (1966b) 8 Deer was born in A.D. 1011 to the ruler of Tilantongo, whose name was 5 Alligator "Rain-Sun." Tilantongo dominated an area in the northern Mixteca Alta. It is possible that this 5 Alligator may have been involved in the military incursion into the Maya area in the tenth century. A certain 5 Alligator is prominent on the fine orange pottery found at Altar de Sacrificios. However, that invader may also have been another, previous 5 Alligator named in the codices or not a Mixtec at all (D. Kelley, personal communication, 1976). In any case, 5 Alligator "Rain-Sun" was a fairly successful militarist. He died in 1030, leaving the throne to his nineteen-year-old son. It may be that a regent acted for 8 Deer in the first few years of his reign. Relatively soon, however, 8 Deer "Tiger Claw" showed outstanding ability and began to put together a political tribute alliance system which was more than that of the standard Mixtec city-state. He may well have been helped by also inheriting the throne of the most important south coast town, Tututepec. In that case, 8 Deer's story is a little less fabulous and more like that of "self-made" millionaires who actually begin with substantial inheritances.

Be that as it may, 8 Deer, with or without striking advantages, came the closest to establishing a Mixtec empire of any Mixtec ruler in prehistory. He conquered various places and allied himself to others by judicious and multiple marriages. As an example of the latter, 8 Deer is recorded in the Codex Bodley to have married 13 Serpent "Serpent of Flowers" in 1051, 6 Eagle in 1053, 11 Serpent in 1060, and two other women. One of the great events in 8 Deer's life was the incident in which he was requested by the ruler of Tula, 4 Tiger, to capture another ruler. With the help of his half-brother, 8 Deer did as requested in 1045 and drove the captive to Tula. It is not known if this was the "Great Tula" or another place named after it. In any case, 8 Deer was rewarded by having his nose perforated and a jade nose plug inserted, signifying his elevation to the rank of *teuctli* ("lord"). At the age of sixty-two, 8 Deer finally went to war once too often and attacked the town of some of his in-laws, who resisted, took 8 Deer prisoner, and promptly sacrificed him, sending him to join the gods. Still, he was a great man and was buried with proper ceremony eleven days after his death. He is shown in Codex Bodley seated in his mummy bundle in a stone chamber with incense pots smoking around him.

The last few pages of Codex Vienna are lined off in red but not filed in, the last entry occurring about 1397. This codex's records were cut short by the Aztec conquest of the area. Apparently the codex was taken back to Tenochtitlan as part of the loot.

Many other interesting histories are set down in the codices. For example, there is the story of the formidable woman ruler 6 Monkey, who, having been insulted by two male rulers, promptly conquered and sacrificed them. Yanhuitlan no doubt had such pre-Columbian records, but they have not survived except in colonial transcriptions.

A number of problems remain in the decipherment of the Mixtec pictorial books, one of the most crucial being that of identifying the places named in the codices with archaeological sites or present-day communities. Mary Elizabeth Smith has made great headway on this problem. Another intriguing possibility is that lords of other ethnic groups (Zapotec, Chatino, Mixe, and so on) are mentioned in the Mixtec codices. For example, Caso has identified some Tlaxcalan lords in the Codex Nuttall. Overlap of dynastic records between the Mixtec and Maya has already been mentioned as another possibility. Caso, unfortunately, is no longer with us, but his work goes on.

In the sixteenth century the Spaniards built one of their principal colonial churches at Yanhuitlan; it was a handsome example of a "fortress" church. They also retained much of the old Mixtec social order as an administrative and exploitative apparatus. It was not until the seventeenth century that the system began to break down under the twin assaults of a drastic population loss in turn linked to a severe economic depression. By 1600, population in the valley had been reduced by all causes to about ten thousand, an 80 percent loss. The tribute system sustaining the old nobility could no longer be supported along with that imposed by the Spanish colonial empire. The decline never relented; the surviving members of the Yanhuitlan ruling family sold off the last of their inherited lands in the mid-nineteenth century (Caso, 1966*a*).

The Coast of Oaxaca and the Isthmus of Tehuantepec

At the time of the Spanish Conquest both the coast of Oaxaca and the Isthmus of Tehuantepec were exceedingly complex areas ethnically, linguistically, and culturally. From Brockington's survey of the coast and Wallrath's work in the isthmus it appears that this fractionation may have been the case since at least the end of the Formative period and perhaps before (Brockington, Jorrin, and Long, 1974; Brockington and Long, 1974; Wallrath, 1967).

On the Oaxaca coast, Spores (1965) notes the presence in the sixteenth century of the Mixteca de la Costa, Chatino, Southern Zapotec, Nahuatl, and Chontal (Tequistlateco) groups. Various origin myths, some recorded and others of oral tradition, mention Nahuatl-speakers coming down to the coast from Tula by way of Jalisco. Other traditions bring in Chontal from Tabasco.

Brockington's survey and excavations, especially at Sipolite near Puerto Angel, show a long and complex occupation of the coast from Late Formative times to the present. The Late Formative ceramics there are vaguely similar to those of Monte Alban I and II. A considerable body of stone sculpture may go with this period's development, with the stone stelae showing some resemblances to the material from the nearby south coast of Guatemala. Some small civic centers consisting of platforms grouped around courtyards also were found on the Oaxaca coast. This seems reminiscent of the West Mexican pattern. Long notes that the relatively undisturbed development of coastal ceramics is upset in the Late Classic and Early Postclassic with the appearance of various fine orange, fine gray, and fine black wares linked to the ceramics of the Tabasco Coast across the isthmus. Long suggests that they represent an intrusion of Maya people from that zone. Long also notes the variability of the local sequences from the several sites. In the Late Postclassic period, some sites have Mixtec pottery, indicating Mixtec trade or presence. This correlates with the fact that Tututepec is known from documents to have made repeated attempts to dominate the coast and was in perennial conflict with the Coastal Range Zapotec town of Coatlan. Thus, the shattered nature of the archaeological regions ties in with the documents, the linguistics, and the ethnographic picture in indicating a marginal but complex area that was continually changing hands or being penetrated by new cultural groups.

The Oaxaca coast continues to the east and becomes part of the plains of the Isthmus of Tehuantepec. In the sixteenth century, Huave, Zapotec, Mixe, Zoque, and Nahuatl groups inhabited the Pacific side of the isthmus. The only major archaeological work there so far has been done by Matthew Wallrath (1967), who established a sequence which runs from 850 B.C. to the present. The earliest known settlements were centered on the lagoons and are approximately contemporary with Chiapa II (Dili) at Chiapa de Corzo. However, as with most of the rest of the sequence, the ceramics show remarkable regionality and do not closely relate to any other known cultural area. Platform building did not begin there until about 100 B.C., appearing in small sites. Presumably we have a long period of village-centered society with small civic architecture through most of the sequence. The four known major Mixteca-Puebla horizon sites include the Guiengola fortress, which has already been discussed in connection with the Zapotec. Again, reconstruction with the data at hand shows us a marginal area that was largely out of the major cultural-historical action for most of the time and was pushed around by events beyond its control in the Late Postclassic period.

The Mixteca-Puebla Style Horizon

"One of the most noteworthy things in their market was the pottery, of a thousand different designs and colors" (López de Gómara, 1964:131). Thus López de Gómara describes Cholula's famed polychrome ceramics, which were distributed throughout central Mexico through a trade and religious network. This style seems to have evolved principally in the Cholula (Puebla) area beginning at least by A.D. 900, but it also seems to have absorbed influences from, and exerted influence on, Mixteca pottery styles. The final result was the broadly connected set of similar style groups spread over Mesoamerica at the time of Spanish contact. Regional variants of the ceramic expression of the style include the Mixtec polychrome of Monte Alban V, Isla de Sacrificios V polychrome, Cholulteca III "policroma firme," and, in the Basin of Mexico, Chalco polychrome pottery. The Borgia group of codices are included in the style by Nicholson (1960), who argues that the Codex Borgia itself was painted in Cholula. Anawalt (1981) has demonstrated that three of the Borgia group of codices come from the Puebla zone. This cluster of three manuscripts is mainly ritual and calendrical in content. In it the gods are depicted, mythological events transpire, and the mysteries of the sacred almanac and yearly calendar are laid out. The Mitla palace murals show strong affinities to the ceramic and codical styles, as do the Tizatlan mural from Tlaxcala and the Santa Rita murals from Belize.

Nicholson has given the concept a definition which expresses Vaillant's original idea. The style is extraordinarily precise in delineation of motifs. Numerous vivid colors are used and are symbolic themselves. Highly characteristic symbols include solar and lunar disks, water, fire, hearts, war symbols, the twenty *tonalpohualli* signs, serpents, jaguars, deer, and many others. The style is distributed from the Huasteca to the Maya Lowlands and possibly even into Central America.

Cholula's position as an exceedingly important pilgrimage center during the Late Postclassic period would alone account for wide distribution.

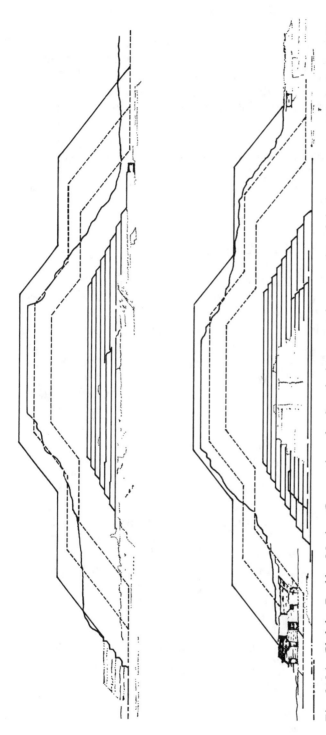

Fig. 8-16. Cholula, Puebla, Mexico. Cross-sections showing the incremental construction of the immense pyramid-platform of this pilgrimage city.

Fig. 8–17. View of an earlier, probably Epi-Classic platform at Cholula and the later, sixteenth-century (Late Postclassic) structure which today supports a colonial Spanish church.

Cholula was the center for the worship of Quetzalcoatl (Figs. 8–16, 8–17). Robertson, as noted before, has characterized the mural style expressed at Santa Rita as a sort of international style of the Late Postclassic period, and it is indeed, being a local variant of the Mixteca-Puebla horizon. The distribution is also a fairly good indicator of the efficiency and vigor of the late prehistoric Mesoamerican trade network along which passed many things not so distinctive as Mixteca-Puebla pottery. The style has no connection with any single ethnic or linguistic group.

Evolution of pottery which seems ancestral to the style at Cholula can be detected near the end of the Late Classic. However, the period of the spread of the developed style outside its heartland of southern Puebla and the northern Mixteca was probably between A.D. 1400 and 1520. Most centers outside the main area acquired the style either as trade wares or as a localized variant and can be dated thereby.

Postclassic and Protohistoric Veracruz

The great Gulf Coast plain of Veracruz was inhabited by at least four major ethnic-linguistic groups at the time of the Spanish Conquest: historic Olmec (their name meaning "rubber people"), Totonac, Huastec, and Nahua groups. We have already seen the difficulties of attempting to equate archaeological cultures with such groups. However, if there is one grand trend in such matters in this area, it is that during the Postclassic, Totonac, Huastec, Uixtotin, and historic Olmec found themselves being compressed into ever smaller territories by expansion of Nahua groups from the highlands. Caution is therefore necessary in dealing with claims of ethnicity projected back through five hundred to fifteen hundred years. Within all coastal areas there was great variability, and multiethnic and multilingual towns are mentioned in historical documents as well as being reported ethnographically.

Withal, this cultural variability can be organized by means of the two major horizons within the area. The first of these horizons is that of the Toltec; it falls between A.D. 1200 and 1450 and is physically marked by the appearance of plumbate ware and the later styles of fine orange pottery as trade wares. The later horizon is that of the Culhua-Mexica (Aztec) empire, beginning about 1450 with the first conquests of the Triple Alliance and extending up to 1519, the date of arrival of Cortés at Cempoala on the central coast. The latest horizon is an areal variant of the Mixteca-Puebla horizon.

Southern Veracruz

Little is known from the historic Olmec area except from documents and ceramics. Needless to say, these Early and Late Postclassic peoples had no necessary connection with the "Olmec" of Early Formative times. Their territory occupied the northern entrance to the trade route across the Isthmus of Tehuantepec.

Early Postclassic pottery found at Tres Zapotes is highly regionalized as the Soncautla complex. This pottery is different in almost every respect from anything earlier at the site and includes large, hollow human effigy figures. The pottery is related to other Early Postclassic pottery found at Isla de Sacrificios. However, the fine orange and plumbate horizon markers are not found. Cremation burial appeared as a new means of disposal of the dead. Taken all together, discontinuity of the ceramic tradition, cremation burials, stylistic linkages of the large clay figures, and other traits suggest that this is possibly the time that the historically known Nahua-speakers moved into the area. Very little is known of architecture or communities of the period, but apparently population was fairly dense, judging by the high frequency of Early Postclassic remains.

To the east, in the Chontalpa Plain of Tabasco, Sanders (1963) excavated a small site named Sigero which may be typical of this period for both areas. The site is a small ceremonial center oriented around a central plaza. A main temple is located on the north edge of the plaza, a residential structure on the west, and a ball court to the east. Small house mounds are scattered over the surrounding countryside and probably represent the population served by the center. There is little evidence of larger centers, and the settlement pattern greatly reminds Sanders of the modern pattern of the area.

The Late Postclassic period is marked by pottery styles related to the general Mixteca-Puebla groups of pottery, associated in this area with Aztec trade and conquest. Brilliant polychromes show up in some zones of the south, but black-on-orange pottery like that of the Basin of Mexico is unknown. Settlement patterns and population sizes were probably the same as for the preceding period. Anawalt (1981) has identified two of the Borgia group of codices, the Codex Fejervary–Mayer and the Codex Laud, as being from central eastern Veracruz. Both are ritual-ceremonial guides. It is not presently known from which centers they may have come.

Sixteenth-century documents indicate a high population of 150,000 to 200,000. Aztec control of the area was typically exercised through native leaders, tax collectors, and garrisons. However, there was no overall Aztec control of the Chontalpa and southern Veracruz. At least one "province" (Coatzalcoalcos) was semiindependent, although it paid tribute to Tenochtitlan. In other words, the political situation matched the linguistic and political fragmentation. The economically important zone furnished rubber, cacao, cotton, and medicinal herbs to the surrounding area and to the central plateau. The people were famous as multilingual traders; Malinche, Cortés's translator, came from this zone. Southern Veracruz and the Chontalpa rapidly became depopulated during the epidemics that followed the Spanish Conquest.

Central Veracruz: Early and Middle Postclassic Centers

The late architectural tradition developed at Tajin was carried on in a transformed version in the Middle Postclassic period (A.D. 1250 to 1450) of central Veracruz, according to José García Payón. This continuity is demonstrated in features such as jutting cornices, columns, friezes with high-relief frets, and communication tunnels. During this period, the Toltec possibly established themselves in the area. Alfonso Medellín-Zenil (1960) and García Payón (1971) attribute the well-preserved pyramid temple at Teayo to the Toltec and say that it was built in A.D. 815, though both the date and ethnic identification seem dubious on the basis of the evidence. From Felipe Solís's recent study (1981) it is fairly clear that Teayo overlaps largely with Aztec sculpture, especially the new body of material from the Great Temple in Mexico City. Moreover, it is clear that Teayo's temple was built in the style of central plateau architecture.

Elsewhere, at the Tuzapan fortress, ceramics are quite close to Toltec-affiliated Mayapan red-and-orange pottery. Other Tuzapan pottery is related to plateau ceramic groups such as Coyotlatelco and Culhuacan black-on-orange wares. Much of this alien pottery is associated with fortified centers. Although there is some doubt about the Toltec identification of Teayo and Tuzapan occupations, then, there is little doubt that central plateau peoples were involved, probably militarily.

During the Early Postclassic period several regional and native styles of pottery were developed, including a particularly lively type of polychrome called Tres Picos I, which was decorated with dancing coyotes and monkeys. The Isla de Sacrificios site off the central coast apparently assumed its function as a sacred burial ground during this period, and a particular tradition of polychrome ware types found there is named after the site (Isla de Sacrificios I, II, III, and IV).

The intrusion of central plateau pottery and formal architectural styles into the sequences of the Veracruz plain may reflect the beginning of the intrusion of peoples from the overpopulated highlands. This trend certainly is historically known for the next period, when it intensified.

The Late Postclassic period in central Veracruz, which began about A.D. 1400, represents the certain emergence of the land of the Totonacs, or El Totonacapan. Major centers of Totonacapan included Quauhtochco, which was conquered by the Aztec between A.D. 1450 and 1472. The site, located in the Orizaba-Cordoba district, has been excavated. Although the ecological setting is semiarid, the site is on a river, as are all of the other major sites of the zone. Although Quauhtochco was founded in Late Formative times, the major period was clearly the latest, when it was under the domination of the Aztec empire. The major temple of the center is much like those found in the Basin of Mexico. For example, the panels on the upper facades of the temple itself are studded with "nailhead" stones, which probably represent stars. Many of the associated ceramics are related to the Aztec III black-on-orange wares and the "lacquer-finish" polychromes of Cholula. It is interesting that the Mixteca-Puebla polychromes at Quauhtochco were made from local clays. Large braziers of coarse, heavy ceramic material served as temple incense burners. Gods represented in the associated clay figurines include many central plateau deities, according to Medellín-Zenil.

Another fifteenth-century center in the same district is the fortress-cemetery of Comapan, built high on an escarpment. The fortifications, like those of Tepexi el Viejo in the Mixteca-Puebla area, consist of high, stone-revetted terraces and free-standing walls. The site includes temples, residential palaces, tombs, shrines, and other architectonic complexities. Unfortunately, it has never been adequately explored or mapped. Historical documents indicate that the fortress goes back to the fourteenth century and that it was occupied by the historic Olmec. Mixteca-Puebla polychrome pottery also occurs at Comapan.

Siemens (personal communication, 1985) has found firm evidence in Central Veracruz for late, intensive, wetland gardening similar to that of the Maya Lowlands in earlier periods.

Cempoala and Quiahuiztlan

The most densely inhabited regions of Totonacapan were dry and warm zones along major rivers which were used as irrigation sources. I. T. Kelly and A. Palerm (1952) have estimated that about 250,000 people lived in the province of Cempoala alone, with between 80,000 and 120,000 in the city. Cempoala was near the coast; the center of Jalapa, further inland, is estimated also to have had about 120,000 persons. Some smaller centers had respectable populations: Colipa had 24,000 and Papantla, 60,000. Although these estimates seem very high, we need more archaeological work before they can be modified.

Based on these density estimates, the descriptions left us by the Spaniards, and the archaeological remains, there is no doubt that Cempoala was a true urban center. The city lies in the bend of the Río Grande de Actopan, which has an interlaced network of wandering channels at this point. Highly productive irrigation agriculture supported the large populations. The site is laid out on the flat flood plain and arranged in at least nine major precincts. These zones are paved areas surrounded by walls which served for both defense and flood control. High platforms elevated the main structures above flood level.

The major group at Cempoala includes five separate temples arranged about three sides of an enclosed courtyard of substantial size. This courtyard was the scene of the crucial battle between Cortés's and Narváez's troops during the Conquest of Mexico. Dance platforms are located in fronts of some of the temples. A round temple base indicates the presence of a structure dedicated to Quetzalcoatl-Ehecatl. At least ten T-shaped tombs are known from the main group. There is a total area of 120,000 square meters (1,292,000 square feet) covered by the formal architecture at Cempoala, with much more represented by domestic housing. It is known that a water system furnished fresh water to each house.

Ceramics associated with the latest period at Cempoala are closely related to late Cholula (Mixteca-Puebla) pottery, and still other types continue the regional Isla de Sacrificios ceramic tradition.

Cempoala was the first major Mesoamerican city to be seen by the Spaniards. Cortes's expedition went there at the invitation of the Totonac leaders and was warmly received by a ruler whom they affectionately called "the Fat Cacique."

Quiahuiztlan, a smaller contemporary site, is located a short march away from Cempoala. Several major temples dominate the fortress center there. Its defense consists of location on a ridge which has been modified by high terrace walls. Quiahuiztlan also contains at least a dozen special cemeteries, which consist of small mausoleums in the form of miniature temples. Secondary burials are found in chambers in the base platforms, and small conduits often lead up to the temple-shrine above. Presumably we have here something paralleling the Maya practice of making sure that the distinguished dead were kept apprised of the latest events and could be appealed to for supernatural aid. At any rate, only the important dead were buried in these small buildings along with their funerary offerings of ceramics and jewelry. Medellín-Zenil (1960) says that animal sculptures are frequently found by the sides of the mausoleums and suggests that these represent the *tonales* ("animal-souls") of the individuals buried inside. This belief in animals souls (*tonal*ism) is ethnographically wide-spread in Mesoamerica, and presumably these cemeteries represent an origin of the belief in the archaeological past.

It was at Quiahuiztlan that Cortés first met representatives of the Aztec empire. These were some very haughty tax-collectors (*calpixques*), who demanded that the Spaniards be refused hospitality. Cortés arranged for their arrest, thereby initiating his first assault on the Aztec political system.

The Huasteca

The vast Huastec area is one of extreme ecological complexity, even for Mesoamerica, and is united only loosely by certain cultural traits and by language. The Huasteca lies in northern Veracruz and southern Tamaulipas and includes both very mountainous and flood-plain topography. The Huastec speak a form of Maya which may have split from the rest of Maya languages about 1500 B.C., according to lexicostatistics. However, aside from the linguistic affiliation, the Huastec followed their own cultural trajectory, which seems closer to that of the rest of Mexico than to their Maya relatives'. One further handicap in understanding the Huastec area is that it is poorly known, and the sample of data from it varies wildly in quality.

The earliest cultural development in the Huasteca has already been discussed in chapter 2, on the development of sedentary life and the domestication of plants. The Tamaulipas caves and villages excavated by MacNeish also have yielded a series of phases which continue from when we left them, 1500 B.C., to about A.D. 1520 (MacNeish, 1971), as shown in Table 8–1.

Population growth accompanied by increasing food production based on domesticated plants provides the archaeological framework for this area from Middle Formative times onward. The area also shows remarkable stabilization of cultural complexity at the village level. In other words, cultural development in the Huasteca was somehow arrested at the Late Formative level for most of its history. The major perturbations are in the direction of deevolution.

In more detail, the Mesa de Guaje phase represents a village-oriented society in which agricultural stability has been achieved, with about 40 percent of the food produced by cultivated plants. The following La

Table 8.1.   Chronological Chart for the Huasteca, 1400 B.C. to A.D. 1750.

Time	Sierra de Tamaulipas	Southwest Sierra Madre
1750	Los Angeles	San Antonio
1300		
		San Lorenzo
900		
	La Salta	
500		
		Palmillas
A.D. 1	Eslabones	
B.C. 1	Laguna	La Florida
500		
		Mesa de Guaje
1400		
		Guerra

SOURCE: MacNeish, 1958

Florida phase shows about the same proportions of wild to domesticated plant foods, but the numbers of communities and their nature changed significantly. MacNeish says that temple-oriented village groups are the normal pattern in that phase. During the Palmillas phase, shortly after A.D. 1, the numbers of villages and people increased further, and a maximum population was reached in the mountains of the Huasteca. Up to fourteen hundred house platforms, each presumably representing a household, have been found there around a single temple. The villages reach their most complex development with the addition of ball courts and possible water storage facilities.

At this time (about A.D. 500) the area reached a degree of complexity equal to that used by other Mesoamerican peoples to launch themselves into the quantum jump to civilization. However, that jump did not happen here, and the period after about A.D. 500 represents a drastic simplification of material culture and of the incipient civic centers. The villages of this time mainly lack the civic centers of the preceding period. The final period from A.D. 1300 to 1750 seems to represent a stabilized version of this impoverished culture and was the situation encountered by the Spaniards during their incursions into the zone during the colonial period.

South and Western Huasteca

To the south and west of the Huastec area in which MacNeish has worked there were more sophisticated developments (MacNeish, 1971). These sites lie in what are now the states of San Luis Potosí, Hidalgo, and Querétaro. The area is thinly known, and the sample is poor in quality.

Ceramics show that the area was occupied by at least the end of the

Late Formative period. Some Teotihuacan contact is indicated by certain forms of pottery. Presumably this part of the Huasteca was exploited by or was a trade area for the Teotihuacanos. Presumably also, the area had gone through much of the same cultural evolution as that which we have seen for the area to the east and north in Tamaulipas. However, it did not stabilize at the same level. By about A.D. 500, a number of ceremonial centers, large and small, had developed. The pattern of site hierarchy is similar to that of the Etzatlan region in West Mexico.

Tamuin, located on a river in San Luis Potosí, is one of the largest of the sites of the Late Classic and Early Postclassic period in the Huasteca. Presumably the center was founded in the Formative period, but the period best known at the site is the Toltec horizon. The site occupies about 17 hectares (42 acres) and has dozens of mounds, but no satisfactory map of it has ever been published. The largest platforms are arranged around the inevitable open courtyards. Excavations have been concentrated around the south platform, which seems to have supported a number of perishable buildings.

One small temple platform at Tamuin produced an interesting mural painted in dark red on a stucco-covered altar. Associated pottery dates the mural to the ninth century A.D. Eleven resplendent personages appear in a line, all facing in the same direction. In this arrangement and theme the painting is similar to the carved Toltec altars noted before at Tula and Toltec Chichen. Five persons are seated, and six stand. All hold diverse and ornamented items which appear to be fans, spear-throwers, and symbols of rank. One individual holds what seems to be a human head by the hair.

A small, nearby structure produced a magnificent piece of sculpture, the so-called Huastec Boy. The appealing naturalism of the piece is strongly modified by intricate low reliefs on various parts of the body, probably indicating tattoos. A child clings to the "boy's" lower back. The "tattoos" are stylistically related to the paintings. Other sculptures from the Huasteca seem to represent life images of a person on one side and a death image on the other.

Tombs were found on both sides of the main staircase of the south platform, all with men and women buried in the fetal position. Only the south line of tombs had offerings, including brand-new vases apparently acquired or made for the occasion.

The Aztec did a great deal of trading with the Huastec in Late Postclassic times. Distinctive pottery then being made in the area features intricate black-on-white designs painted on various forms of jars and vases. Some of the pieces are effigy vessels, and many have pouring spouts and strap handles.

Other large centers such as Tancanhuitz, Tantoc, and Tamposoque are similar to Tamuin but much less known.

The Gulf Coast section of the Huasteca had a long ceramic sequence running back into the Early Formative period. This tropical area is roughly centered about Tuxpan and Tampico. One site is better known than others in the area: La Florida. Only one structure there was dug by Ekholm, principally because most of the site had already been destroyed. The clay platform and perishable, wooden-roofed temple atop it were both round. The latest construction phase dates to the fifteenth century, probably about the time that the Aztec under Motecuhzoma I conquered the zone (A.D. 1460–61).

Ethnohistorical documents state that the Huastec, like the Totonac, had once occupied much more territory than they held in the sixteenth century. It seems clear that a principal reason for this territorial contraction was the fact that Nahua groups, including the later Aztec, had pressed the Huastec northward.

The Valley of Toluca

Although the Valley of Toluca is an attractive place ecologically, the Matlazinca who occupied it during at least the Late Postclassic period were in a truly unenviable position. To the west were located the formidable Tarascan, while the predatory and militaristic Aztec were just over the mountain range to the east.

At the time of the Spanish Conquest, a principal Matlazinca city was Tecaxic, located near Calixtlahuaca. The early historian Ixtlilxóchitl mentions that the Matlazinca were conquered by the Toltec and forced by them to pay tribute. According to several chronicles, the Matlazinca later underwent great difficulties in dealing with their more powerful neighbors during the fifteenth century. Lack of political unity led to disorganization in the face of Aztec aggression during the reign of Axayacatl. A series of wars begun in 1473 led to eventual Aztec domination of the central valley of Toluca and later, in 1476, Malinalco. Tizoc, Axayacatl's successor, had trouble with the Matlazinca and destroyed Tecaxic's temples during his punitive campaign. Tecaxic also made the error in 1510 of rebelling against Motecuhzoma II, who abolished the town. Nearby Calixtlahuaca, which had been favored by the Aztec, assumed Tecaxic's place in the tribute lists.

Having inherited the tributaries in the Toluca Valley, Ahuitzotl, the ruling Aztec emperor, had construction begun in 1501 on the House of the Eagle and Tiger Knights that perched high on its cliff above Malinalco.

The Archaeological Record: Calixtlahuaca and Malinalco

Calixtlahuaca is located on the steep hill called Tenismo, which was anciently terraced. Middle Formative material has been found in the Toluca Valley, but not at Calixtlahuaca. Excavations at the site in the 1930s established a ceramic sequence running from Teotihuacan times to the Aztec conquest period. The ceramic record is supplemented by both architecture and the chronicle information summarized above.

Seventeen major buildings and complexes are scattered without much apparent plan over the terraced areas. One of these, Structure 3, has a round plan and went through four stages of construction. The first stage dates from the period of Teotihuacan, although the building shows no apparent relationship to the architecture of that greater city. The final stage is the platform on which the temple to Quetzalcoatl-Ehecatl, the wind god, was located (Fig. 8–18). Presumably this temple was one of those destroyed by Axayacatl or Motecuhzoma II. A well-done sculptured figure of a man equipped with not much more than the wind god's face mask was found in the ruins of this temple. Structure 17 is actually a complex of many rooms which may have been a true palace structure. It includes many small "patios, living rooms, small shrines, and passageways at different levels" (Marquina, 1964:232).

Malinalco is located in a small valley just to the south of the main Toluca Valley. It is a zone of extraordinary fractured cliffs hung with greenery. High on one of these cliffs, seven hundred feet above the valley

Fig. 8–18. A late temple platform at Calixtlahuaca, the central Mexican capital of a regional state eventually conquered by the Aztecs.

Fig. 8–19. The cult temple of the Eagle and Tiger Knights, elite groups in the Aztec army, at Malinalco, Edo. de Mexico, Mexico. Carved from the rock cliff and embellished inside with eagles and jaguars, this complex of temples was built at a spectacular location.

floor, a complex called the House of the Eagle and Tiger Knights was built on a shelf cut from the rock (Fig. 8–19). Most extraordinarily, major portions of the complex's buildings are themselves cut from the cliff rock in an architectonic concept which is essentially that of a gigantic sculpture. The shelf was cut around a corner, leaving an L-shaped space, and the rock forms the lower parts of the temples, which were roofed with elaborate perishable materials. Channels cut into the cliff rock lead rainwater away from the buildings.

Three of the temples are round in plan. Structure I contains a bench upon which are carved eagles and an ocelot pelt; the building was evidently dedicated to the sun god in spite of the round plan. In Structure III, the front of which is built of masonry, were found the remains of a large mural. The fragments show a line of warriors advancing to the attack with their shields and spears at the ready. The theme harks back to Tula at least, but the style is definitely Aztec.

The present town of Malinalco somehow preserved a magnificent carved wooden drum until the beginning of this century. It is now in the National Museum. Presumably it comes from the temple zone above, but in any case it is appropriately carved with eagles, dancing ocelots, and solar signs.

Malinalco is only one of dozens of shrines and pilgrimage temples which once were scattered throughout Mesoamerica. Some, such as the great temple of Quetzalcoatl at Cholula, drew pilgrims from far and wide. Some, like Malinalco, were dedicated to special activities and are somewhat analogous to the ritual buildings of such organizations as the Masonic order among us today. Still other temples probably were dedicated to gods of only local interest. For example, there is a small Late Postclassic temple located above the present, anthropologically famous town of Tepoztlan. The temple is dedicated to the god of intoxication and pulque, Ome Tochtli (2 Rabbit). The building is known today as the Temple of Tepozteco, and its pilgrims are tourists.

Tepexi el Viejo: A Late Fortress Site

The Tepexi el Viejo fortress is located in southern Puebla near the Mixteca Baja. We will spend perhaps more space on it than seems warranted, but it represents one of the few small states about which we have both archaeological and documentary information, thanks to the work of Shirley Gorenstein (1973). In the vicissitudes of Tepexi we may see mirrored something of the typical dilemmas and resolutions of this type of traditional Mesoamerican community.

Tepexi ("Rocky Place") is mentioned in chronicles as being part of a kingdom of southern Puebla ruled by the city of Quauhtinchan until that place was conquered by Tlatelolco (Tenochtitlan's twin city) in A.D. 1438. Tlatelolco made marriage alliances with various towns of southern Puebla, and one of those was a linkage with the ruling family of Tepexi. In the meantime, Tepexi pursued its traditional rivalries with other small city-states to the south and north, fighting with them over tributaries. The city apparently remained more or less independent until 1503, when the Mexica-Aztec conquered the place and made it tributary to one of their regional garrison points, Tepeaca, located 70 kilometers (43 miles) to the north. The fortress remained in this network of the Aztec tribute system until 1520, when it was conquered by Cortés. Soon after this final disaster, the remaining population was congregated at a village site which replaced Tepexi el Viejo as the regional capital—the town of Tepexi de Rodríguez, also known as Tepexi de la Seda. The latter named comes from the fact that a strong silk (*seda*) industry was introduced by the Spaniards in the early colonial period, as was done in the Mixteca Alta. The silk industry in both areas was successful for a while and then failed because of the population losses during the late-sixteenth-century plagues and the competition of Chinese silk in the European markets.

The Archaeological Record

Tepexi fortress is located atop a steep ridge which is defined by three deep canyons. One canyon is the bed of the Xamilpan River, and most of the cultivable land around Tepexi is located there. *Lamabordo,* a terrace-check dam system for soil conservation, was used on the steep hillsides.

The fortress itself is only the main precinct among five associated hilltop groups of formal architecture. The flattened top of the ridge was retained and expanded by the use of massive outer walls which were as high as 15 meters (50 feet). Formal gates and what may have been guard houses on the walls complete the inventory of fortifications. The height of the walls and the fact that they were plastered were the major functional features of military construction at Tepexi.

Construction methods for the walls and other buildings were of the same nature. A mass of adobe mortar was combined with blocks of caliche. Shaped caliche blocks faced the walls, being laid in the same mortar, and were finished off with a thin plaster. Plazas, pyramidal platforms, and building complexes occupied the space inside the walls. The building complexes are agglomerations of rooms of the sort we have seen repeatedly and which were probably elite-class housing. No burials have been recovered, because most of the tombs were looted in 1949. Counting all of the roofed-over space, Gorenstein estimates that the 62,000 square meters (667,000 square feet) could have accommodated between six thousand and twelve thousand people. In a 1565 census, Tepexi is listed as having ten thousand to eleven thousand people, lending weight to this estimate.

The ceramic sequence at Tepexi runs from A.D. 1300 to 1520, thereby falling entirely within the Late Postclassic period. Ceramics for all three phases indicate heavy reliance on local manufacture for domestic pottery but strong contacts with outside areas for fine pottery. Especially important are Mixteca-Puebla regional polychromes from the Mixteca and Cholula as well as black-on-orange pottery from the Basin of Mexico. Ceramic linkages with Veracruz are confirmed by documentary evidence for two major trails leading from Tepexi to the Veracruz lowlands. One trail connects with Cempoala on the coast, and the other turns southward to the area of the Tuxtlas Mountains.

Gorenstein comments that the tributary system of a small city-state such as Tepexi was decentralized. Although subordinate communities owed economic tribute to the dominant community, they were left more or less alone in their sociopolitical affairs. According to Gorenstein, this decentralization also correlates with the nonspecialized militarism reflected at Tepexi el Viejo. The Aztec had moved beyond the simple economic tribute system and toward control of the sociopolitical affairs of their tributaries. This trend was part of a move to a greater degree of state centralization. In the more traditional characteristics, Tepexi represented a much older and more vulnerable order of society. Both Aztec and Tepexijeño, however, fell before the Spaniards.

The Tehuacan Valley: The Last Phases

The master chronology of the Tehuacan Valley includes a long Postclassic phase called Venta Salada, which runs from A.D. 700 or 800 to A.D. 1520. The Tehuacan project members and Edward Sisson have been able to amass a remarkably detailed amount of data relating to the Tehuacan Valley in the Postclassic period, including details of ordinary life (Sisson, 1973, 1974).

Valley population is estimated by MacNeish (1962:41) to have been between 60,000 and 120,000 just before the Spanish Conquest. This population was supported by intensive agriculture based on a variety of irrigation techniques. The main technique used on the relatively flat valley floor was and is still the canal system. These systems have a dendritic pattern, as seen in Woodbury and Neely's maps (1972), and were usually dependent on springs. Many of the systems have been fossilized by the travertine content of the water. Almost as important were combination terracing and check-dam systems used on hillsides. Large dam building was tried once in the Tilapa River area of Tehuacan but finally given up. The Purron Dam, begun about 700 B.C., with the last phase of the immense structure built about A.D. 300, silted up and was abandoned. Early Postclassic population therefore also abandoned the area. Our own Army Corps of Engineers might do well to study this example.

Of the 456 archaeological sites in the Tehuacan Valley, 357 have Classic and Postclassic remains. Coxcatlan is recorded as one of the principal towns of the area in the sixteenth century and the center of a tributary network. Before the Spanish Conquest it had been a tributary of Teotitlan del Camino in the Mixteca area.

Salt production is mentioned in many colonial documents as being a principal resource of Coxcatlan both then and in pre-Hispanic times. The 1580 production figures are listed as being between 225 and 280 kiloliters (6,400 and 8,000 bushels) per year, some of which was exported to the Basin of Mexico and to mining areas in the north and northwest. No pre-Conquest tribute list notes salt as a tribute item for Coxcatlan, however. Salt was produced by solar evaporation of water from saline wells and by leaching it from mineral-bearing earth. Salt-making sites in the valley are marked by special, coarse pottery salt molds, mounds of earth with pottery tubing probably used for filtering brine, and solar evaporation pans. The pans are still in use in the valley today and are nearly identical to the ancient examples.

Sisson has excavated in the vicinity of many of the small ward temples within Coxcatlan Viejo and other sites. At Coxcatlan Viejo, houses were clustered around what are apparently *calpulli* temple plazas. The remains of looted tombs have been found near the tops of these temples, while dozens of cremation burials in coarse jars and pots are buried in front of them. In one case, ninety-seven cremation burials were found under a plastered apron extending out from the temple base.

The major domestic ceramics of the valley during the Venta Salada period are heavily regionalized. However, Mixteca-Puebla polychromes (Mixtec and Cholulan) and Veracruz ceramics are also found, as at Tepexi el Viejo.

Perhaps the most fascinating part of Sisson's work has been in the common housing areas. These houses were not necessarily mean and humble. One house excavated at the site of San Mateo Tlacuchcalco contained at least 500 square meters (5,400 square feet) and perhaps double that. The pattern is one of several rooms or apartments clustered around an open patio, or even a series of patios. Stucco floors cover the patios, and the interiors of the rooms are plastered. Drains lead rainwater away from open areas. Plastered water storage basins set in floors are nearly identical to those in use in modern Coxcatlan. Several houses have evidence of craft specialties: spinning and weaving and pottery making. One of the few examples of a prehistoric kiln in Mesoamerica was found in a house at Coxcatlan Viejo. An amazing find of a carved greenstone Olmec figure is truly puzzling. No explanation can be readily suggested for the presence of a 2,400-year-old antique being the property of the humble potter in whose house it was found.

Altogether, the housing and artifacts of the Venta Salada period indicate a fairly high standard of living for even common people in the Tehuacan Valley. Sisson makes the point well:

> The patios, open to the sky, must have been the focus for most activities carried out within the residence. Here younger children could play while their mothers chatted and went about their daily activities. Men engaged in certain crafts may have worked on the patio floor. Probably on every clear day, a woman could be found seated on the patio floor weaving, one end of her backstrap loom attached to a circular column of one of the surrounding rooms. In the evening, men returning from the fields or from the hunt would gather in small groups in a neighbor's patio to relax after dinner and to discuss those things which men, and farmers, and hunters always discuss. Finally, each man would return to his wife and children and fall asleep in his family's room located along one side of a patio. Before dawn, the patio would echo with the sound of mano on metate and the patting of masa between bare hands, and the daily cycle would have begun anew. [1974:15]

It was this life-style which ultimately proved the most durable and which still survives today in Mexico, Guatemala, Belize, and El Salvador, the modern political inheritors of ancient Mesoamerica.

CHAPTER 9

THE AZTEC

We welcome you
To this city of Mexico Tenochtitlan
Which is in the great pool of water
Where the eagle sang and the snake hissed!
Where the fishes fly,
Where the blue waters came out to join
the red waters!
—Priests' address to captives of Tepeaca be-
ing led into the city of Mexico, in Durán,
1964:101.

Coming to what all of us saw in this country, a thing that amazed
us was the number of people found here. This was observed by the
Spaniards who came early to this country, before the great plague.
—Durán, 1964:4.

Then Montezuma took Cortés by the hand and told him to look at
his great city and all the other cities that were standing in the water
and the many other towns and the land around the lake. . . . So we
stood looking about us, for that huge and cursed temple stood so high
that from it we could see over every thing very well, and we saw the
three causeways which led into Mexico . . . and we saw the [aqueduct
of] fresh water that comes from Chapultepec, which supplies the city
and we saw the bridges on the three causeways which were built at
certain distances apart . . . and we beheld on the lake a great multi-
tude of canoes, some coming with supplies of food, others returning
loaded with cargoes of merchandise, and we saw that from every house
of that great city and of all the other cities that were built in the
water it was impossible to pass from house to house except by draw-
bridges, which were made of wood, or in canoes; and we saw in those
cities Cues [temples] and oratories like towers and fortresses and all
gleaming white, and it was a wonderful thing to behold!
—Bernál Díaz del Castillo, 1968:218.

THE WONDERFUL capital city of the Aztec is gone. It disappeared in 1521 in the agonizingly brutal Spanish siege of ninety-one days, during which the canals were filled up with the demolished remains of its inhabitants' houses. This was done to open large areas for cavalry operations and fields of fire for artillery. At the end of the siege, the city was a scorched, battered zone with some areas of low, one-story houses left and the fire-marred remains of the larger public buildings. Even these were not allowed to remain, but disappeared rapidly after the Conquest to be used in building the new colonial capital.

The inhabitants of the city were much reduced in number. Many were buried in the ruins of the old city, and the few who remained and the many more Indians from other cities of the valley were impressed into building a new colonial capital. In so doing, they were forced to systematically dismantle the remains of Tenochtitlan. The public buildings of the Aztec not only were unsuitable for the new social structure and administration, but also were looked upon as positively demonic in their associations with the pagan religion. The Spaniards had no interest in preserving any of the ruins, and certainly not the hated remains of the great temple and other buildings where so many of them had died in combat or had been sacrificed to the Aztec deities after capture. Although the city itself is gone, there are two means by which we can reconstruct a picture of the Aztec capital and Aztec culture. One way is through documents written in the early sixteenth century.

First a word about the ethnic and cultural labels which litter this part of the book. The name Aztec collectively denotes the people of the Basin of Mexico in 1519. Many groups made up this culturally diverse area, and each considered itself unique and separate. Chalca, Xochimilca, Tepa-nec, and Acolhua are among the most important of these peoples. Each group was centered on a capital city with its dependent communities. The Mexica (from which comes the name Mexico) are the group most often thought of by the public when the name Aztec is used. Their complete name was Colhua-Mexica, which derived from the city in which they resided for some time, Colhuacan. The Aztec empire refers to the political system built by the Triple Alliance, which was composed of the Mexica (capital at Tenochtitlan), the Acolhua (capital at Texcoco), and the people of the small city of Tlacopan.

The sixteenth century was one of rebuilding of the city of Mexico, but it also was one in which the Church saved and converted thousands of souls daily. At the same time, there were, among these early churchmen, individuals who wished, for various reasons, to record information about the old native culture they were supplanting. One motivation was to be able to avoid the evils of concealed survivals of Aztec religion and its practices. Father Diego Durán wrote two of the best accounts from this motivation with his *History of the Indies of New Spain* (1964, 1967) and *The Book of the Gods and Rites, and The Ancient Calendar* (1971). Bernardino de Sahagún was another scholar-priest who worked at this task of salvage. He produced a series of volumes which are a monumental and invaluable source of reliable information about the Aztec. Nearly as informative as the text are the illustrations that Sahagún commissioned from native artists. Both Sahagún and Durán talked with many Indians who had lived and been important before the Conquest. A crown official, Judge Alonso de Zorita, in his *Life and Labor in Ancient Mexico* (1963), wrote one of the best accounts of Mexican social structure and economics in answer to a government questionnaire. Numerous others wrote documents which preserve the Aztec in both description and illustration. Durán and Sahagún each employed a team of scribes and artists.

The sixteenth-century conquerors also wrote documents, either in self-justification or as memoirs or bureaucratic reports. Cortés's five letters to Charles V (1963) written during the Conquest, Bernal Díaz del Castillo's memoirs (1968) written in his old age, Francisco López de Gómara's *Life of Cortés* (1964), and others are all examples. Paradoxically, then, these men who destroyed and rooted out the civilization of the Aztec also furnish us the means for reconstructing that same culture and give us eyewitness accounts of Tenochtitlan–Mexico City at its height.

Native chronicles are revealing. There are several kinds, including pictorial codices, Nahuatl texts written in Spanish script, and records filed as documents in lawsuits in Spanish courts. Wills, tax records, and bureaucratic reports on native peoples of New Spain all contribute immense amounts of detail and perspective to our picture of the Aztec.

There are frustrations and dead ends in such materials, inasmuch as none of the chroniclers answers all of the questions which we would like answered. For example, none gives an exact figure for the population of the Aztec capital. Possibly the Aztec themselves had no precise idea, although this is unlikely. Possibly the census records perished in the holocaust of the Conquest, and the knowledgeable native scribes and bureaucrats were probably never consulted even if they survived. We are not certain of the exact arrangement of the buildings or even of the number of buildings in the central square of Tenochtitlan. We can come to a fair approximation of an answer to both these questions by comparing the accounts, factoring out error, and weighing the evidence, but in the end we will still be left with a substantial residue of doubt and probable error. This being so, it is well that we have another source of information to which we can turn—archaeology.

Fortunately, the massive Templo Mayor (Great Temple) project of Eduardo Matos Moctezuma has produced enormous amounts of data which are tightly controlled by excellent excavation techniques. This information is supplemented by the subway salvage excavations. The Plaza of the Three Cultures dig gives us still more data, and the general sequence and surveys (cf. Sanders, Parsons, and Santley, 1979) for the Basin of Mexico aids us in reconstructing the ancient city.

Natural Setting

The closed Basin of Mexico before 1519 was physically occupied by a chain of interconnected shallow lakes: three or six, depending on how one splits them up (Map 9–1). The Aztec themselves seem to have spoken mainly of three lakes—Chalco, Texcoco, and Xaltocan, proceeding from south to north. Lake Texcoco was the lowest (deepest), and water flowed to it from the other lakes. The basin is at about 2,200 meters (7,200 feet) above sea level and has an area of about 7,834 square kilometers (3,024 square miles). Of that area about 15 percent was occupied by water. These bodies of water profoundly influenced climate, agricultural systems, population size, and even the social forms developed in the basin.

William Sanders, based on a careful study (1970) and aided by E. E. Calnek, estimates the population of the basin in 1519 to have been between 1 million and 1.2 million. He estimates the population of the city of Tenochtitlan to have been between 122,000 and 200,000, depending on how many tributaries the city called on. The Spaniards have left records indicating that about fifty small city-states existed in the valley in 1519, and Sanders estimates that most of these domains had between 14,000 and 16,000 people. There were also a few large cities besides the Aztec capital. These figures seem well-reasoned, although Sherburne F. Cook and Woodrow Borah (1960) have made higher estimates totaling 2.5 million for the basin.

Whatever demographic estimates one accepts, it is clear that there were substantial numbers of people involved, and the next question is, How were they all fed? This was also a continual question in the minds of the rulers of these vast numbers. The ancient chronicles mention a number of famines brought on by natural disasters—plagues of locusts, droughts, storms, and floods. Between 1450 and 1454 there were particularly bad harvests, and people sold themselves and their children into slavery in order to survive. One answer, then, is that they were not all fed all of the time (Kovar, 1970). Another, as Sanders has pointed out, is that the living standard for many of the lower-class people was even lower than it is for the rural population of central Mexico today. Zorita (1963) mentions the extreme poverty of the lower classes, and Durán (1971) says that one of the tasty feast-day dishes was a bean and corn stew (*etzalli*), which was considered costly enough that not all could afford it. He further says that no people were more capable of eating well at their neighbors' expense and more frugally at their own expense; food, because of its scarcity, was too valuable. Confirmation of this picture of subsistence-level existence for the masses comes from the nearby Tehuacan Valley, in which extensive use was made of cactus (*Opuntia*) fruits and

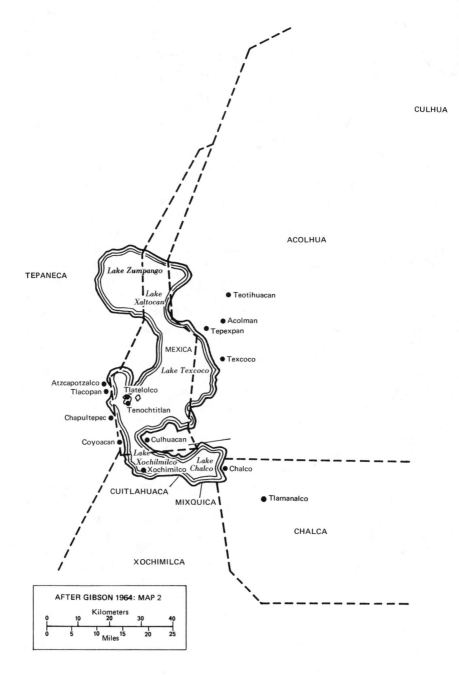

CULHUA

ACOLHUA

TEPANECA

Lake Zumpango

Lake
Xaltocan

● Teotihuacan

● Acolman
● Tepexpan

MEXICA

● Texcoco

Lake Texcoco

Atzcapotzalco ●
Tlacopan ●

Tlatelolco

Tenochtitlan

Chapultepec ●

Coyoacan ●

● Culhuacan

Lake
Xochilmilco
● Xochimilco

Lake
Chalco

● Chalco

CUITLAHUACA

MIXQUICA

● Tlamanalco

CHALCA

XOCHIMILCA

AFTER GIBSON 1964: MAP 2

Kilometers
0   10   20   30   40

0   5   10   15   20   25
Miles

Map 9–1. The Basin of Mexico, showing major cities and ethnic-political divisions in 1519.

grass seeds in the local diet. A Spanish questionnaire of the sixteenth century from the Teotihuacan Valley indicates the same use of wild plant seeds and fruits as staples for poor people. The implication, then, is of a density and level of population which at times exceeded its food supply.

Agriculture and the Chinampas

The Basin of Mexico was one of the most intensely exploited agricultural zones of Mesoamerica. Nearly every agricultural system was used in some ecological zone of the basin. A highland slash-and-burn system was used on the upper slopes of the surrounding mountains. Dry farming was practiced widely. Irrigation systems of both floodwater and canal types were prevalent. Further, the famous *chinampa*, or floating garden, technique was extensively used.

At the time of the entry of the Spaniards into the basin, there were over 10,000 hectares (25,000 acres) of *chinampas* in the southern basin alone (Chalco). The system is one of the most productive and intensive ever devised. Because of studies by Pedro Armillas, Robert West, and Elizabeth Schilling on both archaeological and present-day *chinampa* gardening, we know quite a bit about it (Armillas, 1971; Schilling, 1939; West and Armillas, 1950). Tourists who have floated around Xochimilco on a Sunday afternoon have seen the system in operation although they may not have realized it.

The system is essentially one of land reclamation or swamp drainage, akin, as M. D. Coe (1964) points out, to the drainage of the fens in England or the polders in the Netherlands. These so-called floating gardens never actually floated, but were created by making efficient use of the standing water, rich alluvium, and the marsh grasses and other vegetation in the swamps. Mats of floating water plants growing on the deeper and open ponds in the basin were used to build up the marshy areas for *chinampas*. These mats—long, rectangular strips of vegetation— were towed to suitable sites in the marshes and dragged onto the selected spot for the new *chinampa*. The mats were then anchored by stakes from the native cypress, which took root and eventually became trees, like those which one sees at Xochimilco today (Fig. 9–1). Successive layers of vegetation were dragged into place until the *chinampa* site was raised above water. The sites usually measured about 10 meters by 100 meters (30 feet by 330 feet), and canals were dug on three or four sides of them. They were laid out in a grid pattern which allowed for continual percolation of nutrient-rich water through the entire *chinampa* (Map 9– 2). The next stage of construction was to pile on lake mud from the canal bottom. This mud was periodically renewed and was also rejuvenated by the use of night soil. Special canoe-latrines collected human waste in Tenochtitlan for this purpose. Ditches extended into lakeside land expanded the wetland gardening zone.

Fig. 9–1. Xochimilco, D. F., Mexico. A remnant of an old raised-field (chinampa) *district which still supplies vegetables and flowers to the capital city.* (Courtesy Ford Green)

One of the most efficient aspects of the *chinampa* system was in the use of the farmland thus created. A small section might be set aside in a corner for germination purposes and all crops planted there first. Tomatoes, corn, squashes, and other vegetables would be planted in small squares of mud, and the resultant seedlings would then be transplanted to crop plots elsewhere on the *chinampa*. Thus, germination losses were taken on a relatively small amount of ground, and the transplanted crops were made up of those plants which already had a good start, presumably being the hardiest. The main part of the *chinampa* was devoted to either a variety of truck crops or a main food crop such as corn. Another form of seedbed indeed floated, and it is from these that the legend of the floating gardens no doubt comes. Floating nurseries of reeds, cattails, and other water plants supported the germinating seedlings, which were then towed to the appropriate *chinampa* for transplanting.

Several *chinampas* made up the farmland for one family. This is clear from various maps and documents. The variety of crops indicates that throughout the year there were a number of different foods coming into harvest stage. At Xochimilco, modern *chinamperos* expect about seven crops a year from a plot. Once a crop is harvested, another set of newly germinated plants replaces it in the fertilized soil. In other words, the *chinampa* system allows a year-round productivity of an amazing amount and variety of roots, vegetables, cereals, and fruits. The 10,000 hectares (25,000 acres) of *chinampas* in 1519 in the Chalco zone, Armillas estimates, supported about 100,000 people. However, each family of *chinamperos* did not nearly consume their yearly produce, and over half the crops would be available to feed nonfarming people: the ruling elite, artisans, soldiers, and bureaucrats of the Aztec empire. Sanders (1970:9) estimates that 10,000 hectares would support 180,000 people. In other words, production is estimated at a carrying capacity of 10 to 18 persons per hectare (4 to 7 per acre). J. R. Parsons (1976) has also calculated the similarly sustained population of the Texcoco plain, which brings the total to about 300,000 people living from the produce of swamp reclamation land. Some of the production, however, was of flowers, as at Xochi-

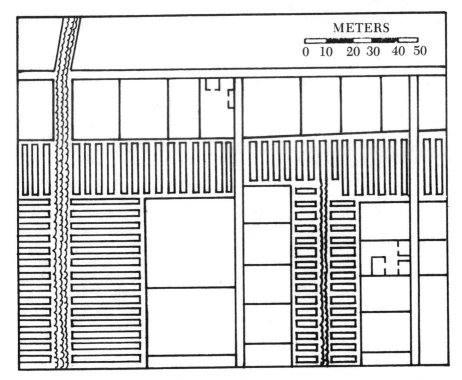

Map 9–2. A section of a central segment of Tenochtitlan which was composed of many raised fields (chinampas) *and house lots.* (After Calnek)

milco today. Durán says that one of the great pleasures of the senses among the Aztec was in smelling flowers: "They find gladness and joy in spending the entire day smelling a little flower or bouquet made of different kinds of flowers; their gifts are accompanied by them; they relieve the tediousness of journeys with flowers" (Durán, 1971:238).

Xochimilco, incidentally, counted among its principal gods two which were associated with the *chinampas* and canals, Amimitl and Atlahua, aspects of the general water god complex (Sahagún, 1970, Book 1:79).

The use of marshes for crops encouraged waterfowl and aquatic animals, both of which were desirable items of the diet. Large numbers of migratory birds used the lakes and were hunted. Vast quantities of fish were taken and were a significant part of the diet. The axolotl, a large salamander (*Ambystoma* spp.), was and is esteemed for its meat in the *chinampa* zones. Sahagún's informants said that they are "good, fine, edible, savory: what one deserves" (Sahagún, 1963, Book 11:64).

The start of the *chinampa* system is possibly in the Preclassic period, dating to the last centuries B.C. Armillas's work (1971) seems to show a sort of a regression in *chinampa* activity from about A.D. 1 to A.D. 1200, and he thinks that this is a result of the rise in the lake level for that period. Such rises are historically known, and if such a rise did occur, it would flood out many of the marshy areas and coalesce the deeper ponds into still larger lakes. About A.D. 1200, however, it is thought that the lake level dropped; and beginning about A.D. 1400, because of the pressures of population, the *chinampa* system was spread into the new marshes under centrally planned guidance. The *chinampa* grids, feeders, and main canals are too well integrated to allow for individual initiative as the prime mover in this expansion.

Small islets dotted the lakes or were created in the marshes by filling cribbing of posts and wickerwork with mud and vegetation. These artificial islands supported households or even communities. Even today, these small sites of Aztec culture can be seen in the form of low mounds as one drives across the flat former lakebed near Chalco. They are locally called *tlateles*. Beginning with some rocky islets, the Aztec built their cities of Tenochtitlan-Tlatelolco in this way.

In the sense that the *chinampa* system uses a drainage technique, it resembles the "drained-field" techniques that are found in the lowlands of the New World, usually in a tropical forest environment. It has been seen that very similar fields are to be found extensively throughout the southern Maya Lowlands. Further, the *chinampa* system seems to have been more widespread in Central Mexico than is generally allowed. Long strips of formerly cultivated fields have been found in Puebla, while the old name of Cuautla in Morelos, Cuautla Amilpas, is suggestive. *Amilpas(n)* means "water-cultivated fields" in Nahuatl, although this term may refer to ditch-irrigated land as well.

The famous "Maguey Map" possibly shows a section of the northwest corner of Tenochtitlan, where a series of household heads are illustrated sitting on their *chinampas*. Calnek (1972) believes that this map belongs to another of the many island "suburbs" in the western embayment. *Chinampas* were definitely part of the main city, in any case, as Calnek demonstrates from legal documents of the colonial period. A striking aspect of this study is that *chinampa* land associated with each household is only enough to produce from 1 to 15 percent of the needs of the estimated population. In other words, the city was heavily dependent on the surrounding *chinampa* and other agricultural areas for support. Indeed, Sanders estimates that from 40,000 to 120,000 of the possible 122,000 to 200,000 population of the city were tributary farmers from outside the city. The core city had a probable nonfarmer population of about 82,000.

The Chalco zone is apparently where the *chinampa* system got its start. The southern basin has fewer killing frosts and is generally better for agriculture because of its greater rainfall. These circumstances would lead to intensification of cropping as population grew. The southern lake was fresh water, and the system requires constant freshwater circulation. Texcoco, the central lake and the location of Tenochtitlan, was more turbulent, deeper, and, most crucial, brackish or saline. A heavy charge of minerals was picked up by the rivers draining into the eastern edge, the deepest section of the lake. The other lakes also overflowed into Texcoco. The ever-accumulating saline waters would usually lie in the eastern, deeper edge of the lake, with the fresh water riding on top. The western edge of the lake was shallow, mostly fresh water, and marshy, a likely spot for *chinampas*. However, before the Aztec arrival in the basin in the thirteenth century, this area had never been extensively used for this purpose, in spite of population pressures, because of periodic floods which drove the saline waters from the eastern side of the lake to the west, penetrating the *chinampas* located there and ruining them for a substantial period until they could be flushed out with fresh water. Even more serious was the inability to control the vast fluctuations in water levels. The western embayment where Tenochtitlan was located was unsuitable for extensive *chinampa* development until these problems were overcome. This was done after the Aztecs rose to power, with the help of the allied city of Texcoco. Civil engineers under the direction of the Texcocan king Nezahualcoyotl built a long dike to close off the western embayment. This effectively controlled most of the flooding problems, but also impeded circulation within the embayment. The aqueduct from Chapultepec, where there were freshwater springs, was built to the center of Tenochtitlan to bring fresh water not only for household use but probably also for the *chinampas*. The chronicles record that it took thirteen years to build the aqueduct and that it was completed in 1466 (Chimalpahin, 1965). A later Aztec emperor undertook to bring still more fresh water from Coyoacan against the advice of the king of Coyoacan. The latter was posthumously vindicated when the flow proved so strong that the Aztec capital suffered severe flooding.

Lake Texcoco was a formidable place, with hot springs, geysers, sudden storms, and other hazards. Some authors mention whirlpools, but this seems to be a figment of Aztec mythology and cosmology. Many of the problems of the Aztec, living on an island in this lake, were hydraulic, and the dikes, aqueducts, canals, causeways, and other developments were all responses to these problems. The *chinampas,* located mainly in the more peaceful southern lake and marshes, provided a great deal of the subsistence base for these later local large-scale efforts at hydraulic engineering. The manpower to carry out such projects and, indeed, the population pressures motivating them were in part fed by the *chinampas.*

Economics, the Market System, and Tribute

The agricultural structure sketched out above may seem complicated and sophisticated, but it was only a part of a vastly more complex system. Distinct ecological zones produced, naturally, distinctive products by different means of cultivation. These products passed into a highly organized marketing system which redistributed them. Agricultural products were also an important part of the tribute system, which was the other major means of redistribution in the area dominated by the Mexica. Although the present-day tourist may be impressed with the diversity and size of the traditional markets of Indian Mexico and Guatemala, they are much simplified remnants of the pre-Hispanic markets.

To begin with, the Valley of Mexico was part of an economically interrelated set of regions which consisted of the surrounding valleys of Morelos to the south, Puebla to the east, the Mezquital to the north, and Toluca to the west. Sanders (1956) calls this the Central Mexican Symbiotic Region. Although many of the food crops produced in any of these areas were the same as those grown elsewhere, each zone had its specialty crops, which it supplied to the others. Thus, in the market of Mexico there were available not only maize, chiles (hot peppers), beans, and tomatoes grown in the valley, but also tropical fruits, cotton, and cacao from the Morelos and Guerrero zones; beans and *chian* from the Puebla area (Atotonilco); and maize and beans from Toluca. Maize surpluses were more common in the far eastern reaches of the Aztec empire, near the Gulf in Veracruz, and they were imported by the state in times of need.

Markets were held religiously (literally and figuratively) at stated periods: usually once each five days—four times each month, according to the native calendar—with daily markets in the larger towns. Every community of any size held markets. These markets, some specialized but all with enormous variety of selection, reflect community craft specialization in the basin as well as imports from outside it. It is known that many small towns, villages, and hamlets combined agriculture with the manufacture of items such as pottery, salt, mats, adobe, and cotton cloth. Slaves were especially to be found at Azcapotzalco and Itzocan, and tasty dogs for eating were sold in the market at Acolman. Durán (1971) reported over four hundred dogs for sale on a slow day and complained of the smell. Craft specialty markets could be found in a number of towns, large and small. Texcoco, across the lake from Tenochtitlan, was noted for cloth, fine gourds, and exquisitely worked ceramics. Cholula, east of the valley, was renowned for jewelry, precious stones, and fine featherwork. The fancier commodities were mainly available through the larger markets.

Bernál Díaz del Castillo says of the market at Tlatelolco, after spending a good deal of ink listing items sold there, "But why do I waste so many words in recounting what they sell in that great market?—for I shall never finish if I tell it all in detail" (1972:197–98). Fortunately for us, he did continue, and he tells us that paper, tobacco, yellow ointments, skins of animals, cooked foods, honey, pottery in a thousand different forms, and all of the other items had special places assigned to them in the marketplace. The Tlatelolco market was open daily.

Tlatelolco itself was a most-favored city within the Aztec domain, since the principal men of the city were long-distance merchants who belonged to a special class. These were the *pochteca*, a group that will be discussed further in considering social organization. The market system was deliberately fostered and protected by the state; no one could transact business outside the market. Order and quality control were kept by special officials, and three judges were in attendance to decide any disputes. Commodities and goods were exchanged in a barter relationship, and there was only a skeletal monetary system based on cloaks, cacao beans, and gold dust. It was fully as rational a system as our own international monetary arrangements. The Valley of Mexico actually was an economic unit before it was politically unified. Another aspect of this unity was that craft guilds in the valley included people from several city-states.

As noted, the tribute system was the other means of redistribution in this nonmonetary economy. It was based on kinship, social, and political units, with the various units assigned specified amounts and kinds of tribute. Zorita mentions maize, chiles, beans, and cotton as tribute. Water, fuel, and domestic service were other forms of tribute. The magnificent Codex Mendoza, named for the first viceroy of New Spain, was made in order that the Spaniards might know how much had been exacted from each community before the Conquest. It was a version of an older Aztec bureaucratic document, which also gave rise to another version, called the *Matrícula de Tributos*.

The tribute was onerous. Sahagún sympathetically cites the dilemma of the commoner overwhelmed by the additional burden of religious tribute in the early colonial period. The amounts and variety of foodstuffs, manufactured items, slaves for sacrifice, raw materials, and other things demanded by the Aztec of their conquered vassals were truly staggering. Based on a study of the quantities of tribute recorded in the Codex Mendoza, it seems that Tenochtitlan received enormous amounts of foodstuffs alone. One year's yields of grains and cereals were approximately as follows: corn, 6,000 metric tons; beans, 4,000 metric tons; *chian*, 4,000 metric tons; and *huauhtli* (amaranth, or "careless weed"), a total of 18,000 metric tons or 19,841 short tons (Barlow, 1949).

Human societies have always regarded some symbolically valuable items as nearly as important as food, or, at times, as life itself. The eagles of Napoleon's regiments and the samurai swords of the Japanese *daimyo* come to mind in this regard. Similarly, the Aztec traded for symbolically valuable items and made considerable efforts to obtain them. A striking example is that even after the Conquest (1575), some 10,000 quetzal feathers were obtained from Alta Verapaz in northern Guatemala. The Codex Mendoza mentions that 3,280 feathers were derived as pre-Hispanic tribute from the same area (Berdan, 1987). Vast quantities of clothing, warrior costumes, honey, jadeite, wood products, and the like were also demanded by the Aztec in pre-Hispanic times.

Physical Plan and Organization of Tenochtitlan-Tlatelolco

Calnek's important study of Tenochtitlan (1972) gives some idea of the physical arrangements of urban life in the city outside the ceremonial precincts. Tenochtitlan shared its artificially created island with Tlatelolco (Map 9–3). The island had been partly built up by *chinampa* construction and by use of small islets and landfill operations around them. However, the main city was only the largest of at least nineteen island communities in the western embayment of Lake Texcoco. As such, it measured at least 14 square kilometers (about 5.4 square miles). All of the other island communities were smaller, and most were agricultural, fishing, and craft-specialist towns. Whereas the interior *chinampa* districts of Tenochtitlan had households that measured about 400 square meters (4,300 square feet) at most, those on the outskirts and presumably of the outer islands averaged about ten times that area. High-density urban buildup was probably largely confined to the main island.

The system of measurement used to lay out the city and to build structures was complex but consistent and practical. An *omitl* ("bone") was equivalent to 0.55 meter (1.8 feet), and a *maitl* ("hand") to 1.65 meters (5.4 feet), or three *omitls* (Aveni, Calnek, and Hartung, 1988).

The heart of Tenochtitlan-Tlatelolco consisted of the two main ceremonial precincts and the large market of Tlatelolco. The precincts were

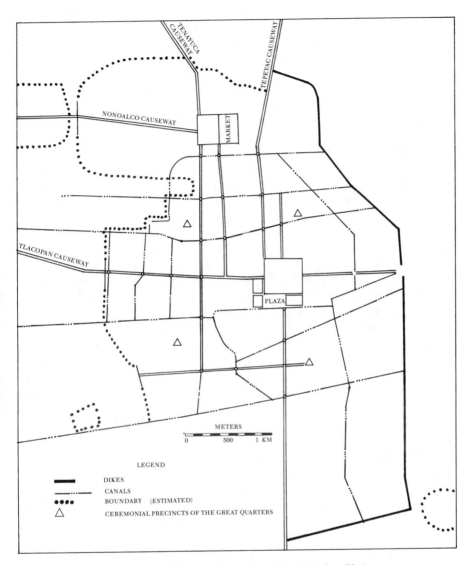

Map 9–3. Major features of Tenochtitlan-Tlatelolco (Mexico City).

actually a series of adjacent plazas around which were arranged the major temples, administrative structures, palaces, and other pieces of monumental architecture. Sahagún lists for Tenochtitlan's center alone some twenty-five pyramid temples, nine attached priests' quarters, seven skull racks, two ball courts, arsenals, shops, and many other features (Marquina, 1960).

The sacred central square of Tenochtitlan formed a secular as well as a religious focus for the Mexica. The recent excavations of Matos Moctezuma (1982) and the studies of Aveni, Calnek, and Hartung (1988) give us considerable information not only on the layout of the precinct but also on the city itself. It appears that Tenochtitlan was planned from the beginning in accordance with certain astronomical principles. These principles were also influenced by certain aspects of the landscape. Finally, the mythical events of the arrival and founding of Tenochtitlan were commemorated by the public architecture.

The planning was carried out as follows. The zero point of city planning was located in front of the Temple of Huitzilopochtli. From this point extended the four major avenues, which ran roughly east-west and north-south (Fig. 9–2). These avenues still exist in the form of the modern streets named Argentina, Seminario, Tacuba, and Guatemala. They divided the city into four great quarters, each apparently marked by four major temples, the sites of which are now marked by major colonial churches. Within the great precinct, the Great Temple (Templo Mayor) was aligned with the rising of the sun at the equinox. There is some problem with determining whether the sun rose over the Temple of Huitzilopochtli, on the south side of the platform, or in the notch between the two temples at the top. The Great Temple is skewed about seven degrees east of true north in order to accommodate such observations. It is also aligned with a notch between Mount Tlaloc and another sacred mountain. Finally, the city layout was also determined by the Aztec system of measurement. Avenues seem to have been laid out at 660-meter (400-*maitl* or 2,160 -foot) intervals, and cross streets were spaced at 220 meters (400 *omitls,* or 720 feet). Walls of the sacred precinct were 220 meters from the zero point noted above. The zero point and the location of the Great Temple were determined in the first place, according to the famous tale of the founding of Tenochtitlan, when a Tenochca priest observed an eagle (the sun) devouring a snake while perched in a nopal cactus. The Great Temple was situated on the calculated spot of the sacred nopal, while other parts of the city were laid out around other, less familiar, events of the myth. The final giant structure was rebuilt and enlarged at least seven times, according to Matos Moctezuma's excavations (1987). The earliest temple dates from about 1428. Continual refurbishment and embellishment means that construction and remodeling also were nearly continuous (Fig. 9–3).

Calnek (1972) shows that the residential areas around the central zones were house-to-house concentrations with no *chinampas.* Farther away from the precincts were the smaller *chinampa*-household plots in which extended families lived. In addition to the gardens, household lots included a low, one-story residence surrounded by a wall which defined a large open space next to the house. Several generations and related families

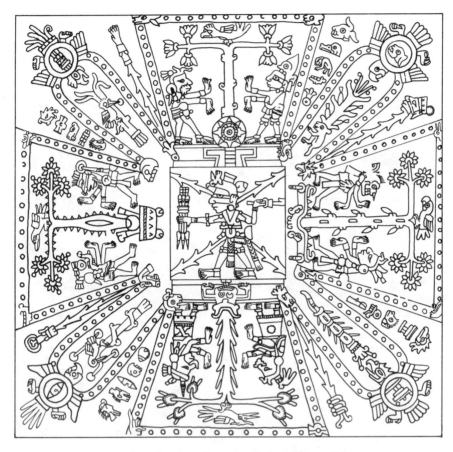

Fig. 9–2. Gods of the five directions from the Codex Fejevary-Mayer.

lived in these buildings, which meant that from ten to thirty people of both sexes and all ages might be found in one household.

Six major canals ran through the city from north to south, with many smaller canals feeding into them. At least two major canals ran east-west through the city. Three major causeway systems connected the city with the mainland and with other island communities, but the best way of getting about was by canoe. Based on several eyewitness sources, it seems that there were tens of thousands of small boats on the lakes, carrying people and supplies. López de Gómara (1964:163–64) mentions two hundred thousand canoes, a figure he may have gotten from Cortés, but this number may be an exaggeration. On the other hand, even in 1580, three thousand to four thousand canoes daily passed Mexicalzingo on their way into Mexico City (Hassig, 1985:62). At any rate, the lakes and

Fig. 9–3. A serpent head, possibly originally from the Great Temple, in a colonial building in downtown Mexico City. (Courtesy Ford Green)

lagoons were an enormous advantage in a land where the alternative to water transport was carrying things on one's back. Hassig (1985:133) calculates that the amount carried by a single canoe with a single man propelling it was about forty times the amount carried by a single porter.

The city was divided into sixty or seventy wards which corresponded to the clans discussed below. Each of these barrios had its own set of communally constructed and maintained buildings, including a temple, a school, and an administrative structure. Judging from this, the numbers of large and formal buildings in Tenochtitlan must have numbered in the hundreds, and the city was probably dotted with smaller plazas around which these ward buildings were grouped.

Across the lake at Texcoco was another, older major city. Nicholson (1987) notes that this city also had a double temple, and one which may have been taller in its last stages than that of Tenochtitlan.

Aztec architecture had flowing lines, and since most of the buildings were only one or two stories, the temples impressively raised their gleaming white bulks above the general mass. The green trees and crops of the *chinampas* lightened the masonry mass of the city, as did the surrounding water of the canals and lake, with the huge causeways stretching into the distance. With the mountain walls and snow-capped volcanoes crowding the horizon in the clear air and the intense blue sky above, it is no wonder that the Spaniards thought themselves marching into an enchanted land like those described in their medieval romances.

Social Organization

Although the *calpulli* (clan) was the basic unit of social organization, and most Mexica belonged to one, apparently not all lineages within the *calpullis* were equal. As noted, the *calpulli* head was elected from a specific lineage. Similarly, noble houses and lineages were ranked in order of prestige. Yopico was a lineage of importance in Tenochtitlan, for example, and seems to have furnished some of the top leadership of the Mexica. Durán (1971) mentions that some of the most prestigious religious duties in the main temple at Tenochtitlan were performed by young men and women who came on an annual basis from six favored wards, which were probably noble houses and not *calpullis*.

There were four principal social categories. At the top were the ruler of the city state and his relatives. These, with the descendants of the preceding rulers, made up the class called the *pipiltin*. Motecuhzoma II (the Aztec ruler at the time of Spanish Conquest) was a member of this class and had been selected as ruler of Tenochtitlan from a specific lineage. There were a great many *pipiltin* by 1519, inasmuch as many of the men had concubines whose children were also considered members of the upper class. Motecuhzoma II had made a great effort to set the elite class apart even more than before. *Pipiltin* boys made up the majority of students at schools called *calmecac*, which also had a certain number of commoner pupils. These schools were directly attached to temples and dedicated to patron gods (Hassig, 1988:34). Instruction in these relatively few schools prepared their inmates for the priesthood (both commoners and nobles) and for careers in the army and politics (nobles only). More intellectual matters were included in the curriculum of the *calmecac* than in that of the *telpochcalli* schools. Besides having a chance at better education, nobles had many other perquisites: polygyny, two-story houses, fancy regalia, and elaborate clothing.

The Calpulli

Although the smallest social group in Aztec society was the nuclear family, a man and wife and their children, it was around the *calpulli* ("big house") that social, political, and religious life revolved for most people. The *calpulli* was the unit that worked the land. Indeed, this communal land management function is still a characteristic of most traditional Indian communities in Mesoamerica today. However, the pre-Hispanic unit was somewhat different. The nature of differences is the subject of one of those scholarly debates which take on the characteristics of a blood feud. There are two main interpretations of the evidence. In what might be called the Zorita school (after its principal source of information), the *calpulli* is looked upon as a more or less autonomous, kinship-oriented, landholding group. In the view of the Carrasco school (after its principal exponent), the *calpulli* was a tribute-paying group linked to a noble house.

Let us first examine the Zorita view. Membership in the *calpulli* was by birth, and generally the *calpulli* was the rural community, or in the city, a ward. Zorita (1963) and Sanders (1965) make the following characterization of this unit. Mexica families who traced their descent through the male line to a common ancestor considered themselves in a lineage. A group of lineages made up a *calpulli,* and the ordinary members married within the *calpulli* (endogamy). One of the lineages traditionally furnished the leader of the *calpulli,* the *calpule* (plural, *calpuleque*). One of the *calpule*'s most important functions was to act as custodian of a set of land maps showing the distribution of the *calpulli* lands. These maps showed the shape of the land and its area, soil qualities, water sources, and other features (Williams, 1980; Williams and Harvey, 1988). The *calpule* was assisted by a council of heads of households. These men enforced the rules of land distribution and redistribution. Landholding by the individual family was only in usufruct, and the amount of land held was enlarged or diminished according to the family's needs. Therefore, as a family added more children, its allotment was increased, and when the children had married and left and the couple was alone, the land allotment was decreased. If the couple was infirm or disabled, or if a man left a widow and orphans, the *calpulli* arranged for the cultivation of the man's land for the benefit of those persons. Social security was thus provided. Other economic functions were served when the men of the *calpulli* worked as a unit on large-scale construction, such as building temples, or maintenance of large-scale irrigation works. Taxes to the associated noble families and to the city-state ruler were paid in labor and produce by the *calpulli*. The *calpule* thus acted as the intermediary for the individual with the state. Traditional crafts were carried on by the *calpulli*. In time of war the *calpulli* went into battle as a unit and was about the size of our modern rifle companies, 200 to 400 men.

According to the Carrasco school (Carrasco, 1976; Hicks, 1982, 1986; Hassig, 1988:29–31) the *calpulli* was a group of commoners attached to a noble house (a *tecpan*). The head of the house controlled its land and distributed the land to the *calpulli* members in return for tribute. The *calpulli* could also be directly attached to a city-state ruler (*tlahtoani*). Again, the *calpulli* was required to render tribute and rotational labor service in order to qualify for the use of land. The internal working of the *calpulli* is regarded as the same in both schools of thought. In the Carrasco viewpoint, the *calpulli* is much more integrated into the aristocratically dominated social structure.

Young men of commoner class (*macehualtin*) were educated in a school called the *telpochcalli*, which was established and maintained by the *calpulli* in a special building. Boys from the traditionally associated noble families also might attend these *calpulli* schools. Instruction emphasized military training. Between 419 and 559 youths were enrolled in each *telpochcalli* in Tenochtitlan in 1519 (Hassig, 1988:31). Each *calpulli* had its patron deity, which was worshiped in a small temple set on a high platform.

From the above it can be seen that the *calpulli* was a fundamental unit of Aztec society. On it all of the larger social organizations—religious, political, economic, and military—were based. These functions are reflected in the architectural assemblage which made up the typical Aztec small community center. All the structures were made of stone and oriented around an open square. The house of the *calpule* was a low, one-story structure with a few rooms and probably a patio. The *calpule* both resided there and used the house as an administrative building. He kept the land maps in his house. Another side of the square was the location of the pyramid-temple, probably with quarters nearby for a resident priest. The young men's school, found on the main square, was both a school and a residence until they married. The building would be found on the main square. The plaza acted as a marketplace if the community were large enough. "The markets in this land were all enclosed by walls and stood either in front of temples to the gods or to one side" (Durán, 1971:275).

A *calpulli* community at Cerro Gordo in the northern basin was explored by Susan Evans (1985), who unfortunately was unable to excavate. In this case, the remains of the community are dispersed over a terraced hillside probably dedicated to maguey cultivation. About 178 mounds were evidently the houses of the *calpulli* members, who numbered an estimated one thousand. Eleven mounds were large enough to be public architecture and probably represent the *calpule*'s house, the young men's school, and other community structures.

The great mass of the population were *macehualtin*, or free men, but as noted above, they were organized on kinship lines into *calpulli*. These free men could move either way in social rank, at least temporarily. Upward mobility was through achievement and service to the state, usually in war, religion, or trade. In this case, the city-state ruler would ennoble the *macehual*, who became a member of a class that the Spaniards called caballeros pardos, "gray knights." The Aztec term was *quauhpipiltin*, or "eagle nobles" (Calnek, 1974:202). These men were nobles with rights and privileges for their lifetimes only; "life peers," in British terminology. They were awarded small private estates with resident labor, serfs. Both land and labor reverted to the state at the death of a gray knight, in contrast to the estates of the *pipiltin*, which were passed on to their descendants. Private ownership of land thus distinguished aristocrat and temporary noble from commoner. It is interesting that the estates of nobles bear a great resemblance to the later haciendas of colonial and republican Mexico. The privilege of building a two-story house was also restricted to the aristocracy.

Zorita mentions that *mayeque* were the serfs working the landed estates of nobility. They were presumably outside the *calpulli* system, being landless peasants with no rights to either usufruct or inherited lands. However, Hicks (1986) suggests that Zorita has confused a rarely used term which was equivalent to that for commoner, *macehualli*. By the sixteenth century nearly all commoners in the Basin of Mexico had been reduced to a state of tribute and labor obligations; *mayeque* to the aristocrats and *macehualtin* to the state.

The bottom of the social scale was occupied by slaves (*tlacotin*), who not only were landless, but who also had lost their individual rights. Enslavement might occur by selling oneself or one's children. This happened not infrequently when famines occurred, families hoping to buy their children survival by this means. Gambling also could lead to slavery, the ultimate wager being one's freedom. Many porters who made the cross-country trips with merchants were slaves. Captives taken in war were occasionally enslaved, but usually they were dedicated to sacrifice and did not last long. Slavery was a reversible status: one could purchase one's freedom, and a slave's children were born free. There were other specified circumstances under which one could regain freedom.

As noted above, one of the distinctions of social ranking was in the disposal of land, private landownership being restricted to certain of the nobility. Much of the rest of the land was held by either individual *calpulli* or their associated noble houses, depending on which view one prefers. However, a significant amount of land was also attached to high public offices, the salaries for which were in the form of produce from this entailed real estate. Other land was set aside for support of temples and schools. Specific towns, devotees of gods, or students from the community schools worked these lands. Some land was also set aside for the defense budget. Especially in conquered communities, the Mexica would thus provide for the support of a resident garrison.

Caso (1963) points out that the so-called military and religious classes of the Aztec did not really exist independently. Instead, one had access to these offices by belonging to a specific lineage or class and also through individual qualifications. Thus, though a man might have qualified through birth to fill an office, he was not necessarily elected or selected for it. There is an inherent tendency toward incompetence in rigidly aristocratic societies if birth is coupled to a right to specific social functions. This can lead to certain dilemmas such as those that occurred in seventeenth-century armies of Europe when military leadership was largely aristocratic. Thus, one was not merely promoted to one's level of incompetence, but was born into it. However, specification of a certain lineage or set of lineages as the social pool from which one draws the candidate for a certain office means that the best man can be chosen. One hopes that the best man will be competent to deal with the job. Different city-states arranged succession differently. With the Mexica, the preference was brother to brother and then down to the sons. Motecuhzoma II was the nephew of the preceding ruler and not the son. Unfortunately, he did not possess the necessary qualities to deal with the unforeseeable event of a Spanish invasion, but he was felt to be the most suitable of the candidates for the leadership of the Aztec state at the time. Cuautemoc, his ultimate successor, might have been more suited by his warlike nature for resisting the Spaniards, especially when they were weakened as they were at various times.

On a lesser level, the possibility of distinction in war or administration left a door open to talent from lower social levels (war was the most important avenue for advancement in the earlier stages of the Aztec empire). In addition, there was the opportunity of trade, and members of the merchant class, the *pochteca*, fitted between aristocrats and plebians. In either case, trade, especially long-distance trade, was a further chance for individual distinction; military intelligence activity was often combined with foreign business dealings, a practice not unknown in our own day. Middle-class occupations also were available in terms of the lower elite specialty jobs in religion, administration, and in certain craft specialties, such as jewelry making. Thus, social mobility was based on personal achievement in the several areas open to distinguished conduct.

To summarize, Mexica society was organized, to a great degree, around the *calpulli* and their associated noble houses. This group had landholding, social security, military, religious, and educational functions. However, this kinship-based unit was only fully in operation in the middle ranks of society. Social strata above and below the *macehualtin* level lacked complete *calpulli* organization, and individuals who had fallen into evil circumstances lost membership. Thus, it was most important to be born a member of a specific aristocratic lineage at the upper levels, in which case one was considered for certain offices and at least had perquisites such as holding private lands. At the lower levels of society it was of little importance to a serf attached to a ruler's estate how adjacent *calpulli* operated. Such a serf had left or been born outside the *calpulli* system and lacked the rights inherent in *calpulli* membership. Slaves, of course, had dropped out of the *calpulli* system but had not forfeited individual rights, although their labor was entailed.

Aztec society seems to have been moving increasingly toward a rigid aristocratic principle, however, especially under the last Motecuhzoma, who made it a crime for a commoner to enter the same waiting room in his palace as nobility. There were other moves toward despotism and the establishment of caste. Each member of the state apparatus had a special dress and badges of rank to set him apart. Warriors were given decorations and different uniforms according to the number of enemies they had captured. The warrior societies called Eagles, Jaguars, and Otomis all had special uniforms and fought as units in time of war. At the same time, there was a rapid expansion in sheer numbers of the *pipiltin* because they were taking large numbers of concubines. These women were often of commoner (*macehualtin*) origin, but their children assumed their father's rank. On the other hand, a *pilli* could not be assured of distinction simply because of birth and might wind up with a very pedestrian administrative job, whereas one of the gray knights could well be placed over him.

Other social categories of people who were at least implicitly recognized were gamblers, thieves, and prostitutes. Gamblers played at the game of *patolli*, a kind of parchesi which invoked numerological symbolism tied up with the sacred calendar. Bets were also placed on the outcomes of ball games played with rubber balls in special courts. Thieves are mentioned as being a certain problem, with a criminal band sometimes terrorizing a household and stripping it of its goods. Prostitutes were at least common enough that those young men who had distinguished themselves in war had the privilege of consorting with them for a short period. Porters, innkeepers, barbers, and beggars fill out the social scene and confirm Tenochtitlan's fully urban status.

Political Organization

In the Basin of Mexico, the ultimate unit of political stability was the city-state. Kingdoms and empires all appeared at various times, but these nearly always were reduced to the city-state, or sometimes were completely destroyed. The fifty city-states in the basin in 1519 were each ruled by a petty king with all the trappings of royalty. A member of the *pipiltin*, he dwelt in a stone palace with a harem, bodyguard, and court ritual. Such a ruler was known as a *tlahtoani*. As was the case with the *calpule*, the *tlahtoani* was supported by cultivation of designated communal lands and also received tribute in the form of labor and services. Being a member of the *pipiltin,* he also had landed estates with serfs, and the production was his to dispose of in support of his household or as reward for services. The small estates reverting to the state by the deaths of the temporary nobles and the acquisition of new lands by war gave him immense power to bind the allegiance of talented men to him. However, religious sanctions also bolstered his position, since most of the *tlatoque*-rulers of the basin claimed descent from the divine Quetzalcoatl through the Toltec. For this reason, Sanders (1965) has argued that the upper classes of the various communities in the basin formed an endogamous caste. One could not marry beneath one's social class. Women of suitable rank were scarce within any community, considering the incest taboo. The common practice was to exchange women among the ruling lineages. These marriages had political implications and remind one of the dynastic marriages of Europe. Nezahualpilli, king of Texcoco, for an example, was married to Motecuhzoma II's sister. Such an alliance did not preclude hostilities. Indeed, Nezahualpilli executed his wife for adulterous conduct, although this act was partly motivated by a desire for revenge on Motecuhzoma, who had betrayed the Texcocan army into an ambush. Compare this system with the circumstances in Europe in 1914 on the eve of World War I; the heads of state of England, Germany, and Russia were then all cousins.

The social and political structure outlined above was the ideal. The reality of the situation depended, as always, on historical circumstance, personality, and the run of fortune. Rules were to be obeyed; they ordered the social universe and, in a sense, reflected the divine order. Larger or smaller units accommodated themselves to special natural circumstances as they did also to the historical circumstances that made them more or less important in the eyes of men. The Aztec had come from very humble beginnings in their rise to domination of the central plateau of Mexico, and the empire was a relatively late political structure built on already existing patterns found when they came into the basin. It seems clear that they followed the historically recorded pattern in building their empire. There had been the Toltec empire of the golden age. There had also been another, greater state earlier, whose name and history had been lost but whose institutions had passed into the tradition of the people of central Mesoamerica—the empire of Teotihuacan. Taking this legacy of organizational tools and concepts, the Aztec developed their own features of governance.

An empire, by simplest definition, is a state that includes, under one administrative umbrella, a diversity of peoples in language and culture. Generally, this means that a vast area is dominated, and thus natural diversity is also characteristic. The empires before that of the Aztec had penetrated northward into the barbarian lands of the Gran Chichimeca, where

Fig. 9–4. *Aztec place-name hieroglyphs from the Stone of Tizoc, which shows the places conquered by that Aztec ruler. The third symbol down in the left-hand column is that of Xochimilco.*

the hunting and gathering peoples of the deserts and mountains lived. Both preceding empires had at least briefly established enclaves of control in the exotic Maya country, both lowlands and highlands. The Toltec and Teotihuacanos had established garrisons and routes of access to far-flung outposts instead of physically controlling all of the intervening country. The Aztec followed this pattern as they expanded outside the central plateau. They eventually ruled over an area of 200,000 square kilometers (77,000 square miles) and a population of from 5 to 6 million people. To govern this vast area there was an elaborate political apparatus built on the kinship, social, and political principles discussed above (Fig. 9–4).

At the top of the Mexica state was dual leadership, religious and military. This reflected the dual hierarchy of offices. Since the state was nearly continuously at war through its later history, the military segment became dominant. The supreme leader was chosen from a special lineage by a set of important men who were members of the *pipiltin* and also heads of state or high officials. Durán says in his *History* (1967) that all of the civil officials attended the election proceedings, but it is quite evident that only the most important had a voice. Brother succeeded brother in the normal order of things. For example, the three sons of Motecuhzoma I served in succession: Axayacatl, Tizoc, and Ahuitzotl. These four were, in turn, related to the other two great expansionist rulers of the Aztec state, Itzcoatl and Motecuhzoma I. Motecuhzoma II was the grandson of Axayacatl. Itzcoatl, who preceded Axayacatl, was the latter's cousin.

The ruler was assisted by a royal court structure which consisted of advisors and administrative heads of the various segments of the state. The state was divided into functionally distinct departments: spiritual, military, justice, treasury, and commerce. These were controlled by the court, which acted as the executive branch. The departments were organized internally in a hierarchical manner, with various classes of officials in each. Such a civil service also had its paperwork. "The nation has a special official for every activity, small though it were. Everything was so well recorded that no detail was left out of the accounts. There were even officials in charge of sweeping . . . And so the officials of the Republic were innumerable" (Durán, 1967:183).

Below the supreme level of government there was a division of the empire into provinces which represented groups of conquered city-states. There were some thirty-eight of these provinces, but also some so-called independent kingdoms. Davies, in his study of these independent pockets within the empire (1968), came to the conclusion that the Aztec controlled their empire much as the British had administered India. That is, the Aztec controlled key points with garrisons, secured the routes through territories, and arranged for tribute to be paid, but usually made no effort to otherwise assimilate conquered peoples. Hassig (1985:92 *et passim*) has pointed out that the empire was not physically occupied by Aztec armies but was controlled by intimidation, which led to an economy of force. To some degree this type of political system was dictated by the difficulties of transport and communication.

Some of the provinces had governors appointed over them, members of the *pipiltin* class, with garrisons to assist them and civil servants. All provinces had tax collectors. The native ruler was often maintained in power as long as he collaborated. Some "independent kingdoms" were actually less crucial polities and in reality were "protectorates" of the Aztec, with varying degrees of independence. Those on the frontiers of the empire tended to be most independent. An example of this type of buffer state was the trading state of Xicalanco, on the Gulf Coast, between Maya country and Nahua-speakers. Others, Tlaxcala and Tututepec, were well placed to menace the Aztec lines of communication and were truly independent. However, most, except for Tlaxcala, had been militarily neutralized. The Tlaxcalans became the original and most constant allies of the Spaniards. In the west, the formidable Tarascan army protected its empire and defeated the Aztec in their attempted incursions. At the time of the Spanish contact, the Aztec were constantly nibbling away at the territories of the independent kingdoms in an obvious attempt to absorb them into the empire tribute system.

Tribute was regulated by the calendar, and payments were made quarterly, semiannually, and annually. Provinces farthest away from Tenochtitlan made payments less often. However, tribute was always given on certain religious festival days, whatever the frequency.

Judicial Branch

The judicial branch is a good example of graded bureaucracy in Aztec political structure. Both aristocrats (*pipiltin*) and commoners were chosen for judgeships, mainly according to their accomplishments and qualities. They were supported by the state. Sahagún described them as the most virtuous of men:

> Such as these the ruler gave office and chose as his judges—the wise, the able, the sage; who listened and spoke well; who were of good memory; who spoke not vainly nor lightly; who did not make friends without forethought nor were drunkards; who guarded their lineage with honor; who slept not overmuch (but rather), arose early; who did nothing for friendship's or kinship's sake, nor for enmity; who would not hear nor judge a case for a fee. The ruler might condemn them to death; hence they performed their offices as judges righteously." [Sahagún, 1954, Book 8:54]

Inasmuch as society was rigidly graded and because there was a partial caste system in effect, a two-level system of courts was necessary to take care of justice at all social levels. The Aztec judiciary seems to have functioned something like the modern European continental system, with its pretrial review, magistrates, and higher courts. Common folk were able to use the lower courts, the *teccalli*, to lodge complaints. The judges acted as magistrates on this level. They decided matters of lesser importance, arrested offenders, and did the preliminary work on complex cases. A careful record of the proceedings of the lower courts was made in hieroglyphic writing by a secretary, which record was then forwarded to the higher court for disposition. Appeals from the lower courts were also sent up for review.

The higher court (*tlacxitlan*) consisted of twelve distinguished judges and the city-state ruler and met each twelve days. This higher court was responsible for review of cases and decisions on complex cases, it called witnesses and examined testimony, and it was expected to detect miscarriages of justice. Princes and great lords were tried by the *tlacxitlan*. The final decisions and appeals were handled by the ruler.

Offenses were social and ideological, the latter including religious offenses. For example, sacrilegious people who stole items from temples were tried, and if condemned, they were dragged by the throat with a rope and thrown into the lake. Three of the titles of the superior court are also those of religious officials, indicating that the higher officers of the church participated in the judicial system (Sahagún, 1954, Book 8:54). Judges were also found in the marketplaces and immediately acted on such matters as false measure or the sale of stolen goods.

Of the ordinary judges, Zorita says: "The Indian judges of whom I spoke would seat themselves at daybreak on their mat dais, and immediately begin to hear pleas. The judges' meals were brought to them at an early hour from the royal palace. After eating they rested for a while, then returned to hear the remaining suitors, staying until two hours before sundown" (1963:126). Zorita also states that each province was represented in the capital city of the empire by two judges.

Police were appointed by the wards or *calpulli*. Persons accused of a crime and waiting for trial were confined in wooden cages, where they received little or no food and water. When a person was found guilty and condemned, execution was carried out by special personnel appointed by the ruler. Lesser sentences were jailing, mutilation, and slavery.

Even the highest person in society was not exempt from justice. The previously mentioned case which involved the sister of Motecuhzoma II, wife of Nezahualpilli, ruler of Texcoco, occurred not long before the arrival of the Spaniards. Her extramarital affairs had become notorious, and her husband had her tried in 1498, presumably by the *tlacxitlan*. She and her current lovers were condemned and executed.

Religion and Cosmology

The people of central Mexico generally believed that there had been several worlds before the present one: four "suns," each with different types of inhabitants. Each of these preceding worlds had perished through

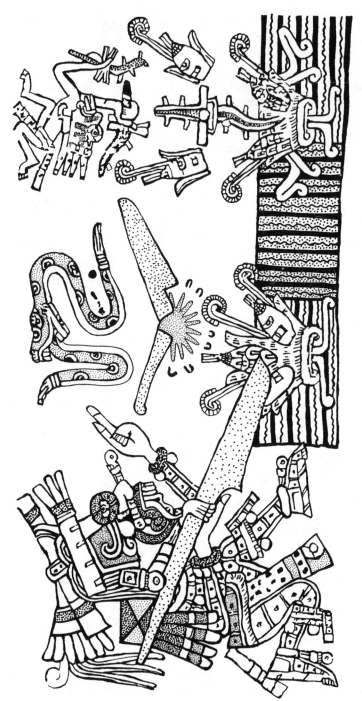

Fig. 9–5. A page from Codex Borgia, a sixteenth-century book possibly from the Tehuacan Valley. Tlaloc, the rain god, cultivates his fields, in which the sacred corn plants grow.

its own imperfections, and the fifth sun or world, in which man now dwelt, would also perish—through a series of devastating earthquakes. It was not known when this end would come, but it was known that the ultimate catastrophe would occur at the end of a particular calendrical cycle, the fifty-two-year cycle. The famous Aztec calendar stone depicts the four suns that have preceded the present sun, which is in the center of the stone.

The earth was visualized as a crocodilelike monster floating in the primeval sea, the edges of which turned up to support the sky. The heavens were arranged in a pyramidal manner with either nine or thirteen layers. There were also nine underworlds. All of this was fairly standard and Mesoamerica-wide ideology.

A jostling, busy, and generally malevolent crowd of deities made up the Aztec pantheon. Nicholson (1971a, 1971b) has analyzed them in terms of fundamental characteristics, cult themes, and deity clusters, brilliantly bringing some order out of this supernatural chaos. Most deities were invisible and made manifest only in dreams and visions and by other special means. Most gods were in human form, at least in part, and dwelt in the celestial sphere. There were specific underworld deities, and occasionally some others went to the underworld temporarily. The rain gods, the *tlaloque,* resided in particular mountains which generated the rain clouds (Fig. 9–5). Mount Tlaloc, in fact and according to some authorities (Aveni among them), seems to be aligned with the former location of the Tlaloc shrine on top of the Great Temple in Tenochtitlan.

A basic conception, again Mesoamerica-wide, was that of multiple aspects of most gods. Creator deities come in pairs and in both sexes. Most gods had four or five aspects which directly related to the four directions and the zenith (the fifth direction). All world directions were associated with different colors. These associations between directions, colors, and aspects of divinities led to such conceptions as the Red Tezcatlipoca of the west, who also took the name of Xipe. The White Tezcatlipoca of the east also was Quetzalcoatl. History and a philosophy of protean existence combined to make special patron relationships with certain sociopolitical units such as city-states, craft groups, or *calpulli.* Huitzilopochtli, the patron god of the Mexica, became extremely important with the rise of the Mexica to power and, according to Padden (1967), began to absorb the attributes formerly belonging to other gods, especially the sun.

Three major cult themes pervaded Aztec religion, according to Nicholson. The first had to do with celestial creativity and divine paternalism and was the most abstract, poetic, and philosophical segment of the whole body of religious thought. It is to this cult theme that such relatively well known material as the writings of Nezahualcoyotl, the philosopher-king of Texcoco, belong. The fierce, capricious Tezcatlipoca also belongs in this category. This deity was a supernatural magician and associated with the things of the night and darkness. "No deity better expressed the pessimistic, fatalistic *weltanschauung* which prevailed in pre-Hispanic Central Mexico. . . . It can be argued that this god, true to his name (smoking mirror), mirrors in his supernatural personality the essential ethos of the whole culture" (Nicholson, 1971*a*:231).

The second major cult theme had to do with rain, moisture, and agricultural fertility. This cult undoubtedly had deep roots in the past, being tied to fundamental affairs of life-giving plants, rain, soil, and water. The rain god complex, Tlaloc and all his helpers, is especially important. Another group of deities clustered about the maguey plant and the fermented cactus juice it produced. One bunch was known as "400 rabbits," which may have been how one felt after sufficient pulque. A whole roster of female deities is also present, many of whom are aspects of rain and water or personifications of the various stages of growth of the maize plant.

The dreadful Xipe-Totec complex, dreadful in its sacrificial aspect of the flayed human victim, was clearly an expression of the idea of death and rebirth, rest and growing seasons. It is thought to have been introduced from the Guerrero area. Many of the female deities of these complexes were represented by the multitudinous small clay figurines made and used in home worship. It might be noted that this practice of figurine making continued into early colonial times, except that instead of Coatlicue, the mother of the gods, the Virgin Mary was depicted. I have even found a small figurine of a man on horseback in an early colonial Indian tomb in the highlands of Guatemala.

Quetzalcoatl, the great patron deity of the Toltec, was a unique deity because he crossed many of the lines drawn above. He was a creator deity, associated with the war-and-blood nourishment cult, and also was conceived of as being a great culture hero. He provided humanity with maize and other gifts. There seems little doubt that here we are dealing with the mythological apotheosis of a historical personage. The story of Quetzalcoatl was taken up in the consideration of the Toltec in chapter 7.

The third cult theme was that of state-fostered blood nourishment of the sun and earth by war and sacrifice. The justification of human sacrifice was preservation of the very existence of the universe. The sun had to be kept nourished by the blood of victims, or else the end of the world, the fifth sun, would come about. Incessant war was necessary to gain a constant supply of such quantities of victims. The death god complex was of course an important deity cluster, but so also was Tonatiuh, the sun god complex. Tonatiuh was the patron of the warrior societies, the eagle and jaguar "knights." Appropriately, both the eagle and the jaguar were symbols of the sun in his various aspects. Huitzilopochtli became the supreme supernatural power in his guise as the god of war. Tezcatlipoca was also important in this group as the patron of young warriors.

There was a basic ritual pattern to nearly all of Aztec religious life. The great spectacles and liturgies were mainly elitist in orientation: most of the many and continuous ceremonies involved only a few members of the state-supported church or, at most, were attended by upper-class members. A ceremony usually started with a preparation by fasting and other abstentions. The main business of the ceremony varied, but it usually involved offerings, processions, deity impersonations, dancing, singing, mock combats, and human sacrifice. Feasts usually followed, and more secular dancing and singing were featured then.

Ceremonies were both calendrical and noncalendrical. The calendrical ceremonies of the 365-day calendar were called "fixed" ceremonies by the early Spaniards and occurred in each of the eighteen months of the year. The 260-day sacred calendar had "movable feasts" which rotated in relation to those of the 365-day year. Movable feasts were somewhat like the Christian Easter, which shifts in the 365-day calendar according to lunar cycles. Noncalendrical ceremonies were usually tied to the individual's life cycle, crises, homecoming ceremonies, domestic rituals, curing ceremonies, and so forth. Again, many of the small clay figurines so common in the Basin of Mexico were made for curing ceremonies, according to Sahagún. They were also strung over the fields for fertility purposes, according to Durán.

The major ceremonies were, of course, held in the temple precincts, with and under direction of special personnel, and were patronized by the state and elite leadership. The Spanish friars concentrated upon this part of the religious structure when they engaged in the first generation's massive conversion efforts. Several aspects of Aztec religion seemed especially remarkable to them because of similarities to Christianity. One such feature was the use of confession of sins among the Aztec, although this was done infrequently. Another parallel was the use of a sacred dough which was often made into an image of a god and ultimately eaten by the participants. The similarity of the concepts of the mother of the gods, Coatlicue, and of the Virgin Mary has been remarked. Indeed, the shrine to the Virgin of Guadalupe presently occupies the site of the old center of worship of Tonantzin, an aspect of Coatlicue.

The Aztec felt themselves surrounded by and acted upon by the supernatural. Religion permeated every aspect of life. The gods were in this world, and were unknowable and capricious; man was at the mercy of their whims. The future was perhaps divinable if one knew enough to detect the cycles of time, events, and ritual. Life might be controlled to some degree, or at least foreseen, if one had such knowledge. The small town of Malinalco was noted for its sorcerers and fortune-tellers, some of whom used the device of staring into tubs of water. The calendars were inextricably bound up with life, and one's whole life pattern to a large degree was bound up with one's birthday and its lucky or unlucky aspects.

Small shrines dotted the countryside, much as Catholic shrines are still found in profusion throughout Mesoamerica today. Shrine worship in the mountains was especially dedicated to the rain gods, the *tlaloque*. Even the emperor and his court repaired at a certain time of the year to a remote and gloomy precinct in a forest on Mount Tlaloc for a ceremony dedicated to the rain god. Long-distance merchants on a trip worshiped their Pinocchio-nosed god, Yacateuctli, asked his protection from the dangers of the trip, and made a temporary shrine to him each evening with their staves and clay images of the god's face; one still finds these small clay masks as far south as the highlands of Guatemala. The agriculturalist, of course, felt the wrath or beneficence of the gods in all his activities. The *chinampero* had his own patron deities. The breath of cooling air which preceded the rain squall was Quetzalcoatl in his guise as the wind god sweeping the road before the moisture of the rain god Tlaloc.

The world was mysterious and awful in many ways, but there was an explanation for nearly everything. The universe was in order and man was meant to help keep that order by proper worship and sacrifices. The regularity and the pageantry and drama of Aztec religion went far to allay anxieties about the essential hostility and unpredictability of the world and served also to bind the commoner's allegiance to the state.

War and Imperialism

Much of what follows is derived from Ross Hassig's recent study, *Aztec Warfare* (1988). The practice of war by the Aztec has been given a number of constructions which are nearly as divorced from reality as the myth of the "peaceful" Maya. Idealization of the ideological elements, the "sacred war" to save the world and the sun, is a common misconstruction. Characteristics of the "flowery wars" of the nobility carried out between formally declared wars are sometimes confused as part of the expansionist wars of the empire. Both of these elements were present, of course, but they seem to have been justifications for the real practicality of warfare, the aim of which was to gain tribute payers and tribute for the empire.

The empire, as noted, was loosely controlled physically but held in taut control by intimidation and the perception of overwhelming power. Hassig notes that this made for a great economy of force, just as it did for the British in India, where no immense standing armies or large numbers of garrisons were needed.

It has been argued that the Aztec had no professional army. This is basically a matter of definition. Modern armies of industrial states are clearly not the sort of force that the Aztec developed. Neither are the small professional armies of Europe of the seventeenth and eighteenth centuries an appropriate model. Perhaps we may look to the more traditional armies of ancient states, an eighteenth-century survival of which were those of the Maharattas of India.

All Aztec males were militarily trained, either in the *telpochcalli* or *calmecac* schools. Further training was under the tutelage of a more experienced warrior. Social prestige and advancement for both commoner and noble were available through military exploits. It was much more likely, however, that a noble would distinguish himself because of his access to better training and because of more military opportunities afforded him. The military societies were graded according to noble or commoner membership. Titles given for achievement were not necessarily equivalent to chain-of-command rank. The military societies were not groups of officers, although nobles made up more of their membership than did commoners. Nobles were not necessarily officers, either. Kinship, social status, military achievement, and personality determined rank, and these elements seem to have occurred in different mixes, all of which made the Aztec armies unendingly fluid and volatile organizations. At any rate, no matter who commanded in a particular campaign or battle, a set of principles governed conduct and made clear responsibility for all the necessary tasks. War was patterned in its process from inception to conclusion, victorious or otherwise.

Declarations of war were often kept within Aztec society in order to gain surprise in an offensive attack. Efficient mobilization depended on several elements. One was the existence of a body of trained men, which was provided by the men's schools and military orders, and another was intelligence, which was gathered by spies, merchants, diplomats, and others familiar in our own day. Communication for political purposes could also be used in time of war; relay messengers stationed about 4.2 kilometers (2.6 miles) apart passed information rapidly through the empire. Finally, logistics had to be adequate, and supply lines carefully calculated according to the campaign. Supplies were taken from dumps prepared in advance by tributary towns along the line of march. Armories in Tenochtitlan provided the weapons.

Selected numbers and proportions of nobles and commoners were used in actual combat, depending on the enemy to be confronted. Armies of seven thousand to eight thousand were commonly drawn from a calculated total military manpower pool of perhaps half a million. Only in an emergency, usually a defensive situation, was nearly the whole of the military organization brought into play. Full mobilization occurred during the Spanish Conquest, of course.

The sophistication, courage, discipline, and numbers of the Aztec are repeatedly mentioned in the Spanish accounts of the Conquest. All of these characteristics had been developed during the period of empire building under a series of strong leaders. At first, however, the Aztec did not hold any notable advantages except for the élan that they always displayed in combat. At the end, they had developed a great army, but one which was more attuned to political expansion for the purpose of tribute than to defense. Spanish tactics and weapons, combined with Cortés's strategic genius, finally prevailed.

Historical Summary

Like many imperial peoples suddenly reaching gloriously improved circumstances, the Aztec-Mexica looked back on the past and found it lacking. In fact, at one point they went so far as to burn as many of the older history books as were available and then rewrote their own history. Therefore, much of what comes down to us is in the form of the official chronicle of the Aztec and is as they themselves wished to be seen. Fortunately, other histories have survived from city-state archives, of Chalco and Texcoco for example, which give us a chance to balance more realistic or different versions against the chest-beating tone of the official record.

The Aztec considered themselves part of a group of seven Chichimec tribes which left a semimythical place to the west of Mexico, Aztlan. It is from the latter place name that "Aztec" is derived. The Aztec were also called Mexica after a famous leader named Meci. All seven tribes eventually arrived in the basin of Mexico, but the Aztec, after several generations of wandering and adventuring, following their tribal deity, Huitzilopochtli, arrived last in about A.D. 1193. It is difficult to say exactly what the status of the Aztec was at that time, but there seems little doubt that it was a politically weak, militarily aggressive, and probably tributary group. Sanders (personal communication) has expressed the opinion that the Aztec may have been in the valley all along but had the status of a pariah or outcast ethnic group. In any event, until about 1427 the Aztec barely maintained themselves in this precarious and politically fragmented condition. One group of them is said to have settled with the civilized people of the venerable city-state of Colhuacan. Another group settled on a rocky group of islets in the western embayment of Lake Texcoco and founded what became the city of Tlatelolco, Tenochtitlan's sister city. The Plaza of the Three Cultures in Mexico City today reveals the remnants of that ancient town.

Tenochtitlan was founded in marshland that belonged to three powerful city-states, Azcapotzalco, Texcoco, and Colhuacan. The Aztec had located the place after many vicissitudes, largely of their own making, when they found the promised sign of an eagle nesting on a prickly pear cactus in a swamp. They built their initial shrine to Huitzilopochtli, who had led them through all of those years. That shrine probably is still buried beneath the earliest temples exposed in the excavations of the

Templo Mayor. "Although the wood and stone were not sufficient, the Aztec began to build their temple. Little by little they filled in and consolidated the site for the city. They built foundations in the water by driving in stakes and throwing dirt and stone between the stakes" (Durán, 1967:23). The city was divided into four districts corresponding to the four world quarters; each district was home to several *calpulli*.

At this point, having established and developed their town to some extent, the Aztec requested a king from Colhuacan. It seems clear that they needed someone of the necessary distinguished genealogy who could lend status to their ruling class—that is, someone who could claim descent from the Toltec. Acamapichtli became king in about 1364, married a Colhuacan princess of Toltec ancestry, and ruled until 1404. During that time the Aztec were tributaries of Azcapotzalco and paid heavy tribute to that city-state. Huitzilhuitl, Acamapichtli's successor, married a daughter of the ruler of Azcapotzalco and thereby gained a means of reducing the onerous tribute due Azcapotzalco. The daughter begged her father to remit the taxes, and he agreed to do so.

During these years the Aztec made a distinct effort to live in peace with their more powerful neighbors, establishing relationships with them by inviting people from other city-states to settle in Tenochtitlan. On the other hand, they also served as mercenaries and established a reputation as fierce and skillful warriors. Commerce was also encouraged, with much coming and going among the various regional markets of the basin, and that of Tlatelolco-Tenochtitlan became more important. About 1417 the third king, Chimalpopoca (Smoking Shield), took office upon his father's death and continued the peaceful development of the city.

After about ten years, a crisis took place which threatened the very existence of the Aztec as a separate state. More water was needed for the increasingly large *chinampa* zone and the growing population of the city, and an aqueduct-causeway was planned and attempted. However, the Aztec needed help and requested it of Azcapotzalco. Whether or not the request was insolently phrased, it was said to be, and Azcapotzalco took this incident as a good chance to destroy a growing rival. Azcapotzalco sent assassins who killed Chimalpopoca and his son, and the older city instituted an economic blockade. At this point, the first of the great conqueror-kings of the Aztec, Itzcoatl, ascended the throne, and the ferocious personality of his nephew Tlacaelel made its appearance. Together, the new king and Tlacaelel first resisted and then, with the immense help of Texcoco, conquered Azcapotzalco. For the first time the Aztec were an independent city-state, free of tributary obligations.

Itzcoatl was the first of six rulers who presided over Aztec imperial expansion. According to some sources, Tlacaelel was first general and then chief counselor to all but Motecuhzoma II, the next to last pre-Hispanic ruler. In point of fact, Tlacaelel was emperor-ruler in all but name for most of his lifetime. The Aztec state and its ultimate form, ideology, social structure, and accomplishments are very much the achievement of this extraordinary personality. It was Tlacaelel who planned and, at first, largely carried out the military campaigns which subjugated the basin for the Aztec and who then spread the empire beyond the basin. Tlacaelel, according to R. C. Padden's interpretation (1967), was also responsible for the psychopathic emphasis on human sacrifice as an instrument of terror and political and social control. However, this interpretation is disputed by other scholars, who see Tlacaelel as much less influential (cf. Hassig, 1988:189). Demarest has more recently developed this theme in an anthropological context and argues that the real difference between the Aztec and the other central Mexican cultures was ideological (Conrad and Demarest, 1984). By this means he claims to have put the element of human volition (stimulated by an ideology) back into evolutionary explanations. Undoubtedly this factor has been underestimated, but an ideological base without a solid economic base is not a long-term winner in competitive situations, as shown by the Japanese-American war of 1941–1945. The situation was nothing if not competitive in fifteenth-century Mesoamerica.

A balanced treatment of cultural evolution probably means that economics and ideology will be found to be interactive in most cases. The use of the land of the conquered city-states by the Aztec relieved their hunger, and the tribute exacted from the same conquered places provided the economic support for the rapidly expanding aristocracy (*pipiltin*), bureaucracy, and church. Much of the expenditure of the state was in the form of extravagant building: glorious architectural monuments that embellished the capital city and provided the physical stage upon which the pageantry of social and religious (ideological) activities were acted out.

The above reconstruction of Aztec history is almost wholly derived from the official version. However, according to other city-state chronicles, the initial struggle with Azcapotzalco was successful only because of an alliance with two other city-states, Texcoco and Tacuba. Texcoco was the home of another extraordinary personality, the ruler Nezahualcoyotl, who was also an accomplished engineer and warrior. Much of the initial domination of the basin and the Central Plateau of Mexico was attributable to this man's achievements, it appears. However, it also appears that the Aztec expurgated the history books to omit both the historical and the cultural accomplishments of the rival city of Texcoco. Unfortunately, the great library of Texcoco was destroyed in the course of the Spanish Conquest.

It seems quite clear that shifting power balances took place within the century of Aztec expansion, 1427–1519, among the allies of the basin. Although Texcoco retained its reputation and eminence in cultural achievements, it had become politically and economically subordinated to Tenochtitlan by the late fifteenth century.

Padden argues that the Aztec state by that time had also become a mad world of bloody terrorism based on the cynical, psychopathic policies of the high imperial rulers. Coronation ceremonies of the later kings were accompanied by the offering of fantastic quantities of human victims to the gods. These victims were purchased slaves from Aztec society itself, coerced members of a society who played the parts of god impersonators, and the collected captives from the constant foreign campaigns of the Aztec armies. Some eighty thousand captives are said to have been sacrificed at the dedication of the enlarged Great Temple housing Huitzilopochtli in 1487. While that is probably an exaggerated figure, the true number was undoubtedly horrifyingly large. Incredibly, the Aztec elite invited rulers of hostile states to view the spectacle as honored guests— "enemies of the house." The consumption of human flesh by the *pipiltin* has been argued to have been massive, and it is said that one reason pork was so popular after 1521 was its similarity in taste to human meat. The expansion of the *pipiltin* class, the increasing tribute loads on the *macehualtin*, the growing stresses of ever more far-reaching military campaigns, and the increasing hostility of the conquered provinces all produced internal and external strains on the empire that set the stage for its fall in 1521 (Padden, 1967).

Tlacaelel died in 1496, and Motecuhzoma II came to power in 1503. The latter had ascended the religious route to supreme authority. He moved almost immediately to deify himself. Durán (1964) records that he asked an old man what the emperor Motecuhzoma looked like, and the old one replied that he in truth did not know, not having dared to look on Motecuhzoma's face. Much of the later majesty, elaborate protocol, and almost Byzantine court procedure were Motecuhzoma's creation. He arranged for the assassination of most of the court officials who had served his predecessor, Ahuitzotl. Those men knew too much to accept his divinity.

The king of Texcoco, Nezahualpilli, became an enemy—covert, but powerful. He made dire predictions, moreover, about the end of Aztec hegemony; it would come within a few years, he said, although he himself would not see it. Whether or not this was psychological warfare, it certainly upset Motecuhzoma. Many other upsetting events occurred in the years shortly before the appearance of the Spaniards. A bird with a mirror in its head was brought to the emperor, who gazed into it and saw first a starry constellation and then men on horses. A fire broke out in a temple dedicated to Huitzilopochtli, and it burned to the ground. A great comet was seen in the sky. These and other omens reminded Motecuhzoma of the now-dead Nezahualpilli's prophecy and also of the ancient traditions that the god Quetzalcoatl would one day return or send his sons back to reclaim his patrimony. The appearance of Spanish exploring vessels in the period 1507–10 greatly alarmed the empire's ruler.

The extraordinary story of the Conquest of Mexico by Cortés and how it was aided by the psychological preparation mentioned above and by the internal stresses of the Aztec system is well known. It took Cortés only two years to reduce the Aztec to slaves and their marvelous city to malodorous rubble. As well as the cultural and political destruction figured in the Conquest, there was a horrific population loss during the Conquest period and for the next 160 years of the colonial era. It is estimated that the Indian population of the basin was reduced from about 1.2 million in 1519 to some 70,000 in 1680. This was accomplished by numerous causes: war, slavery, disease, overwork, malnutrition, and famine. The basin was not alone in suffering this process. It is estimated on good grounds that the total population loss in Mesoamerica during the same period was on the order of 85 to 95 percent in some areas (Cook and Borah, 1960).

The Spaniards retained the collaborating native elites for the first part of the colonial period. Increased tribute, reduced populations, and depressed economic conditions, however, rapidly reduced these descendants of the *pipiltin* to poverty-stricken remnants hardly distinguishable from their former vassals and serfs. One wonders if the sadness and bitterness of the worldview of much of Indian culture today in the highlands is not the legacy of this disastrous past, which has not yet been fully redeemed.

> They have been destroyed by the great and excessive tribute they have had to pay, for in their great fear of the Spaniards they have given all they had. Since the tribute was excessive and continually demanded, to make payment they sold their lands at a low price, and their children as slaves. When they had nothing left with which to pay, many died for this in prison; if they managed to get out, they emerged in such sorry state that they died in a few days. Others died from being tortured to tell where there was gold or where they had hidden it. They have been treated bestially and unreasonably in all respects. [Zorita, 1963:207]

EXPLANATORY AND ANALYTICAL TOOLS FOR UNDERSTANDING THE PAST

There is no intention in this section of being original. Indeed, my aim is just the opposite: to be unoriginal. That is, I mean to outline the commonly accepted theoretical and analytical patterns. Therefore, most of the material I present here is standard, used by most archaeologists in part or as a whole. This statement applies to the "new" archaeologists and to the "pragmatists." The distinction made above is one which is most often insisted upon by the "new" archaeologists, who consider themselves explicitly committed to the "scientific" method or the hypothetico-deductive system of research. The rest of the profession, which is not so specifically committed and is willing to use anything that comes to hand, I have grouped into a loose category under the label "pragmatists." Wishing to avoid the polemics that have often characterized the debate between the two groups, I shall do no more than refer the reader to a few articles and books which outline the distinctions in more detail. I cannot refrain from one comment, however, and that is that most of us do not take professional epistemology as seriously as we do our religions, unless they happen to be the same.[1]

There are three elements with which an archaeologist deals. These are time, space, and content. A multitude of structures of hierarchically organized units is concerned with each of these qualities. These elements give us some control over the materials, and with them many inferences are possible and testable. Without such control, nothing is certain. We will consider time first.

Relative and absolute time distinctions are important. The former can be determined by means of the most useful field technique ever developed: stratigraphy, a principle borrowed from geology. Simply stated, stratigraphy means that physical deposits and the cultural materials they contain can be ordered by their physical ordering as found in excavation. This

---

1. The literature on the "new archaeology" versus the traditional or pragmatic archaeology is long and acrimonious. Some major statements can be found in Binford and Binford (1968) and in Fritz and Plog (1979), and a comment is in R. E. W. Adams (1969) from a Mesoamericanist point of view. Watson, LeBlanc, and Redman (1971) strike a more moderate stance, although still avowedly "scientific."

means that the latest deposits are on top and the earliest on the bottom of a pit. There are many permutations to the technique, but that is the essence of it, and with it one can establish relative time. The lowest material in a pit thus is usually the oldest, the highest is the youngest, and the order of the rest of the materials—say, pottery—falls in between in the order indicated by the deposits. By this, then, we can determine that pottery type 3-R is more recent than type 7-X and that both come before type 2-A.[2]

Absolute time can be inserted into the relative time sequence by the use of several sources of information. History may aid us, as do native calendars such as the Maya calendar. However, physical science has provided us with the majority of independent checks on the absolute dating of archaeological materials. Carbon 14, thermoluminescence, obsidian hydration, tree-ring analysis, and other wonderful and arcane techniques lead to dating.

Content comprehends all of the various items and kinds of information that an archaeologist digs up. At the most basic, it means artifacts and their contexts. Artifacts are classified further according to style. Thus, we have stone, bone, antler, pottery, textiles, basketry, wood, and other classes of artifacts. Within these classes, there are taxonomically or descriptively organized units. For example, red-slipped pottery, which makes up a large amount of the ceramics in the Maya Lowlands, is distinguished by varieties of forms, color variants, surface decoration (punctuation, incision, and so on), wall thickness, tempering (grog) qualities, and other characteristics. Thus, a type known as Sierra Red has a certain range of forms and associated qualities that distinguish it from all other red pottery specifically and all other pottery generally. By stratigraphic means it is known that Sierra Red occurs before polychrome pottery decoration was developed and after the height of white-slipped pottery's popularity. This constitutes the establishment of relative dating. Similarly, one classifies other kinds of artifacts and associated information such as house types, art styles, estimated population sizes, and so on. By these means one arrives at an organized inventory of the entire material content of a specific place at a particular time.

It is obvious that all of the above types of artifacts are specifically located in space. One digs at a site or a series of sites and the distribution of pottery and associated materials, together with data from one's colleagues or predecessors, allows one to draw rough boundaries on a map. Thus, for example, we know that Sierra Red pottery is most common in the Maya Lowlands but also occurs in the Chiapas Lowlands. Further,

2. For more on the technical and theoretical aspects of fieldwork, see Hole and Heizer (1973) and Hester, Heizer, and Graham (1975).

stratigraphy has repeatedly shown that these types occur at about the same time.

It is obvious that ancient peoples did not use just one type of pottery at any one time. Usually there were up to twenty types of pottery in use simultaneously. Once one has established the contemporaneity of a group of pottery or lithic or wooden artifact types, then one has established a ceramic, lithic, or wooden artifact complex. Putting all the contemporary complexes together defines the entire known artifact inventory of a specific place at a particular time. At this point one has the necessary information for the establishment of that most useful of all archaeological units, the phase. The phase is the unit in which all three elemental qualities (time, space, and content) are combined. A phase is defined as a distinctive body of content located in a specific place (or region) and with a specified length of duration. It follows that all phases are nct of the same length. Depending on circumstances, the archaeologist makes the phases as short as possible, but they may range from a thousand years in length to twenty.

A series of such phases constitutes a sequence. Sequences are often referred to in this book, and they usually mean sequences at a particular site, but sometimes they are region-wide, as is the case with the Tehuacan phases. The problem is obviously one of sampling, and indeed, as I have said in another context, archaeology can be viewed as a kind of grand sampling game. Usually the archaeologist is dealing with only a 1–2 percent sample at best, and often the excavated material from a site is far less than that proportion.

Archaeological reconnaissance over large zones can extend our knowledge. Surface collecting of pottery and other artifacts and test pits at other sites may greatly expand the site or regional sequence. Cross-tying regional sequences into larger sequences is accomplished by use of horizons. Horizon styles are widely spread in space but fairly short-lived in time. For example, the Mixteca-Puebla style is a Protohistoric example from Mesoamerica, and the widespread use of slab-footed, tripod, cylindrical vases with lids is an example from the Teotihuacan period. By these means and absolute dating, large stages, developmental epochs, are established with roughly contemporary events from throughout the Mesoamerican area.

The specific meanings of these stages and periods are discussed in the introductory chapter. However, it bears repeating here that periods are regarded simply as large blocks of time applicable to all of Mesoamerica, and they have no specific evolutionary or culture-historical implications.

Levels of organizational development. Certain terms are used in the body of this book to refer to levels of complexity in social, political, and economic organization. Most of these terms are derived from the general body of ethnological theory. There are several problems with these labels, however. One is that there is no stable agreement about what constitutes a tribe, say, across all world culture areas. Therefore, one cannot automatically say that tribal level of organization in the Tehuacan valley at a specific time meant that it had all of the same characteristics that have been cross-culturally defined for us by such scholars as Murdock and Service (1962).

Furthermore, there is a problem with the differences between the nature of archaeological evidence and the character of definitions based on ethnological data. Sanders and Price (1968) have ably discussed this matter. Ethnologists tend to deal with nonmaterial evidence derived from the observation of living societies. Archaeologists are constrained to deal with a fragment of the material remains of extinct societies. Therefore, any statements about social organization of archaeological cultures are usually and mainly inferential, and consequently there is an obvious incongruity in the nature of the two sets of organizational labels. A partial solution to the problem would be to pay more attention to the material correlates of organizational levels of living societies. But there is another problem, and one more fundamental. Our ethnological record is small in sample and somewhat uneven in quality. Further, it is largely, although not entirely, confined to the past hundred years of anthropological work. For these and other reasons, the resultant cross-cultural and universalistic categories of social organization may well be inappropriate to apply to the archaeological cultures of the past.

The early cultures must have gone through many stages that were only relatively fleeting and unstable. However, the peculiarities of these transitional stages may have had lasting effects on the later stylistic and functional characteristics of developed cultures. For example, the Olmec culture arose in a world largely free of the intense competition that the later Mixtec states faced. The Olmec culture may be regarded as a form of "pristine state," one which was by nature transitory. However, as we now see it, certain crucial features of Olmec social organization may have been perpetuated in Classic Maya civilization, lasting until the collapse at about 900 A.D. For these reasons, then, it is proposed here that archaeologists must eventually work out their own typologies and sequences of social organizations which will be largely independent of ethnological categories, though the matching of archaeological and ethnological categories would be a still further and comparative step toward the understanding of both conceptual frameworks.

The new data from almost all of Mesoamerica indicate that the sequence of community development was village to regional center to ceremonial center and/or urban center (city). These archaeologically detectable entities indicate the increasingly complex nature of Mesoamerican societies. On the other hand, the question is left open for a parallel interpretation of the nature of the society represented by the site.

In the meantime, however, we are left, at least for the purposes of this book, with a terminology derived from ethnology which carries a load of possible misinformation. In Service's (1962) terminology the evolutionary scale runs from band (simplest) to tribe to chiefdom to primitive state. In a sense, the definitions of these levels are too detailed, with the kind of evidence extremely unlikely to show up in the archaeological record. On the other hand, they are not refined enough to take account of the apparent variation in the crucial transition stages of passage from the chiefdom to the state or from the tribe to the chiefdom. In practice, it is exceedingly difficult to distinguish between villages inhabited by people organized into tribes and those organized into chiefdoms or even states. Therefore, the reader will often encounter terms such as *village-oriented society* as a euphemism which leaves open the social organizational possibilities.

GUIDE TO PRONUNCIATION

The reader who is confronted with the names of Mixtec (MEESH-tek) or Aztec deities is liable to be dismayed at first sight. This guide is intended to allay that feeling. However, there is no substitute for buckling down, slowly taking apart some words, and getting something of the verbal rhythm of those rich languages. If this book is used in a classroom, the student will, at the least, be able to make a connection between the written word and the word as it is spoken by his or her instructor.

The reader may find some solace in the fact that the first Spaniards had an equally difficult time with Nahuatl, the Aztec language. Indeed, most of them never did master it, judging by the book written by that old conqueror, Bernal Díaz. Huitzilopochtli, the principal Aztec deity, became Huichilobos in many sixteenth-century Spanish accounts.

Sixteenth-century Spanish was different from modern Spanish and had an *x* used to represent a *sh* sound. Thus, Tlaxcala is Tlash-KAH-lah, and Texcoco is Tesh-KOH-koh. Xaltocan is Hal-TOH-kahn today, but in preconquest times was Shal-TOH-kahn. The letter *a* is nearly always long, as in *ah*, and all other vowels are long, with *i* being pronounced *ee*, as in Huitzilopochtli (Weet-see-low-POCH-tlee). Nahuatl words are not accented except in the case of those that end with *e*. Because of the fact that Spanish-speakers are our major sources for Nahuatl, it has become customary to stress the penultimate syllable, as in Spanish. Thus, Xochimilco is pronounced Shoh-chee-MEEL-koh, and Tenochtitlan is Taynoch-TEET-lahn.

In Maya the accent is often on the last syllable, as in Chichen Itza (Chee-CHEN Eet-ZAH), or Becan (Bay-KAHN). The *x* in Maya words is nearly always pronounced *sh*, as in Iximche (Eesh-eem-CHAY). A *u* on the beginning of words takes a *w* sound, as in Uaxactun (Wah-shock-TOON).

Mixtec words are complicated by the use of the Spanish tilde (˜) over some *n*s, indicating an *ny* sound; thus, Yucuñudahui is Yoo-koon-yoodah-WHEE, and Ñuiñe is NYOO-een-yea. The reader may take some small comfort from knowing that at least he or she is not required to pronounce Parangaricutirimicuaro.

Examples of many of the most commonly encountered deity and place names follow:

Maya Deities

Written	*Pronounced*
Ah Kin	Ah Keen
Ah Puch	Ah Pooch
Bacabs	Bah-KAHBS
Chac	Chahk
Ek Chuah	Eck Choo-AH
Hunab Ku	Hoo-NAHB Koo
Itzamna	Eet-zahm-NAH
Ixchel	Eesh-CHEL
Kinich Ahau	Kee-NEECH Ah-HOW
Kukulcan	Koo-kool-KAHN
Xamen Ek	Sha-MEN Eck
Yum Cimil	Yoom Kee-MEEL

Nahuatl Deities

Coatlicue	Ko-ah-TLEE-kway
Huitzilopochtli	Weet-see-low-POCH-tlee
Mixcoatl	Meesh-KOH-ahtl
Quetzalcoatl	Kayt-zahl-KOH -ahtl
Tezcatlipoca	Tez-ca-tlee-PO-ka
Tlaloc	TLAH-lokh
Xipe Totec	SHEE-pay TOH-teck
Xochipilli	Sho-chee-PEEL-lee
Xolotl	SHOH-lohtl

Western Mesoamerican Place-Names

If names have changed, the original version is given in parenthesis.

Aztlan	AHS-tlan
Azcapotzalco	Ahz-ka-po-TZAHL-koh
Cempoala (Cempohallan)	Sem-po-WAHL-ah (Sem-po-WAHL-lan)
Cholula (Cholollan)	Choh-LU-lah (Choh-LOL-lan)
Chupicuaro	Choo-PEE-kwar-oh
Coxcatlan	Kosh-KAH-tlan
Cuicuilco	Kwee-KWEEL-koh
Malinalco	Mah-lee-NAHL-koh
Popocatepetl	Poh-poh-kah-TAY-petl
Santa Isabel Iztapan	Eez-TAH-pahn
Tajin	Tah-HEEN
Tamuin	Tah-MOO-een
Tehuacan	Tay-WAH-kahn
Tehuantepec	Tay-wahn-TAY-peck
Tena yuca (Tenayocan)	Tay-nah-YUC-ah (Tay-nah-YOH-kahn)

Tenochtitlan	Tay-noch-TEE-tlan
Teotihuacan	Tay-oh-TEE-wah-kahn
Teotitlan del Rio	Tay-oh-TEE-tlahn
Tepexpan	Tay-PESH-pahn
Tequixquiac	Tay-KEESH-kee-akh
Tilantongo	Tee-lahn-TOHN-goh
Tlatelolco	Tlah-tay-LOHL-koh
Tlatilco	Tlah-TEEL-koh
Tula (Tollan)	TOO-lah (TOL-lan)
Tzintzuntzan	Tzeen-tzoon-TZAHN
Valsequillo	Vahl-say-KEEL-yoh
Xochicalco	Shoh-chee-KAHL-koh
Xochimilco	Shoh-chee-MEEL-koh
Zacatenco	Zah-kah-TEN-koh

Eastern Mesoamerican Place-Names

Acanceh	Ah-kahn-KAY
Chiapa de Corzo	Chee-AH-pah day KOHR-zoh
Chichen Itza	Chee-CHEN Eet-ZAH
Chixoy River	Chee-SHOY
Dzibilchaltun	Dzee-beel-chahl-TOON
Holmul	Hohl-MOOL
Iximche	Eesh-eem-CHAY
Jaina	High-NAH
Kaminaljuyu	Kah-mee-nahl-hoo-YOO
Kohunlich	Koh-hoon-LEECH
Nebaj	Nay-BAH
Oxkintok	Osh-keen-TOHK
Palenque	Pah-LEN-kay
Quirigua	Kee-ree-GWAH
Seibal	Sigh-BALL
Uaxactun	Wah-shock-TOON
Tho	Tu-HOH
Usumacinta	Oo-soo-mah-SEEN-tah
Uxmal	Oosh-MAHL
Xunantunich	Shoo-nahn-too-NEECH
Yaxchilan	Yash-chee-LAHN
Zaculeu	Zah-koo-LAY-oo

Maya Manuscripts

Chilam Balam of Chumayel	Chee-LAHM Bah-LAHM Choo-mah-YEL
Popol Vuh	Poh-POL Vooh

COMPARISON OF DAY NAMES AND THEIR MEANINGS FROM VARIOUS PARTS OF MESOAMERICA
(after Caso, 1967, and Thompson, 1950)

Mexica (Tenochtitlan)	Lowland Maya	Zapotec
1. Cipactli (crocodile)	Imix (earth monster)	Chilla (crocodile)
2. Ehecatl (wind)	Ik (wind)	Quij (arm)
3. Calli (house)	Akbal (darkness)	Guela (night)
4. Cuetzpallin (lizard)	Kan (ripe maize)	Ache (lizard)
5. Coatl (serpent)	Chicchan (serpent)	Zee (serpent)
6. Miquiztli (death)	Cimi (death)	Lana (black)
7. Mazatl (deer)	Manik (hand)	China (deer)
8. Tochtli (rabbit)	Lamat (Venus)	Lapa (rabbit)
9. Atl (water)	Muluc (water)	Niza (water)
10. Itzcuintli (dog)	Oc (dog)	Tella (dog)
11. Ozomatli (monkey)	Chuen (monkey)	Loo (monkey)
12. Malinalli (grass)	Eb (Bad rain)	Pija (drought)
13. Acatl (reed)	Ben (growing maize)	Quij (reed)
14. Ocelotl (ocelot)	Ix (jaguar)	Geche (jaguar)
15. Cuauhtli (eagle)	Men (moon/eagle)	Naa (eagle)
16. Cozcaquautli (vulture)	Cib (wax)	Loo (crow)
17. Ollin (earthquake)	Caban (earth)	Xoo (earthquake)
18. Tecpatl (flint knife)	Etznab (knife)	Opa (cold)
19. Quiauitl (rain)	Cauac (storm)	Ape (cloudy)
20. Xochitl (flower)	Ahau (lord)	Lao (flower)

GLOSSARY

AGUADA. A waterhole, most often in the Maya Lowlands; shallow, weedy rain catchment which may dry up between rainy seasons. An *aguada* often was improved in ancient times by deepening and lining with clay and stone.

ALTARS. Stone monuments, which may be sculptured, found commonly in nearly all regions of Mesoamerica within urban or ceremonial centers. An inaccurate name for what probably were thrones.

AMARANTH. A small-seeded, bushy plant now considered a weed in most of the United States but prehistorically harvested by New World groups, including many Mesoamerican societies.

ATLANTEAN FIGURES. Carved human figures in the form of large or small columns. These columns may hold up roofs (as at Tula) or low table-altars (as at Chichen Itza). They are mainly of the Toltec period.

ATLATL. A spearthrower device, very ancient and spread throughout the New World. Operates as an extension of the arm and as a lever, pushing the butt of the spear's shaft, thus increasing accuracy, length of throw, and striking power.

ATOLE. A corn gruel, nourishing and palatable, used widely in ancient and modern Mesoamerica. Used especially for infants and the elderly because of its easy digestibility.

BACKFRAME. A wooden frame strapped to the back of a person to which were attached feathers and other symbolic and ornamental items. Usually part of elaborate elite-class costuming.

BAJO. A periodic swamp in the Maya Lowlands. Up to 42 percent of the lowlands in the south is covered by such low areas, which fill with water during the rainy seasons. *Bajos* possibly were once shallow lakes which silted in because of erosion during the Maya Classic period.

BAKTUN. A period of 144,000 days, or about four hundred years, in the Maya long-count calendar. The original Maya term for this period is unknown.

BALL GAME. A game played throughout Mesoamerica with a solid rubber ball in a formal court. Rules and courts varied, but generally the game was used for divination, with the future indicated by the outcome. It was also recreational. Earliest ball courts date from Chiapas about 1200 B.C. The game was most popular among the Classic Maya, to judge from the number of their courts, although the Toltec also were addicted to it.

BIOME. Broadly defined as a whole community of plants and animals; for example, a temperate deciduous forest or a tropical rain forest. Each *biome* is made up of many specifically adapted biotic communities. Usually, these communities contain a great deal of variation, as discussed in the section on development of agriculture.

CACAO. Beans of the cacao tree (*Theobroma cacao*), used to produce chocolate. Native to Mesoamerica.

CALDERA. A volcanic crater.

CALENDAR ROUND. A shortened form of date which gives the day within the 260-day almanac and within the current 365-day calendar. However, these dates repeat themselves each fifty-two years. The Maya developed the *long count* in order to specify time more exactly.

CALICHE. Secondary calcium carbonate deposit usually found in lower soil zones and precipitated out of groundwater or irrigation waters.

CALMECAC. Aztec school for young men and women of the nobility. These schools were attached to specific temples.

CALPULE. The head of a CALPULLI. A principal duty of the *calpule* was to be custodian of the land maps of the *calpulli*. He reported to the city-state ruler.

CALPULLI. The Aztec social-residential unit, which had landholding, military, labor, religious, and political functions. Patrilineal clans.

CANDELERO. A small, usually crudely made incense burner found in quantity at Teotihuacan. Associated with the apartment compounds and therefore assumed to have been part of home worship.

CAUSEWAY. A raised road of stone. Aztec causeways were dikes and roads through the lakes. Maya causeways, or SACBES, were elevated roads across land.

CELT. A form of small stone axe, common as a manufactured item from Olmec times on. Usually highly polished.

CENOTE. The Maya term for a sinkhole; a solution cavity in the limestone area of the Maya Lowlands where the bedrock has collapsed and exposed the water table.

CEREMONIAL BAR OR STAFF. Bars or staffs which are usually richly ornamented and which apparently served as symbols of authority among Mesoamerican rulers. Equivalent in function to scepters of European rulers.

CEREMONIAL CENTER. A collection of temple, administrative, and elite residence structures that served as the focus of a dispersed urban center. Most of the population lived out in the country and congregated in the ceremonial center for markets and religious and political events. Centers were once and mistakenly thought to be characteristic of Olmec and Maya cultures. At least the latter are now known to have had true cities. Probably characteristic of all Mesoamerican Formative cultures.

CHACMUL (CHACMOOL, CHACMOL). Literally, "red tiger." Actually, a stone sculpture of a reclining human figure with an offering plate on the stomach.

These figures are characteristic of Toltec-period culture and sat in front of temple doorways to receive initial offerings.

CHAPALOTE. A primitive type of popcorn still grown in Mexico. The early wild corn found in the Tehuacan caves is *chapalote*.

CHIAN. A bushy plant of the *Salvia* family which produces seeds. Used by the ancient Mesoamericans for oil and as a drink.

CHICHIMECA (GRAN CHICHIMECA). The northern mountain and desert lands beyond the limits of Mesoamerican civilization and inhabited by so-called barbarians. In reality, the inhabitants were a mixture of nomadic hunting-gathering groups, intermittent and marginal farmers, and farming communities. Interspersed among them were Mesoamerican trading and mining colonies. The Aztec and other Mesoamericans originally may have been Chichimec immigrants from the north and west.

CHICLE. Sap from the zapote tree of the Maya Lowlands. Boiled down to make chicle, it is the ingredient in chewing gum that gives it "bounce."

CHINAMPA. An agricultural field developed by swamp drainage, extensive irrigation, or filling operations along the edges of lakes. A form of raised or drained field. It is especially characteristic of the Basin of Mexico, but also found elsewhere in the central highlands, and it is one of the most productive of all intensive agricultural techniques developed in ancient Mesoamerica.

CHULTUN. Underground, bell-shaped chamber dug in ancient times in the Maya Lowlands. Through experimentation, the multiple-chambered types possibly were storage places for ramon (breadnut tree) nuts or smoked corn. Some examples in northern Yucatan hold as much as 19 kiloliters (5,000 gallons) and are lined with stucco for use as cisterns.

CLOISONNÉ. Decorative technique by which a surface zone of a clay pot is scraped away while the pot is still soft. The zone is then filled with colored paint, and with differing zones and differing colors, complex designs are created. The technique is especially characteristic of western Mexico and the Toltec period.

COA. A wooden spadelike instrument used in the Valley of Mexico and the central highlands generally for cultivation of fields.

COATEPANTLI. Literally, "serpent wall." Both Toltec Tula and Aztec Tenochtitlan had such walls, which set apart the ceremonial precinct from the rest of the civic structures. In both cases, the wall was decorated with serpents.

CODEX. A hand-drawn manuscript. In Mesoamerica, a screen-fold illustrated book of indefinite length, made of either native paper (*amate* bark) or animal skin, lightly coated with plaster. Used for historical, religious, and tribute information, codices were made both prehistorically and for a short time after the Spanish Conquest. *See also* LIENZO.

COMAL. Flat griddle made of pottery for the express purpose of cooking tortillas or flat, thin cakes of corn flour.

CONVERGENCE. A phenomenon wherein two unrelated complex cultures independently developed similar features. These features are usually stylistically similar but functionally different; for example, wheels used on toys in Mesoamerica and wheels used on carts in the Old World.

COPAL. Maya word for incense made from pine resin. Used extensively in ceremonies throughout Mesoamerica and still in use in the Maya Highlands in religious affairs.

COPROLITE. Dried-out human feces, often found in cave sites and useful for laboratory study of prehistoric diet.

CORBEL VAULT. Vault made without the use of the keystone principle. It is constructed by erecting two parallel stone walls and then gradually edging parallel courses of stone inward towards one another until the space can be closed by a single capstone. In general, the technique was confined to the Classic Maya.

CORD MARKING. Pottery decoration technique achieved by wrapping a paddle with string. The soft clay of the unfired pot is patted with the paddle, and the string leaves twisted marks.

DANZANTES. Bas-relief sculptures from Monte Alban, Oaxaca, dating from the period of about 500 to 200 B.C.

DIFFUSION. Anthropological concept in which it is assumed that complex inventions or ideas are only likely to be invented once. The diffusion or spread of such ideas and inventions can be traced archaeologically.

EARSPOOLS OR EARPLUGS. Both terms refer to jewelry or decorative items commonly worn by both male and female Mesoamericans in pierced ears. Jade, feathers, gold, copper, and other materials were used.

EMBLEM GLYPHS. Glyphs in Maya writing which identify cities or the ruling lineages of those cities. Deciphered by Heinrich Berlin in 1958.

FRESCO. Used synonymously with *mural* (wall painting); the European technique of painting on a still-damp plastered surface. Maya murals were painted this way.

GLYPH. A drawn symbol in a writing system. In Mesoamerican systems, a glyph may stand for a syllable, a sound, an idea, a word, or a combination of these qualities.

GRAPHEME. A minimum unit of written meaning.

HACHA (SPANISH: "AXE"). An axelike small stone sculpture usually carved into a human or animal likeness. Found most commonly in the Veracruz lowlands and Guatemalan highlands in Classic times.

HIEROGLYPH. A term derived from Egyptology meaning literally, "priestly writing." Adopted in Mesoamerican archaeology to mean the depictive, art-related systems of writing developed there. Hieroglyphs are the units themselves. *See* GLYPH.

INCENSARIO. An incense burner. Mesoamerican ceremonies, both religious and political, involved incense burning in special vessels made of pottery and sometimes of stone. These *incensarios* are often decorated with elaborate religious symbolism.

INITIAL SERIES. Maya inscriptions of the Classic period often open with the complete designation of a point in time, using the LONG COUNT. This statement is the initial series.

KATUN. A period of 7,200 days (about twenty years) in the Maya LONG COUNT calendar. Used in the period A.D. 1250–1520 as an abbreviated notation system for the longer dates used in the Classic period.

KIN (MAYA: "SUN"). The single day unit in the Maya calendar.

LIENZO. A large, maplike document made of cloth or animal skin, similar to a codex. It was often a map showing the traditional landholdings of a native community or family. The famous *Lienzo de Tlaxcala,* however, shows the Spanish Conquest and the important part played in it by the Tlaxcalans, traditional enemies of the Aztec. A *lienzo* differs from a codex only in physical characteristics, being rectangular or irregular in shape instead of a long screen-fold of indefinite length.

LINTEL. A beam of wood or stone supporting the wall above a doorway. In many Mesoamerican areas, it is carved with scenes and written texts.

LONG COUNT. The Classic Maya system of dating, which could specify a point in time to infinity. Such a date is usually noted as being in a specific BAKTUN (cycle of about four hundred years), KATUN (cycle of about twenty years), TUN (cycle of 360 days), and UNINAL (cycle of 20 days) and on a specific day (KIN). In addition, the day was specified in the cycles of eighteen months of 20 days each, 20 named days, and 13 numbers.

LOST WAX PROCESS. A metal casting technique much used by Mesoamericans of Protohistoric times. A wax sculpture is made, then a pottery casing is formed around it, with several vents left in the casing. Metal is poured in one of the vents; melted wax and heat leave by the other vents. The cooling metal assumes the shape of the wax sculpture by filling the inside form of the pottery casing.

LUNAR SERIES. The part of the text following the date specification (initial series) of a Classic Maya inscription. The subject matter consists of dating the moon phase and notation of the associated god or gods.

MACEHUALLI (PL., MACEHUALTIN). A member of the Aztec commoner class and invariably a member of a CALPULLI. Theoretically, a *macehualli* was a free man, but with obligations as a CALPULLI member and also through it to the city-state.

MANIKIN SCEPTER. Badge of office often held by Maya rulers depicted in Classic sculpture. The "manikin scepter deity" may be a corn god.

MAYE (PL., MAYEQUE). A member of the Aztec serf class, attached to the private estates of the aristocratic class and therefore landless. Apparently a *maye* did not belong to a **calpulli.** However, it may be that this word is a synonym for *macehualli.*

MAZAPAN WARE. Toltec (Postclassic) horizon marker in Central Mexico. Pottery of orange color was decorated with multiple, parallel, wavy red lines. Most often on **molcajete** forms.

MEGAFAUNA. Giant forms of animal species characteristic of the Pleistocene. At least three kinds of elephant and a giant species of bison existed in North America and either died out or were replaced by smaller species toward the end of the Ice Age.

METATE AND MANO. Food-grinding apparatus of all Mesoamericans. METATES were slab- or trough-shaped stones, and MANOS were loaf-shaped stones used to grind the substance (for example, corn) against the METATE. These implements are still in wide use in Mexico and Guatemala, although they are being replaced by village mills.

PERCUSSION. Technique by which stone flakes are removed from a block usually of flint or obsidian. A blow is struck with a stone at the edge of the block (direct percussion), or a hammer stone is used to tap a chisel against the edge of the block (indirect percussion).

PETATE. Mat woven of reeds or grass and usually used for floor covering and as a sleeping mat. *Petates* are still in use today.

PILLI (PL., PIPILTIN). A member of a current or former ruling lineage of the Aztec upper class.

PISOTE. Coatimundi; a medium-sized mammal, related to the raccoon, common in the tropical forests of Mesoamerica. It is one of many animals used by the Maya as models for their glyphs.

PLEISTOCENE. The last major stage is the Wisconsin glaciation. Generally dated as beginning about one hundred thousand years ago and having lasted until about seven thousand years ago.

PLUMBATE. Pottery type, decorated with a lead-colored glaze, manufactured in the Izapa-Tajumulco zone and widely traded throughout Mesoamerica in Postclassic times.

POCHTECA. The long-distance merchants of Tlatelolco, the twin city of Aztec Tenochtitlan. The term is used also generically for all long-distance merchants in Mesoamerica. The merchants were a privileged and often aristocratic class sponsored by the state. They often acted as military and intelligence units.

POSOLE. A drink in which maize dough is dissolved in water. The difference between ATOLE and POSOLE is one of degree, the latter being more diluted and the former having additional sweetening and spices added.

POT IRRIGATION. A simple irrigation method by which a pot of water is poured upon each plant in a narrow field around which are dug wells to the water table.

POX POTTERY. Pottery the surface of which is dimpled with pockmarks created by poorly controlled firing. Expansion of the clay in the pottery caused bits of the surface to flake away, leaving the dimples.

PRECLASSIC. Synonym for Mesoamerican Formative.

PUNCTATION. Pottery decoration technique by which the surface of a pot is indented using a sharply pointed instrument or even fingernails.

PUTUN (MAYA). Chontal-speaking Maya from the Tabasco zone of the Gulf Coast. Natives from Poton-chan, a capital of the Chontal in the sixteenth century. They may have invaded the Classic Maya Lowlands at the end of the Classic period.

QUIDS. Mouthfuls of early corn, which was chewed for its juices, being such a small plant. The residues of chewed vegetable matter were discarded as *quids*. These residues are often found in the dry caves of Mesoamerica.

REPOUSSÉ. Technique by which thin sheets of metal, usually gold or copper, are decorated. Cold hammering of the metal from the back raises the front of the piece into a design.

RESIST PAINTING. Pottery decoration technique in which the vessel is painted with the design in wax or grease. A slip or thin paint is then applied to the pot. Upon firing, the paint resting on the waxed areas is burnt away, leaving the design subtly shown in the unslipped areas.

ROCKER STAMPING. Technique of pottery decoration especially in vogue in Early and Middle Formative times. The rounded edge of a shell or sherd was rocked back and forth over the wet surface of a pot to form a continuous in-and-out line.

ROOFCOMB. A free-standing wall built atop Maya temples with the function of providing broad areas for modeling human figures and hieroglyphs in stucco. It apparently fulfilled the same purpose as the *stelae*.

SACBE (MAYA: "WHITE WAY"). Raised causeway-roads which connect many Maya cities, both internally and externally.

SETTLEMENT PATTERN STUDIES. Studies of the disposition of houses and communities over the landscape. These patterns reveal relationships and hierarchical structures from which archaeologists deduce information about social and political arrangements, for example.

SHELL MIDDEN. Heaps of discarded shell at prehistoric sites where the principal food used was shellfish.

SHORT COUNT. The same as the calendar round; an abbreviated Maya date.

SLATE WARE. Pottery ware of the northern and intermediate lowlands of the Maya Lowlands. Handsome, greenish white pottery, which may be decorated.

SLIP. A solution of clay and pigment either painted on a pot or into which a pot is dipped to give it a color other than that of its natural clay.

STELA (PL. STELAE). Erect stone monument, often sculptured. *Stelae* were most often used by the Maya, Olmec, and Izapan cultures.

STIRRUP JAR. Jars with spouts shaped to form a stirrup; a single orifice allows a flow of liquid.

SWIDDEN. Synonym for the slash-and-burn system of agriculture, in which forest is cut down and the land is cultivated for a time, abandoned, and allowed to recover, after which the cycle is repeated.

TALPETATE. A soil level in the Guatemalan highlands which is made up of compacted volcanic ash, yellowish and claylike in its characteristics.

TALUD-TABLERO. Architectural feature characteristic of the Teotihuacan Classic period. Used on terraced platforms in which each terrace slopes upward (the TALUD) toward a recessed vertical panel (the TABLERO).

TAMALE. A delicious dish in which a preparation of chopped meat is encased in cornmeal dough, wrapped in a corn shuck, and steamed. It is eaten piping hot after the shuck is discarded.

TECCALLI. Lower judicial court for Aztec commoners. See also TLACXITLAN.

TECOMATE. Literally, a gourd vessel, or a pottery vessel which looks like a gourd with the neck cut off. One of the earliest forms of pottery.

TECUHTLI (Nahuatl: "lord"). A honorific title given to various kinds of Aztec nobility, usually in combination with a modifying title; for example, *amiztlato-tecuhtli*, "lord of the hunt."

TEMPLE MOUND/PYRAMID. Mesoamerican "pyramids" are actually platforms which are usually terraced and are never truly pyramidal in shape, as are Egyptian pyramids. The platforms almost invariably supported temples of wood or stone and are sometimes known as temple mounds. Archaeologists prefer to call them "temple structures."

TEOSINTE. A grass, and closest relative of maize or corn. There is argument over its relationship to corn concerning whether it is an ancestor or an offspring.

TLACHTLI. The Aztec word for the ball court in which the Mesoamerican ball game was played. Each town seems to have had at least one.

TLACXITLAN. Aztec higher judicial court used for appeals from the TECCALLI. Also the principal law court for aristocrats.

TLALOQUE (PL.). The Aztec rain gods. The term usually refers to the multitude of smaller helpers to the great rain god, *Tlaloc*.

TLATOQUE (PL. TLATOANI). A city-state ruler of the Basin of Mexico and member of the aristocratic PIPILTIN class. Usually from a hereditary leadership lineage within the class.

TONALPOHUALLI. The Nahuatl name for the 260-day sacred almanac.

TORTILLAS. Flat, thin, corn-dough cakes cooked on a griddle (COMAL). Perhaps a relatively late and regional development in the use of corn flour in Mesoamerica, tortillas substituted for wheat bread in ancient Mexico and Guatemala.

TRAIT. A distinctive and notable cultural characteristic, such as a pottery decorative motif. The term is often used in old-fashioned diffusion studies of archaeological cultures. The preference is now to study functionally related groups of traits.

TRIPSACUM. Member of the grass family and a relative of corn and TEOSINTE.

TUMPLINE. A band of leather or woven grass which can be attached to a heavy load. The load is lifted onto the lower back of the human porter, and the band is placed around the forehead. At a dog trot, a Mesoamerican merchant could travel considerable distances with respectable loads. Tumplines are still used today by itinerant merchants in the Maya Highlands.

TUN. A 360-day period in the Maya *long count* dating system.

TZOLKIN. The 260-day calendar among the Maya (who may not have used this word). It was made up of 20 named days and 13 numbers ($20 \times 13 = 260$ combinations).

TZOMPANTLI. Nahuatl word for skull rack. The Aztecs displayed the skulls of their sacrificial victims on wooden frames in their town squares.

UAYEB. The last, unlucky five days of the year in the Maya calendar.

UINAL. A twenty-day period in the Maya *long count* system of dating.

VOLADOR CEREMONY. A ritual still practiced today in Mexico. Dancers dressed as birds ascend to the top of a tall pole, from which they launch themselves into the air upside down, attached to the top of the pole by ropes. The ropes have been wound intricately around the pole and gradually unwind, bringing the dancers to the ground once more. In ancient times there was much calendrical symbolism in the number of dancers, the number of revolutions in their descent, and other variables.

WERE-JAGUAR (AS IN WEREWOLF). The major deity cluster of the Formative Olmec culture, characterized by combined jaguar and human figures.

YOKE-PALMA-HACHA. Small stone sculpture complex from Classic-period lowland Veracruz cultures. Yokes all may be associated with important dress used by ball players in ritual associated with the ball game.

ZONED DENTATE STAMPING. Technique of pottery decoration by which a zone was marked off by incised lines on the surface of a pot. The zone was then filled with marks that resemble those that would be left by a modern hair comb if the teeth were repeatedly jabbed into the wet clay. Especially favored in the Early and Middle Formative.

REFERENCES

Abbreviations

AMN   *Anales del Museo Nacional de México,* Mexico City.
BAE   Bureau of American Ethnology, Smithsonian Institution, Washington, D.C.
CIW   Carnegie Institution of Washington, Washington, D.C.
HMAI *Handbook of Middle American Indians,* 13 vols. Ed. Robert Wauchope. Austin: University of Texas Press, 1964–74.
ICA   International Congress of Americanists (meets every three years and alternates between New and Old worlds).
IDAEH Instituto de Antropologia e Historia de Guatemala.
INAH Instituto Nacional de Antropología e Historia, Mexico City.
MARI Middle American Research Institute, Tulane University, New Orleans.
NWAF New World Archaeological Foundation, Provo, Utah.
PMP   Papers of the Peabody Museum, Harvard University, Cambridge, Mass.
UCAFR University of California Archaeological Research Facility, Berkeley, California.
VUPA Vanderbilt University Publications in Anthropology, Nashville, Tennessee.

Abascal, R.; P. Davila; P. J. Schmidt; and D. Z. de Davila
  1976   *La arqueología del sur-oeste de Tlaxcala (primera parte).* Communicaciones de la Fundación Alemana para la Investigación Científica, No. 11. Puebla, Mexico.
Acosta, Jorge R.
  1956   "Resumen de los informes de las exploraciones arqueológicas en Tula, Hidalgo, durante las VI, VII, VIII temporadas, 1946–1950." *Anales del INAH* 8:37–115.
  1964   "La decimotercera temporada de exploraciones en Tula, Hgo." *Anales del ANAH* 16:45–76.
  1972   "Exploraciones en Zaachila, Oaxaca." *INAH Boletin,* Epoca II, No. 3.
  1974   "La piramide de El Corral de Tula, Hgo." In Matos Moctezuma, 1974, pp. 27–50.
Adams, R. E. W.
  1969   "Maya Archaeology, 1958–1968: A Review." *Latin American Research Review* 4:3–45.
  1970   "Suggested Classic Period Occupational Specialization in the Southern Maya Lowlands." In Bullard, 1970a:487–98.
  1971   *The Ceramics of Altar de Sacrificios.* PMP, vol. 63, no. 1.
  1974a "A Trial Estimation of Classic Maya Palace Populations at Uaxactun." In Hammond, 1974:285–96.
  1974b (Ed.) *Preliminary Reports on Archaeological Investigations in the Río Bec Area, Campeche, Mexico.* MARI Publication No. 31:103–46.
  1977a (Ed.) *The Origins of Maya Civilization.* Albuquerque: University of New Mexico Press.

1977*b* "Río Bec Archaeology and the Rise of Maya Civilization." In R. E. W. Adams, 1977*a*:77–99.
1981 "Settlement Patterns of the Central Yucatan and Southern Campeche Regions." In Ashmore, 1981:211–57.
1986 (Ed.) *Río Azul Reports No. 2: the 1984 Season.* San Antonio: Center for Archaeological Research, University of Texas.
1987*a* (Ed.) *Río Azul Reports No. 3: the 1985 Season.* San Antonio: Center for Archaeological Research, University of Texas.
1987*b* "The Río Azul Archaeological Project, 1985 Summary." In R. E. W. Adams, 1987*a*:1–27.

Adams, R. E. W.; W. E. Brown, Jr.; and T. P. Culbert
1988 "Radar Mapping, Archeology, and Ancient Maya Land Use." *Science* 213:1457–63.

Adams, R. E. W., and J. L. Gatling
1964 "Noreste del Peten: un nuevo sitio y un mapa arqueológico regional." *Estudios de cultura Maya* 4:99–118.

Adams, R. E. W. and R. C. Jones
1981 "Spatial Patterns and Regional Growth among Classic Maya Cities." *American Antiquity* 46:301–22.

Adams, R. E. W., and James Karbula
1988 "Estimated Populations at Río Azúl, Guatemala, Based on Covered Space Calculations." Manuscript.

Adams, R. E. W., and W. D. Smith
1981 "Feudal Models for Classic Maya Civilization." In Ashmore, 1981:335–49.

Adams, R. E. W., and Aubrey Trik
1961 *Temple I (Str. 5D–1): Post-Constructional Activities.* Tikal Reports, No. 7 Philadelphia: Univ. Museum.

Adams, R. McC.
1961 "Changing Patterns of Territorial Organization in the Central Highlands of Chiapas." *American Antiquity* 26:341–60.

Adelhofer, Otto
1963 *Codex Vindobonensis Mexicanus I.* Graz: Akademische Druck- und Verlagsanstalt.

Andovasio, J. M.; J. D. Gunn; J. Donahue; and R. Stuckenrath
1978 "Meadowcroft Rockshelter, 1977: An Overview." *American Antiquity* 43:632–51.

Agrinier, P.
1960 *The Carved Human Femurs from Tomb 1, Chiapa de Corzo, Mexico* NWAF Paper No. 6.

Anales de Cuauhtitlan
1945 In *Códice Chimalpopoca.* Trans. from Nahuatl to Spanish by Primo Feliciano Velásquez. Mexico City: Imprenta Universitaria.

Anawalt, P.
1981 "Costume Analysis and the Provenience of the Borgia Group Codices." *American Antiquity* 46:837–52.

Anderson, W. F.
1971 "Arithmetic in Maya Numerals." *American Antiquity* 36:54–63.

Andrews, A. P.; T. Gallareta N.; F. Robles C.; R. Cobos P.; and P. Cervera R.
1988 "Isla Cerritos: An Itza Trading Port on the North Coast of Yucatan, Mexico." *National Geographic Research* 4:196–207.

Andrews, E. W., IV
1965 "Archaeology and Prehistory in the Northern Maya Lowlands." In *HMAI* 2:288–330.

1970   *Balankanche, Throne of the Tiger Priest.* MARI Publication No. 32.

Andrews, E. W., V
1981   "Dzibilchaltun." In Sabloff, 1981:313–41.

Andrews, E. W., V; W. M. Ringle; P. Barnes; A. Barrera R.; and T. Gallareta N.
1984   "Komchen, an Ancient Maya Community In Northwest Yucatan." In *Investigaciones recientes en el area Maya* 1:73–92. XVII Mesa Redonda, Sociedad Mexicana de Antropología, San Cristóbal de las Casas, Mexico.

Anonymous Conqueror
1917   *Narrative of Some Things of New Spain and the Great City of Temestitan, Mexico.* New York: Cortés Society.

Armillas, P.
1971   "Gardens on Swamps." *Science* 174:653–61.

Ashmore, W. (ed.)
1981   *Lowland Maya Settlement Patterns.* Albuquerque: Univ. of New Mexico Press.
1984   "Quirigua Archaeology and History Revisited." *Journal of Field Archaeology* 11:365–86.

Aufdermauer, J.
1970   *Excavaciones en dos sitios preclasicos de Moyotzingo, Puebla. Comunicaciones* de la Fundación Alemana para la Investigación Científica, No. 1. Puebla, Mexico.
1973   Aspectos de la cronología del Preclasico en la cuenca de Puebla-Tlaxcala. *Comunicaciones* 9:11–24. Fundación Alemana para la Investigación Científica. Puebla, Mexico.

Aveleyra Arroyo de Anda, Luis
1964   "The Primitive Hunters." In *HMAI* 1:384–412.

Aveni, A. F.; E. E. Calnek; and H. Hartung
1988   "Myth, Environment, and the Orientation of the Templo Mayor of Tenochtitlan." *American Antiquity* 53:287–309.

Ball, J. W.
1974   "A Coordinate Approach to Northern Maya Prehistory." *American Antiquity* 39:85–93.
1977   "The Rise of the Northern Maya Chiefdoms: A Socioprocessual Analysis." In R. E. W. Adams, 1977a: 101–32.
1985   "Campeche, the Itza, and the Postclassic: A Study in Ethnohistorical Archaeology." In Sabloff and Andrews 1985:379–408.

Ball, J. W., and J. D. Eaton
1972   "Marine Resources and the Prehistoric Lowland Maya: A Comment." *American Anthropologist* 74:772–76.

Barlow, R. H.
1949   *The Extent of the Empire of the Culhua Mexica.* Ibero-Americana 28. Berkeley and Los Angeles: Univ. of California Press.

Baudez, Claude F. (ed.)
1983   *Introducción a la arqueología de Copan, Honduras.* 3 vol. Tegucipalpa: Secretaría de Estado en el Despacho de Cultura y Turismo de Honduras. (Distributed in the United States by MARI.)

Baudez, Claude F., and P. Becquelin
1973   *Archéologie de Los Naranjos, Honduras.* Collection Etudes Mesoamericaines, 2. Mexico City: Mission Archéologique et Ethnologique Française au Mexique.

Beadle, G. W.
1972   "The Mystery of Maize." *Field Museum of Natural History Bulletin* 43, no. 10:2–11.

Becker, M. J.
1971   "The Identification of a Second Plaza Plan at Tikal, Guatemala, and Its Implica-

tions for Ancient Maya Social Complexity." Ph.D. diss. Univ. of Pennsylvania. Ann Arbor: Univ. Microfilms (BWH71–25982).

Becquelin, P.
1969   *Archéologie de la Region de Nebaj.* Paris: Univ. de Paris.

Bell, B.
1971   "Archaeology of Nayarit, Jalisco, and Colima." In *HMAI* 11:694–753.
1974a   (Ed.) *The Archaeology of West Mexico.* Sociedad de Estudios Avanzados del Occidente de Mexico, A. C. Ajijic.
1974b   "Excavations at El Cerro Encantado, Jalisco." In Bell 1974a:147–67.

Benson, Elizabeth P. (ed.)
1968   *Dumbarton Oaks Conference on the Olmec.* Washington, D.C.: Dumbarton Oaks Research Library and Collection.

Berdan, Frances
1987   "The Economics of Aztec Luxury Trade and Tribute." In *The Aztec Templo Mayor,* pp. 161–83. Ed. Elizabeth Boone. Washington, D.C.: Dumbarton Oaks.

Berlin, Heinrich
1958   "El glifo 'Emblema' en las inscripciones mayas." *Journal de la Société des Américanistes de Paris* 47:111–19.

Bernal, I.
1949   "Exploraciones en Coixtlahuaca, Oaxaca." *Revista mexicana de estudios antropológicos* 10:5–76.
1964   "Introduction." In Diego Durán, *The Aztecs: The History of the Indies of New Spain.* New York: Orion Press.
1965a   "Archaeological Synthesis of Oaxaca." In *HMAI* 3:788–813.
1965b   "Architecture in Oaxaca after the End of Monte Albán." In *HMAI* 3:837–48.
1969   *The Olmec World.* Berkeley and Los Angeles: Univ. of California Press.
1980   *A History of Mexican Archaeology.* London: Thames and Hudson.

Binford, L. R., and S. R. Binford
1968   *New Perspectives in Archaeology.* Chicago: Aldine.

Blanton, R. E.
1978   *Monte Albán: Settlement Patterns at the Ancient Zapotec Capital.* New York: Academic Press.

Blanton, R. E., and S. A. Kowalewski
1981   "Monte Albán and After in the Valley of Oaxaca." In Sabloff, ed., 1981:94–116.

Boone, E.
1987   (Ed.) *The Aztec Templo Mayor.* Washington, D.C.: Dunbarton Oaks.

Bove, F. J.
1978   "Laguna de los Cerros: An Olmec Central Place." *Journal of New World Archaeology* 2:1–56.

Bray, W.
1977   "From Foraging to Farming in Early Mexico." In *Hunters, Gatherers and First Farmers Beyond Europe.* Ed. J. V. S. Megaw. Leicester, England: Leicester Univ. Press.

Bricker, V.
1986   *A Grammar of Maya Hieroglyphs.* MARI Publication No. 56.

Brockington, D. L.
1973   *Archaeological Investigations at Miahuatlan, Oaxaca.* VUPA No. 7.
1974   "Spatial and Temporal Variations of the Mixtec-style Ceramics in Southern Oaxaca." Paper prepared for the 41st ICA. Mexico City.

Brockington, D. L.; M. Jorrin; and J. R. Long
1974   *The Oaxaca Coast Project Reports: Part I.* VUPA No. 8.

Brockington, D. L., and J. R. Long
   1974   *The Oaxaca Coast Project Reports: Part II. VUPA* No. 9
Bronson, B.
   1966   "Roots and the Subsistence of the Ancient Maya." *Southwestern Journal of Anthropology* 22:251–79.
Brown, K. L.
   1980   "A Brief Report on Paleoindian-Archaic Occupation in the Quiche Basin, Guatemala." *American Antiquity* 45:313–24.
Brunhouse, R. L.
   1973   *In Search of the Maya: The First Archaeologists.* Albuquerque: Univ. of New Mexico Press.
Bullard, W. R., Jr.
   1960   "The Maya Settlement Pattern in Northeastern Peten, Guatemala." *American Antiquity* 25:355–72.
   1970a   (Ed.) *Monographs and Papers in Maya Archaeology.* PMP, vol. 61.
   1970b   "Topoxte: A Postclassic Maya Site in Peten, Guatemala." In Bullard, 1970a:245–307.
   1973   "Postclassic Culture in Central Peten and Adjacent British Honduras." In Culbert, 1973:221–41.
Cabrera, R.; I. Rodríguez; and N. Morelos (ed.)
   1982   *Teotihuacan, 80–82: primeros resultados.* INAH.
Calnek, E. E.
   1972   "Settlement Pattern and Chinampa Agriculture at Tenochtitlan." *American Antiquity* 37:104–15.
   1974   "The Sahagún Texts as a Source of Sociological Information." In *The Valley of Mexico: The Work of Sahagún,* pp. 189–204. Ed. M. S. Edmundson. Albuquerque: Univ. of New Mexico Press.
Campbell, L., and T. Kaufman
   1976   "A Linguistic Look at the Olmecs." *American Antiquity* 41:80–89.
Carlsen, R.
   1986   "Analysis of the Early Classic Period Textile Remains—Tomb 19, Río Azúl, Guatemala." In R. E. W. Adams, 1986:122–55.
   1987   "Analysis of the Early Classic Textile Remains from Tomb 23, Río Azúl, Guatemala." In R. E. W. Adams, 1987:152–58.
Carmack, R. W.
   1973   *Quichean Civilization.* Berkeley: Univ. of California Press.
Carmack, R. M., and J. J. Weeks
   1981   "The Archaeology and Ethnohistory of Utatlan: A Conjunctive Approach." *American Antiquity* 46:323–41.
Carneiro, R.
   1970   "A Theory of the Origin of the State." *Science* 169:733–38.
Carr, R. F., and J. E. Hazard
   1961   *Map of the Ruins of Tikal, El Peten, Guatemala. Tikal Reports,* No. 11. Philadelphia: Univ. Museum.
Carrasco, P.
   1971a   "Social Organization of Ancient Mexico." In *HMAI* 10:349–75.
   1971b   "The Peoples of Central Mexico and Their Historical Traditions." In *HMAI* 11:459–73.
   1976   "Los linajes nobles del México antiguo." In *Estratificación social en la Mesoamérica prehispanica.,* pp. 19–36. Ed. P. Carrasco and J. Broda. INAH.
Caso, A.
   1942   "El paraíso terrenal en Teotihuacan." *Cuadernos americanos* 6:136–37.
   1949   "El mapa de Teozacoalco." *Cuadernos americanos* 8:145–81.

426

1960   *Interpretation of the Codex Bodley 2858.* Mexico City: *Sociedad Mexicana de Antropología.*

1963   "Land Tenure among the Ancient Mexicans." *American Anthropologist* 65:863–78.

1965   "Zapotec Writing and Calendar." In *HMAI* 3:931–47.

1966a   "The Lords of Yanhuitlan." In Paddock, 1966a:313–335.

1966b   *Interpretación del Codice Colombino* (includes English version). Mexico City: Sociedad Mexicana de Antropología.

1967   *Los calendarios prehispanicos.* Serie de cultura Nahuatl, Monografía No. 6. Mexico City: Univ. Autonoma de Mexico, Instituto de Investigaciones Historicas.

1969   *El tesoro de Monte Albán.* INAH Memoria No. 3.

Caso, A., and I. Bernal

1952   *Urnas de Oaxaca.* INAH Memoria No. 2.

Chadwick, R.

1971   "Archaeological Synthesis of Michoacan and Adjacent Regions." In *HMAI* 11:657–93.

Chamberlin, R. S.

1948   *The Conquest and Colonization of Yucatan.* CIW Publication No. 582.

Chase, A. F., and D. Z. Chase

1987   *Glimmers of a Forgotten Realm: Maya Archaeology at Caracol, Belize.* Orlando: Univ. of Central Florida.

Chase, A. F., and P. M. Rice (eds.)

1985   *The Lowland Maya Postclassic.* Austin: Univ. of Texas Press.

Chase, D.

1985   "Ganned but Not Forgotten: Late Postclassic Archaeology and Ritual at Santa Rita Corozal, Belize." In, A. F. Chase and P. M. Rice, 1985:104–49.

Chilam Balam of Chumayel

1967   *The Book of Chilam Balam of Chumayel.* Trans. Ralph L. Roys. Norman: Univ. of Oklahoma Press.

Chilam Balam of Tizimin, *See* Makemson, 1951.

Childe, V. G.

1950   "The Urban Revolution." *Town Planning Review* 21:3–17.

Chimalpahin Quauhtlehuanitzin, D. F.

1965   *Relaciones originales de Chalco Amaquemecan.* Mexico City: Fondo de Cultura Económica.

Cline, H.

1973   "Selected Nineteenth-Century Mexican Writers on Ethnohistory." In *HMAI* 13:370–427.

Cobean, R. H.

1974   "The Ceramics of Tula." In Diehl, 1974:32–41.

Cobean, R. H.; M. D. Coe; E. A. Perry, Jr.; K. K. Turekian; D. H. Kharkar

1972   "Obsidian Trade at San Lorenzo, Tenochtitlan, Mexico." *Science* 174:666–71.

Codex Bodley. *See* Caso, 1960.

Codex Nuttall. *See* Nuttall, 1975.

Codex Vienna. *See* Adelhofer, 1963.

Coe, M. D.

1956   "The Funerary Temple among the Classic Maya." *Southwestern Journal of Anthropology* 12:387–493.

1957   "The Khmer Settlement Pattern: A Possible Analogy with That of the Maya." *American Antiquity* 22:409–10.

1960   "Archaeological Linkages with North and South America at La Victoria, Guatemala." *American Anthropologist* 62:363–93.

1964 "The Chinampas of Mexico." *Scientific American* 211:90–98.
1965a "Archaeological Synthesis of Southern Veracruz and Tabasco." In *HMAI* 3:697–715.
1965b "The Olmec Style and Its Distribution." In *HMAI* 3:739–75.
1968 *America's First Civilization*. New York: D. Van Nostrand.
1970 "The Archaeological Sequence at San Lorenzo, Tenochtitlan." In *Contributions* of the Univ. of California Archaeological Research Facility, No. 8:21–34.
1977 "Olmec and Maya: A Study in Relationships." In R. E. W. Adams, 1977a:183–95.
1981 "San Lorenzo Tenochtitlan." In Sabloff, 1981:117–46.
Coe, M. D., and R. A. Diehl
1980 *In the Land of the Olmec*. Austin: Univ. of Texas Press.
Coe, M. D.; R. A. Diehl; and M. Stuiver
1967 "Olmec Civilization, Veracruz, Mexico: Dating of the San Lorenzo Phase." *Science* 155:1399–1401.
Coe, W. R., III
1959 *Piedras Negras Archaeology: Artifacts, Caches, and Burials*. Univ. Museum Monographs. Philadelphia: Univ. Museum.
1965a "Tikal, Guatemala, and Emergent Maya Civilization." *Science* 147:1401–19.
1965b "Tikal: Ten Years of Study of a Maya Ruin in the Lowlands of Guatemala." *Expedition* 8:5–56.
Colby, B. N., and P. L. van den Berghe
1969 *Ixil Country*. Berkeley and Los Angeles: Univ. of California Press.
Conrad, G. W., and A. A. Demarest
1984 *Religion and Empire*. Cambridge: Cambridge Univ. Press.
Cook, O. F.
1921 *Milpa Agriculture, A Primitive Tropical System*. Annual Report of the Smithsonian Institution, 1919. Washington, D.C.
Cook, S. F.
1949 *The Historical Demography and Ecology of the Teotlalpan*. Ibero-Americana 33. Berkeley: Univ. of California Press.
Cook, S. F., and W. Borah
1960 *The Indian Population of Central Mexico, 1531–1610*. Ibero-Americana 44. Berkeley: Univ. of California Press.
Cortés, Hernán
1963 *Cartas y documentos*. Mexico City: Editorial Porrua.
Coulborn, R.
1956 *Feudalism in History*. Princeton, N.J.: Princeton Univ. Press.
Covarrubias, M.
1946 *Mexico South: The Isthmus of Tehuantepec*. New York: Knopf.
1957 *Indian Art of Mexico and Central America*. New York: Knopf.
Cowgill, G. L.
1963 "Postclassic Period Culture in the Vicinity of Flores, Peten, Guatemala." Ph.D. diss., Dept. of Anthropology, Harvard Univ.
1964 "The End of Classic Maya Culture: A Review of Recent Evidence." *Southwestern Journal of Anthropology* 20:145–59.
1979 Processes of Growth and Decline at Teotihuacan: The City and the State. In *Los procesos de cambio*, 1:183–93. XV Mesa Redonda, Sociedad Mexicana de Antropología, Mexico City.
Cowgill, Ursula M.
1961 "Soil Fertility and the Ancient Maya." In *Transactions of the Connecticut Academy of Arts and Sciences* 42:1–56.

1962   "An Agricultural Study of the Southern Maya Lowlands." *American Anthropologist* 64:273–86.
1971   "Some Comments on Manihot Subsistence and the Ancient Maya.," *Southwestern Journal of Anthropology* 27:51–63.

Craine, E. R., and R. C. Reindorp (trans. and eds.)
1970   *The Chronicles of Michoacan.* Norman: Univ. of Oklahoma Press.

Culbert, T. P.
1965   *The Ceramic History of the Central Highlands of Chiapas, Mexico.* NWAF Paper No. 19.
1973   (Ed.) *The Classic Maya Collapse.* Albuquerque: Univ. of New Mexico Press.
1977   "Early Maya Development at Tikal, Guatemala." In R. E. W. Adams, 1977a27–43.
1988   "The Collapse of Classic Maya Civilization." In Yoffee and Cowgill, 1988:69–101.

Davies, C. N. B.
1968   *Los señorios independientes del imperio azteca.* INAH.
1973   *The Aztecs.* London: Macmillan.

DeBloois, E. I.
1970   *Archaeological Researches in Northern Campeche, Mexico.* Ogden, Utah: Weber State College.

Demarest, A. A., and R. J. Sharer
1982   "The Origins and Evolution of the Usulutan Ceramic Style." *American Antiquity* 47:810–22.

Denevan, W. M.
1970   "Aboriginal Drained-field Cultivation in the Americas." *Science* 169:647–54.

Díaz del Castillo, B.
1968   *Historia verdadera de la conquista de la Nueva España.* 2 vol., 6th ed. Vols. 6 and 7. Mexico City: Editorial Porrua. Translated to English by A. P. Maudslay in 1908; of that translation there are various abridged editions, including (1972) *The Discovery and Conquest of Mexico,* New York: Farrar, Strauss, and Giroux.

Díaz Oyarzabal, C. L.
1986   La presencia teotihuacana en las estelas de Tepecuacuilco. In *Arqueología y ethnohistoria del estado de Guerrero,* pp. 203–208. Ed. R. Cervantes-Delgado. INAH.

Diehl, R. A. (ed.)
1974   *Studies of Ancient Tollan: A Report of the University of Missouri Tula Archaeological Project.* Columbia: Department of Anthropology, Univ. of Missouri—Columbia.
1981   "Tula." In *HMAI, Supplement, Archaeology* , pp. 277–95.
1983   *Tula, the Toltec Capital of Ancient Mexico.* London: Thames and Hudson.

Diehl, R. A.; R. Lomas; and J. T. Wynn
1974   "Toltec Trade with Central America: New Light and Evidence." *Archaeology* 27:182–87.

Dillehay, T. D.
1986   "Monte Verde Excavations." Cited in "Current Research," *American Antiquity* 51:180.

Di Peso, C. C.
1968   "Casas Grandes and the Gran Chichimeca." *El Palacio* 75:47–61.
1974   *Casas Grandes: A Fallen Trading Center of the Gran Chichimeca.* Dragoon, Ariz.: Amerind Foundation Publication.

Drucker, P.
1943a   *Ceramic Stratigraphy at Cerro de las Mesas, Veracruz, Mexico.* BAE Bulletin 141.
1943b   *Ceramic Sequences at Tres Zapotes, Veracruz, Mexico.* BAE Bulletin 140.

1955 *The Cerro de las Mesas Offering of Jade and Other Materials.* BAE Bulletin 157:25–68.
1981 "On the Nature of Olmec Polity." In *The Olmec and Their Neighbors,* pp. 29–47. Ed. E. Benson. Washington, D.C.: Dumbarton Oaks.

Drucker, P.; R. Heizer; and R. J. Squier
1959 *Excavations at La Venta, Tabasco, 1955.* BAE Bulletin 170.

Durán, Diego
1964 *The Aztecs: The History of the Indies of New Spain.* Trans. with notes by Doris Heyden and Fernando Horcasitas. New York: Orion Press.
1967 *Historia de las Indias de Nueva España e islas de la tierra firme.* Ed. and annotated by Angel Ma. Garibay K. in 2 vols. Vols. 36 and 37. Mexico City: Biblioteca Porrua. (Includes the *History, The Book of the Gods and Rites,* and *The Ancient Calendar.*)
1971 *Book of the Gods and Rites, and The Ancient Calendar.* Trans. F. Horcasitas and Doris Heyden. Norman: Univ. of Oklahoma Press.

Eaton, J. D.
1975 "Ancient Agricultural Farmstead in the Río Bec Region of Yucatan." *UCARF Contributions* 27:56–82.
1978 *Archaeological Survey of the Yucatan-Campeche Coast.* MARI Publication No. 46.
1980 "Operation 2011: Investigations Within the Main Plaza of the Monumental Center at Colha." In *The Colha Project, Second Season: 1980 Interim Report,* pp. 145–61. Ed. T. R. Hester, J. D. Eaton, and H. J. Shafer. San Antonio: Center for Archaeological Research, Univ. of Texas.

Ekholm, G.
1944 *Excavations at Tampico and Panuco in the Huasteca, Mexico.* Anthropological Papers of the American Museum of Natural History 38, no. 5.

Evans, S. T.
1985 "The Cerro Gordo Site: A Rural Settlement of the Aztec Period in the Basin of Mexico." *Journal of Field Archaeology* 12:1–18.

Flannery, K. V.
1968 "The Olmec and the Valley of Oaxaca: A Model for Inter-regional Interaction in Formative Times." In Benson, 1968:79–110.
1973 "The Origins of Agriculture." *Annual Reviews of Anthropology* 2:271–10.
1982 (Ed.) *Maya Subsistence: Studies in Memory of Dennis E. Puleston.* New York: Academic Press.
1983a "Monte Negro: A Reinterpretation." In Flannery and Marcus, 1983:99–102.
1983b "The Development of Monte Albán's Main Plaza in Period II." In Flannery and Marcus, 1983:102–104.
1986 (Ed.) *Guila Naquitz.* New York: Academic Press.

Flannery, K. V.; A. V. Kirby; and A. W. Williams, Jr.
1967 "Farming Systems and Political Growth in Ancient Oaxaca." *Science* 158:445–54.

Flannery, K. V., and J. Marcus (eds.)
1983 *The Cloud People: Divergent Evolution of the Zapotec and Mixtec Civilizations.* New York: Academic Press.

Flannery, K. V.; J. Marcus; and S. A. Kowalewski
1981 "The Preceramic and Formative of the Valley of Oaxaca." In *HMAI, Supplement, Archaeology,* pp. 48–93.

Fletcher, L. A.; J. M. Hau; L. M. Florey Folan; and W. J. Folan
1987 *Un análisis estadístico preliminar del patrón de asentamiento de Calakmul.* Campeche, Mexico: Univ. Autonoma del Sudeste.

Folan, W. J.; L. A. Fletcher; and E. R. Kintz
1979 "Fruit, Fiber, Bark and Resin: The Social Organization of a Maya Urban Center: Coba, Quintana Roo, Mexico." *Science* 204:697–701.

Folan, W. J.; J. Gunn; J. D. Easton; and R. W. Patch
1983 "Paleoclimatological Patterning in Southern Mesoamerica." *Journal of Field Archaeology* 10:453–68.

Folan, W. J.; E. R. Kintz; and L. A. Fletcher
1983 *Coba: A Classic Maya Metropolis.* New York: Academic Press.

Ford, J. A.
1969 *A Comparison of Formative Cultures in the Americas.* Smithsonian Contributions to Anthropology, Vol. 11, Washington, D.C.: Smithsonian Institution.

Fowler, Melvin L.
1987 "Early Water Management at Amalucan, State of Puebla, Mexico." *National Geographic Research* 3:52–68.

Freidel, D. A., and L. Schele
1988 "Kingship in the Late Preclassic Maya Lowlands." *American Anthropologist* 90:547–67.

Fritz, J. M., and F. Plog
1979 "The Nature of Archaeological Explanation." *American Antiquity* 35:405–12.

Furst, P. T.
1974 "Some Problems in the Interpretation of West Mexican Tomb Art." In Bell, 1974:132–46.

Gallegos, R.
1962 "Zaachila: The First Season's Work." *Archaeology* 16:226–33.

Gann, T.
1900 "Mounds in Northern Honduras." *19th Annual Report of the BAE,* Part II:665–92.

Garcia Cook, A.
1981 "The Historical Importance of Tlaxcala in the Cultural Development of the Central Highlands." *HMAI, Supplement, Archaeology,* pp. 244–76.
1986 *Guía oficial: Cacaxtla-Tizatlan.* INAH.

García Payón, J.
1957 *El Tajin: guía oficial.* INAH.
1971 "Archaeology of Central Veracruz." *HMAI* 11:505–42.

Gibson, C.
1971 "Structure of the Aztec Empire." *HMAI* 10:376–94.

Gibson, E. C.; L. C. Shaw; and D. R. Finamore
1986 *Early Evidence of Maya Hieroglyphic Writing at Kichpanha, Belize.* Working Papers in Archaeology, No. 2. San Antonio: Center for Archaeological Research, Univ. of Texas.

González Lauck, Rebecca
1988 "Proyecto arqueológico La Venta." *Arqueología* No. 4. Monumentos Prehispanicos. INAH.

Gorenstein, S. S.
1973 "Tepexi el Viejo: A Postclassic Fortified Site in the Mixteca-Puebla Region of Mexico." *Transactions of the American Philosophical Society,* n.s., vol. 63, pt. 1.

Gorenstein, S. S., and H. P. Pollard
1983 *The Tarascan Civilization.* VUPA.

Graham, Ian
1967 *Archaeological Explorations in El Peten, Guatemala.* MARI Publication No. 33.

Graham, J. (ed.)
1966 *Ancient Mesoamerica: Selected Readings.* Palo Alto, Calif.: Peek Press.
1978 *Abaj Takalik 1976: Exploratory Investigations.* UCARF Contributions No. 36.

Green, D. F., and G. W. Lowe
1967 *Altamira and Padre Piedra: Early Preclassic Sites in Chiapas, Mexico.* NWAF Paper No. 20.

Grosscup, G. L.
1961 "A Sequence of Figurines from West Mexico." *American Antiquity* 26:390–406.

Grove, D. C.
1969 "Olmec Cave Paintings: Discovery from Guerrero, Mexico (Juxtlahuaca)." *Science* 164:421–23.
1970a "The San Pablo Pantheon Mound: A Middle Preclassic Site in Morelos, Mexico." *American Antiquity* 35:62–73.
1970b *The Olmec Paintings of Oxtotitlan Cave, Guerrero, Mexico.* Studies in Pre-Columbian Art and Archaeology, No. 6. Washington, D.C.: Dumbarton Oaks.
1981 "The Formative Period and the Evolution of Complex Culture." *HMAI, Supplement, Archaeology,* pp. 373–91.
1987 (Ed.) *Ancient Chalcatzingo.* Austin: Univ. of Texas Press.

Guillemin, J. F.
1966 *Iximche: capital del antiguo reino cachiquel.* Guatemala: IDAEH.

Hall, G. D.; S. M. Tarka; W. J. Hurst; D. Stuart; and R. E. W. Adams
In press "Ancient Maya Vessels from Río Azúl, Guatemala, Yield Residues of Cacao." *American Antiquity.*

Hammond, Norman
1974 (Ed.) *Mesoamerican Archaeology: New Approaches.* Austin: Univ. of Texas Press.
1977 "Ex Oriente Lux: The View from Belize." In R. E. W. Adams, 1977a:45–76.
1982 "The Prehistory of Belize." *Journal of Field Archaeology* 9:349–62.

Harrison, P. D.
1974 *Archaeology in Southwestern Quintana Roo: Interim Report of the Uaymil Survey Project.* Peterborough, Ontario, Canada: Department of Anthropology, Trent University.
1981 "Some Aspects of Preconquest Settlement in Southern Quintana Roo, Mexico." In Ashmore, 1981:259–86.

Hassig, R.
1985 *Trade, Tribute, and Transportation.* Norman: Univ. of Oklahoma Press.
1988 *Aztec Warfare.* Norman: Univ. of Oklahoma Press.

Hatch, Marion Popenoe
1987 "Un análisis de las esculturas de Santa Lucía Cotzumalguapa." *Mesoamerica* (Antigua Guatemala) 14:467–509.

Haviland, W.
1968 *Ancient Lowland Maya Social Organization.* MARI Publication No. 26:93–107.
1977 "Dynastic Genealogies from Tikal, Guatemala: Implications for Descent and Political Organization." *American Antiquity* 42:61–67.

Healan, D. M.
1974 "Residential Architecture at Tula." In R. A. Diehl, 1974.

Healy, P. F.; J. D. H. Lambert; J. T. Arnason; and R. J. Hebda
1983 "Caracol, Belize: Evidence of Ancient Maya Agricultural Terraces." *Journal of Field Archaeology* 10:397–410.

Heizer, R. F.
1968 "New Observations on La Venta." In Benson, 1968:9–36.

Hester, T. R.; R. F. Heizer; and J. A. Graham
1975 *Field Methods in Archaeology.* Palo Alto: Mayfield Press. (Also in a Spanish edition published in Mexico in 1988.)

Hester, T. R.; T. C. Kelly; and G. Ligabue
1981 *A Fluted Paleo-Indian Projectile Point from Belize, Central America.* Working Paper 1, Colha Project. San Antonio: Center for Archaeological Research, Univ. of Texas.

Hicks, F.
1983   "Tetzcoco in the Early Sixteenth Century: The State, the City, and the Cal-
polli." *American Ethnologist* 9:230–49.
1986   "Prehispanic Background of Colonial Political and Economic Organization in
Central Mexico." In *HMAI Supplement, Ethnohistory*, pp. 35–54.
Hirth, K.
1984   "Xochicalco: Urban Growth and State Formation in Central Mexico." *Science*
225:579–86.
Hole, F., and R. F. Heizer
1973   *An Introduction to Prehistoric Archaeology*. Third ed. New York: Holt, Rinehart,
Winston.
Hooton, A.E.
1940   "Skeletons From the Cenote of Sacrifice at Chichen Itza." In C. L. Hay, ed.,
The Maya and Their Neighbors, pp. 272–80. New York: D. Appleton-Century.
Iceland, Harry B.
1989   "Stone Tools at the Teotihuacan Merchants' Barrio: Considerations of Technology and Function." M. A. thesis, Univ. of Texas at San Antonio.
Ixtlilxóchitl, Fernando de Alva
1952   *Obras históricas*. Mexico: Editoral Nacional.
Jennings, J. D., and E. Norbeck (Eds.)
1964   *Prehistoric Man in the New World*. Chicago: Univ. of Chicago Press.
Jiménez-Moreno, W.
1941   "Tula y los Toltecas segun las fuentes historicas." *Revista de la Sociedad Mexicana de Antropología* 5:79–83.
1966a   "Mesoamerica Before the Toltecs." In Paddock, 1966a.
1966b   "Los imperios prehispanicas de Mesoamérica." *Revista de la Sociedad Mexicana
de Antropología* 20:179–95.
Jones, C.
1977   "Inauguration Dates of Three Late Classic Rulers at Tikal, Guatemala." *American Antiquity* 42:28–60.
1987   "The Life and Times of Ah-Cacau." In *Primera Conferencia de Epigrafía y
Arqueología Maya*. Asociación Tikal, Guatemala.
Jones, G. C.; D. S. Rice; and P. M. Rice
1981   "The Location of Tayasal: A Reconsideration in Light of Peten Maya Ethnohistory and Archaeology." *American Antiquity* 46:530–47.
Kampen, M. E.
1972   *The Sculptures of El Tajin, Veracruz, Mexico* Gainesville: Univ. of Florida Press.
Kelley, David H.
1962   "Glyphic Evidence for a Dynastic Sequence at Quirigua, Guatemala." *American
Antiquity* 27:323–35.
1976   *Deciphering the Maya Script*. Austin: Univ. of Texas Press.
Kelley, J. Charles
1971   "Archaeology of the Northern Frontiers: Zacatecas and Durango." In *HMAI*
11:768–801.
Kelly, I.
1974   "Stirrup Pots from Colima: Some Implications." In Bell, 1974:206–11.
Kelly, I., and A. Palerm
1952   *The Tajin Totonac*. Part 1: *History, Subsistence, Shelter and Technology*. Smithsonian Institution, Institute of Social Anthropology Publication No. 13. Washington, D.C.
Kidder, A. V.; J. Jennings; and E. M. Shook
1946   *Excavations at Kaminaljuyu, Guatemala*. CIW Publication No. 561.
Kidder, A. V., and A. L. Smith
1951   *Excavations at Nebaj, Guatemala*. CIW Publication No. 594.

Kirchhoff, Paul
1943 "Mesoamérica, sus límites geográficos, composición étnica y caracteres cultur-
ales." *Acta Americana* 1:92–107. (Republished in 1974 by Students Association, Escuela Nacional de Antropología e Historia, Mexico City. English
translation in Graham, 1966.)
1961 "Der Beitrag Chimalphains zur Geschichte der Tolteken." In *Beitrage zur
Völkerforschung. . . . Berlin: Academie-Verlag.*
Kirchhoff, P.; L. Odena G.; and L. Reyes G. (eds.)
1976 *Historia tolteca-chichimeca.* INAH.
Knorozov, Y.
1958 "The Problem of the Study of Maya Hieroglyphic Writing." *American Antiquity* 23:284–91.
Kovar, Anton
1970 "The Physical and Biological Environment of Basin of Mexico." In Sanders et
al., 1970:13–101.
Krickeberg, Walter
1956 *Las antiguas culturas mexicanas.* Mexico City: Fondo de Cultura Económica.
Krieger, Alex D.
1964 "Early Man in the New World." In Jennings and Norbeck, 1964.
Kroeber, A. L.
1963 *Configurations of Culture Growth.* Berkeley: Univ. of California Press.
Krotser, P., and G. R. Krotser
1973 "The Life Style of El Tajin." *American Antiquity* 38:199–205.
Kubler, G.
1967 *The Iconography of the Art of Teotihuacan.* Studies in Pre-Columbian Art and
Archaeology, No. 4. Washington, D. C.: Dumbarton Oaks.
Kurjack, E. B.
1979 *Introduction to the Map of the Ruins of Dzibilchaltun, Yucatan, Mexico.* MARI
Publication No. 47.
Kurjack, E. B., and S. Garza T.
1981 "Pre-Columbian Community Form and Distribution in the Northern Maya
Area." In W. Ashmore, ed., *Lowland Maya Settlement Patterns,* pp. 287–309.
Albuquerque: Univ. of New Mexico Press.
Landa, Diego de
1941 *Relación de las cosas de Yucatán.* Ed. Garibay, 1966, Mexico City: Editorial
Porrua. (English trans. and notes by A. M. Tozzer, PMP, vol. 18.)
Lange, F. W.
1971 "Marine Resources: A Viable Subsistence Alternative for the Prehistoric Lowland Maya." *American Anthropologist* 73:619–39.
Lehmann, H.
1968 *Mixco Viejo.* Guatemala: Editorial Malvina.
León-Portilla, Miguel
1961 *Los antiguos mexicanos, a traves de sur cronicas y cantares.* Mexico City: Fondo
de Cultura Económica.
1969 *Pre-Columbian Literatures of Mexico.* Trans. Grace Lobanov and M. León
Portilla. Norman: Univ. of Oklahoma Press.
Lister, R. H.
1958 *Archaeological Excavations in the Northern Sierra Madre Occidental, Chihuahua
and Sonora, Mexico.* Boulder: Univ. Colorado Studies, Anthr. Ser. No. 7.
Litvak-King, J.
1970 "Xochicalco en la caida del Clasico: una hipotesis." In *Anales de antropología,*
pp. 101–24. Mexico City: Univ. Autonoma de México.
Long, Austin; B. F. Benz; D. J. Donahue; A. J. T. Jull; and L. J. Toolin
1989 "First Direct AMS Dates on Early Maize from Tehuacan, Mexico." *Radiocar-*

bon 31:3. In Austin Long and Rene Kra, eds., *13th International Radiocarbon Conference* Proceedings.

López de Gómara, Francisco
1964   *Cortés: The Life of the Conqueror by His Secretary.* Trans. and ed. Lesley Byrd Simpson from *Istoria de la conquista de México.* Berkeley and Los Angeles: Univ. of California Press.

Lothrop, S. K.
1952   *Metals from the Cenote of Sacrifice, Chichen Itza, Yucatan.* Peabody Museum Memoirs, vol. 10, no. 2. Cambridge: Harvard Univ.
1964   *Treasures of Ancient America.* New York: Skira.

Lounsbury, F. G.
1973   "On the Derivation and Reading of the 'Ben-Ich' Prefix." In *Mesoamerican Writing Systems,* pp. 99–143. Ed. E. P. Benson. Washington, D.C.: Dumbarton Oaks.

Lowe, G. W.
1962   *Mound 5 and Minor Excavations, Chiapa de Corzo, Chiapas, Mexico.* NWAF Paper No. 12.
1971   "The Civilizational Consequences of Varying Degrees of Agricultural and Ceramic Dependence Within the Basic Eco-systems of Mesoamerica." In *Contributions of the University of California Archaeological Research Facility,* No. 11:211–48. Berkeley.
1977   "The Mixe-Zoque as Competing Neighbors of the Early Lowland Maya." In R. E. W. Adams, 1977*a*:197–248.

Lowe, G. W.; T. A. Lee, Jr.; and E. Martínez E.
1982   *Izapa: An Introduction to the Ruins and Monuments.* NWAF Paper No. 32.

Lowe, J. W. G.
1985   *The Dynamics of Apocalypse: A Systems Simulation of the Classic Maya Collapse.* Albuquerque: Univ. of New Mexico Press.

Mace, C.E.
1973   "Charles Etienne Brasseur de Bourbourg, 1814–1874." In *HMAI* 13:298–325.

McLeod, Murdo J.
1973   *Spanish Central America: A Socioeconomic History, 1520–1720.* Berkeley: Univ. of California Press.

MacNeish, R. S.
1954   *An Early Archaeological Site near Panuco, Veracruz.* Transactions of the American Philosophical Society, n.s., vol. 44, pt. 5. Philadelphia.
1958   *Preliminary Archaeological Investigations in the Sierra de Tamaulipas, Mexico.* Transactions of the American Philosophical Society, n.s., vol. 28, pt. 6,. Philadelphia.
1964   "Ancient Mesoamerican Civilization." *Science* 143:531–37.
1966   "Speculations about the Beginnings of Village Agriculture in Meso-America." *35th ICA* 1:181–85. Seville.
1970   (Ed.) *The Prehistory of the Tehuacan Valley,* Vol. 3, *Ceramics.* Austin: Univ. of Texas Press.
1971   "Early Man in the Andes." *Scientific American* 224:36–46.
1972   (Ed.) *The Prehistory of the Tehuacan Valley,* Vol. 4, *Chronology and Irrigation.* Austin: Univ. of Texas Press.

MacNeish, R. S., and A. Nelken-Terner
1983   "The Preceramic of Mesoamerica." *Journal of Field Archaeology* 10:71–84.

MacNeish, R. S.; S. J. K. Wilkerson; and A. Nelken-Terner
1980   *First Annual Report of the Belize Archaic Archaeological Reconnaissance.* Andover, Mass.: Phillips Academy, Robert S. Peabody Foundation.

Makemson, M. W.
1951   *The Book of the Jaguar Priest: A Translation of the Book of Chilam Balam of
        Tizimin with Commentary.* New York: Henry Schuman.
Mangelsdorf, Paul C.
1974   *Corn: Its Origin, Evolution, and Improvement.* Cambridge: Belknap Press, Har-
        vard Univ. Press.
1983   "The Mystery of Corn: New Perspectives." *Proceedings of the American Philo-
        sophical Society* 127:215–47.
Mangelsdorf, P. A.; R. S. MacNeish; and W. C. Galinat
1967   "Prehistoric Wild and Cultivated Maize." In *The Prehistory of the Tehuacan
        Valley,* Vol. 1, *Environment and Subsistence.* Ed. R. S. MacNeish. Austin: Univ.
        of Texas Press.
Marcus, J.
1973   "Territorial Organization of the Lowland Maya." *Science* 180:911–16.
1976   *Emblem and State in the Classic Maya Lowlands.* Washington, D.C.: Dumbarton
        Oaks.
1980   "Zapotec Writing." *Scientific American,* February, pp. 50–64.
1983a   "Monte Alban II in the Macuilxochitl Area." In Flannery and Marcus,
        1983:113–15.
1983b   "The Conquest Slabs of Building J, Monte Alban." In Flannery and Marcus,
        1983:106–108.
1983c   "Rethinking the Zapotec Urn." In Flannery and Marcus, 1983:144–48.
1983d   "Teotihuacan Visitors on Monte Alban Monuments and Murals." In Flannery
        and Marcus, 1983:175–81.
1983e   "Changing Patterns of Stone Monuments after the Fall of Monte Alban, A.D.
        600–900." In Flannery and Marcus, 1983:191–97.
1987   *The Inscriptions of Calakmul.* Technical Report 21. Ann Arbor: Univ. of Michi-
        gan Museum of Anthropology.
Margain, C. R.
1971   "Pre-Columbian Architecture of Central Mexico." In *HMAI* 10:45–91.
Marquina, I.
1960   *El Templo Mayor de México.* INAH.
1964   *Arquitectura prehispanica.* Second ed. INAH Memoria No. 1.
1970   (Ed.) *Proyecto Cholula.* INAH Investigaciones, No. 19.
1971   "The Paintings at Cholula." *Artes de Mexico,* No. 140:32–40.
Martin, P. S., and P. J. Mehringer, Jr.
1965   "Pleistocene Pollen Analysis and Biography of the Southwest." In *The Quater-
        nary of the United States: Biogeography, Phytogeography and Palynology, Part II,*
        pp. 433–51. Ed. H. E. Wright, Jr., and D. G. Frey. Princeton: Princeton
        Univ. Press.
Mastache, A. G., and R. H. Cobean
1985   "Tula." In *Mesoamerica y el centro de México,* pp. 273–307. Ed. J. Monjaras-
        Ruiz, R. Brambila, and E. Perez-Rocha. Collección Biblioteca del INAH.
        Mexico City.
Matheny, R.
1980   *El Mirador, Peten, Guatemala.* NWAF Paper No. 45. Provo, Utah.
1983   *Investigations at Edzna, Campeche, Mexico.* NWAF Publication No. 46. Provo,
        Utah.
Matos Moctezuma, E.
1974   (Ed.) *Proyecto Tula (1a parte).* INAH Colección Científica No. 15. Mexico
        City.
1982   (Ed.) *El Templo Mayor: excavaciones y estudios.* INAH.
1987   "Symbolism of the Templo Mayor." In E. Boone, 1987:185–207.

1988   *The Great Temple of the Aztecs.* London: Thames and Hudson.
Medellín-Zenil, Alfonso
1960   *Ceramicas del Totonacapan.* Veracruz: Univ. de Veracruz.
Meggers, Betty J., and Clifford Evans
1962   "The Machalilla Culture: An Early Formative Complex on the Ecuadorian Coast." *American Antiquity* 18:186–92.
Meighan, Clement
1972   "Matanchen Complex: New Radiocarbon Dates on Early Coastal Adaptation in West Mexico." *Science* 275:1242–43.
1974   "Prehistory of West Mexico." *Science* 184:1254–61.
1976   *The Archaeology of Amapa, Nayarit.* Los Angeles: Institute of Archaeology, Univ. of California.
Melgar y Serrano, J. M.
1869   "Antigüedades Mexicanas." In *Boletin de la Sociedad Mexicana de Geografía y Estadística*, No. 2a, Epoca I:292–97.
Merwin, R. E. and G. C. Vaillant
1932   *The Ruins of Holmul, Guatemala.* Peabody Museum Memoirs, vol. 3, no. 2. Cambridge: Harvard Univ.
Michels, J.
1979a   (Ed.) *Settlement Pattern Excavations at Kaminaljuyu, Guatemala.* University Park: Pennsylvania State Univ. Press.
1979b   *The Kaminaljuyu Chiefdom.* University Park: Pennsylvania State Univ. Press.
Miller, Arthur G.
1973   *The Mural Painting of Teotihuacan.* Washington, D.C.: Dumbarton Oaks.
1982   *On the Edge of the Sea: Mural Painting at Tancah-Tulum, Quintana Roo, Mexico*, Washington, D.C.: Dumbarton Oaks.
1988   "Pre-Hispanic Mural Painting in the Valley of Oaxaca, Mexico." *National Geographic Research* 4:233–58.
Millon, Clara
1972   "The History of Mural Art at Teotihuacan." In *Teotihuacan*, 2:1–16. XI *Mesa Redonda*, Sociedad Mexicana de Antropología.
1973   "Painting, Writing, and Polity at Teotihuacan, Mexico." *American Antiquity* 38:294–314.
Millon, Rene
1967   "Teotihuacan." *Scientific American* 216:38–49.
1970   "Teotihuacan: Completion of Map of Giant Ancient City in the Valley of Mexico." *Science* 170:1077–82.
1973   *The Teotihuacan Map*, Vol. 1, Part One, *Text*. Austin: Univ. of Texas Press.
1981   "Teotihuacan." In *HMAI, Supplement, Archaeology*, pp. 198–243.
1988   "The Last Years of Teotihuacan Dominance." In Yoffee and Cowgill, 1988:102–64.
Millon, R.; B. Drewitt; and G. Cowgill
1973   *The Teotihuacan Map*, Vol. 1, Part Two, *Maps*. Austin: Univ. of Texas Press.
Moore, C. B. (ed.)
1974   *Reconstructing Complex Societies.* Supplement to the Bulletin of the American Schools of Oriental Research, No. 20. Cambridge: Harvard Univ.
Morley, S. G.
1937–38   *The Inscriptions of Peten.* CIW Publication No. 437. 5 vols.
1946   *The Ancient Maya.* Palo Alto: Stanford Univ. Press.
Morris, Ann Axtell
1931   "Murals from the Temples of the Warriors and Adjacent Structures." In E. H. Morris, J. Charlot, and A. A. Morris, *The Temple of the Warriors at Chichen Itza, Yucatan*, pp. 437–85. CIW Publication No. 406.

Navarrete, C., and L. Lujan M.
    1986   *El Gran Monticulo de la Culebra en el Valle de Guatemala.* Instituto de Investigaciones Antropológicas, Academia de Geografía e Historia de Guatemala, Serie Antropológica No. 72. Mexico City: Univ. Nacional Autonoma de México.

Nicholson, H. B.
    1960   "The Mixteca-Puebla Concept in Mesoamerican Archaeology." In J. Graham, 1966.
    1971a "The Religious-ritual System of Late Prehispanic Central Mexico." *38th ICA* 3:223–38. Stuttgart.
    1971b "Religion in Prehispanic Central Mexico." In *HMAI* 10:395–446.
    1973   "Eduard Georg Seler, 1849–1922." In *HMAI* 13:348–69.
    1987   Symposium discussion. In *The Aztec Templo Mayor*, pp. 463–79. Washington, D.C.: Dumbarton Oaks. Ed. E. H. Boone.

Niederberger, C.
    1976   "Early Sedentary Economy in the Basin of Mexico." *Science* 203:131–42.

Noguera, Eduardo
    1965   *La cerámica arqueológica de Mesoamérica.* Instituto de Investigaciones Historicas, No. 86. Mexico City: Univ. Nacional Autonoma de México.

Norman, Garth
    1973   *Izapa Sculpture*, Part 1, *Album.* NWAF Paper No. 30.
    1976   *Izapa Sculpture*, Part 2, *Text.* NWAF Paper No. 31.

Nuttall, Zelia
    1975   *Codex Nuttall.* New York: Dover Press.

Oliveros, José Arturo
    1974   "Nuevas exploraciones en el Opeño, Michoacán." In Bell, 1974:182–201.

Padden, R. C.
    1967   *The Hummingbird and the Hawk: Conquest and Sovereignty in the Valley of Mexico, 1503–1541.* Columbus: Ohio State Univ. Press.

Paddock, John
    1966a (Ed.) *Ancient Oaxaca.* Palo Alto: Stanford Univ. Press.
    1966b "Oaxaca in Ancient Mesoamerica." In Paddock, 1966a: 83–242.
    1966c "Mixtec Ethnohistory and Monte Albán V." In Paddock, 1966a: 367–85.
    1974a "Mesoamérica no es el Valle de México." Paper prepared for the 41st ICA, Mexico City.
    1974b "Mixtec-Puebla Culture in the Valley of Oaxaca." Paper prepared for the 41st ICA, Mexico City.
    1983a "The Oaxaca Barrio at Teotihuacan." In Flannery and Marcus, 1983:170–75.
    1983b "Lambityeco." In Flannery and Marcus, 1983:197–204.

Palerm, Angel, and Eric Wolf
    1960   "Ecological Potential and Cultural Development in Mesoamerica." *Social Science Monographs* 3:1–38. Washington, D.C.: Pan American Union.

Parsons, J. R.
    1968   "Teotihuacan, Mexico, and Its Impact on Regional Demography." *Science* 162:872–77.
    1974   "The Development of a Prehistoric Complex Society: A Regional Perspective from the Valley of Mexico." *Journal of Field Archaeology* 1:81–108.
    1976   "Settlement and Population History of the Basin of Mexico." In Wolf, 1976:69–100.

Parsons, Lee A.
    1967   *Bilbao, Guatemala: An Archaeological Study of Pacific Coast Cotzumalhuapa*
    –69   *Region.* Milwaukee Public Museum Publications in Anthropology, Nos. 11 and 12.

Pasztory, E.
1974 "The Iconography of the Teotihuacan Tlaloc." In *Studies in Pre-Columbian Art and Archaeology,* No. 15. Washington, D.C.: Dumbarton Oaks.
1983 *Aztec Art.* New York: Abrams.

Pendergast, David M.
1962 "Metal Artifacts from Amapa, Nayarit, Mexico." *American Antiquity* 27:370–79.
1981 "Lamanai, Belize: Summary of Excavation Results, 1974–1980." *Journal of Field Archaeology* 8:29–53.
1985 "Stability through Change: Lamanai, Belize, from the Ninth to the Seventeenth Century." In Sabloff and Andrews, 1985:223–49.

Peterson, D. A., and T. B. MacDougall
1974 *Guiengola: A Fortified Site in the Isthmus of Tehuantepec.* VUPA No. 10.

Piggott, Stuart
1965 *Ancient Europe.* Chicago: Aldine.

Piña Chan, R.
1958 *Tlatilco, 1,* INAH Investigaciones Nos. 1 and 2.

Pollard, H. P.
1980 "Central Place and Cities: A Consideration of the Protohistoric Tarascan State." *American Antiquity* 45:677–96.

Pollock, H. E. D.
1965 "Architecture of the Maya Lowlands." In *HMAI* 3:378–440.
1980 *The Puuc: An Architectural Survey of the Hill Country of Yucatan and Northern Campeche, Mexico.*, Peabody Museum Memoirs, No. 19. Cambridge: Harvard Univ.

Pollock,, H. E. D.; R. L. Roys; T. Proskouriakoff; and A. L. Smith (eds.)
1962 *Mayapan, Yucatan, Mexico.* CIW Publication No. 619.

Popol Vuh
1971 *The Book of Counsel: The Popol Vuh of the Quiche Maya of Guatemala.* Trans. Munro Edmonson. MARI Publication No. 35.

Porter, James B.
1989 "Olmec Colossal Heads as Recarved Thrones: 'Mutilation,' Revolution and Recarving." Manuscript, Department of Anthropology, Univ. of California, Berkeley.

Porter, M. N. [Muriel Noe Porter Weaver]
1953 *Tlatilco and the Preclassic Cultures of the New World.* New York: Viking Fund Publications in Anthropology, No. 19.

Potter, David F.
1976 "Prehispanic Architecture and Sculpture in Central Yucatan." *American Antiquity* 41:430–448.
1977 *Maya Architecture of the Central Yucatan Peninsula, Mexico.* MARI Publication No. 44.

Proskouriakoff, T.
1960 "Historical Implications of a Pattern of Dates at Piedras Negras, Guatemala." *American Antiquity* 25:454–75.
1961 "The Lords of the Maya Realm." *Expedition* 4:14–21.
1962 "Civic and Religious Structures of Mayapan." In Pollock et al., 1962:87–163.
1963 "Historical Data in the Inscriptions of Yaxchilan, I." *Estudios de Cultura Maya* 3:149–67.
1964 "Historical Data in the Inscriptions of Yaxchilan, II." *Estudios de Cultura Maya* 4:177–201.
1974 *Jades from the Cenote of Sacrifice, Chichen Itza, Yucatan.* Peabody Museum Memoirs, Vol. 10, No. 1. Cambridge: Harvard Univ.

Puleston, D. E.
  1977   "The Art and Archaeology of Hydraulic Agriculture in the Maya Lowlands." In *Social Process in Maya Prehistory*, pp. 449–79. Ed. N. Hammond. New York: Academic Press.
Quirarte, J.
  1973   *Izapan-style Art: A Study of Its Form and Meaning.* Studies in Pre-Columbian Art and Archaeology, No. 10. Washington, D.C.: Dumbarton Oaks.
  1977   "Early Art Styles of Mesoamerica and Early Classic Maya Art." In R. E. W. Adams, 1977a:249–84.
  1982   "The Santa Rita Murals: A Review." In *MARI Occasional Papers* 4:43–59.
Rands, R. L.
  1973   "The Classic Maya Collapse: Usumacinta Zone and the Northwestern Periphery." In Culbert, 1973:165–206.
  1977   "The Rise of Classic Maya Civilization in the Northwestern Zone: Isolation and Integration." In R. E. W. Adams, 1977a:159–80.
Rathje, W. L.
  1971   "The Origins and Development of Lowland Classic Maya Civilization." *American Antiquity* 36:275–85.
  1977   "The Origin and Development of Lowland Classic Maya Civilization." *American Antiquity* 36:275–85.
  1973   "Classic Maya Development and Denouement: A Research Design." In Culbert, 1973:405–56.
Rattray, E. C.
  1987   "The Merchants Barrio, Teotihuacan." Preliminary Report submitted to INAH and Instituto de Investigaciones Antropológicas, Univ. Autonoma de México, Mexico City.
Redmond, E. M., and C. S. Spencer
  1983   "The Cuicatlan Cañada and the Period III Frontier of the Zapotec State." In Flannery and Marcus, 1983:117–20.
Reina, R.
  1967   "Milpas and Milperos: Implications for Prehistoric Times." *American Anthropologist* 69:1–20.
Reina, R., and R. M. Hill
  1980   "Lowland Maya Subsistence: Notes from Ethnohistory and Ethnography." *American Antiquity* 45:74–79.
Relación de Michoacan: See Caine and Reindorp, 1970.
"Religion en Mesoamerica."
  1972   In *Revista Mexicana de estudios antropológicos.* Mexico City.
Ringle, W. M., and E. W. Andrews V
  1982   "Formative Residences at Komchen, Yucatan, Mexico." In Wilk and Ashmore, 1982:171–98.
Robertson, D.
  1970   "The Tulum Murals: The International Style of the Late Post-Classic." *38th ICA* 2:77–88. Stuttgart.
Robertson, R. A., and D. A. Freidel (eds.)
  1986   *Archaeology at Cerros, Belize, Central America,* Vol. 1, *An Interim Report.* Dallas: Southern Methodist University Press.
Romero Quiroz, J.
  1963   *Teotenanco y Matlatzinco (Calixtlahuaca).* Mexico City: Ediciones del Gobierno del Estado de México.
Roys, L.
  1934   "The Engineering Knowledge of the Maya." CIW Publication No. 436. *Contributions* No. 6.

Roys, Ralph
1957 *The Political Geography of the Yucatan Maya*. CIW Publication No. 613.
1962 "Literary Sources for the History of Mayapan." In Pollock et al., 1962:25–86.
1965 "Lowland Maya Native Society at Spanish Contact." In *HMAI* 3:659–78.
1966 "Native Empires in Yucatan: The Maya-Toltec Empire." *Revista de la Sociedad Mexicana de Antropología* 20:153–77.
1972 *The Indian Background of Colonial Yucatan*. Norman: Univ. of Oklahoma Press.
Ruppert, K., and J. H. Denison
1943 *Archaeological Reconnaissance in Campeche, Quintana Roo and Peten*. CIW Publication No. 543.
Ruppert, K.; J. Eric S. Thompson; and T. Proskouriakoff
1955 *Bonampak, Chiapas, Mexico*. CIW Publication No. 602.
Rust, W. F., and R. J. Sharer
1988 "Olmec Settlement Data from La Venta, Tabasco." *Science* 242:102–104.
Ruz L., A.
1973 *El Templo de las inscripciones, Palenque*. INAH Colleción Cientifica, No. 7.
Sabloff, J. A. (ed.)
1981 *Handbook of Middle American Indians, Supplement 1, Archaeology*. Austin: Univ. of Texas Press.
Sabloff, J. A., and D. A. Friedel
1975 "A Model of a Pre-Columbian Trading Center." In J. A. Sabloff and C. C. Lamberg-Karlovsky (Eds.), *Ancient Civilizations and Trade*. Albuquerque: Univ. of New Mexico Press.
Sabloff, J. A., and E. W. Andrews V (eds.)
1985 *Late Lowland Maya Civilization*. Albuquerque: Univ. of New Mexico Press.
Sahagún, Bernardino de
1950 *Florentine Codex: General History of the Things of New Spain*. English trans.
–70 Charles E. Dibble And Arthur J. O. Anderson. 12 vol. Provo: The School of American Research and the Univ. of Utah.
Sanchez, George I.
1961 *Arithmetic in Maya*. Austin, Texas: privately printed.
Sánchez del Real, C.
1987 *Cacaxtla*. Tlaxcala, Mexico.
Sanders, W. T.
1956 "The Central Mexican Symbiotic Region." In *Settlement Patterns in the New World*. Ed. G. R. Willey. New York: Viking Fund Publication in Anthropology No. 23.
1963 "Cultural Ecology of the Maya Lowlands, Part II." *Estudios de Cultura Maya* 3:203–41.
1965 *Cultural Ecology of the Teotihuacan Valley*. University Park: Department of Sociology and Anthropology, Pennsylvania State Univ.
1970 "The Population of the Teotihuacan Valley, the Basin of Mexico, and the Central Mexican Symbiotic Region in the Sixteenth Century." In Sanders et al., 1970:385–487.
1973 "The Cultural Ecology of the Lowland Maya: A Reevaluation." In Culbert, 1973:325–65.
1977 "Environmental Heterogeneity and the Evolution of Lowland Maya Civilization." In R. E. W. Adams, 1977a:287–97.
Sanders, W. T.; A. Kovar; T. Charlton; and R. A. Diehl (eds.)
1970 "The Natural Environment, Contemporary Occupation and 16th Century Population of the Valley." *The Teotihuacan Valley Project, Final Report*, Vol. 1. Occasional Papers in Anthropology, No.3. University Park: Department of Anthropology, Pennsylvania State Univ.

Sanders, W. T., and J. W. Michels
    1969   *Kaminaljuya Project—1968 Season*, Part 1, *The Excavations*. Occasional Papers
            in Anthropology, No. 2. University Park: Department of Anthropology,
            Pennsylvania State Univ.
    1977   (eds.) *Teotihuacan and Kaminaljuyu*. University Park: Pennsylvania State
            Univ. Press.
Sanders, W. T.; J. R. Parsons; and R. S. Santley
    1979   *The Basin of Mexico: Ecological Processes in the Evolution of a Civilization*. New
            York: Academic Press.
Sanders, W. T., and Barbara J. Price
    1968   *Mesoamerica: The Evolution of a Civilization*. New York: Random House.
Satterthwaite, L., Jr., and E. K. Ralph
    1960   "Radiocarbon Dates and the Maya Correlation Problem." *American Antiquity*
            26:165–84.
Saul, Frank P.
    1972   *Human Skeletal Remains of Altar de Sacrificios*. PMP Vol. 63, No. 2.
    1973   "Disease in the Maya Area: The Pre-Columbian Evidence." In Culbert,
            1973:301–24.
Schele, L.
    1982   *Maya Glyphs: The Verbs*. Austin: Univ. of Texas Press.
Schele, L., and M. Miller
    1986   *The Blood of Kings*. Dallas: Kimball Museum of Art.
Schilling, Elizabeth
    1939   "Die 'Schwimmenden Garten' von Xochimilco." *Schriften des Geographische
            Institut des Universität Kiel*, Vol. 9, No. 3. Kiel.
Scholes, F. V., and R. L. Roys
    1948   *The Maya Chontal Indians of Acalan-Tixchel*. CIW Publication No. 560.
Sejourne, Laurette
    1966   *Arquitectura y pintura en Teotihuacan*. Mexico City: Siglo Veintiuno Editores.
Seler, Eduard
    1904   "The Wall Paintings of Mitla, a Mexican Picture Writing in Fresco." In
            Mexican and Central American Antiquities, Calendar Systems and History, pp.
            247–324. Ed. C. P. Bowditch. BAE Bulletin 28.
    1960   "Die Ruinen auf dem Quie-ngola." *Gesammelte Abhandlungen* 2:184–99.
            Graz, Austria: Akademischeruck und-Verlags Anstalt.
Service, Elman R.
    1962   *Primitive Social Organization: An Evolutionary Perspective*. New York: Random
            House.
Shafer, H. J., and T. R. Hester
    1983   "Ancient Maya Chert Workshops in Northern Belize, Central America." *American Antiquity* 58:519–43.
Sharer, Robert J.
    1974   "The Prehistory of the Southeastern Maya Periphery." *Current Anthropology*
            15:165–87.
Sharer, Robert J., and D. W. Sedat
    1973   "Monument 1, El Porton, Guatemala, and the Development of Maya Calendrical and Writing Systems." In *UCARF Contribution* 18:177–94.
Sheets, P. D.
    1971   "An Ancient Natural Disaster." *Expedition* 14:24–31.
Shimkin, D.
    1973   "Models for the Downfall: Some Ecological and Culture-historical Considerations." In Culbert, 1973:269–300.
Shook, E. M., and A. V. Kidder
    1952   "Mound E-III–3, Kaminaljuyu, Guatemala." *CIW Contributions* 9:33–128.

Siemens, A. H.; R. J. Hebda; M. Navarrete H.; Dolores R. Piperno; J. K. Stein; and M. G. Zola B.
    1988   "Evidence for a Cultivar and a Chronology from Patterned Wetlands in Central Veracruz, Mexico." *Science* 242:105–107.

Siemens, A. H., and D. E. Puleston
    1972   "Ridged Fields and Associated Features in Southern Campeche: New Perspectives on the Lowland Maya." *American Antiquity* 37:228–39.

Sisson, Edward B.
    1973   *First Annual Report of the Coxcatlan Project.* Andover, Mass.: R. S. Peabody Foundation for Archaeology.
    1974   *Second Annual Report of the Coxcatlan Project.* Andover, Mass.: R. S. Peabody Foundation for Archaeology.

Smith, A. L.
    1950   *Uaxactun, Guatemala: Excavations of 1931–1937.* CIW Publication No. 568.

Smith, M. E.
    1973   *Picture Writing from Ancient Southern Mexico.* Norman: Univ. of Oklahoma Press.

Solís, Felipe
    1981   *Escultura del Castillo de Teayo, Veracrúz, México: catalogo.* Mexico City: Univ. Autonoma de México.

Spores, Ronald
    1965   "The Zapotec and Mixtec at Spanish Contact." In *HMAI* 3:962–87.
    1967   *The Mixtec Kings and Their People.* Norman: Univ. of Oklahoma Press.
    1969   "Settlement, Farming Technology, and Environment in the Nochixtlan Valley." *Science* 166:557–69.
    1972   *An Archaeological Settlement Survey of the Nochixtlan Valley, Oaxaca.* VUPA No. 1.

Spores. R., and K. V. Flannery
    1983   "Sixteenth Century Kinship and Social Organization." In Flannery and Marcus, 1983:339–42.

Stark, B. L.
    1977   *Prehistoric Ecology at Patarata 52, Veracruz, Mexico: Adaptation to the Mangrove Swamp.* VUPA No. 18.
    1981   "The Rise of Sedentary Life." In *HMAI, Supplement, Archaeology,* pp. 345–72.

Steele, D. Gentry
    1986   "The Skeletal Remains from Río Azul, 1984 Season." In *Río Azul Reports,* No. 2, *The 1984 Season,* pp. 111–16. Ed. R. E. W. Adams. San Antonio: Center for Archaeological Research, Univ. of Texas.

Stephens, J. L.
    1949   *Incidents of Travel in Central America, Chiapas, and Yucatan.* New Brunswick, N.J.: Rutgers Univ. Press.
    1963   *Incidents of Travel in Yucatan.* New York: Dover.

Steward, J. H.
    1938   *Basin-Plateau Aboriginal Sociopolitical Groups.* BAE Bulletin 120.
    1955   *Theory of Culture Change.* Champaign: Univ. of Illinois Press.
    1961   "The Urban Focus: Is There a Common Problem and Method in Studies of City Development—a Science of Urbanology?" *Science* 134:1354–56.

Stirling, M. W.
    1943   *Stone Monuments of Southern Mexico.* BAE Bulletin 138.
    1965   "Monumental Sculpture of Southern Veracruz and Tabasco." In *HMAI* 3:716–38.

Sugiyama, Saburo
    1989   "Burials dedicated to the Old Temple of Quetzalcoatl at Teotihuacan, Mexico." *American Antiquity* 54:85–106.

Taylor, W. W.
    1948 *A Study of Archaeology.* Memoirs of the American Anthropological Association.
Thompson, E. H.
    1938 *The High Priest's Grave, Chichen Itza, Yucatan, Mexico.* Field Museum of Natural History Anthropological Series, Vol. 27, No. 1, pp. 1–64. Chicago.
Thompson, J. E. S.
    1950 *Maya Hieroglyphic Writing: An Introduction.* CIW Publication No. 589. Reprinted, Norman: Univ. of Oklahoma Press.
    1966 *The Rise and Fall of Maya Civilization.* Second ed. Norman: Univ. of Oklahoma Press.
    1970 *Maya History and Religion.* Norman: Univ. of Oklahoma Press.
    1972 *Maya Hieroglyphs Without Tears.* London: British Museum.
    1974 " 'Canals' of the Río Candelaria Basin, Campeche, Mexico." In Hammond, 1974:297–302.
Tolstoy, P., and L. I. Paradis
    1970 "Early and Middle Preclassic Culture in the Basin of Mexico." *Science* 167:344–51.
Torres Guzmán, M.
    1972 "Hallazgos en El Zapotal, Ver." *INAH Boletin,* Epoca II, No. 2.
Tozzer, A. M.
    1941 *See* Landa, 1941.
    1957 *Chichen Itza and Its Cenote of Sacrifice: A Comparative Study of Contemporaneous Maya and Toltec.* Peabody Museum Memoirs, Vols. 11 and 12. Cambridge: Harvard Univ.
Troike, N. P.
    1978 "Fundamental Changes in the Interpretation of the Mixtec Codices." *American Antiquity* 44:229–305.
Turner, B. L., II
    1974 "Prehistoric Intensive Agriculture in the Mayan Lowlands." *Science* 185:118–24.
Turner, B. L., II, and P. D. Harrison (eds.)
    1983 *Pulltrouser Swamp.* Austin: Univ. of Texas Press.
Vaillant, G. C.
    1962 *The Aztecs of Mexico.* Second ed. revised by Suzannah B. Vaillant. New York: Doubleday.
Velazquez, P. F. (trans.)
    1945 *Codice Chimalpopoca: anales de Cuauhtitlan y leyenda de los Soles.* Mexico City: Instituto de Historia, Univ. Nacional Autonoma de México.
Vogt, E. Z.
    1969 *Zinacantan.* Cambridge: Harvard Univ. Press.
    1971 "The Genetic Model and Maya Cultural Development." In Vogt and Ruz, 1971:9–48.
Vogt, E. Z., and A. Ruz L.
    1971 *Desarrollo cultural de los Mayas.* Second ed. Mexico City: Univ. Nacional Autonoma de México, Centro de Estudios Mayas.
von Winning, H.
    1961 "Teotihuacan Symbols: The Reptile's Eye Glyph." *Ethnos* (Stockholm) 26:121–66.
    1974 *The Shaft Tomb Figures of West Mexico.* Southwest Museum Papers, No. 24. Los Angeles.
von Winning, H., and O. Hammer
    1972 *Anecdotal Sculpture of Ancient West Mexico.* Los Angeles: Ethnic Arts Council of Los Angeles.

Wallrath, M.
  1967   *Excavations in the Tehuantepec Region, Mexico.* Transactions of the American
         Philosophical Society, n.s., Vol. 57, Part 2. Philadelphia.
Watson, P. J.; S. A. LeBlanc; and C. L. Redman
  1971   *Explanation in Archaeology: An Explicitly Scientific Approach.* New York: Colum-
         bia Univ. Press.
Wauchope, R.
  1938   *Modern Maya Houses: A Study of Their Archaeological Significance.* CIW Publica-
         tion No. 436.
  1965   *They Found the Buried Cities.* Chicago: Univ. of Chicago Press.
Weaver, M. P. (*See also* Porter, M. N.)
  1981   *The Aztecs, Maya, and Their Predecessors.* Second ed. New York: Academic
         Press.
Webb, M. C.
  1973   "The Peten Maya Decline Viewed in the Perspective of State Formation." In
         Culbert, 1973:367–404.
Webster, D.
  1974   "The Fortifications of Becan, Campeche, Mexico." In R. E. W. Adams,
         1974b:123–28.
Weigand, P. C.
  1968   "The Mines and Mining Techniques of the Chalchihuites Culture." *American
         Antiquity* 33:45–61.
  1974   "The Ahualulco Site and the Shaft-Tomb Complex of the Etzatlan Area." In
         Bell 1974.
West, Robert
  1964   "Surface Configuration and Associated Geology of Middle America." In
         HMAI 1:33–83.
West, Robert, and Pedro Armillas
  1950   "Las chinampas de México." *Cuadernos americanos* 50:165–82.
Wilk, R. R., and W. Ashmore (eds.)
  1988   *Household and Community in the Meosamerican Past.* Albuquerque: Univ. of
         New Mexico Press.
Wilkerson, S. Jeffrey K.
  1975   "Pre-Agricultural Village Life: The Late Preceramic Period in Veracruz."
         UCAFR Contribution No. 27.
  1987   *El Tajin: A Guide for Visitors.* Veracruz: Museum of Xalapa.
Willey, G. R.
  1962   "The Early Great Styles and the Rise of the Pre-Columbian Civilizations."
         American Anthropologist 64:1–14.
  1967   *Alfred Vincent Kidder, 1885–1963: A Biographical Memoir.* Washington, D.C.:
         National Academy of Sciences.
  1973   *The Altar de Sacrificios Excavations: General Summary and Conclusions.* PMP,
         vol. 64, no. 3.
  1974   "The Classic Maya Hiatus: A 'Rehearsal' for the Collapse?" In Hammond,
         1974:313–34.
  1987   *Essays in Maya Archaeology.* Albuquerque: Univ. of New Mexico Press.
Willey, G. R., W. R. Bullard, Jr., J. B. Glass, and J. C. Gifford
  1965   "Prehistoric Maya Settlements in the Belize Valley." *PMP,* No. 54.
Willey, G. R.; R. Millon; and G. Ekholm
  1964   "The Patterns of Farming Life and Civilization." In *HMAI* 1:446–98.
Willey, G. R., and D. B. Shimkin
  1973   "The Maya Collapse: A Summary View." In Culbert, 1973:457–503.

Williams, B. J.
    1980   "Nahuatl Soil Glyphs from the Codice de Santa María de Asunción." *42nd ICA* 7:27–37. Paris.
Williams, B. J., and H. R. Harvey
    1988   "Content, Provenience, and Significance of the Codex Vergara and the Codice de Santa María Asunción." *American Antiquity* 53:337–51.
Winfield Capitaine, Fernando
    1988   *La Estela 1 de La Mojarra, Veracruz, Mexico.* Research Reports on Ancient Maya Writing, No. 16. Washington, D.C.: Center for Maya Research.
Winter, Marcus C.
    1974   "Residential Patterns at Monte Albán, Oaxaca, Mexico." *Science* 186:981–87.
Wolf, E. R. (ed.)
    1976   *The Valley of Mexico.* Albuquerque: Univ. of New Mexico Press.
Woodbury, R. B., and J. A. Neely
    1972   "Water Control Systems of the Tehuacan Valley." In MacNeish, 1972:81–153.
Woodbury, R. B., and A. S. Trik
    1953   *The Ruins of Zaculeu, Guatemala.* Richmond, Va.: United Fruit Company and William Byrd Press.
Wright, H. T., and G. A. Johnson
    1975   "Population, Exchange, and Early State Formation in Southwestern Iran." *American Anthropologist* 77:267–89.
Yoffee, N., and G. L. Cowgill (eds.)
    1988   *The Collapse of Ancient States and Civilizations.* Tucson: Univ. of Arizona Press.
Zorita, Alonso de
    1963   *Life and Labor in Ancient Mexico: The Brief and Summary Relation of the Lords of New Spain.* Trans. and intro. by B. Keen. New Brunswick, N.J.: Rutgers Univ. Press.

Index

Abaj Takalik: 49, 73, 80–81, 93
Abejas phase: 34
Acalan: 312; see also Chontal Maya
Agriculture: techniques of, 19; history of, 31ff., 40; slash-and-burn, 53, 54, 128, 140–45, 369; irrigation, 54, 100–101, 110, 111, 129–30, 145–47, 200, 234, 264, 277, 312, 352, 362, 367; terracing, 110, 146, 264, 333, 340, 361; Maya, 140–47, 264; yearly cycle, 141–45; raised fields, 145–47, 200, 264, 312; chinampas, 203, 220, 369–74ff.; at Teotihuacan, 203, 219–20; Aztec, 367–74; in Basin of Mexico, 369–74; religion and, 396
Ah Muzencabob (bee gods): 396
Ahuachapan: 81
Ahualulco: 118
Ahuitzotl: 357, 387, 401
Ajuereado phase: 33, 34
Almanac, sacred: 110, 177, 235, 240, 242, 243
Altamira: 38, 42
Altar de Sacrificios: 131, 344; burials at, 183; invasion of, 267, 287
Altar Vase: 183
Amalucan: 110
Amapa: 322ff.
Anales de Cuauhtitlan: 271, 272
Animals, domestication of: 37, 40; as food, 33, 34; hunting of, 29
Anonymous Conqueror: 3
Apartment compounds: 209, 212ff.
Apatzingan: 323
Apoala: 343–44
Aqueducts: 100–101, 373–74, 399
Archaic stage: 22; sequence, 39
Arenal phase: 115, 117–18
Aristocracy: see elite class
Art: Izapan, 92–93; narrative, 92–93; Maya, 188ff.; Cotzumalhuapan, 227;

Oaxacan, 242; Toltec, 282–84; Toltec-Maya, 282–84; see also specific art forms, e.g., murals
Astronomical year: 177
Atetelco, murals at: 218
Avocados: 33, 143
Awatovi: 285
Axayacatl: 357, 389
Axolotl: 372
Azcapotzalco: 257, 321, 375, 398, 399ff.
Aztec: 364–402; history of, 321, 398–402; tax collectors, 354; ethnic composition, 365; agriculture of, 367–74; population of, 367, 373; measurement, 376; social structure, 381–86; political organization of, 386–90; legal system, 390–91; religion, 391–96; warfare of, 394, 399ff.; empire of, 396–98; alliances of, 399, 400; expansion by, 400; conquest of, 402
Aztec black-on-orange pottery: 276, 281, 351, 352
Aztlan: 397

Bajio phase: 45, 49
Balankanche Cave: 286
Ball game: Classic Maya, 162; at Tajin, 233–34; courts for, 281, 314, 323, 332, 334, 336; at Chichen Itza, 291–92; in art, 335
Balsas River phase: 115
Bar-and-dot notation: 89, 91, 178–79, 282
Bari sites: 41, 49
Barra phase: 42, 47
Batres, Leopoldo: 6
Baul: 93, 227, 228
Beans: 37, 143, 220
Becan: 127, 130, 158ff., 228–29
Becerra: 27, 28, 29
Bees: 309